SECURITY THREATENED

Public opinion has played a crucial role in the transitions from war to peace in Israel since the 1967 Six Days war. *Security Threatened* is the first major analysis of the interactions among opinion, politics, and policy in that period, based on opinion surveys of thousands of adult Jews carried out in the 33-year period between 1962 and 1994.

The author documents the public division during these years between militant hardliners and those maintaining more conciliatory security positions. Power either shifted between, or was shared by, the right-wing Likud and left-of-center Labor parties. In the late 1980s and early 1990s, with the onset of the intifada, the collapse of the Soviet Union, and the American victory in the Gulf war, all segments of the Israeli public became more conciliatory.

Policy initiatives reflected shifts in political power which in turn magnified changes in public opinion. Leaders were constrained by public opinion and by perceptions of threat, but they could also alter policy if they had the will because opinion was rather equally divided; since most people had their minds made up, the opposition could not block their policy.

CAMBRIDGE STUDIES IN POLITICAL PSYCHOLOGY AND PUBLIC OPINION

General Editors

JAMES H. KUKLINSKI and ROBERT S. WYER, JR. University of Illinois, Urbana-Champaign

Editorial Board

STANLEY FELDMAN State University of New York, Stony Brook

ROGER D. MASTERS Dartmouth College

WILLIAM J. MCGUIRE Yale University

NORBERT SCHWARZ Zentrum für Umfragen, Methoden und Analysen, ZUMA, Mannheim, Germany

DAVID O. SEARS University of California, Los Angeles

PAUL M. SNIDERMAN Stanford University and Survey Research Center, University of California, Berkeley

JAMES A. STIMSON University of Minnesota

This series has been established in recognition of interest in political psychology in recent years. The series will focus on work that pertains to the fundamental question: What kinds of mental processes do citizens employ when they think about democratic politics and respond, consciously or unconsciously, to their political environments? We will also include research that explores the macro-level consequences of such processes.

We expect that many of the works will draw on developments in cognitive and social psychology and relevant areas of philosophy. Appropriate subjects would include the use of heuristics, the roles of core values and moral principles in political reasoning, the effects of expertise and sophistication, the role of affect and emotion, and the nature of cognition and information processing. The emphasis will be on systematic and rigorous empirical analysis, and a wide range of methodologies will be appropriate: traditional surveys, experimental surveys, laboratory experiments, focus groups, in-depth interviews, as well as others. We intend that these empirically oriented studies will also consider normative implications for democratic politics generally.

Politics, not psychology, will be the focus, and it is expected that most works will deal with mass public and democratic politics, although work on nondemocratic publics will not be excluded.

OTHER BOOKS IN THE SERIES

James DeNardo *The Amateur Strategist*

John Hibbing and Elizabeth Theiss-Morse *Congress as Public Enemy*

Robert Huckfeldt and John Sprague *Citizens, Politics, and Social Communication*

George E. Marcus, John L. Sullivan, Elizabeth Theiss-Morse, and Sandra L. Wood *Experimenting with Tolerance: How People Make Civil Liberties Judgments*

Paul M. Sniderman, Richard A. Brody, and Philip E. Tetlock *Reasoning and Choice: Explorations in Political Psychology*

John Zaller *The Nature and Origins of Mass Opinion*

SECURITY THREATENED

*Surveying Israeli Opinion on Peace
and War*

ASHER ARIAN
The City University of New York and the University of Haifa

Jaffee Center for Strategic Studies
TEL AVIV UNIVERSITY

and

CAMBRIDGE
UNIVERSITY PRESS

Published by the Press Syndicate of the University of Cambridge
The Pitt Building, Trumpington Street, Cambridge CB2 1RP
40 West 20th Street, New York, NY 10011-4211, USA
10 Stamford Road, Oakleigh, Melbourne 3166, Australia

©Jaffee Center for Strategic Studies, Tel Aviv University, 1995

First published 1995

Printed in the United States of America

Library of Congress Cataloging-in-Publication Data
Arian, Asher
Security threatened : surveying Israeli opinion on peace and war /
Asher Arian.
p.   cm. – (Cambridge studies in political psychology and public
opinion)
Includes bibliographical references.
ISBN 0-521-48314-X. – ISBN 0-521-49925-9 (pbk.)
1. National security – Israel – Public opinion.   2. Israel – Military
policy – Public opinion.   3. Public opinion –
Israel.   I. Title.   II. Series.
UA853.I8A755   1995
355'.03305694–dc20   94-47414
                                                                  CIP

A catalog record for this book is available from the British Library.

ISBN 0-521-48314-X hardback
ISBN 0-521-49925-9 paperback

THE JAFFEE CENTER FOR STRATEGIC STUDIES (JCSS)

The Center for Strategic Studies was established at Tel Aviv University at the end of 1977. In 1983 it was named the Jaffee Center for Strategic Studies in honor of Mr. & Mrs. Mel Jaffee. The objective of the Center is to contribute to the expansion of knowledge on strategic subjects and to promote public understanding of and pluralistic thought on matters of national and international security.

The Center relates to the concept of strategy in its broadest meaning, namely, the complex of processes involved in the identification, mobilization, and application of resources in peace and war, in order to solidify and strengthen national and international security.

To Carol

– who outdid herself (Proverbs 31:29)

Contents

Acknowledgments

Many people aided me with their collaboration, cooperation, and encouragement while I wrote this book, and I am very grateful to them.

Michal Shamir and I have discussed the topics of this volume for years and many of the themes were presented in articles we published jointly. Specifically, I refer to Chapters 3 and 4 on the panel study of the influence of the intifada on attitudes in Israel (Arian, Shamir, and Ventura 1992), to Chapter 5 on politics (Arian and Shamir 1993), and to Chapter 8 on values (Shamir and Arian 1994); in the last of these, her innovative ideas were especially important.

Carol Gordon developed the notion of threat in a protracted conflict in her work, and it influenced mine. That influence is especially evident in the sections on the Gulf war in Chapter 3 and in Chapter 7, some of which was published as Arian and Gordon 1993. Raphael Ventura did much of the preliminary work on the nuclear weapons section of Chapter 3 and was one of the coauthors of the intifada article mentioned above.

In addition to those, earlier versions of some of the analyses appeared in articles I published in the *Journal of Conflict Resolution,* the *Public Opinion Quarterly,* and in the volume edited by Avner Yaniv, as listed in the bibliography. All are used here with the permission of the respective publishers.

The Jaffee Center for Strategic Studies has been an ideal sponsor for the National Security and Public Opinion Project, which funded most of the surveys, and under whose auspices this volume is published. Initiated by Amiram Nir when he was active with the center, the project had the constant support and encouragement of Ahrele Yariv and Yossi Alpher. The scientific committee of the center has been diligent and helpful in reviewing drafts of questionnaires and manuscripts.

Mina Zemach of the Dahaf Research Institute was a pleasure to work with in the data-gathering stages of the project. Her industry and tact helped overcome problems and delays that at times seemed insurmountable. The contribution of Ruth Amir was considerable and much appreciated; thanks also to Joel Lefkowitz.

xii*Acknowledgments*

Those mentioned above, and Arthur Goldberg, Zeev Maoz, Avner Yaniv, and Alan Zuckerman, were good listeners and readers at various points in this project.

Unfortunately, after having acknowledged all the help and support, errors of fact and interpretation remain mine alone.

Haifa, Israel

1

Security Threatened

ISRAELI OPINION ON PEACE AND WAR

Public opinion in Israel on security questions is malleable, and politicians deemed legitimate can lead opinion precisely because of this fluidity. This proposition explains the support for seemingly surprising developments: the Camp David accords of 1978 between Israel's Prime Minister Menachem Begin and Egypt's President Anwar Sadat that stipulated Israeli withdrawal from the Sinai Peninsula and the signing of a peace treaty with Egypt, and the accord of joint recognition signed in 1993 on the White House lawn by Israel's Prime Minister Yitzhak Rabin and Yasir Arafat of the Palestine Liberation Organization.

These processes were deemed improbable by most observers months before – and even days before – they began. But considered in light of the cumulative record of public opinion survey findings, such developments take on a different complexion. It is not that the breakthroughs on the long path toward peace could have been predicted from the survey data; but a careful reading of the findings indicates that public opinion also presented no obstacle to progress along the tortuous path of negotiation, compromise, and concession. It is not the intention of this volume to "predict the past" once policies change: that is too easy. But it is also too facile to project political paralysis on the basis of a finding that a population is nearly evenly divided on an important matter. Based on the data of Israeli public opinion to be presented here, it has been reasonable to conclude that diplomatic breakthroughs would be accepted if pursued by a legitimate leadership, *and/or* that a toughening of security policy would be supported, if that case were convincingly made.

Two trends characterized security opinion in Israel in the years after the Six Days war of 1967, and especially in the late 1980s and early 1990s. They were a hardening of short-term positions regarding matters which could be perceived to have immediate implications for security, on the one hand, and a softening of positions regarding long-term political issues, on the other. Illustrations of short-term issues included insistence on control over day-to-day security (such as border crossings), the reaction to the Arab uprising in the territories (the intifada), the fight against terror, and efforts to achieve personal safety; examples of conciliation regarding long-term issues included the growing willingness to return some territories for peace, negotiations with the PLO, and the possible creation of a Palestinian state.

These distinctions between short-term and long-term are fluid and much more discernible after the fact, but they underscore the two key elements which formed the basis of the tension in the area: the simultaneous quest for both peace and security. It is the mix of these two which generated much of the political heat, and at times bloody violence, of the period. Was peace possible? What price security? Was there an interlocutor with whom to negotiate? How best to encourage the emergence of one? If concessions were made, would they make Israel appear more forthcoming or more vulnerable? Could such concessions be reversed, or were they simply points on the compass in the oft-mentioned plan of stages by which the Arabs intended to dismember Israel? And on and on.

The notable dynamic of the story was the slow but consistent movement toward mutual recognition and negotiations for peace. This momentum was very sporadic and was interspersed with violent eruptions of animosity and war. However, with the United States consistently propping up the Israel Defense Forces (IDF) with military hardware and aid, along with the no less insistent prodding of Israel by the Americans to be prepared to concede the fruits of the 1967 war in favor of peace accords, the time finally seemed ripe in the mid-1990s. After the dissolution of the Soviet Union in 1989, and the defeat of Iraq in the Gulf war in 1991, the policy of hanging tough on the battlefield was to be augmented by the equally exhausting endeavor of reaching acceptable agreements between long-standing enemies.

Israeli public opinion accommodated itself to these changes. It would be wrong to say that opinion caused such changes, but it would be equally incorrect to claim that policy shifts consistently brought about changes in public opinion. The pattern was much more complex and subtle, with one pattern more dominant in one situation, and the other more clearly manifesting itself in another. The interplay of the two patterns was facilitated in the case of Israel by the widespread interest in the issues at hand, and by the almost even split in Jewish public opinion regarding two very different visions of the future. Were Israeli public opinion on security questions not malleable, politicians could neither afford policy paralysis at certain times nor shift into action based on tough decisions at others.

These generalizations can be understood properly only in terms of four further clarifications:

1. The security threat to Israel was great, attested to by the extent and power of the armies and armaments Israel faced. Still, the public's perception of that threat varied among groups and over time.
2. On many security issues there was a high level of consensus, bolstered by an ideology called the People Apart Syndrome. This ideology facilitated coping with the security threat perceived, and was braced by that threat. As perceived threat increased, the circle turned in on itself, to form a tighter knot.
3. The question of the future of the territories taken by Israel in the 1967 Six Days war was key to understanding Israel's security. For many, the issue was emotional, and even religious. But others had more pragmatic arguments: some doves, for instance, tended to stress demographic trends of an expanding Arab population, and the wisdom of seeking durable political solutions to forestall military confrontation; hawks tended to see military confrontation as inevitable, and hence preferred the strategic depth afforded by retaining the territories. Regardless of argument, there was little doubt that public opinion on the issue was divided, and this division gave politicians more, not less, latitude in forming security policies. Public opinion split in a manner that appeared to lead to standstill and paralysis, but that same situation could be mustered by a legitimate leadership into a policy which would commit the nation one way or the other. The more or less equal division of an alert polity may empower a leadership determined to decide, or may be the excuse of one bent on avoiding decision.
4. The demographic cleavages of Israel were useful, if imperfect, guides to an individual's policy position; hawks tended to be younger, less educated, lower-class, more religious, sephardi (Jews of Asian and African origins), while doves were disproportionately found among the older, more educated, higher-class, more secular, ashkenazi (Jews of European origins). Events such as Sadat's coming to Jerusalem, the intifada, and the Gulf war affected opinion; generally this change of policy position had an impact on all groups in the same direction. Shifts seemed to be along the spectrum of more or less, with few individuals changing previous positions in a radical manner. Events often produced polarization, but that took place most noticeably at the extremes of the continuum; the bulk of the population moved in tandem according to a more universal calculus.

SURVEYING THE ISRAELI PUBLIC, 1962–1994

The analyses presented in this book are based largely on public opinion surveys of representative samples of adult Jews in Israel, numbering thousands of respondents (see Appendix I). Carried out in the 33-year period between 1962 and 1994, the surveys were almost always based on representative samples of the adult Jewish population of Israel, excluding individuals from kibbutzim and from the territories occupied by Israel after the Six Days war of 1967. Special supplementary material included a 1962 survey of 300 kibbutz members, and a 1990 survey of West Bank residents. In addition, a two-wave panel (1987 and 1988) and a three-wave panel (1987, 1988, and 1990), in which the same respondents were reinterviewed, were analyzed.

The time period covered by this study ranges over decades laden with "historical" events, and these events affected the way the public reacted to policy issues. Perspective is a gift conferred by time and distance; it is very difficult to discern the importance of developments when in close proximity. But there can be little doubt that the Six Days war of 1967 will always be identified as a decisive turning point in Israeli history; the events of the decades following that war obviously played a critical role in defining the country's future.

Public opinion reacted differently to different stimuli. Sometimes the reaction to events was crisp, as with Sadat's visit to Jerusalem in 1977, and sometimes slower, as with the intifada 10 years later (Stone 1982; Shamir and Shamir 1992). The beginning of the Arab-Israeli peace talks in 1991, following the Gulf war, and the signing of the peace accord with the Palestine Liberation Organization in 1993, marked other junctures of potential change. All of these highlighted, and were highlighted by, the threats perceived by Israelis as being both of war and of peace. Public opinion reacted to events, and adjusted to the changing view of security over the years (Handel 1973; Yariv 1980; Horowitz 1982; Yaniv 1987a; Horowitz 1993).

A habit of confrontation is perhaps as difficult to give up as any other habit. The ways of peace are difficult for those disciplined in war. As international relations changed in the post-cold-war world, there was no doubt that Israel's security dilemmas were also changing. Israel was faced with the challenges attendant upon entering into situations of peace or pseudo peace with many of its neighbors, of forgoing immediate gratification for promises of future tranquillity, of believing the promises of leaders of countries which in the not distant past had expressed enmity and disdain. Should Israel take those risks? Part of the answer rested with how such threats were perceived, and the lessons learned, by public opinion in Israel in the past. Another part depended on the quality of the leadership and the direction it chose to take. Public opinion could be led, but it was neither deaf nor dumb.

The 1967–94 years were different from the two decades which followed independence in 1948. The earlier period was characterized by feelings of military insecurity regarding threats from neighboring countries; the development of a secure and stable, if insulated, domestic scene; and the political, economic, spiritual, and cultural dominance of the party in power at the time of independence, Mapai (later known as the Labor party). The period between 1967 and 1994 saw a change in each category: in its international setting, Israel experienced a growing sense of security after the trauma of the Yom Kippur war in 1973. This sense of security was underscored by the initiation of massive American aid, and the signing of peace treaties with Egypt in 1979 and with Jordan in 1994. In 1982 Israel even initiated war in Lebanon against the PLO and the Lebanese army, risking the wrath of the Syrians and the other powers of the Eastern front. In the 1991 Gulf war, even though it was attacked, Israel did not participate, mostly because of American pressure. The U.S.-led coalition against Iraq, which included Egypt, Syria, and Saudi Arabia, might have fallen apart had Israel acted. During this same period, in addition to the SCUD missiles raining down on the country in 1991, Israel was subject to terrorist attacks from outside the country (which was not new), and to the uprising of the Arab population in the territories occupied by Israel in the 1967 Six Days war, intifada, which began in 1987 (which was new). And it went from dominance to competitiveness in electoral politics.

Table 1.1 lists the security and political highlights of the 1967-94 period. Six of Israel's first eight prime ministers were active in this period. All but the first two, David Ben-Gurion and Moshe Sharett, who were in power until 1963, led the government at various times during these years. Labor gained electoral strength at the end of the 1960s, but declined in the 1970s until it lost power in 1977. Then it began a slow and unsteady recovery; the Likud's record was the mirror image of Labor's.

As already noted, the analyses in this volume are based on surveys of attitudes of representative samples of Israeli Jews. Two topics this study does *not* deal with are Arab opinion and elite opinion. Arab citizens of Israel (not territories residents) constitute almost 20 percent of the population of Israel, and some 17 percent of the electorate. However, they do not take part in the security debate in Israel, although they are sometimes a topic in that debate (Smooha 1978, 1989, 1992; Rouhana 1989; Al-Haj 1995), and hence they are not included in these analyses. What this exclusion says about Israeli society, and about whether or not it is "democratic" to omit Arabs from the security debate in Israel, are topics beyond the scope of this book. But in terms of research strategy, it certainly makes good sense to focus on Jewish respondents. Israel defines itself as a Jewish state and one of its cherished values is to prepare itself as a home for future Jewish immigrants. Arabs do not serve in the armed forces, nor is it legitimate in the Israeli political culture for a governing coalition to rely on the support of Arab political parties to provide the swing votes in decisions about territories and peace proposals.

The reasons why such a large minority group can be excluded in a study of public opinion in a democracy explain a good deal about the political culture of Israel and about the limitations of public opinion in its strict sense. If only numbers mattered, then most Israelis (half the Jews and all the Arabs) would support dovish policies. But more than numbers matter: distribution, concentration, intensity, and leadership also matter. Most important, politics matters.

Table 1.1. *Security and Political Highlights 1967-1994*

Security and foreign affairs	Domestic politics
	1963-69 - Levi Eshkol prime minister
1967 - Six Days war	
1968-69 - War of Attrition	1967-70 - National Unity Government including Dayan and Begin
	1969 - Golda Meir prime minister
	1969 - Labor's biggest victory
1973 - Yom Kippur war	
	1973 (after war) - Labor wins but strength diminished
1974 - disengagement agreements	1974 (after agreements) - Yitzhak Rabin prime minister
	1977 - Likud victory; Menachem Begin prime minister
1977 - Sadat visit to Jerusalem	
1978 - Camp David accords	
1981 - cease-fire agreement with PLO in Lebanon	1981 - close race; Likud victory; large 2-party vote
1982 - Lebanon campaign	
	1983 - Yitzhak Shamir prime minister
	1984 - close race; Labor victory but smaller 2-party vote; rotation agreement; Shimon Peres prime minister
	1986 - Shamir again prime minister
1987 - intifada begins	
1991 - January: Gulf war - October: peace conference in Madrid	1988 - close race; Likud victory but smaller 2-party vote
1993 - mutual recognition ("Jericho-Gaza first") accord with the PLO	
1994 - Syria expresses willingness for peace treaty; peace treaty signed with Jordan	1992 - Labor victory; Rabin again prime minister

The views of the political elite are on display in the positions taken by their parties, by the speeches they make, and by the policies they advocate (Heradstviet 1974; Brecher 1972, 1980; Yaniv and Pascal 1980; Peri 1983; Yishai 1987; Inbar 1991; Shamir 1991). The strengthened linkage over time between them and the public is expressed in the growing importance of issue-based voting in Israel, analyzed in Chapter 5. In this study, many questions relate to the assessment of leaders, parties, and policies, but the questions are asked only of the public.

The years under consideration represent more than half of the years of Israel's existence up to this time. It was a period characterized by conflicting trends: steady growth of the Jewish population yet faster growth of the Arab population under Israel's jurisdiction; a strengthened security position yet increasing dangers from nonconventional weapons; a growing economy over time yet one which was not spared the occasionally grave problems of inflation, unemployment, and erratic growth.

Israel's population within its pre-1967 borders increased by 77.3 percent from 1969 to 1993 (see Table 1.2); growth in the territories was greater at 83.9 percent. Change stemmed from the natural growth of births over deaths, from the waves of immigration of Jews, especially the mass immigration from the former Soviet Union since 1989, and from emigration. Table 1.2 includes inhabitants in pre-1967 Israel and in the territories (the West Bank and Gaza) taken in the Six Days war (see Benvenisti 1986, 1988). The population of pre-1967, Jews and Arabs (line 2), were citizens of Israel and had the right to vote in elections; the surveys on which the analyses of this book are based focus on Jews only (line 2.a).

Jews and Arabs within the pre-1967 borders generated different growth rates during this period (see Table 1.2 and Figure 1.1). Both populations grew, for the Jews at about 69 percent, and for Arabs above 125 percent. In 1969, Jews made up about 64 percent of the total population, and 86 percent within the pre-1967 borders. The corresponding figures for 1992 were 63 percent and 82 percent. In the pre-1967 borders, the Arab population more than doubled its size between 1969 and 1992, while Jews were only two-thirds again as numerous; from 14.4 percent of Israeli citizens in 1969, Arabs constituted 18.3 percent in 1992.

The imbalance between Jews and non-Jews grew despite the efforts of the Israeli government to increase Jewish population by encouraging immigration and by discouraging Israeli Jews from leaving, or by granting them benefits if they returned. Not only Jews left Israel; there has been a steady out-migration of Arabs as well; the Arab Christian community has especially shrunk in size, although it never made up a large fraction of the Arab population. Many Arabs of the territories, living under military occupation and facing uncertainties of livelihood in a politically charged

Table 1.2. *Population in Israel and Territories, 1969-1992 (in 000s)*

	1969	1973	1977	1981	1984	1988	1992	Increase 1969-1992
1. Total population	3,892	4,392	4,800	5,179	5,503	5,961	6,965	79.7%
2. Pre-1967 borders	2,930	3,338	3,653	3,978	4,200	4,477	5,196	77.3%
a. Jews	2,507	2,845	3,077	3,320	3,472	3,659	4,243	69.2%
b. non-Jews	423	493	576	658	728	818	953	125.3%
3. Territories (a+b)	962	1,054	1,147	1,201	1,303	1,484	1,769	83.9%
a. West Bank	598	652	696	732	793	895	1,052	75.9%
b. Gaza Strip	364	402	451	469	510	589	717	96.8%
c. Jews	[a]	2	11	27	46	66	110	[a]
Jews as % of total (2a+3c/1, in %)	64.4	64.8	64.3	64.6	63.9	62.5	62.5	[c]
Jews[b] as % in pre-1967 borders (2a/2, in %)	85.6	85.2	84.2	83.5	82.7	81.7	81.7	[c]
Territories of total (3/1, in %)	24.7	24.0	23.9	23.2	23.4	24.9	25.4	[c]

[a] No 1969 population.
[b] Numbers include Jews in territories.
[c] Not relevant.
Source: Compiled from *Statistical Abstracts of Israel*, various years.

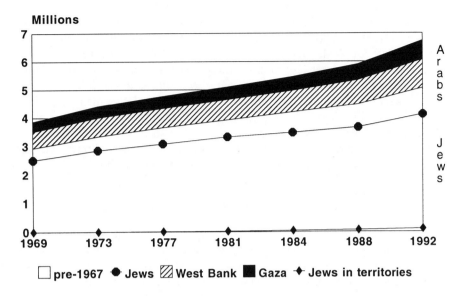

Figure 1.1. Population of Israel, 1969–1992.

environment, opted to leave. Fertility rates (representing the average number of children a woman may bear during her lifetime) fell for all groups in Israel, but mostly among Moslem Arabs: the total fertility rate for that group in 1970 was 8.95 and 4.70 in 1990. The comparable figures for Arab Christians and Jews, respectively, were 3.62 and 2.57, and 3.41 and 2.69. Despite the falling Arab fertility rate and the dual policy of encouraging the immigration of Jews and the emigration of Arabs, the higher rate of Arab population growth was not stemmed (Friedlander and Goldscheider 1979; Goldscheider 1992a, 21, and 1992b).

The Israeli economy grew dramatically in the same period, and the standard of living rose for all in the population, although after the 1973 Yom Kippur war the growth of per capita product began to drop (Aharoni 1991). Inflation soared in the 1980s, unemployment in the 1990s (Shalev 1992, 239–40); by the mid-1990s growth had picked up impressively and unemployment was shrinking. The gross domestic product per capita in constant prices was 14,424 for 1969 and 22,435 for 1991 (*Statistical Abstracts of Israel*). While both groups showed improvement, growth among Jews was higher than among Arabs. In 1994, a World Bank report of the standard of living of the nations of the world listed Israel in 18th place (*Ha'aretz*, January 21, 1994).

Military expenditure as a percentage of gross national product fell to

12.8 percent in 1989 and continued downward in the 1990s; it was as high as 24.4 percent in 1984 and 25.5 percent in 1982 (*Encyclopedia Britannica Yearbooks*); the world percent rates of military expenditure as a percentage of GNP for those years were 4.9, 5.9, and 6.0 percent, respectively. This decline expressed less military budget relative to a national budget burdened with many other pressures; it also could be lowered because of the growth in the size of the economy, and the relative lessening of hostility levels of Israel's neighbors. But given the military threats Israel faced and the political risks it considered taking, it was not surprising that the downward slide of the military budget caused concern in many quarters. These and other factors are the backdrop for change in public opinion.

POLICY MAKING IN A DEMOCRACY

Shrewd politicians have two eyes on the target: one on where the public is, and one on where the public is going. Politicians clearly respect, fear, and try to manipulate public opinion. The leaders of every state – and certainly every democracy – are concerned with the reaction of the public to their policies, and it is the public which will ultimately enjoy or suffer the fruits of these policies. The political leadership of a democratic regime will stand for election in the not too distant future. In the analysis of security policy, the role of public opinion seems marginal compared to political, military, and economic factors. But politicians understand that there is truth in the old adage "all politics is local politics"; politicians are correct in according public opinion an important place in their considerations (Russett 1990).

Public opinion does not make policy; policy is made by politicians; the distribution of public attitudes is thus a crucial datum for politicians and decision-makers (Holsti and Rosenau 1984, 1986; Lijphart 1984). In democracies, the impact of public opinion on policy is through the selection of politicians who will ultimately make decisions. Policy, in turn, affects public opinion; the leadership has the authority to define the security agenda, and has access to the media. As the next elections approach, this situation is balanced to a degree, but it still favors those who wield power. As Key (1966, 2, 7) points out:

The voice of the people is but an echo. The output of an echo chamber bears an inevitable and invariable relation to the input . . . [But] voters are not fools . . . the electorate behaves about as rationally and responsibly as we should expect, given the clarity of the alternatives presented to it and the character of the information available to it.

There has been a spirited debate among those who study opinion about the public. Earlier U.S. studies characterized the citizenry as uninformed and uninterested, while scholars now tend to see the public in a more positive manner. The conclusions of the literature on public opinion has shifted in the past few decades from one dominated by a pessimistic reading of the public's role in decision making, to a more optimistic tone. This change parallels the pattern of change which occurred in the voting behavior literature. Those studies tended to characterize voters in the United States in the 1950s and 1960s as "nonideological" (Campbell, Converse, Miller, and Stokes, 1960; Converse 1964), only to be challenged and partially replaced, or at least augmented, by a literature that explored and found higher levels of issue voting in the 1970s and 1980s (Nie, Verba, and Petrocik, 1979; Smith 1989; Mayer 1992; Niemi and Weisberg 1993). The parallel shift in the characterization of public opinion regarding foreign and security policy saw a move from an ignorant and apathetic public whose attitudes did not hang together in a logical manner (Almond 1960; Verba and Brody 1970; Merritt 1973) to one that is knowledgeable (Wittkopf 1990) and even "rational" (Page and Shapiro 1992).

It may be that both positions are correct, but for different periods of time. One of the most pernicious fallacies to which social science researchers are prone is to believe that their findings are valid in other times and different places. It may be that the former depiction was accurate in the post–World War II period in the United States, but as conditions forced a change of focus from the postwar euphoria to the troubling issues of social and racial unrest and Vietnam, as the war generation was replaced by their children, the latter portrayal became more fitting.

The Israeli case does not seem to have undergone similar changes. The Israeli public was, and continues to be, informed, interested, alert, and argumentative; skeptical, yet prepared to sacrifice for security. This is a constant of the political culture of Israel, despite tremendous changes in population size, demographic composition, economic development, and security position. The available data and anecdotes suggest that the Israeli public was always informed and involved. There have been periods of great cynicism, and even though many in the Israeli public knew what they wanted and expressed that desire, the result of this informed activity was official vacillation between one policy pole or another, or shared power by politicians who chose to defer decisive action. Many in the system felt thwarted, but no new party emerged to deal with the security issue in a new way. Without an available policy alternative, politicians were rotated rather than replaced.

It would be desirable to make a clear statement here about the interaction between the opinions of that public and policy. One of the most fascinating in the academic study of public opinion, the issue has far-reaching implications for practitioners and for the theory of democracy.

Unfortunately, a sharp, clear-cut answer is beyond our grasp. Opinion sets general limits or, in Stimson's (1991) phrase, "zones of acquiescence." These may change over time, but it is within these limits that government acts (Schattschneider 1942, Truman 1951, Key 1961). Public opinion plays a crucial role in policy formation – but not a direct one. As Almond (1960) states, public opinion supports policy, but does not initiate it:

> The function of the public in a democratic policy-making process is to set certain policy criteria in the form of widely held values and expectations. It evaluates the results of policies from the point of view of their conformity to these basic values and expectations. The policies themselves, however, are the products of leadership groups ("elites") who carry on the specific work of policy formulation and policy advocacy.

Saying that leaders are aware of public opinion is not the same as saying that public opinion affects policy. On the contrary; Coplin (1974) points out that politicians know that they can influence public opinion rather easily and generate positive feedback for the policies they have initiated.

A fascinating paradox emerges from the consideration of public opinion and policy; and it is all the more fascinating because it applies regardless of whether the public is found to be apathetic or involved. Democratic theory has no answer to the paradox that in the face of either apathy or involvement, if the will of the public is equally divided, the politicians may ignore it with impunity.

The pessimistic version of this paradox of democracy portrays the public as uninformed, misinformed, or misled; people are not concerned and not about to discover their will, let alone express it to the leaders. Elites decide as they see fit, with little or no accountability or threat of reprisal from an incensed public. But even in the optimistic scenario, with citizens informed, interested, and articulate, politicians are still free to do as they choose when the distribution of opinion is relatively balanced. Under these conditions, "elections are virtual lotteries because the two sides cancel each other out" (Rabinowitz and MacDonald 1989, 115), and precisely because of the balanced division of public opinion, the elite can do as it sees fit.

Elections can thus foster experiments in public policy, with no direct relationship to the party platform or the campaign. This has happened in Israeli elections and is the root explanation of why the fit between public opinion and policy is less than good. The vote is the important ingredient in determining who will decide, but not in determining the direction policy will take.

It is thus inaccurate to argue that Menachem Begin rode into power in Israel in 1977 on a wave which demanded that a hard-line, nationalist approach be applied to Israel's foreign policy. That interpretation is as problematic as the one attributing Begin's electoral success to a groundswell in public opinion which directed him to reach a peace treaty with Egypt in 1979 at the expense of returning the Sinai Peninsula, restoring to Egypt the oil fields of the Sinai, and uprooting Jewish settlements there. Nor would it be accurate to analyze Labor's victory in 1992 solely in light of the less militant platform of that party. While it is true that after the 1992 elections Labor party leaders strained to turn their parliamentary majority into peace agreements with Arab neighbors, it is simplistic to think that they exerted these efforts because they were given a mandate to do so. The links between public opinion, policy, and political outcomes are much more complex.

It is more to the political point to recall that the hard-line Begin was able to get 95 of the 120 members of the Knesset to support the crucial portion of the treaty with Egypt, while the more pragmatic Rabin had ample reason to be apprehensive about the political correctness in Israel's political culture of cutting a deal with Arab states and the Palestinians based on a bare majority of the Knesset, with some of those votes likely to come from Arab Knesset members. Rabin's call for a referendum if significant territorial concessions on the Golan Heights were to be part of a peace treaty with Syria reflected this same apprehension. Promising to turn to the public for its judgment regarding the peace deal that he could strike with Syria gave Rabin a reprieve from the relentless pressure of a large part of the Jewish public (almost all readings portrayed it as a majority of the public) that opposed significant territorial concessions on the Golan, made the point for the Syrians that the fate of the negotiations went beyond the preferences and personalities of the negotiators, and underscored the democratic underpinnings of the Israeli system. Few pointed out that in a future referendum on the Golan, some 20 percent of the voters would be Arab.

The crucial difference in these stories involves politics, not public opinion. While the support of public opinion cannot be a good predictor of policy outcome, the absence of favorable public opinion for the policy direction the leader chooses to take is almost always a bad sign for the policy initiative being pursued.

Elections are sometimes portrayed as a referendum regarding an important issue, and in Israel in the post-1967 period elections were often described as referenda regarding the future of the territories taken in the Six Days war. However, this portrayal is largely inappropriate. Voters are regularly faced with the one-vote many-issues dilemma, in which a single vote is provided a voter to express his or her opinion on a range of issues, and on the leadership itself. There is no empirical support for the proposition that all voters in any election are simultaneously motivated by one issue in reaching their decisions about the vote. Moreover, one would have

to accept herculean assumptions about the ability of the electorate to define issues and to order parties in a unidimensional space, and then to
translate these abilities of defining and ordering into the vote, in order to
accept the proposition.

Public opinion defines the parameters within which policy is set. Its
mandates are vague, rather than specific. We might expect that many have
a position on autonomy for Palestinians, but not necessarily on the size of
the police force which should be agreed to for that autonomous region.
Public opinion deals in principles, policy deals in details. Opinion affects
policy on strategic long-term issues, but policy affects opinion on short-
term tactical ones. The task of the leader is to affect long-range change of
opinion on strategic issues by instituting policies which in turn will move
opinion in the direction desired (Zaller 1992).

MEASURING OPINION

The technological revolution of the last part of the twentieth century has
profoundly affected the practice of public opinion survey research and has
encouraged the mushrooming of reports on what people think. This trend
has accelerated the accumulation of data regarding public opinion and
facilitated its analysis. We probably know more today about the responses
(if not the thoughts) of the common man than at any other period of
history. The revolution is truly startling. Consider two examples, one
grand-scale, the other small-scale: (1) I was recently told by a colleague
with prodigious work capacity that he had undertaken a series of surveys
which would sample, for the first time in human history, the attitudes of
more than half the population of the planet; (2) in the 1969 Israeli elections, there were 16 reports on polls in the Israeli press; in 1992, the
parallel number was 421. The space allocated for reporting these polls in
column inches jumped from 172 in 1969 to 9,411 in 1992 (Weimann 1995).

The easily accessed power to analyze amounts of data unthinkable only a
few years ago should alert us more strongly than ever to the dangers of
scientific hubris. The concept of public opinion has always been loaded
with difficult methodological and epistemological problems, and the new
facility with which we can "measure" public opinion makes it even more
seductive. One key question is whether I am discovering a phenomenon
(public opinion) which is a feature of the real world, or am I discussing
something I created and labeled?

Since we are interested in questions such as whether policy is produced
by public opinion or is influenced by it, the issue of whether or not public
opinion is created or invented is important. Is there such a thing as public opinion out there, or do we, in our zeal to measure and to analyze public

opinion, create it by making up questions which are in turn answered by cooperative citizens? Do my surveys discover the contours of a "real" public opinion, or do their results create something I call public opinion, useful enough for me and others to understand something about public matters, but with no clear empirical referent?

Probably the "true" answer to the question of created or discovered is ultimately unknowable, and therefore we must behave as if the correct answer were "created" since that posture intrudes less on reality; that the concept is one developed for my purposes, with no discernible proof that public opinion "really" exists. We shall discuss public opinion in this book, its contents and its correlates, in a real-life context and regarding a life-and-death topic, but we must recall that public opinion exists only as we define it and measure it. The goal should be a high degree of accuracy in measurement, and a healthy degree of cognizance of the limitations of the method.

Social scientists are familiar with such problems, but the manner in which the issues are raised regarding public opinion is unusually sharp. Many social science concepts are abstractions of reality and have no direct, or only indirect, referents in empirical reality. For example, one cannot see power, or an election, or a parliament, but one can see those who wield power, or those who are declared winners in an election, or those who were voted into the parliament, and the volumes of laws which the members of the parliament passed, and the building in which the members meet.

No one has ever seen public opinion, and the empirical referent for that concept is as elusive as any, if not more so. In practice, we often (too often?) accept the results of public opinion polls as evidence of the existence of public opinion. Yet its reality – let alone its impact – is a matter of definition and interpretation and not of direct observation. This places an extraordinary burden and opportunity on those who define and measure public opinion, and on those who read their work. Among the many pitfalls that await those who deal with the term, we must remember that the use of the public opinion concept is very loose and is often used in other senses, such as when a noisy demonstration or an articulate spokesman on television are depicted as evidence of public opinion.

The concept "public opinion" has a scientific air about it, but it is applicable only if the data were collected in a professionally acceptable manner. A properly drawn sample with a good questionnaire administered by trained and trustworthy interviewers will produce a snapshot of opinion as close to the actual distribution of the moment as is possible to obtain. But it will be a static picture, and "reality" might change in the nanoseconds following the completion of the survey. One colleague gave me well-intentioned advice which goes to the heart of this issue: "Gather your data in periods in which security incidents do not occur." If I knew enough to do that, I would not have to conduct the surveys at all. A good public opinion survey is like a good snapshot rather than a movie, showing accurately enough what it shows, but not being able to show what happened before, what happened later, or what was not shown. A movie, while also incomplete, is more complete.

There are methods to contain some of these problems. The analyses in this book are based largely on answers to identically worded questions collected from interviews of independent samples of the same population following the assumption of sampling theory that well-drawn samples of the same population will be equivalent within known bounds of probability. In addition, a panel design which calls for interviewing the same people a number of times was employed. Both methods attempt to introduce a dynamic dimension into the study of public opinion. Using identical questions over time is an important technique, but not a foolproof one. Suppose the reality about which the questions were asked changes. The question remains, but the stimulus has been altered. For example, we shall present the results of questions probing the response of Israelis concerning participation in an international peace conference. When broached before 1991, the socially acceptable response in Israel was to oppose participating in the conference because the Arab states refused to take part on terms acceptable to the Israeli government. In 1991, the Madrid conference convened, and the question took on a different meaning. Before Madrid, a no response indicated support for the government position; after Madrid, to agree with government policy meant giving a yes response.

A panel design – interviewing the same respondents again – will also be used, and while better, it too has limitations. There is a natural attrition rate in the reinterview stage, perhaps because respondents cannot be located, or because they refuse to cooperate a second time.

Are opinions expressions of "real" attitudes or are they merely reactions to the probings of a newly met interviewer? Are opinions part of larger belief systems or are they autonomous answers to questions? Are opinions stable over time? What is the meaning of a public opinion "mood"? What are the relations among values, beliefs, attitudes, and opinions? How do attitudes change? These questions permeate the literature of public opinion (Zaller 1992), and each of them will be addressed in this book.

Converse (1964, 107) observed that attitudes are unstable over time because there is a "major component of random answering in most survey data." He developed the notion of "non-attitudes" to account for people responding to surveyors on issues they hadn't thought much about. Converse saw non-attitudes as a feature of modern society and accordingly was dismissive of the opinions of most of the public since these random attitudes could hardly be characterized by constraint or driven by structure.

This skepticism about the integrity of attitudes for most of the public is raised by the intriguing finding that there tend to be "modest individual level stability together with remarkably high aggregate stability" (Inglehart 1990, 106) in many panel studies. It seems that although the attitudes of individuals may change in a seemingly random matter, the total distribution of a properly drawn sample will show much greater stability. This fascinating notion is reformulated by Page and Shapiro (1992, 16–17) when they assert that "even if individual opinions or survey responses are ill-informed, shallow, and fluctuating, collective opinion can be real, highly stable . . . and it can be measured with considerable accuracy by standard survey techniques." That individuals may fluctuate more than well-drawn samples is an important axiom of survey research and allows Page and Shapiro to assert that public opinion is rational (they really mean stable, although they write about rationality), and even wise.

It is a huge leap from doing careful sampling and analysis to the assertion that public opinion is an aggregate different from the sum of its parts, and that assertion should cause us pause. The statement is open to the charge of reification; public opinion has no empirical referent independent of the polls we collect and study. Asserting "rationality" and "wisdom" assumes a reality that is knowable and a nexus between policy and politics that can be observed beyond our own value preferences. More cautious, and therefore more attractive, is Dahl's formulation (1985): "It is true that a democratic regime runs the risk that the people will make mistakes. But the risk exists in all regimes in the real world, and the worst blunders of this century have been made by leaders in non-democratic regimes."

Mood is an especially attractive and elusive concept in public opinion research. In his chapter entitled "The Instability of Mood," Almond (1960, 76) maintains that under normal circumstances the American public tended to be indifferent to matters of foreign policy because such issues seemed far away from everyday interest and activities. He argued that only immediate threats break into the focus of attention, and that the moment the pressure is reduced there is a "swift withdrawal, like the snapping back of a strained elastic" (76). Converse's argument about the unstructured nature of American opinion and Almond's interpretation of mood argue against the primacy of public opinion. A public that gyrates capriciously between isolationism on the one hand, and involvement on the other, cannot be taken too seriously if a stable and reasonable foreign policy is desired (see also Miller and Stokes 1963; Caspari 1970; Sniderman, Brody, and Tetlock 1991; Stimson 1991).

That depiction was never a good characterization of the realities in Israel, whether or not it was true for Americans then or now. As will be amply demonstrated, the Israeli public generated high levels of structure and constraint of security attitudes, and very high levels of knowledge and interest in security and political matters.

How does opinion change come about? A catalogue of reasons of how collective opinion changes might include the possibility that individual opinion remains the same but the composition of the population changes; many individuals change opinion in the same direction at the same time reflecting shared personal experience; many individuals slowly undergo changes in experiences and life circumstances so that their needs, values, and beliefs change and bring about corresponding changes in policy preferences. The political world changes in ways that alter the perceived costs and benefits of policy alternatives for many citizens at once, with the introduction of new technology, or international crisis, or war. Public opinion may change temporarily because of dramatic events which impress a lot of people at once and cause a sudden blip in public opinion before it fades from memory (see Page and Shapiro 1992, 31–4; Chapter 8 this volume).

My use of public opinion surveys is not simply an exercise in tallying how many say one thing, and how many another, although there is intrinsic interest in that too. I shall also broach analytical issues relating to thought patterns and beliefs about security, to the role of threat, and to relations between politics and public opinion. These topics are central to a better understanding of Israeli society and politics because attitudes regarding security play such a central role in shaping the reality of the country, and because those beliefs are encapsulated in a rich tapestry of image and hope, of fantasy and fear.

The approach used here sees the public as having indirect influence on the policy process. While decision making in Israel is highly centralized, public opinion does play a role. This role is both nourished and restrained by the difficult dilemmas faced by Israel's policy makers, by the high cost of a wrong decision, and by the nightmare of the Jewish past, which has been part of the conceptual baggage of every Israeli decision maker since independence.

THEMES

This book presents mounds of data and numerous figures and tables. To steer the reader through the material, the following overview is offered, outlining the plan of the book and its guiding propositions.

Chapter 2 discusses the capacity of Israelis to be simultaneously apprehensive about the aspirations of the Arabs and yet optimistic about their own ability to overcome these threats. Over the decades, a slight downward trend in confidence regarding the destiny of the nation was discerned; however, the severity of threat perception, although persistent, was somewhat relieved over the years.

Using another measure of mood and morale, there seem to have been two other parallel developments during these years. On the one hand, there was a positive, upbeat quality when one was asked to evaluate one's personal position, and on the other a concurrent deterioration in the estimate of the nation's circumstances. This pattern, similar to those generated in other postindustrial societies, reflected the emergence of a me-now mentality in Israel. It was an orientation buttressed by an expanding consumer economy, and by social policies of the various ruling parties, each of which vied for the votes of the middle class. In addition, the public was affected by the challenge of the intifada and by the complexities of superpower developments.

Issues of peace and war are explored in Chapter 3. Israelis' expectations of peace were juxtaposed to the dangers of war. In addition, the way that the samples conceived of peace was assessed. Surprisingly, the cold peace with Egypt surpassed the minimal expectations of most in the samples.

The Israel Defense Forces, one of the most respected institutions in Israel, was held in high esteem by the samples, although it was not immune from criticism. Israelis were ready to make sacrifices for security, up to a point. They were also anxious to take tough measures in the territories and against terrorists, and were critical of Israeli governments whose policies were considered too soft on the whole. They were also willing to develop nuclear weapons and to use them; at the same time, their desire for peace and their belief in its possible achievement increased over the years.

In the four political-security events considered here – Lebanon, the intifada, the Gulf war, and the peace accord with the PLO – the population showed high levels of initial support for the position of the government. This is especially important because at the outset of these events, governments led by different parties were in control, underscoring the theme of the malleability of public opinion. In the case of protracted conflicts (Lebanon and the intifada), the initial support by the population faded, to be replaced by a polarization closely following the political contours of the public debate. In the case of the Gulf war, much shorter and with only passive Israeli involvement, support for the government position remained strong.

Chapter 4 scrutinizes the basic attitudes of the security policy domain in the 1980s and early 1990s in Israel. Focusing on the future of the territories and the political implications of policy positions – such as the appropriate posture of the IDF in the territories, or the civil rights to be granted Arabs if the territories were annexed, and the stance toward the Palestine Liberation Organization and the idea of establishing a Palestinian state – a nine-item policy scale was developed. Using the policy scale scores, the oscillations of attitude over the 1987–93 period were plotted. What emerged was

a pattern of increasing militancy in the late 1980s and a creeping conciliation in the early 1990s; the score peaked (was most hawkish) in 1988, a year
after the intifada began. On the whole, people seemed to differentiate their
responses depending on the implied time-frame of the stimulus: on short-
term issues, militant positions were taken; on long-term goals, more conciliatory stands were adopted and became more prominent.

The shift in the policy score was not caused by a disproportionate movement of one group; instead, the pattern represented a rather consistent
shift by all groups in the direction of conciliation. The swing of respondents
with various social, economic, and political characteristics was uniform on
the whole; events and moods affected most of the groups, and in much the
same manner. Over all, groups changed in the dovish direction; while
background variables were helpful in predicting the original relative degree
of dovishness or hawkishness, background variables made no difference in
ascertaining the direction of change during the period under study.

The opinion-election-policy nexus is examined in Chapter 5. This is a
crucial theme of the book: policy is not made by public opinion alone; it is
made by politicians elected to office. Policy flows from election results
because the elections empower those who make policy. Elections are the
beginning of the process of setting policy for the nation, not the end of the
process. Policy decisions are specific and elections are diffuse, so it is
usually incorrect to view elections as a referendum on a given issue. Obviously, the phenomenon is cyclical since policy also interacts with later
voting decisions, and decision makers keep at least one eye on the election
calendar and one ear open to the musings of the media and the roar of the
streets.

The Israeli case is an excellent example of this. While public opinion is
catered to, monitored, and studied, policy decisions impact public opinion
and not only reflect it. Menachem Begin in the late 1970s and early 1980s
made difficult and unprecedented decisions (Camp David, the Lebanese
war) because he had the political will and the parliamentary majority to do
so. Yitzhak Rabin in 1993 did the same in agreeing to mutual recognition
with the PLO. In Begin's case, public opinion went along regarding the
peace treaty with Egypt, but balked at the Lebanese war. Rabin made his
move with a fragile parliamentary majority, and a shifting public opinion.
But the strength of his own party in the Knesset in a relative sense (compared to other parties and to other likely coalitions) gave him the opportunity to alter Israeli history. Public opinion backed him at first, then shied
away from the deal cut with the PLO. But the crucial test would be the next
election and not the next opinion poll, and the crucial answer would be the
relative strength of his party and those other parties which supported him,
and not the absolute number of votes won. Thus, the few thousand voters

who swing the balance of electoral power one way or another, have within their power to set the stage for a leader's bold move. The swing voters, and the wedge issues which move them, then, become crucial in understanding how the system works. These swing voters in Israel of 1977 and 1992 are studied in Chapter 5.

Chapter 6 explores the mechanisms Israelis use to facilitate feeling threatened and confident – both at the same time. Also considered is the distribution of rational and religious patterns of thought in Israel, and their relations to the complex world of security alternatives. Using a combination of four mechanisms, Israelis seem to have been able to achieve cognitive harmony between feelings of being threatened and of believing in the country's ability to overcome: perceived success, denial, differentiation, and a belief system called here the People Apart Syndrome.

For respondents to the surveys, that syndrome was a most pervasive mechanism for overcoming the anxieties about the security situation in Israel. The syndrome was composed of two constructs, here called God-and-us and go-it-alone. The first related to the special, mystical relation perceived by many between God, Israel, and Jewish history; and the second, to feelings of isolation and to the belief that ultimately Jewish destiny depends on the Jews themselves. The protracted conflict with its Arab neighbors in which Israel found itself seemed to activate mechanisms of group solidarity and ideological consensus which contributed to the ability of the nation's citizenry to persist. The structure of the ideology and the attitudes it comprised seemed well designed to withstand long periods of frustration and stubborn resistance. This appeared to be a key factor in how such a small community could withstand so many pressures for such a long time.

The Jewish population of Israel shared many of these values even though they disagreed about policy positions. Politicians, journalists, and observers tended to focus on the divergence of opinion, but this focus overlooked the overarching agreement – the ideological glue – which permitted the system to hold together. Only by recalling that most politicians operated in the ooze of the accepted values can we understand how political change could have occurred during this period.

Aspects of political psychology, tapped by the People Apart Syndrome, seem much more effective in explaining policy position than do sociodemographic variables. Education and religiosity were related to these variables, social class more weakly related, and gender and age not at all. Those with low levels of education and high levels of religious observance were most likely to support nonconciliatory policy positions and to score highest on the People Apart constructs.

Threat is also related to policy choices, and this connection is considered in greater depth in Chapter 7. Knowing the degree of perceived threat and the individual's assessment of the likelihood that an event will occur form the basis of the model presented there. Using the model, an attempt is made to specify the conditions under which an individual would take a conciliatory position rather than a militant one. Rational choice theory was found wanting in predicting these decisions made under risk. Prospect theory, on the other hand, which uses a descriptive psychological analysis of judgment and choice that departs from rational theory, was more effective. Prospect theory takes into account emotional factors as opposed to the rational actor model of rational choice theory; since prospect theory predicts risk aversion in the domain of gains, and risk seeking in the domain of losses, it provides greater sensitivity to losses than to gains, whereas rational choice theory predicts risk aversion independent of the reference point.

Applied to the security domain, and to a lesser degree to the domestic ramifications of the religious-secular domain, the model provided insight into the political psychology of the respondents. For both the security and the religious domains, threat was a good predictor of policy position: support for returning the territories was highest among those least threatened by that eventuality, and having public life run by religious law was supported at the highest rates by those threatened by the separation of religion and state. The model successfully predicted the differences within the threatened group with those who thought the occurrence was likely generating the highest levels of support for the policy; both threat and likelihood worked together in predicting the rate of support for the policy proposition. The higher the rate of threat, the lower the support; among the threatened, the more likely the occurrence, the higher the rate of support. Policy position and likely outcome were good predictors of level of threat.

The findings offer intriguing implications for leaders intent on pointing an anxious population in new directions. For those already convinced of the cause, the emphasis should be on averting future dangers (such as war and terror, or civil war); for the hesitant and fearful, stressing that the conclusion is inevitable (returning the territories, for example) can focus the mind of the threatened on cutting down potential loss from international sanctions or isolation. Obviously, there are enormous political risks in projecting a dual message for the leadership, but it may be worth the try.

Values in conflict is the theme of Chapter 8. In many political situations, the question is not whether one agrees or disagrees with a value but, rather, what priority is given to it. Many values may be cherished, but they may be ordered in different ways. It is the hierarchy of values that orders people's positions on specific issues. Value priorities are not random; rather, they are structured by politics and ideology, with certain value combinations more prevalent and more enduring than others.

Value hierarchies significantly structure policy preferences and the changes that take place among them, as shown by the issues of the Israeli-Arab conflict. The more salient or acute the value conflict, the greater the correspondence between the hierarchy and the structure. This value trade-off approach presents a picture of Israeli public opinion which is very different from that usually portrayed: one of a population firmly supporting a Jewish majority in their state, with a very strong desire for peace. The values of land (territory) and democracy (equality) are shown to be much less important.

Chapter 9 investigates the connections among opinion, security, and democracy. Since Israeli democracy provides a mixture of great attention to formal matters such as majority rule and elections, but more cavalier concern for the underpinning values of democratic life such as civil liberties and minority rights, the maintenance of democratic government throughout its history must be considered as one of Israel's finest achievements. As in other democratic countries, civil rights were upheld by Israeli public opinion, especially in their abstract form. As they became more concrete, support for these principles dwindled. There was ambivalence regarding civil rights: a large and growing segment thought they should be extended to Arabs in the territories if those territories were annexed, yet they also thought that Jews should be granted preferential treatment.

Israelis were found to be very knowledgeable about security matters, and yet they were tentative about their security attitudes and felt they had little influence on security matters. Data for other countries, especially the United States, show low rates of information, interest, and participation. Israelis were prolific consumers of the news media and they were attentive to security issues. They also believed that they must be supportive of government and obey orders, even though they were skeptical about politicians and even army chiefs.

Israelis placed great importance on consensus during times of national security stress. By 1994, however, as issues regarding the future of the territories became more salient, there were signs that this pattern was changing. The propriety of obeying orders to remove Jews from settlements in the territories generated more division than other matters asked about in the past, and a third of the respondents admitted that in their opinion a civil war among Jews in Israel was likely. There might have been a greater sense of national security in the country, but political anxiety seemed to be on the rise. Israeli Jews who had been accustomed to religious fractionalism and security solidarity were faced with the possible breakdown of this pattern.

2

Overcoming Threat

– Woe to those who are at ease in Zion. (Amos 6:1)

Considering the advantages of Israel's adversaries in terms of population and natural resources, one might expect Israelis to view their security future with feelings of low confidence. On the whole, however, this has not been the case. Israelis were generally confident when it came to their perceptions of potency in the long confrontation with their neighbors. Part of this confidence rested on the unquestioned success of much of the record. Since it had looked bleak in the past and somehow the worst was averted, the gap between the threat perceived and the belief in the ability to overcome peril was narrowed. The consistent generalization, even though there were fluctuations in the details, was that Israelis felt secure in an objectively threatening situation.

The mood eroded over the decades; political solutions seemed unattainable, terror continued and even intensified, and the military threat persisted. Simultaneously, the limitations of national power in dealing with these issues seemed to become clearer, and the opening of dialogue with the enemies of the recent past seemed to engender a more realistic assessment. By the mid-1990s the mood appeared to be more in keeping with the enormity of the challenges facing the country. Over the years, there were swings between euphoria and pessimism; the assessment often proved too glum when there was danger, and too exuberant when the danger momentarily passed (Levy 1994). But based on the overall record, the persistent belief in the ability of the country to prevail was well founded.

THREAT

Arab Aspirations

Defining the threat perceived by a nation entails labeling states which are trying to prevent the realization of your national goals as enemies, or those who are willing or able to aid you in your attempt to achieve national goals as allies. Cantril (1953) points out that "people in one nation are hostile towards another nation not because they have unfavorable stereotypes;

rather, they develop negative stereotypes because they perceive that others are preventing them from achieving their self- or national-interest."

There were fascinating shifts in the assessment by the Israeli public of the security situation during the period studied; confidence levels were high on the whole, but tended to fluctuate in a downward direction. On the whole, the perception of the aspirations of the Arabs did not change much.[1]

Israelis demonstrated a very somber appraisal of the aspirations of the Arabs. The wording of the question in the surveys was purposely left vague; were Arab states to be asked about, or Palestinian organizations, or the Arab masses, the response would likely be affected. Asking about "the Arabs" allowed the respondent to focus on aspirations without involving a discussion of intergroup and intragroup differences. Unfortunately no measure exists for the "actual" aspirations of the Arabs (Harkabi 1986). If we had such a measure, we could discuss Mandel's (1986) "relative rationality" or Gordon's (1989) "stereotyping" defined as the difference between an individual's perception and the opponent's/other's perception of the same set of circumstances.

The ranking of the aspirations by the public was relatively unchanged over time. A small minority of about 10 percent thought that the ultimate goal of the Arabs was to recapture some of the territory lost in the Six Days war of 1967. A slightly larger group (between 20% and 30%) reported that they thought the Arabs aspired to a return of all the territories they lost in that war. For a larger group (about 25% to 30%), the Arabs wanted to conquer the State of Israel. The largest group by far, representing in one case almost half the sample, thought that the Arabs really wanted to conquer the State of Israel and to destroy most of the Jews living there. In fact, that percentage grew between 1986 and 1991, and dropped again in 1992, 1993, and 1994 (see Figure 2.1).

The aspirations of the Arabs have long been viewed with suspicion by Israelis, and the beginning of the peace process in 1991 did not seem to ameliorate that sense.[2] In the two election years of 1988 and 1992, low levels of the most extreme answer were recorded. Not coincidentally, important developments were taking place and some in the Arab world were turning a conciliatory face toward Israel. In November 1988, the Palestine National Council, meeting in Algiers, officially accepted the 1947 UN Partition Plan, thus recognizing a two-state solution to the Palestine problem. In 1992, the preliminaries regarding the peace talks were set and negotiations were about to begin. In September 1993, Prime Minister Yitzhak Rabin of Israel, and Yasir Arafat, head of the Palestine Liberation Organization, shook hands on the White House lawn in Washington after signing an accord granting mutual recognition and spelling out in a vague manner the steps which would lead to peace between the two parties. In January 1994

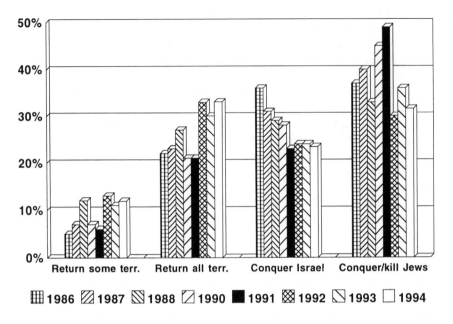

Figure 2.1. Aspirations of Arabs, 1986–1994.

in Geneva, with President Bill Clinton at his side, President Assad of Syria indicated willingness to achieve peace with Israel based on evacuation of the Golan Heights and a settlement of other disputes involving Israel in the region.

Despite these developments, between one-third and one-half of Israel's Jews believed that in the end the Arabs wanted to ravage Israel and slaughter the Jews in it, yet the Israeli public also saw the possibility for peace (or the absence of war) grow as the years went by (see Chapter 3). Moreover, when forced to choose between initiating peace talks and strengthening military capacity, the overwhelming majority chose the path of peace. These counterintuitive findings are all the more impressive because of their stability over time. They portray basic patterns of the Israeli public of the late 1980s and early 1990s. This was also the period in which pressures were applied to solve the problems resulting from the 1967 victory in the Six Days war that put much territory and many Palestinians under Israeli control. Especially after the 1991 Gulf war, these pressures seemed to mount, with George Bush, the president of the United States, and James Baker, his secretary of state, intent on curbing Israeli behavior regarding the settlements in the territories and progressing toward a solution of the Palestinian problem.

The picture presented, then, was of a population deeply distrustful of the aspirations of its adversaries; aware of the stark challenges faced by the country; quite optimistic regarding the ability of the country to overcome a series of dire situations; wary about the eventuality of war, but hopeful about the possibility of peace (Kimmerling 1993).

Israelis were aware that they faced long odds concerning security. They demonstrated two different patterns regarding the situation in which the country found itself. On the one hand, they perceived (in varying degrees) that the country faced threats. But they were very confident that Israel could overcome almost all of these security hazards. This point is fully developed in the next section, but there are additional indicators. For example, most (89% in 1986; 96% in 1987) expressed assurance in Israel's long-range existence; 85 percent in 1986 and 74 percent in 1987 assessed as nonexistent or low the probability that the State of Israel would be destroyed; in most of the surveys respondents were asked if they wanted to continue to live in Israel, and about 9 in 10 respondents consistently answered in the affirmative.

In 1986, 82 percent thought there was absolutely no chance (42%) or only little chance (40%) that the Jewish people would face another Holocaust. Regarding the possibility of another successful surprise attack by Arab armies such as occurred in 1973, the distribution was more normal in the statistical sense: 41 percent thought there was (33%) or definitely was (8%) a chance of another surprise attack; 59 percent thought there was not (38%) or was definitely no chance (21%) that Israel might be surprised again.

Much of the Israeli public generated a skewed picture regarding feelings of vulnerability, on the one hand, and judgments of the capacity to overcome challenges, on the other. A fundamental objective of the Zionist revolution was to change the status of the helpless Jew who was oppressed by his neighbors to a free and independent Jew who would be secure in his homeland. One irony of the history of Zionism is that while the Jews achieved freedom and independence in their land, they did not shake off their perception that opposition to them and struggle with them was owing to their Jewishness. Even mainstream Zionist parties still tend to reject a geopolitical explanation of international conflict and persist in analyzing the Israel-Arab conflict in the spirit, and often in the lexicon, of the persecution suffered by Jews in most European countries and in some of the countries of the Moslem world.

While the threat perceived is reminiscent of the Crusades, the pogroms, and the Holocaust, the response is biblical. No longer passive and meek, the response of Israel and Israelis is one of armed power, retaliation, and retribution. The Lord of Hosts is again at the head of the army of Israel and His hand is outstretched and His arm is mighty. These images are, of course, nourished by Israel's impressive military victories over various combinations of Arab nations. The few against the many have – and shall, in the opinion of an overwhelming number of Israelis interviewed – overcome. The "threat" and "overcome" constructs were shown to be distinct.[3] The threat of war and the hope for peace, on the one hand, and the belief that Israel can overcome, on the other, are central components in understanding public opinion and national security policy in Israel.

Talk or Fight

There are two foundations to the edifice of national security consensus in Israel (Shapira 1992). One stems from the risk which goes along with seeking peace and conducting negotiations; the other, from the hazards associated with war and hostility. For example, the late prime minister Menachem Begin responded to the Middle East plan presented in September 1982 by President Ronald Reagan in a manner which is a prototype of this war-oriented reaction. Begin's response was "The battle for *Eretz Israel* has begun" (Schiff and Ya'ari 1984, 233). On the other hand, in his September 13, 1993, speech on the White House lawn, Prime Minister Rabin declared, "We who have come from a land where parents bury their children; we who have fought against you, the Palestinians – we say to you today, in a loud and a clear voice: enough of blood and tears. Enough!" (*New York Times*, September 14, 1993, A12).

These competing orientations fit in well with feelings of threat and ideology. In each of the surveys, the following question was asked: "What is the best way to prevent another war?" Two answers were offered the respondents: to do all that is possible to initiate peace negotiations or to increase Israel's military power. As discussed in Chapter 4, between 1986 and 1993 two-thirds and three-fourths of the samples selected peace talks when forced to choose. In 1994, with peace talks going on, there was a severe decline to 52 percent.

The relationship between the negotiation choice and the perception of low threat was very high and was evidently on the increase, as demonstrated by the analyses of the 1987 and 1993 data (see Table 2.1). Those who felt threatened split almost evenly between the two options, while those whose score on threat was low split 4:1 in favor of initiating peace negotiations (Margalit 1988).

In the 1986 sample, the correlation between low perceptions of threat and willingness to return the territories was .36, and between low threat and readiness to grant civil rights to inhabitants of the territories, .33. The two issues of the territories – land and people – were themselves closely

Table 2.1. *Threat and the Talk/Fight Choice, 1987, 1993*

A. 1987 data; $N = 1,082$

	Sample Total	Threat[a]		
		High 35%	Medium 35%	Low 30%
To prevent war with Arabs				
Initiate peace negotiations	68%	55	71	79
Increase military power	32%	45	30	21
Gamma = .36				

B. 1993 data; $N = 1,127$

	Sample Total	Threat		
		High 35%	Medium 32%	Low 33%
To prevent war with Arabs				
Initiate peace negotiations	63%	41	67	83
Increase military power	37%	59	33	17
Gamma = .58				

[a] Threat was operationalized as the sum of the responses to the questions regarding the possibility of peace between Israel and the Arab countries in the near future, Israel's ability to influence the Arabs' willingness for peace, and the assessment of Arab aspirations. In 1987, 59% felt that peace with Arab states was possible in the near future; 62% thought that Israel could influence, by its behavior, the willingness of the Arabs to reach a genuine peace. The sample was then divided into thirds. Those in the high category regarded peace as unlikely and the goals of the Arabs far-reaching.

interrelated (.34). Those on the right of the political spectrum were most likely to feel threatened (.34).[4] The lower the perceived threat, the greater the willingness to cede land and to grant civil rights.

Right to the Land

A better approximation of the relationship among these variables is obtained by considering them in conjunction with other questions. One of them has to do with reasons used to keep the territories. The sample was told that "right to the land" was one of four reasons used by people who want Israel to continue to hold the territories. Other reasons were "to prevent the establishment of a Palestinian state," "to maintain strategic depth for military operations," and "to use in future negotiations." The respondents were asked to rank the importance of these reasons. In Figure 2.2, the first choice of the samples between 1986 and 1994 are arrayed. The

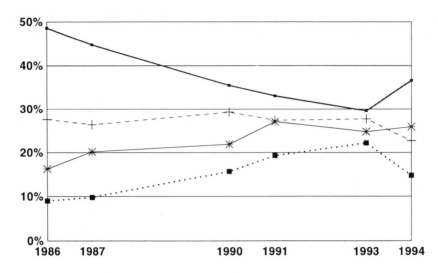

⊷ Right to land ╋ No Palestinian State ＊ Strategic Depth ▪ Negotiation

Figure 2.2. Reasons for keeping the territories, 1986–1994.

ranking of the four responses is almost identical during the years, but the gap between them diminishes dramatically until 1993, and then a new pattern emerges.

Thus, almost 50 percent in 1986 said that Israel has a "right to the land" and that is the reason to hold on to the territories; by 1993, only 30 percent selected that as the chief reason. By contrast, only 9 percent gave the "negotiation" reason in 1986; that reason steadily rose and reached more than 20 percent by 1993. By 1994, with negotiations under way, and the territories on the negotiating table, the percentage which cited the territories as a bargaining chip fell back to 15 percent, while the ideological "right to the land" reason revived, and was mentioned by 36 percent.

Two things were happening in this period: the percentage that identified the reason to keep the territories as "right to the land" decreased until negotiations actually began; in addition, among those who used the "right to the land" justification, the percentage refusing to return the land was *decreasing*. In 1986 and 1987, more than 40 percent of the samples mentioned "right to the land" as the reason to keep the territories, and among those who used that reason, fewer than 30 percent expressed willingness to return territories. In 1991 and 1993, however, with about a third of the samples giving the "right to the land" reason, about 40 percent were willing to return territories. This represents an important shift on both dimensions. Not only was the "right to the land" camp in retreat, but in addition there was a softening of commitment to retaining the land among those who remained in that ideological grouping. The effect of the dual process of a shrinking of the size of those that asserted the "right to the land" argument and the growth of the conciliatory posture of Israeli public opinion in general provided the background for the political events which occurred.

And why would people want to return the territories? That question was asked in 1994 for the first time, and the responses follow:

To lower the risk of war	39%
There is no alternative	27%
To preserve Israel as a Jewish state	17%
Palestinians and Israelis both have the right to live here	17%

There was a clear preference for practical reasons such as lowering the risk of war, or that there was no alternative; the two "ideological" responses were chosen by only a third of the respondents (17% plus 17%).

Analysis of the responses of six of the surveys between 1986 and 1994 indicates that the perception of threat in the samples remained high until 1991; in 1993 and 1994 a different, more subdued pattern was evident (see Table 2.2). From highs of 5.5 in 1986 and 1987, the threat score fell for 5.0 in 1993, and to 4.8 in 1994. While the overall perception of threat was down, threat resonated differently among those who chose the various reasons for not giving back the territories. First, those who claimed a right to the land consistently reported higher levels of threat and their level stayed the most level over the years, even as their portion in the population was falling off, as we have seen. Second, a middle category emerged regarding the reasons for returning territories and the perception of threat as the years went by. In 1986, the level of threat for the first three categories was quite similar, but later the middle category, composed of preventing a Palestinian state and strategic depth, became more articulated in terms of threat perception. The threat rates for those two reasons were clearly between the threat rates for the "right to the land" reason and the "use in future negotiations" reason.

The three elements of right to the land, willingness to return territories, and threat are tied together, as demonstrated in the analyses for the 1987 and 1993 surveys in Table 2.3. Respondents were sorted on the threat construct and on whether or not they mentioned the right to the land as the most important reason for retaining control of the territories. The hypothesis was that those who believed that Israel had a right to the land and had a high perception of threat would be the least willing to return territories, and that those who had perceptions of threat and did not see the right to the land as an important reason for holding on to the territories, would be

Table 2.2. *Threat[a] by Reason for Keeping Territories[b]*

	1986	1987	1990	1991	1993	1994
Mean threat score, total sample	5.5	5.5	5.4	5.3	5.0	4.8
Mean threat score for those whose response was:						
Right to the land	5.6	5.8	5.7	5.7	5.5	5.4
To prevent the establishment of a Palestinian state	5.6	5.5	5.5	5.2	5.1	4.6
To maintain strategic depth for military operations	5.4	5.2	5.3	5.2	5.0	4.6
To use in future negotiations	4.8	4.8	4.7	4.8	4.4	3.9

[a] Threat here was measured by the sum of the responses to the questions concerning the possibility of peace between Israel and the Arab countries in the near future, and the assessment of Arab aspirations. The question regarding Israel's ability to influence the Arabs' willingness for peace was not asked in some of the years under consideration and was hence omitted from the measure. The higher the mean, the greater the perceived threat.
[b] The question was "Which of the following reasons seems most important to you for keeping the territories?"

Table 2.3. *Threat, Right to Land, and Return Territories, 1987, 1993*

A. 1987 data; N = 971

		Threat[a]		
	Sample	High	Medium	Low
Right to the Land	Total	35%	35%	30%
Most important[b]	45%	17	28	33
Not most important	55%	42	51	75

B. 1993 data; N = 1,093

		Threat		
	Sample	High	Medium	Low
Right to the Land	Total	33%	32%	35%
Most important	29%	29	44	60
Not most important	71%	43	67	87

[a] See note a, Table 2.2.
[b] The number in each cell represents the percentage willing to give up territories for peace. Of the total sample, 43% favored returning territories for peace in 1987, 58% percent in 1993.

the most likely. The responses proceeded in a regular and consistent manner through the steps of threat and the perceived importance of the right to the land. More than that, the magnitude of willingness to return the territories doubled for each level of threat depending on whether or not the respondent mentioned the right to the land. Perhaps even more relevant in policy terms was that in both "right to the land" categories the rate of willingness to cede land doubled as perceived threat dropped in 1987; in 1993, the same patterns were generated but because the level of willingness to return land was higher, the increments were less extreme.

The ideology of the land (whether based on Zionist, historical, religious or military might premises) operated with perceptions of threat in ordering an individual's political preference. It is the intersection of these two – the ideological belief in a right and the perception of threat – which seemed to drive the Israeli public.

LADDER RATINGS

The General Population

How are we doing? How do we feel? What will be? These are the familiar questions of everyday conversation and they express the anxieties felt about our own futures, and the future security of the nation. Obviously, the answers to the trilogy of questions are interrelated. Assessing one's position, taking into account one's reaction to that position, and speculating about the effect of these on the future are all very human reactions to situations confronted in life (Stone 1982, chapter 4).

The data at hand afford a method of calibrating these feelings and the changes in them; unfortunately, there are wide gaps in the years of data collection, but even so the overall impression is striking. There appears to be an underlying mood of confidence; this was especially true for the evaluation of personal fortune, although over the years, optimism regarding the future of the nation seemed to slip.

How an individual thinks things are going, or how well a person thinks the country is doing, are assessments which go beyond the specific questions asked. The patterns of these answers for the entire society give us a glimpse of the values of the society.

Some societies have magnified the importance of the collectivity at the expense of the individual; others have reversed the priorities. Still others justified past privation and demanded sacrifice in the present for the future benefit of self and society. Other, more individualistic, societies provide esteem for individual effort and well-being, assuming that if the parts of the whole are content and prosperous, then it follows that the collectivity is also thriving.

We can explore some of these notions more fully using the technique developed by Hadley Cantril (1965) to test levels of aspiration and frustration in societies. In Cantril's method, each respondent is interviewed at length regarding personal hopes and fears and is then shown a ten-rung ladder; the respondent is told that the top of the ladder represents the best possible life as just depicted, and that the bottom is the worst life envisaged. The respondent is then asked to indicate the appropriate rank for his or her position today, which rank it was five years ago, and which rank is foreseen five years hence. After a similar discussion of the nation, the ladder device is applied to the respondent's perception of the position of the country today, five years ago, and five years from the time of the interview. In each case, the reality world has been defined by the respondent, and the ladder ratings are relative to the subjective definition of the ladder provided by the respondent.

However, since the concept of a ladder, of up and down, or higher and lower, seems to be universal, Cantril applied this simple yet perceptive technique to comparative research across very different countries. Based on Cantril's data of 1962, it was possible to compare responses in Israel with those of other countries (Cantril 1965) and to analyze differences among groups in Israel (Antonovsky and Arian 1972). Over the years the technique has been applied in other research in Israel, almost always using the same format.[5] With the ladder method, the patterns of personal and national optimism and pessimism can be assessed over time, and the extent and importance of the changes that have occurred can be ascertained.

Reviewing the Cantril findings from the 1960s indicates possible patterns among the means of the six ladder ratings (see Table 2.4). The Americans interviewed generated the most consistently high means. Their differences between past and present were small, although the present seemed better than the past, and the future even brighter. The range of scores for the nation was much flatter than it was for their personal situations; personally, the past was worse than was the nation's, the present about the same, and the personal future was seen to be brighter than the national future. (These are projections made by Americans in the 1960s; today's responses for them and others might be very different.)

The Brazilian pattern was different. Brazilians started from the lowest personal point, and their national plight in the present was not perceived to be much better. The future, however, rose to the same level as the other countries, and even a little higher. The same pattern of progress from past to present to future was evident for Brazilians regarding the personal ladder. In fact, their increase was highest because their starting mean was so low.

Table 2.4. *Mean Ladder Ratings in Four Countries, 1962*

	Past	Present	Future
National			
United States	6.5	6.7	7.4
Brazil	4.9	5.1	7.6
Egypt	3.5	5.9	7.5
Israel	4.0	5.5	7.5
Israel 1967[a]	5.0	7.5	8.0
Israel 1968[b]	3.8	6.5	7.5
Personal			
United States	5.9	6.6	7.8
Brazil	4.1	4.6	7.3
Egypt	4.6	5.5	8.0
Israel	4.7	5.3	6.9

[a] Asked immediately after the Six Days war in June of a national urban sample. "Past" refers to Independence Day in May 1967 when the prewar tension was building, "future" to one month ahead.
[b] Asked in surveys conducted in spring 1968 and again in December 1968 of national urban samples. "Past" refers to Independence Day in May 1967 when the prewar tension was building, "future" to one year ahead.
Source: Antonovsky and Arian, 1972, 20.

Israelis ranked themselves between the Americans and the Brazilians in the 1960s, and somewhat closer to the Brazilians. Mean Egyptian scores on past and present were almost identical with Israeli scores in 1962. All four populations expressed a sense of personal progress in the five-year period, most notably the Egyptians. Israelis and Americans foresaw solid and intensified progress in the satisfaction of personal aspirations in the next five-year period, but neither was quite as optimistic as the Brazilians or Egyptians.

"Five years before" the interviewing in the early 1960s coincided with the Sinai campaign of 1956. Despite a striking military victory and a letup of terrorist activity, nothing much had changed for the Israelis. They had been forced to give up their territorial gains and they did not perceive that they had achieved political ones. They ranked the past a low 4.0. The Egyptians shared this view of the past; they had suffered military defeat, had become isolated from the West, and were yet to enjoy massive Soviet political, military, and economic support. Americans starting from a high base point, and Brazilians from a low one, reported almost no progress from national past to present; Israelis indicated considerable and Egyptians very great improvement.

Israelis, starting from a low base, were optimistic about past progress and even more so about anticipated progress. Americans were at the other extreme; they started out high and saw only slight positive change. Brazilians did not think much had changed in the past, but were extremely hopeful for the future. Egyptians saw themselves worse off in the past, expressed a sense of great achievement, and saw future movement in the same direction, though not at quite the same pace.

An additional insight is obtained by considering data collected in June 1967, immediately after the Six Days war. In this survey, the past referred to Independence Day 1967 (May 15), when the prewar tension was beginning to build, and the future to one month ahead. The questions were asked twice again in 1968, with identical results each time. Then the past referred to Independence Day 1967, and the future to one year ahead. For these three surveys, the Egyptian pattern was evident: the bulk of the anticipated improvement from past to future already had been achieved. The euphoria of the tremendous victory was evident in these postwar data; even the memory of the tense Independence Day took on a relatively rosy hue.

The important difference between the Israelis and others was that the personal past ranked higher than the national past; in the present, the two ratings were about the same; in the future the national rating was higher. Further, the overall progress of the country from past to future was greater than the personal progress. For the Americans the reverse was true; the country made less progress than the respondent did, and in the future, the sample members think they will be better off than the country. Brazilians also saw more overall personal progress, although the nation was consistently ranked higher. The Egyptians shared with the Israelis in the 1960s the feeling that the country would progress more than the respondents, although the personal future mean rank was higher than that of the country's.

We termed this 1962 Israeli pattern "compensation." We wrote:

How does one adapt to this sense of dissatisfaction? How does one make oneself feel better? . . . [A] partial answer . . . [is] compensation.

The pattern of compensation emerges in two ways. It can first be seen in a comparison of the present ladder ratings for oneself and for the nation. One way to reduce the sense of discomfort reflected in a low personal rating is to rate the nation high. It is as if one were saying, "I may not be in such good shape, but at least my country is in good shape, and this makes me feel better." Thus, for example, the lowest education subgroup, with the lowest mean present personal rating (4.4), has the highest mean present national rating (5.8). True, it is not always the case that this happens, but this is a rather stringent test. A fairer test of the compensation notion is to compare the present personal-national differences. In doing so we find great consistency: the gap is almost always greater for the marginal than for the more dominant groups in the society. The latter, in fact, often tend to rank the state of the nation lower than their own position. For example, the lowest occupation group (Group 5) has a mean personal ranking of 4.0 and a mean national ranking of 5.6, a difference of +1.6. For occupation group 4 the difference is +0.6; for group

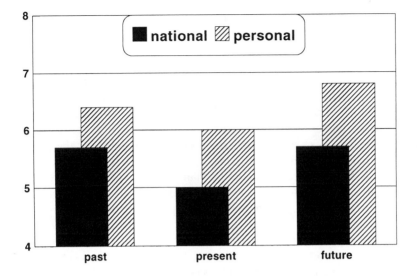

Figure 2.3. Ladder means for national and personal optimism-pessimism, 1994 ($N = 1,239$).

3, +0.3. The sign becomes reversed for occupation group 2, the national rating being higher than the personal (a difference of −0.8); the difference in the highest occupation groups is −1.4. Or, to take the Israeli-born social class groups as another example: the lower class difference is +0.3; that of the middle class, −0.8; and that of the upper class, −1.4.

A second way in which the compensation pattern is expressed is with regard to the future. True, all groups without exception are optimistic, both for themselves and for the nation. The future ratings are always higher than the present ratings. But . . . marginal groups . . . show anticipation of considerable progress. (Antonovsky and Arian, 160–1)

What we found for groups can be extended to nations. Focus on the future glory of the nation can compensate for feelings of deprivation in one's personal life. Alternatively, a narrower range of difference might result from a more sanguine acceptance of the positions of the nation and the self. Keeping this in mind, we turn to the available data on Israel, which cover the years 1962 to 1994.

Figure 2.3 displays the mean ladder positions for the 1994 sample. It shows that the sample generated a national past and national future mean score that was identical (5.7). The mean present score of 5.0 was the lowest of the six scores. The personal mean scores showed that the present was lowest (6.0), followed by the past (6.4), and then future (6.8).

Over the years, this set of questions was posed to some 10,000 respondents. However, the samples were distributed very unevenly over time, with most of them in the 1986–94 period; only 15 percent of the total were in the 1960s; the 1970s, a very tumultuous period in Israeli history, were not registered at all.[6] The accumulated means of the respondents must be considered with prudence since they average together many different surveys that have different results. Certain patterns are nonetheless worthy of note. Almost all the mean scores were at or above the number 5 rung of the ladder, which is the median point.[7] For each series, the personal mean scores were higher than the national mean scores. However, those who participated in these surveys generated different patterns for the personal and national topics, respectively. The general pattern for the personal condition was that the present is better than the past and the future will be even better. The 1994 pattern was an exception to the general pattern in that both the personal present and national present means were lower than the personal past and national past means, respectively. The 1993 means were more typical: progress was seen in all the personal categories, from 6.0 in the past, to 6.2 in the present, and 6.8 in the future. On the other hand, the national present (5.6) was *lower* than the past (5.8); the future followed the pattern of improvement, increasing to 6.2.

Thirty-two years of dramatic change in social, economic, military, and political conditions, and the attendant turnover of population and of survey respondents, would lead us to expect shifts in the ladder ratings. And change there was. For the national means, the record low was the 4.0 for the past for the respondents questioned in 1962, and the registered high was 7.9 for the national future for those questioned in 1969. The accumulated personal means ranged between a low of 4.7 for the past in 1962, and a high of 7.6 regarding the future for the respondents of 1991.

Comparing Figures 2.4 and 2.5 demonstrates how the graphs presented here were generated and how they are to be understood. In Figure 2.4, the means for the personal and national past responses are plotted by year of interview. The points are connected by the appropriate line denoting either the national or personal focus. Figure 2.5 is based on the same data, and the points are displayed as in Figure 2.4 The difference is that the lines for national means and personal means do not touch the data points but are placed to indicate the trend line. The technique displays the lines that best fit the data points (Campbell 1990, 114) calculated by the least-squares method. In other figures, only the trend lines are presented, but the connecting line can be readily imagined because the data points are also presented.[8]

In each year the mean assessment of the personal past was higher than for the nation, except in 1981 when they were tied (see Figure 2.4). We see that this regularity generates a curved pattern, with the high point in 1991. The trend lines and their statistical significance (see Figure 2.5) demonstrate the propensity of Israelis to perceive the past for both personal and

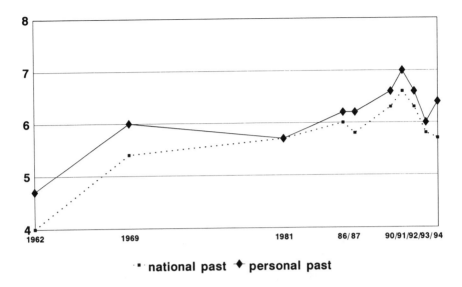

Figure 2.4. Past ladder means for national and personal optimism-pessimism, 1962–1994. (Mean scores on 9-point scale: 9 = best, 1 = worst).

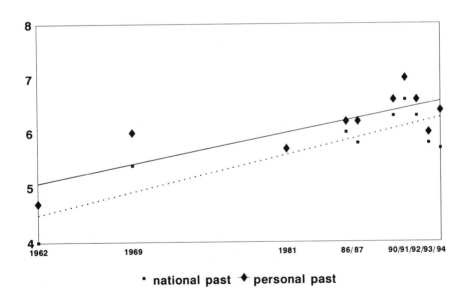

Figure 2.5. Past ladder means – trends, 1962–1994. (Mean scores on 9-point scale: 9 = best, 1 = worst.)

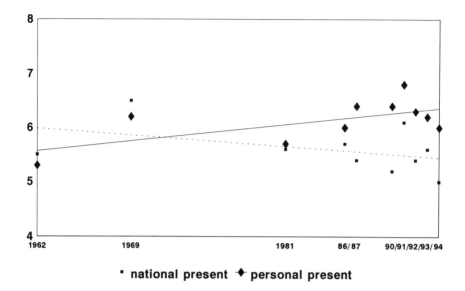

· national present ✦ personal present

Figure 2.6. Present ladder means – trends, 1962–1994. (Mean scores on 9-point scale: 9 = best, 1 = worst.)

national assessments more positively over time, with a deterioration of the pattern in 1993 and 1994. This is a good measure of increasing retrospective optimism.

The corollary of this tendency to a increasingly favorable view of the period five years past was a differentiated view of the present and the future. The personal trend was like the one for the past evaluation (see Figure 2.6) and was also statistically significant, but at a lower level of statistical significance. As the years went by, the samples tended to see their personal present position improving. The national present trend seemed to generate a negative tilt, although the set of differences was not found to be statistically significant. As time went by, samples tended to give the position of the nation a lower score at the moment of the interview than did earlier respondents. The tendency for the personal ladder means was clearly on the incline, while the pattern for the national ladder means seemed to be on the decline. Evaluations regarding the country and its security have gone *down* on the whole over time, while Israelis felt *better* about themselves and their personal chances.

The differentiation between personal and national chances was evident regarding the situation four or five years from the period of posing the question. Figure 2.7 indicates that the two responses regarding the future

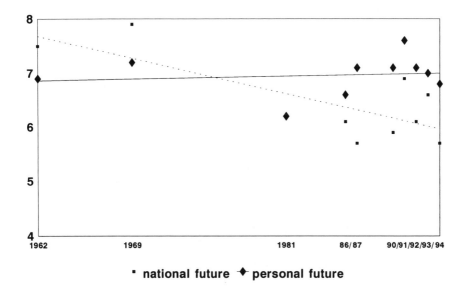

Figure 2.7. Future ladder means – trends, 1962–1994. (Mean scores on 9-point scale: 9 = best, 1 = worst.)

seemed to be tending in different directions. The overall pattern is an increasing spread between the personal and the national ladder ratings.[9] The trend of the national future ladder means was on a downward slide and the graphic presentation of these data in Figure 2.7 easily passes Tukey's "interocular traumatic test" (findings pass this test when they hit the re-searcher between the eyes; Putnam 1993, 13). Much occurred in the 1970s, most notably the enormous political and security changes occasioned by the Yom Kippur war of 1973. The public mood soured, the 1967 euphoria vanished, the economy was altered because of the need to invest in an army which could meet the postwar challenges, and the foreign policy of the country was in retreat. The data in these figures probably indicate that during those years a more realistic assessment of the past, and a dampened optimism regarding the present and future, set in. The net effect of all these changes was that the spread of the means over time for the personal and national expanded, although the personal future trend line was not statistically significant.

The Yom Kippur war was likely the turning point. Unfortunately, di-rectly comparable data for the 1970s are not available. But there is strong evidence nonetheless. In the May 1973 survey ($N = 1939$), five months before the war, respondents were asked about the same topics in a direct manner. They were asked whether, in their opinion, the country's situation had improved compared to four years ago, stayed the same, or become worse. Then they were asked about their personal situations. According to their answers, the country was doing much better before the Yom Kippur war than were the respondents. Almost two-thirds of the respondents said that the national situation had improved, compared with only 12 percent who opined that it had gotten worse, and another 23 percent who said that it had stayed the same. Regarding the personal situation, a third said it had improved, 21 percent responded it got worse, and 41 percent thought it had stayed the same. After the war, the shock tremors were clearly evident. In the November 1973 survey ($N = 642$), almost half the respondents thought that Israel's situation had changed for the worse as a result of the Yom Kippur war, 11 percent saw no change, and 19 percent thought it had improved (4% improved a great deal, and 15% improved).

The compensation pattern of the 1960s did not characterize the Israeli case in the 1980s and 1990s. There was an important reversal between the rankings of the two periods. In the 1960s, the personal past ratings were always higher than the national rankings, but for the present and the future, the national rankings were higher than the personal ratings.

By the 1980s, the nation was no longer the object of hope and the focus of progress to the degree it had been in the 1960s. Rather, the future of the nation became more uncertain over time. In the 1960s, the future was seen as better than the present, which was perceived to be better than the past. Since 1986, the national past consistently has ranked higher than the present. That pattern held for the personal rankings as well for every year but 1987. Most important, optimism regarding the personal future seemed to have replaced hope for nation, reflecting the rise of individualism in Israeli society and the emergence of a me-now generation. This pattern, similar to those generated in other postindustrial societies, was buttressed by an expanding consumer economy and by social policies of the various ruling parties, each of which vied for the votes of the middle class. In addition, the public was affected by the challenge of the intifada and by the complexities of superpower developments.

In summary, we have observed change in two senses, one time-specific and the other having to do with the subject of the query. First, for the past rankings, the personal stayed above the national, and the two increased together over time; for the present and the future in the 1960s, the national was above the personal, and in the 1980s and 1990s that pattern was reversed. Second, the lines tended in opposite directions for the personal and national assessments of the present and future. The personal lines were tilting up, the national lines down. This was especially obvious for the future, but was evident for the present as well.

Two explanations, possibly intertwined, suggest themselves. An optimistic explanation would posit that as a collectivity Israelis evidently felt more secure and realistic about their security position after successfully coming through the anxieties of the Six Days war and the uncertainties of the Yom Kippur war and generated a pattern similar to that of the dominant groups just discussed. As with those groups, Israelis tended to rank the state of the nation lower than their own positions in the 1980s and 1990s. Precisely because the security challenge had been met they could afford to concentrate on their personal lives. This trend was encouraged by a succession of governments led by the major parties, which historically sought the vote of the large middle class by promoting consumption and a rising standard of living.

A less optimistic reading would point out that the public perceived the situation with less hope and promise over time, and with good reason. The curse that accompanied the blessing of the 1967 victory would not go away; the territories issue festered and infected every aspect of Israeli life. The army was less able to meet the challenges the country faced (Wald 1992). The intifada was an extreme manifestation of this, but not the only one. The eventual introduction of weapons of mass destruction into the Israeli-Arab conflict preyed on the minds of Israelis. Although the demise of the Soviet Union deprived the Arab enemy of its major source of military and political support, that collapse coincided with evolution of the United States – Israel's chief ally – into a superpower whose will and stamina were showing worrying signs of atrophy. Even after a peace accord with the dominant Palestinian groups was signed, terrorism continued to pose questions about the extent of security and the safety of life and limb. Accordingly, assessments of the national future became less rosy, and Israelis escaped this by concentrating on their personal lives. Of course, both of these explanations may be correct, at least in part.

Two Special Samples

Special samples were drawn twice during the course of the research at widely different times and among very different populations. Considering their responses can highlight changes in the mean ladder ratings for the entire population.

The first was a 1962 sample of 300 kibbutz members; the second was a 1990 sample of Jewish residents of the territories taken in the 1967 war. These groups can be thought of as vanguards during the respective periods of data collection. The kibbutz movement represented the ideology of the socialist Zionist pioneers who founded the important institutions of the country and led it to independence; in the early 1960s their political, social, and economic power was still considerable, although soon to wane. The territories settlers were the end-of-the-century pioneering group dominant in the country. Largely religious rather than socialist, their nationalism was as fervent in the late 1980s as was that of the kibbutz movement in the late 1930s. Like the kibbutz movement after statehood, their leaders were very well connected with the country's political leadership, and benefited from government policies of land allocation and financial support. Often the pioneering leadership was critical of the politicians because they did not support the pioneers even more.

Ultimately, the movements became stigmatized as having too much power, and of being out of touch with the realities of the country. When the Labor and Likud parties fell from power in 1977 and 1992, respectively, the popular perception was that the successes of the movements and their perceived excesses were partially to blame. Whether or not that assessment was fair, it was clear that these two vanguard movements had impact well above their small numerical sizes. Both embodied ideals important to many in the population at the time of the surveys. Not everyone in the general population agreed with the opinions of the special groups, nor was the motivation of each member of the special groups (the kibbutz members and the territories settlers) entirely ideological. Yet, in a general sense, these groups represented a leadership cadre of the society, and as such, the comparison of their ladder ratings with those of the general population is of interest.

The kibbutz sample of 1962 rated the personal position for all three time periods very high in comparison to the general sample (Antonovsky and Arian 1972, 128–30). However, the kibbutz sample was lower in its evaluation of the national ladder positions than was the general population (see Figure 2.8). This was especially important because the kibbutz sample showed less change between the past and the future in the two topic areas than did the general sample. But unlike the general sample, the kibbutz sample perceived the personal future to be much rosier than the national future.

Different patterns were seen for the settlers. Compared to the breadth of spread between kibbutz members and the population in 1962, there were very similar patterns for the settlers and the general sample in 1990 (see Figure 2.9). With the exception of the past position for the settlers, means for the personal ladders were consistently higher than were means for the national ones. For both the general sample and the territories sample, the mean for the national present was lower than for the national future, and both of those were lower than the mean of the national past. No compensation here, and no great optimism either. Horizons had narrowed by 1990, and the focus of hope was on the personal, if on anything.

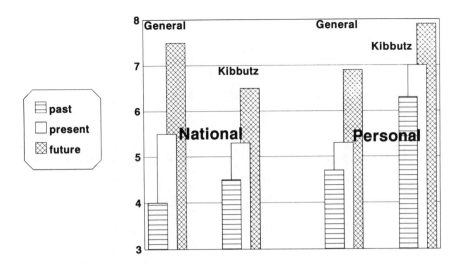

Figure 2.8. Ladder means – general population and kibbutz samples, 1962. (Mean scores on 9-point scale: 9 = best, 1 = worst.)

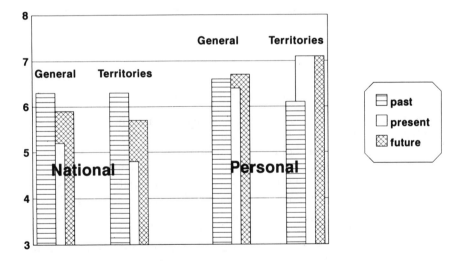

Figure 2.9. Ladder means – general population and territories samples, 1990. (Mean scores on 9-point scale: 9 = best, 1 = worst.)

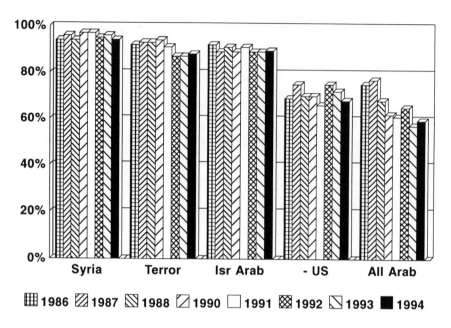

Figure 2.10. "Israel can overcome" – confidence under various threats, 1986–1994.

TO OVERCOME

The General Population

National security matters have elicited a dual reaction from Israelis. On the one hand, Israelis are aware of the numerical superiority of their adversaries, to which the oft-heard phrase "the few against the many" is testimony. On the other hand, Israelis were certain of their ability to overcome (see Figure 2.10) a war with Syria, terror, uprisings of Arabs under Israel's jurisdiction, the lessening of United States aid, and a war against all Arab states. However, the rates of confidence varied for the latter two situations from year to year, and this variation was especially palpable regarding war against all Arab states. In 1993, 58 percent believed that Israel had the ability to wage war successfully against all of the Arab states, but this was 20 points lower than the percent recorded in 1987.

Israel could also contend with a war against the countries of the Eastern front – Syria, Jordan, and Iraq – according to the respondents (see Figure 2.11). At a lower level, Israel could overcome United Nations economic sanctions supported by the United States; only for the eventuality of the

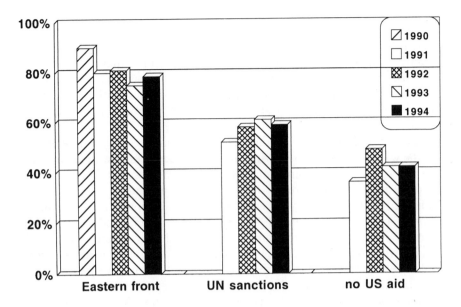

Figure 2.11. "Israel can overcome" – confidence in waging war, 1990–1994.

United States stopping all aid did a majority of Israelis think that Israel could not overcome.

These data are especially important because of the relative stability of the findings over time. In the eight surveys reported here, these questions were repeated and the response pattern was reproduced. The period of these surveys, of course, was hardly uneventful. The first survey, in 1986, was conducted soon after the withdrawal from Lebanon; the second, in 1987, at the beginning of the intifada; the fourth one, in 1991, immediately before and after the Iraqi invasion of Kuwait; the one in 1993, after the beginning of the peace talks; and the last one, in 1994, after the mutual recognition accord with the PLO. Through all of this, the security confidence of the public, and the general stability of its ranking of the problems, persisted.

In addition, 9 in 10 respondents consistently reported that they wanted to live in Israel. But the price of Israel's security is paid not only in terms of personal and economic sacrifice, but also in a social coin. The level of out-migration from Israel was high and the burden of defense was often mentioned as a reason for the drain. In the 1986 survey those in the sample were asked what they thought was the major reason to contemplate leaving the country. The results are interesting because they provide evidence for the social science debate about the effects of prolonged conflict. Do such conflicts lead to greater solidarity or do they hasten destabilizing processes? In the Israeli case, based on responses of the sample, the security issue is by no means the major reason for considering leaving the country. Almost three-quarters thought it was the economic situation which was primarily on the minds of those who wanted to leave, only 14 percent answered the security situation, 10 percent, the social situation, 2 percent, the role of religion in the state's affairs, and 1 percent, antidemocratic tendencies in the country.

The picture generated was complex. True, confidence was high, and had, on the whole, been retained. Moreover, when confronted with an immediate threat like the Iraqi invasion of Kuwait, confidence levels appeared to increase rather than decrease. However, three additional sets of findings indicate that the picture was really much more complex. First, the panel surveys between 1987 and 1990, in which the same individuals were reinterviewed and asked the same questions, indicated an erosion of confidence over time. Second, the 1990 survey allowed the assessment of attitudes before and after the Iraqi invasion of Kuwait. In that case, the portion interviewed after the Iraqi invasion was slightly more confident than the one interviewed before. Third, in tandem with the 1990 survey a special sample of Jewish residents in the territories was interviewed. These settlers generated a pattern different – and less optimistic – than that of the general population.

The 1987–1988 Panel

As mentioned, the impact of time and situation was assessed using the replies of the panel respondents. For the 1987, 1988, and 1990 surveys, a panel design was used: the same respondents were asked the same questions at different points in time. Data were available for this type of analysis from 416 respondents from the 1987 and 1988 samples who were interviewed twice. In 1990, 213 of these same respondents were reinterviewed (see Appendix I).

The six overcome items that repeated in all three surveys for the 213 respondents who were interviewed three times were examined by constructing an "overcome" scale. The questions were dichotomous, "can overcome" and "cannot overcome"; the scale was formed by totaling the number of times the respondent reported that Israel could overcome. Comparing these scores over time provided an indication of the extent to which panel respondents persisted in their belief that Israel could overcome the challenges presented in the surveys.

While most of the respondents remained stable from time period to time period, there was movement (see Table 2.5). This movement can be

Table 2.5. *Overcome Questions and Scale, 1987, 1988, 1990*
(Panel Respondents, N = 213)

	Total % stable	% Stable more confident	% Stable more doubtful	Change to more confident	Change to more doubtful	Net change[a]
1. *Overcome war with Syria*						
1987 to 1988	91	91	0	4	4	0
1988 to 1990	90	90	0	4	5	-1
1987 to 1990	90	90	0	4	5	-1
2. *Overcome terrorist organizations*						
1987 to 1988	89	89	1	6	4	+2
1988 to 1990	89	89	0	4	7	-3
1987 to 1990	88	87	1	6	6	0
3. *Overcome revolt of Israeli Arabs*						
1987 to 1988	86	84	2	10	5	+5
1988 to 1990	85	84	1	5	10	-5
1987 to 1990	84	81	3	8	8	0
4. *Overcome less U.S. aid*						
1987 to 1988	68	62	6	16	16	0
1988 to 1990	64	54	10	13	24	-9
1987 to 1990	63	54	9	12	25	-13
5. *Overcome war with all Arab countries*						
1987 to 1988	68	59	8	13	19	-6
1988 to 1990	63	50	14	14	22	-8
1987 to 1990	67	54	13	9	24	-15
6. *Overcome massive USSR support to Arab countries*						
1987 to 1988	61	45	16	26	13	+13
1988 to 1990	61	47	14	16	24	-8
1987 to 1990	56	37	19	25	19	+6
Overcome Scale						
1987 to 1988	70	56	15	16	13	+3
1988 to 1990	61	48	13	15	24	-9
1987 to 1990	62	46	15	15	23	-8

[a] Positive net change is in overcome direction; negative change is in doubtful direction.

thought of as changes in the panel's confidence level. Subtracting the percentage that shifted from a more confident position to a less confident one from those who moved in the opposite direction generated the confidence-doubt differential. Using this measure, we can ascertain that confidence increased between 1987 and 1988; and that between 1988 and 1990, it decreased, resulting in a net decrease for the 1987–90 period – the one which stretched from the outbreak of the intifada to the outbreak of the Gulf war. The confidence-doubt differential was +3 for 1987 to 1988, and −9 for 1988 to 1990. For the entire three-year period, the differential was −8. Confidence was high, but in decline.

The decline in confidence manifested itself in two ways: first, the level of stable scores for the "overcome" scale between two periods shrank from 70 percent between 1987 to 1988 (56% categorized as confident of overcoming in both periods, 15% nonconfident in both periods), to 61 percent between 1988 and 1990 (48% categorized as confident of overcoming in both periods, 13% doubtful of both). Second, the percentage of panel members who moved from more confident to doubtful jumped from 13 percent in the 1987 to 1988 period, to 24 percent for the 1988 to 1990 period, while the percentage who shifted from less confident to more confident remained the same at 15 percent for both time periods.

The items which composed the overcome scale contributed in differing ways to the overall pattern of weakened confidence. War with all the Arab countries, and the reduction of United States aid, contributed the most by far to the decay in overcome scores. The confidence-doubt differential regarding war with all Arab countries was −6 for 1987 to 1988, and −8 for 1988 to 1990, and −15 for the entire 1987 to 1990 period. Between 1987 and 1990, the confidence that Israel could withstand the challenge of war with all the neighboring Arab states, waned. In 1987, 78 percent of the three-wave panel respondents thought that Israel could overcome such a conflagration, compared to 70 percent in 1988, and 62 percent in 1990. While it is true that almost two out of three panel respondents retained their confidence even in 1990, the 16-point fall-off from the 1987 level among the very same people was dramatic.

The shift regarding the decrease in American aid was much less gradual than in the case of war with all the Arab states. The suddenness of the shift was probably occasioned by the election of George Bush in 1988, and the anticipated shift in American policy from the one pursued during the presidency of Ronald Reagan. The confidence-doubt differential between 1987 and 1990 among panel members for overcoming Israel's problems regardless of diminished United States aid was −13; for the 1988 to 1990 period it was −9. Between the 1987 and 1988 surveys those who shifted to a more confident stance balanced out those who shifted in a less confident direction, and the differential was 0. Over time, fewer panel respondents thought the country could overcome a substantial reduction in American aid. In 1987, 79 percent of the three-wave sample said that Israel could manage with less U.S. aid; in 1988, 77 percent thought so, and by 1990, only 67 percent expressed that opinion.

The larger two-wave panel of 416 respondents questioned in 1987 and again in 1988 provided revealing insights into the changes which took place during the period. Two questions whose response rate differed between the two asking periods were a decrease of United States aid to Israel, and the effect of a massive Soviet supplying of arms to Arab nations at war with Israel. The panel changed on both of these issues in the 10-month period between surveys (discussed in Arian et al., 1992). In the case of U.S. aid, the movement was away from a belief that Israel would be able to overcome a decrease in support: in 1987, 78 percent said that, and in 1988, only 73 percent thought so. The panel respondents thought that Israel could overcome Soviet involvement; the difference between the two measurements was statistically significant to a high degree. The percent who thought Israel would be successful in the face of Soviet aid to its Arab enemies rose from 57 in 1987 to 72 in 1988. Perhaps this was evidence of a greater degree of reality awareness on the part of Israelis (Richards 1971; Simon 1985). Maybe the realization of the enormous dependence of Israel on American aid, on the one hand, and the less antagonistic, inward-looking policies of Gorbachev's Soviet Union, on the other, were reflected in these changes.

The 1990 Samples

Two features of the 1990 sampling design permitted a more complete understanding of the public's orientation to security threats. First, 54 percent of the interviews were conducted before August 2, the day of the Iraqi invasion of Kuwait, and 46 percent afterward. The interview period stretched out between March and October in order to achieve a national sample with a maximum number of reinterviews. An unanticipated consequence of this protracted period was that the interview spanned the time before and immediately after the incursion into Kuwait. Second, a special sub-sample of 119 Jewish respondents living in the territories of the West Bank was also drawn. Breaking down the perceptions of Israel's ability to overcome the challenges just described depicts the extent to which Israeli public opinion is sensitive to ongoing security events and is affected by special circumstances (compare Keis 1975; Guttman 1978; Stone 1982).

The respondents questioned after the invasion of Kuwait were *more* certain of Israel's ability to overcome these dangers than were those asked before the incursion. The increase between the respondents asked before the invasion and those asked after the invasion ranged between 2 and 7 percent. Moreover, the difference was greatest between the two groups for the challenges with the lowest rate of certainty of overcoming. The lower the rank of the item in terms of the percentage of respondents who thought that Israel could prevail, the higher the increment after danger was perceived.

For example, war with Syria could be won according to 96 percent of those interviewed before the invasion, and by 98 percent of those questioned after the invasion. That two-percentage-point difference is so small, it could have easily occurred by chance. Two greater differences involved war with all Arab states and the increased supply of aid to the enemy by the Soviet Union. For each of these, 7 percent more thought that Israel could overcome the situation. In the case of war with all the Arab states, the augmentation was from 59 percent before the invasion, to 66 percent after it. Confidence regarding Soviet support jumped from 67 percent to 74 percent.

Danger seemed to steel Israeli confidence. National assurance was high in general, and it tended to be augmented in times of peril for those topics about which misgivings were more prevalent before the threat. To be certain, differences of this small magnitude are not to be celebrated in public opinion research. Page and Shapiro, for example, use a six-point difference as their definition for attitude change (1992, 44). Still, since all change was in the same direction and since the overall rates of confidence were so high, it is at least worth considering the impact on confidence of an event like the threat of war.

It is also important to note that respondents of the special sub-sample of Jews living in the territories generated very similar rates of confidence, compared with the general sample, of Israel's ability to overcome four of the seven situations: war with Syria, battling terror, overcoming an Arab uprising, and massive Soviet military assistance to Arab states at war with Israel. But for the other three situations – war with all the Arab states, decreased American aid, and war against the Eastern front countries – the respondents in the territories were much less optimistic compared with the general sample. The belief of the settlers in the ability of the country to overcome these situations was 19, 16, and 14 percent lower, respectively, than the respondents in the general sample. Many who favor settlements in the territories see them as a contribution to Israel's security; those living there (based upon this sample and these measures) expressed anxiety about the security future; they seemed to sense that in the long run the continued control over the territories was doubtful. In spite of this, or maybe because of it, many of their other responses on security issues and the territories were hawkish and right-wing in the Israeli context.

Both findings are probably correct. Situational context matters; imminent danger may increase reported confidence. Living in a more dangerous environment (such as the territories) for a prolonged period may sensitize respondents to dangers to which the general population is less attentive. In the former case, reported confidence grew; in the latter, it contracted.

This chapter has demonstrated the simultaneous capacity of Israelis both to be apprehensive about the Arabs' aspirations and yet to hold positive assessments of the country's ability to overcome threat. Personal fortunes seemed rosier than national ones over time, although on the whole the acuity of threat slackened. We turn now to the hope of peace and to the specter of war.

3

Peace and War

War and Peace

War and peace are the constants of security policy. Chapter 2 has made it clear that Israelis feel secure in the nation's ability to win in war. That a country so beleaguered should find the psychological and moral strength to continue its struggle for security for more than four decades is at least as impressive as Israel's record in successfully recruiting political and material support for its cause. Even though the nation has been preoccupied with war for so many years, there are optimistic overtones in the responses regarding peace and war.

War and peace are matters of social learning as much as they are issues of interest or power decisions. As Boulding (1964, 70) puts it, "Peace, no matter its nature, is a feature of the social system and not of the physical or biological systems. Moreover, it is a feature of some social systems and not of others." Israelis display a widespread consensus regarding issues of war and peace. The establishment view, taught in the schools and widely accepted in the culture, is that Israelis are peace-seeking, sacrificing, and, at the same time, work industriously to maintain their security because of the hostile environment in which the nation finds itself. Wars are fought in self-defense, and constant preparedness is a necessity. Even the divisive Lebanese war of 1982 is seen as proving that successful wars must be based on consensus. Spasms of terror restrict the belief that the other side is serious about peace, and policies in the territories or retaliatory acts are viewed as understandable reactions to provocation, and not as evidence of a diminished desire for peace.

Some opposition politicians and a school of "new history" proponents have called this view into question (Flappan 1987; Morris 1988; Shlaim 1988; also see Rabinovich 1991), but on the whole these have not been contentious issues in Israeli politics. The widely held view was that the government had done all it could to achieve peace. The establishment position that the Arab states rejected Israel and the potential of peace, and that Israel persistently and patiently waited for a breakthrough, was the generally accepted view. The breakthroughs came in 1977 when President Sadat of Egypt visited Jerusalem, in 1991 when the peace conference between Israel and neighboring states was convened in Madrid, co-sponsored by the United States and the Soviet Union (although the latter was in serious decline and on the verge of dissolution), and then again in September 1993 when Israel and the Palestinian Liberation Organization signed an accord of mutual recognition in Washington.

Opportunities missed, as revisionist historians relate, include the period immediately after the founding of the state, and then again in the early 1970s. The public at large evidently did not agree with this criticism, backing the stance of the governments of Israel which combined a reputed willingness to talk with a militant posture capable of fighting and winning. Israeli public opinion clearly supported the establishment position. The Arabs were unfriendly and intransigent neighbors who would not recognize Israel's right to exist. As described in Chapter 2, a hostile interpretation of the aspirations of the Arabs was accepted by most Israelis.

In general, the distribution of Israeli public opinion saw *both* the likelihood of war and the hope for peace (or the absence of war) grow as the years went by (see Figure 3.1). In 1987, 57 percent thought that war was probable or very probable between Israel and an Arab state in the following three years; by 1990, the number had climbed to 68 percent; after the Gulf war the corresponding percentage was only 54, and by 1994 it was 43 percent. Peace, in contrast, was perceived as more likely as time went on. From 57 percent in 1986, the numbers rose dramatically until, after the war, more than three of four respondents believed that peace was possible, and in 1994 it remained high at 73 percent.[1] The likelihood of war was down; in the public mind these two issues seemed to go together.

The Israeli public is very sensitive to political developments (Keis 1975; Guttman 1978; Stone 1982; Yishai 1987; Shamir and Shamir 1992), as these two questions show.[2] The 1990 survey, with its before and after August 2 segments, the date of the Iraqi invasion of Kuwait, also demonstrated this sensitivity. For those interviewed before August 2, two of three respondents thought it likely that war would break out; after that date, the figure was three of four. The steady growth of optimism about peace which had been evident over the years was arrested, with the same percentage reporting that peace was possible before and after August 2. After the war, the peace surge resumed, and the assessment that war was likely continued to plummet.

Another indicator of the public's sensitivity to changing conditions was the manner in which the proposed solutions to the Arab-Israeli conflict were evaluated in relation to the chances that war would break out. The

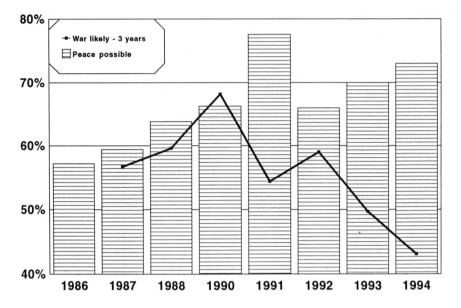

Figure 3.1. Likelihood of war and hope for peace, 1986–1994.

chances of war in 1994 were seen highest if the territories were annexed, or if the status quo were pursued. The creation of a Palestinian state was also seen as very dangerous. Autonomy posed less of a risk of war; the lowest risk would be to turn the territories over to Jordan (see Figure 3.2).

Figure 3.2 shows that using this measure as well, the chances of war were perceived to be down over time. The growth of the assessment that the options of annexation and the status quo would more likely lead to war underscored the increasing relaxation about the chances of war and undermined support for these alternatives. By contrast, the Jordanian option had become much more attractive in this context. Even a Palestinian state or autonomy showed a slight decline over the years.

Israelis thought it was up to them to ensure their security. When asked in 1986 if Israel should buy arms systems abroad or make its own, four of five respondents chose the latter. An example of this involved the Lavi fighter, planned and developed in Israel, but relying heavily on American funding and technology. When the question of continuing its production was being debated, after the United States administration indicated it would not continue funding its development, 60 percent of the 1987 sample favored proceeding with its production. Eventually, of course, the project was abandoned.

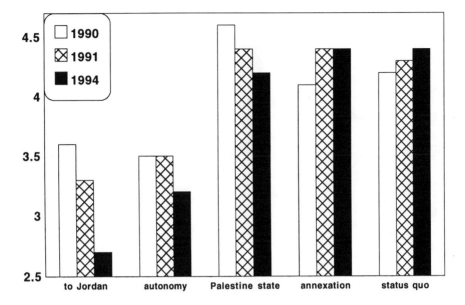

Figure 3.2. Outbreak of war perception versus various solutions to Israeli-Arab conflict, 1990, 1991, 1994. (Mean scores on 7-point scale: 7 = high, 1 = low.)

Israelis liked the idea of arms control regarding nonconventional weapons, but much less so regarding conventional armies. Seventy-two percent of the sample supported each of two ideas: to abandon all nonconventional weapons if the other countries of the region did, and to give up nonconventional weapons (except nuclear) if the other nations relinquished all of their nonconventional weapons (including nuclear ones). Regarding other arms control proposals, Israelis were less enthusiastic. Sixty-six percent supported preventing all outside arms supply to nations of the region. Sixty-eight percent promoted enlarging demilitarized areas, but only 58 percent backed reducing the size of armies in the area. These rates were very similar to the ones recorded in the 1991 survey.

Wanting Peace

Peace was the clear choice of Israelis over the years. Even when respondents were forced to choose between the two alternatives of either initiating peace talks or strengthening military capacity, the preference for peace talks was strong and consistent until 1994 when the talks were under way: 64 percent chose peace talks in 1993, the same percent as in 1986, 1988, and

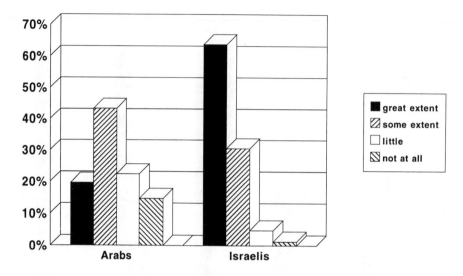

Figure 3.3. Wanting peace, Arabs and Israelis (1994 survey)

1990, compared with 68 percent in 1987 and 74 percent in 1991 and 1992. In 1994, only 52 percent chose talks, and the rest seemed intent to retain the military option, just in case (see Chapter 4).

Almost all respondents reported in 1994 that Israelis wanted peace, but they were divided about the extent to which the Arabs did (see Figure 3.3). Sixty-three percent thought the Arabs wanted peace to a great extent (20%) or to some extent (43%), while 95 percent thought the Israelis wanted peace. ("Most Arabs" was the phrase used to tap the generalized feeling toward Arabs; previous research indicated that "Israelis" were understood as "Jews in Israel" in this type of sample.)

Once the negotiations were under way in 1993, almost all Israelis supported continued participation in the peace process. Only 11 percent opposed; 89 percent were either very much in favor (56%) or in favor (33%) of persevering. Not only were they supportive, they were also interested in the process: 82 percent said that they were very interested (48%) or somewhat interested (34%); only 5 percent reported having no interest at all. By 1994, interest remained high, but consternation was expressed by those who opposed dealing with the PLO or those unsettled by the direction of the talks.

In 1994, a plurality of 43 percent supported the "Gaza-Jericho first" plan with the Palestinians, 32 percent were opposed, and a quarter were not certain. The wording of the question was identical to that used by the

Table 3.1. Reaction to the "Gaza-Jericho First" Plan (%)

Date in 1993	N	Support	Oppose	No opinion	Event
August 29	523	53	45	2	Agreement announced
August 31/					
September 1	550	53	44	3	Details revealed
September 7-8	508	57	41	2	
September 14	523	61	37	2	After signing
September 27	a	60	38	2	
November 19	488	48	47	5	
December 13	a	48	46	6	

[a] Not available.

Nablus-based Center for Palestine Research and Studies, and the pattern of response was similar to the results of their poll conducted in the West Bank and Gaza; their December 1993 poll ($N = 1,137$) had 42 percent supporting the "Gaza-Jericho first" plan, 38 percent opposed, and 20 percent not certain.

The Dahaf Research Institute asked Israeli Jews about the accord a number of times using a slightly different wording. In that version, only the support and oppose categories were offered the respondent. Support peaked at the time of the signing; the approval rate for the agreement was clearly on the decline, and the "no opinion" category grew (see Table 3.1).

Interpreting the surveys together, support for the accord seemed more resilient than opposition to it. The 43 percent rate of support reported in the 1994 poll was a deterioration in the rate of support from all earlier polls, yet the rate of opposition fell at an even sharper rate between these two surveys, from 46% in December to 32% in the current survey. It seems that more of those who supported the accord felt comfortable with that position; when given the option to chose the "not certain" answer, more of those who said they opposed the accord did so.

But how serious were the talks? Would they really make a difference and end the Arab-Israeli conflict? In 1993, before the signing of the mutual recognition agreement with the PLO, respondents were asked just that question, and their responses indicated that though they supported continuing the talks, the purpose of the peace process had not yet crystallized in Israeli public opinion. When asked if peace treaties would mean the end of the Arab-Israeli conflict, 48 percent said definitely (10%) or likely (38%), and 52 percent said unlikely (20%) or definitely not (32%). This had not changed after months of negotiations with the PLO: in the 1994 survey, the corresponding numbers were 10, 37, 18, and 35.

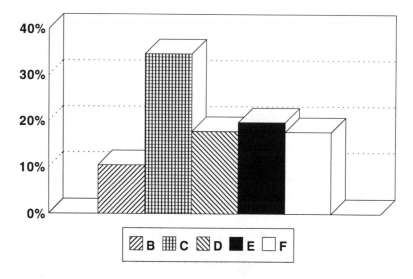

Figure 3.4. The nature of peace – minimal conditions (1994 survey).

The Nature of Peace

The nature of peace was probed by positing a series of five concentric circles. The definition of peace for the respondent would be the innermost point which the respondent mentioned, assuming that the outer regions would be included in a cumulative manner. Accordingly, respondents were asked to identify the minimal conditions which would define for them a situation of peace. (In certain instances, a "no peace" or "peace will never happen" response was legitimate.) The peace prototypes, with the inner limit in *italics*, were

[A. No peace.]
B. *No war*, and no peace treaty
C. No war, and *a peace treaty with security provisions*
D. No war, a peace treaty with security provisions, and *the exchange of ambassadors*
E. No war, a peace treaty with security provisions, the exchange of ambassadors, and *trade and tourism*
F. No war, a peace treaty with security provisions, the exchange of ambassadors, trade and tourism, and *a feeling of closeness between the citizens of the countries involved.*

Most respondents in 1994 (35%) identified C as sufficient to meet their minimal conditions for peace (see Figure 3.4). This was followed by E (20%), D (18%), F (18%), and B (10%).

Peace is, of course, at least a two-actor game, and so it is important to

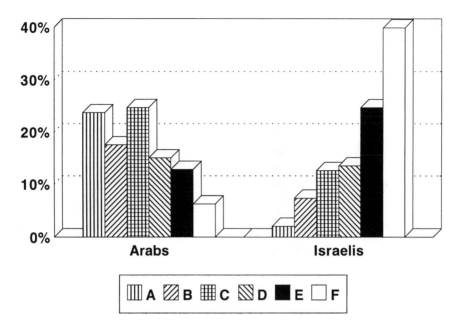

Figure 3.5. "Which peace do they want?" Minimal conditions, Arabs and Israelis compared (1994 survey).

know what the perception of the potential partner is. (Unfortunately, no comparable Arab sample was available.) According to these Jewish respondents, most Arabs would choose a much more minimalist interpretation of peace than would the Jews; on the other hand, most Israelis would want a maximalist rendition (see Figure 3.5). Respondents thought that most Arabs would settle for C (25%) or even B (18%), while they thought that Israelis would prefer F (40%). Importantly, 18 percent (down from 26% in 1993) of the sample thought that Arabs would not want peace at all (A), as compared to only 2 percent in both surveys who thought that Israelis would not want peace.

If these are the minimal conditions, how is the peace with Egypt regarded? Surprisingly, that peace far surpassed the expectations of the minimal conditions for peace in the minds of the respondents (see Figure 3.6). The largest percentages for the Egyptian peace are E (trade and tourism; 42%), and D (exchange of ambassadors; 33%). Peace with Syria, if attained, would more closely fit the pattern of the minimal conditions, although 15 percent (21% in 1993) chose A, indicating they did not believe that peace with Syria would be reached at all.

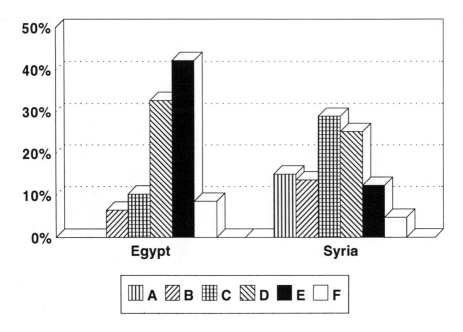

Figure 3.6. Peace with Egypt and with Syria – minimal conditions (1994 survey).

Most Israelis recognized that the peace process was interactive and that Israel's behavior could affect the Arab position. The following question was asked over the years: "Can Israel by its behavior influence the desire of the Arabs for true peace?" The responses are revealing and indicate a growing sense of Israel's role in achieving peace: in 1986 and 1987, 62 percent agreed; in 1988 and 1992, 69 percent concurred.

THE ISRAEL DEFENSE FORCES

The IDF is a major influence in the life of Israelis. Many serve and almost all Jewish Israelis have relatives or friends who do. The army is seen as the vital actor in ensuring the existence of the state. It is little wonder that Israelis have opinions about the IDF, its activities, and its effectiveness. However, these opinions are not examples of blind support; some are critical of its policies, and much less supportive than is sometimes thought. They indicate a knowledge of and sensitivity to developments within the army, and to changes in the role of the armed forces in the country. Respondents do not see the IDF as an institution different from others in the society. Perhaps because of the involvement of many Israelis in it, the IDF

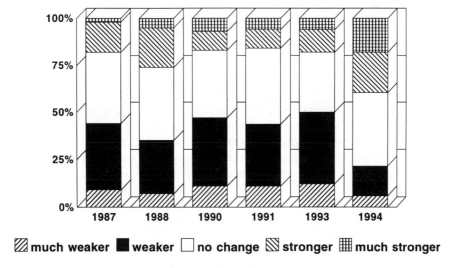

Figure 3.7. Israeli Defense Forces and public opinion over time, 1987–1994.

probably is evaluated more critically by Israelis than it is by many of its non-Israeli admirers. Paralleling the trend of anxiety about the country's security future revealed in Chapter 2, in the judgment of the samples the IDF has been weakened over the years, although the rate of expression of this opinion has been unstable (see Figure 3.7). In 1994, the same question was asked about the future rather than the past, and the assessment was more favorable for the IDF. Almost 40 percent thought the IDF would get stronger in the next five years, another 40 percent thought it would stay the same, and some 20 percent thought it would get weaker. This change could be interpreted as a dividend of the peace accord.

The tone of the assessment regarding the IDF was quite critical. When asked in 1986 if there was more waste in the IDF than in other institutions in Israeli society, 40 percent said yes, another 39 percent thought that the IDF was like the rest of the country, and only 21 percent thought there was less waste in the IDF. Moreover, in the 1986, 1987, and 1988 samples, only half thought that the defense burden of military service was equitably distributed among members of the society. In 1986 and 1987 only half said that in their opinion efficient use was made of the reserve military service period. Among other things, this relates to the deferral of some ultra-Orthodox yeshiva students (in effect they are exempted from army service) while they are studying. This is a source of great concern for many Israelis: when asked in 1992 if active service in the IDF should be universal for all

Jewish males in Israel, 95 percent agreed. In case this was not understood and respondents were merely identifying with the principle of universal military service, the question was asked in a more pointed manner: Should yeshiva students of recruitable age be exempted from active IDF service? Even then, 87 percent said no.

Compulsory service for Jews (three years for most males; two years at the time for non-observant females) was about right, according to 3 out of 4 of the respondents, to a question posed in 1986 and repeated in 1987. About 1 in 5 reported that it was too long, with a handful saying it was too short. The term for women was reduced in 1994. It seemed likely that if political agreements with Arab countries reduced tension, and with a growing population and more sophisticated weapons systems, other compulsory terms of service would also be reduced. The debate among planners concerned with cost-effectiveness will be whether Israel can still afford universal conscription, or whether a smaller, professional, voluntary army would suffice. Since the topic touches on basic myths and values in the Israeli culture, including community, personal sacrifice, and collective self-defense, it is unlikely that the topic will get a full public hearing. More likely, decisions of an ad hoc, incremental nature will be taken, and the army will attempt to meet its needs without taking on the society's value system in the process.

Respondents were asked in the 1986 and 1987 surveys if the defense budget should be increased or decreased or stay the same as it was. Three in 10 favored increasing, 1 in 10 wanted to decrease it, and about 6 in 10 thought it was just right. In 1987, an additional question asked about the size of the defense budget if the economy got worse. The distribution changed then, with only 1 in 10 favoring more spending, and 2 in 10 favoring less. When budget reduction was considered in 1987 in a different form, support for the military was seen as less strong. The question was asked whether the respondent would agree to cut social services in order to increase the defense budget: almost two-thirds opposed the idea.

In 1992, the same topic was broached differently. Respondents were asked regarding several topics whether the government should spend more, less, or about the same as it does. To minimize the chances for a response set of "spend more" on all items, respondents were first asked whether they supported a tax increase which would mean paying more taxes. Only 26 percent supported paying more taxes in general; regarding security, 68 percent wanted to spend more, 8 percent wanted to spend less, and 24 percent thought that the amount was about right (see Chapter 5). But when the two questions are taken together, that is, when the willingness to increase taxes was factored in to the desire to increase the defense budget, only 24 percent were willing to increase defense spending. That rate was lower than those registered in 1986 and 1987. While the decline was not

Table 3.2. *Agree to Increase Taxes and Military Service for Added Security*

Increase for more security	1986	1987	1993
Taxes	48%	56%	42%
Reserve service	37%	34%	37%
Compulsory service	34%	30%	[a]

[a] Not asked.

great, and different questions were used, the level of support for increased defense spending seemed to have eroded.

Although fewer were ready to pay more taxes for more security, the readiness for more reserve duty was stable. The percentages of those who agreed to increase a number of items in order to ensure higher levels of security are displayed in Table 3.2.

MAKING WAR

Initiating War

Peace is one side of the coin, war is the other. The likelihood of war motivates nations to arm and to deal with issues of national security. One distinction made between the war in Lebanon and previous Israeli wars was that in 1982 Israel had a choice and that Israel had chosen war. (Some have suggested that the Sinai campaign of 1956 also fell into that category.) The conditions under which it is justifiable to initiate war is a major theme in the public debate over security (Levite 1990). What type of war would be supported by the public, and what of the specter of nuclear war?

A strong case can be made, based on these surveys, that Israelis are willing to risk much in order to *avoid* war. One might have reasonably expected a great degree of bellicosity in the sample's responses after so many years of national struggle. However, when faced with the hypothetical situation in the 1986 survey of Israel's military power being far superior to that of the enemy's, 92 percent of the sample refrained from supporting the suggestion of a preventive strike.

Hypothetical situations regarding initiating war were presented in the 1986 and 1987 surveys. The responses to these situations clustered into three groups, with men − and especially young men − more likely to support the initiation of war. The first category seemed to point to the use of war in a reactive or defensive sense (see Table 3.3). The values in the public mind that supported these propositions by two-thirds or more were existence, security, and opposition to being forced to alter political arrangements by the use of

Table 3.3. *Conditions for Initiating War*

"Is it justifiable or not justifiable for Israel to initiate war in each of these situations?"[a]	1986	1987
In defense, to prevent the country's destruction	89%	94%
To prevent or stop a war of attrition	76%	81%
To prevent recapture of the territories	75%	79%
To destroy terrorist infrastructure aimed at Israel	[b]	66%
In response to an increase in border attacks	47%	[b]
To destroy enemy's war-making capacity to prevent future threats	44%	62%
In response to intelligence reports regarding intentions by neighboring states to increase border attacks	40%	50%
To capture territories to increase country's security	26%	36%
To topple a hostile regime in support of a friendly leader who will agree to make peace	23%	33%
In response to a request from the United States to protect American interests in the region	[b]	31%
To help friendly forces in the region	[b]	23%

[a] Each question had 4 responses. The sum of "definitely justified" and "justified" is reported.
[b] Not asked.

force, such as relinquishing control of the territories by war or as a result of terrorist acts.

A second category, which included hypothetical examples of using war in a limited offensive manner, generated lower levels of support for the use of war, in the ranges of 40 and 50 percent. About half the samples supported the initiation of war to prevent present or future threats to Israel's security. The lowest level of support was registered for initiating war in a manifestly offensive manner: to capture additional territories, to overthrow a hostile regime, or to go to war to achieve the interests of an ally.

Terror and Terrorists

Israel's history has been accented with bloody terrorist attacks. Terror is especially frustrating to fight because its purposes and personnel are so different from those of a regular army. Its method is to sow fear and panic, and its practitioners are shadows rather than clear targets. Some politicians tried to educate the Israeli public that the primary means to fight terror were political ones, rather than military means; others however argued

Table 3.4. *Actions in the Fight Against Terror*

"Do you support or not support each of these actions in the fight against terror?"[a]	1987	1993
Destroying houses of those who hide known terrorists	88%	79%
Deporting those in contact with terrorist organizations	90%	77%
Bombing terrorist bases outside of Israel even if civilians are likely to be hit	53%	68%
Deporting all residents of villages from which terror attacks originate	[b]	27%
Destroying Arab villages from which terror attacks originate	[b]	21%

[a] Each question had 4 responses. The sum of "definitely support" and "support" is reported.
[b] Not asked.

that with proper military action terror would be controlled. The public was, not surprisingly, divided. The view that terrorism can be put down by military force or that its effects can be minimized has been consistently supported by a large majority of the samples. In the 1986 and 1987 surveys, a question was asked about the effectiveness of military moves against terrorism. In 1986, 13 percent thought that it could stopped, 72 percent said terror could be reduced, and 16 percent replied that confronting terror militarily would result in more terror. The 1987 survey used slightly different response categories, and then 16 percent thought that terror could be deterred, 56 percent related that it could diminished, 16 percent said it would make no difference, and 12 percent felt that it would increase terror. There was no clear-cut preference for how to confront terrorism. One-third said that attacks should be initiated on terrorists and their bases before they strike, 39 percent called for defensive strikes that would prevent further attacks, and 28 percent favored reaction only after terrorist incidents.

The pattern of opinion seems to have changed slightly regarding the deterrence of terrorists and collective punishment when the data of the 1987 and 1993 surveys are compared. The Israeli public seems to have mellowed somewhat regarding acting against individuals who have aided terrorists, but a larger percentage is ready to act against terrorist bases even if civilians would be hit. A quarter of the sample was prepared to support collective punishment (see Table 3.4).

The death penalty for terrorists has regularly been supported by respondents. The question was first asked in 1984 and 80 percent agreed with the proposition then. In 1987 and 1990 the percentages were 79 and 77 respectively. In 1991 and 1993 the question was slightly amended to stipulate that it would apply to terrorists who had been convicted of murder; the response rate barely changed, however. In 1991, 80 percent agreed with the amended version, and in 1993 the rate was 74 percent.

Policy in the Territories

The overwhelming majority of the respondents felt that the intifada could be put down or at least restricted by military effort. After its onset in 1987, a question was posed in these surveys about containing it militarily. Even more than with terror in general, Israelis felt that military force was the tool to be used to confront the intifada. In the 1988, 1991, and 1993 surveys, about a third of the samples reported that the intifada could be completely contained by military means; an additional 43–46 percent replied that it could be restrained but not eliminated by these efforts, 9–12 percent felt that military activity would have no impact, and 8–11 percent answered that any move to arrest these activities would in fact lead to greater efforts against Israel.

Respondents were also upset and dissatisfied regarding the policies of the army and the government in achieving personal safety for the population. Feelings of personal safety were slightly higher in 1994, but still very low. In the 1993 survey, 85 percent reported that they were worried about being hurt by an Arab in their day-to-day activities, compared with 76 percent in 1994. Respondents replied to the query of how worried they were that they or members of their family would be injured by terrorist action as follows: very worried 37 percent; worried 39 percent; not worried 18 percent; not at all worried 6 percent. The corresponding percentages in 1993 were 48, 36, 13, and 2.

At the same time, the prevalent opinion was that the measures used in the territories had been too soft (see Figure 3.8). This feeling appeared to grow, and the 1993 rate was the highest recorded. And this was before the bloody month of March 1993, in which 15 Israeli citizens were killed; in 1994, after the peace accord, that trend receded. However, when asked in 1994 about government policy toward Jewish settlers in the territories, many more felt that the treatment was too harsh.

Of great significance was the fact that those who served in the territories also felt that the policy was too soft, and at a rate higher than the general population (see Figure 3.9). Previous investigations have failed to uncover any systematic connections between active service in war and attitude change in Israel and in other countries (Schild 1973; Horowitz and Kimmerling 1974; Kirkpatrick and Regens 1978; Kimmerling 1985a, Arian,

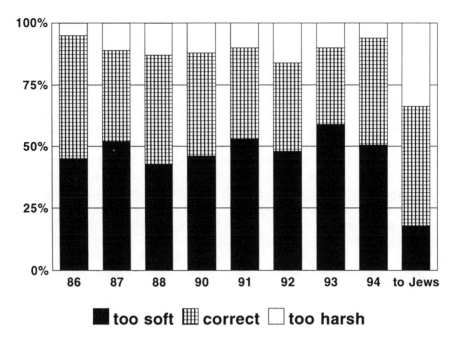

■ too soft ▦ correct ☐ too harsh

Figure 3.8. Attitudes toward policy in the territories. 1986–1994.

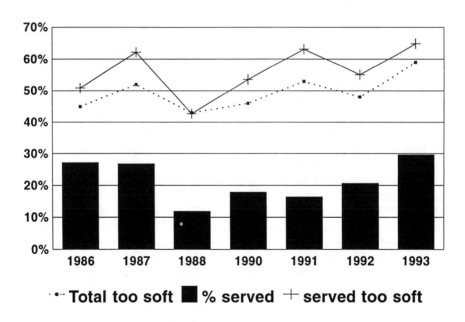

∙•∙ Total too soft ■ % served ┼ served too soft

Figure 3.9. Attitudes toward policy in the territories and IDF service in the territories, 1986–1993.

Talmud, and Hermann 1988). That it is evident here is a measure of just how frustrated and anxious the population was.

Figure 3.9 also displays the percentage of respondents who reported that they had served in the territories between 1986 and 1993. This percentage was stable in the pre-intifada years of 1986 and 1987; in the first years after the onset of the intifada at the end of 1987, the percentage of respondents sent to serve in the territories was lower than in the past. With time, however, the policy of the IDF reacted to the complaints of certain units that their soldiers spent long months of reserve service in the territories while others did not serve there at all. In 1986, 55 percent thought that reserve service was justly distributed; in 1987 that percentage fell to 44 percent, and recovered to 50 percent in 1988. As already noted, slightly less than half the 1986 and 1987 samples thought that the reserve forces were efficiently used. The experience of serving in the territories seems to have become more widespread as evidenced by the larger percentage for 1992 and 1993.

Nuclear Weapons

One of Israel's most closely kept secrets has to do with nuclear military capability. Although it has evidently been the topic of policy discussions since the 1950s, whether or not Israel has a nuclear capacity has never been acknowledged by the government, and no political party has ever raised the issue in an election campaign (see Feldman 1982; Aronson 1977, 1984; Beres 1986; Yaniv 1987a; Shimshoni 1988; Cohen 1993). Shrouding the issue in a veil of secrecy can be understood as a means of preventing a nuclear arms race with Arab neighbors, although the argument is also made that admitting nuclear capability would be a greater deterrent. Israel's official reaction to queries is that it will not be the first power to introduce nuclear weapons into the Middle East; although Foreign Minister Yigal Allon complicated the already unclear issue when he added that Israel would also not be the second power to introduce such weapons into the area. Although this statement is open to various interpretations, the fact is that Israel has not signed the treaty for the nonproliferation of nuclear weapons. Interestingly, however, and equally ambivalent in its meaning, is that in the 1994 survey, 72 percent of the sample supported the proposition that Israel should sign that treaty (35% strongly support, 37% support), compared to 28 percent who opposed (12% strongly opposed, 16% opposed).

Most experts are convinced that Israel has a nuclear capacity, yet the orientation of the public to the topic of nonconventional weapons, and especially nuclear ones, was remarkably dormant before the Gulf war. It was a non-issue, uninformed by public debate. Yet, when called upon to

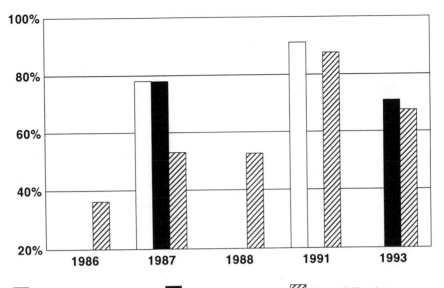

☐ **Should develop** ■ **Keep secret** ▨ **Justified to use**

Figure 3.10. Changes in public opinion toward nuclear weapons, 1986–1993.

express an opinion, the public was ready and able to do so. The rate of nonresponse was low and similar to other questions, between 1 and 3 percent. On the open-ended question of the major issue to be addressed by the government asked over the years and discussed in Chapter 5, the issue of nuclear weapons *never* came up, compared with a 10 percent rate in American surveys (Schuman, Ludwig, and Krosnick 1986).

The fact that nuclear policy is a non-issue in Israeli politics is buttressed by the strict military censorship regarding the matter. Uncertainty and censorship has meant that most of the debate on the subject was carried on abroad, and then reported in Israel as news items from foreign newspapers. That, ironically, is permitted under Israeli practice.

When asked in 1986 about using nuclear weapons (if Israel has nuclear weapons), only 36 percent recognized circumstances under which they would justify such use. In 1987, the number was 53 percent, and in the 1991 survey done after the Gulf war, it was dramatically up to 88 percent, and in 1993 it settled back to 67 percent (see Figure 3.10). Regarding developing nuclear capacity, 78 percent of the Israeli population supported the idea in 1987; by 1991, the size of the group that supported such development rose to 91 percent. Seventy-one percent supported the notion of keeping Israel's nuclear plans secret in 1993, compared with 78 percent in 1987.

Table 3.5. *Conditions for Use of Nuclear Weapons*[a]

	1986 36%[b]	1987 53%[b]	1991 88%[b]	1993 67%[b]
In response to nuclear attack	c	99%	99%	98%
In response to gas or biological attack	c	c	85%	84%
In a desperate military situation	91%	c	c	c
To avoid defeat in conventional war	c	60%	53%	58%
To save many lives	63%	53%	48%	41%
To save few lives	18%	19%	20%	17%
Instead of using the regular army	13%	13%	12%	8%
If the Golan Heights were taken	c	c	c	18%

[a] Data include only those who replied that there existed conditions under which the use of nuclear weapons would be justified, assuming Israel had such weapons. Based on Likert scale with four response options; "definitely justified" and "justified" reported here.
[b] Percentage of total sample for year shown.
[c] Not asked.

Regarding the conditions under which nuclear weapons might be used (if Israel has such weapons), there was a clear pattern. The percentages in Table 3.5 are presented as a proportion of those who indicated that there ever might be a justification for using nuclear weapons. The numbers in the table were calculated by multiplying the percentage of respondents who reported that there were conditions under which the use of nuclear weapons was justified (provided in the column heads) by the percent who agreed to use nuclear weapons in that particular context. As these numbers are read, one must keep in mind that the complement to the number in the column head is the size of the sample opposed to the use of nuclear weapons in any situation.

The small geographical dimensions of the Middle East argue against developing the strategic weapon-of-last-resort, but the fear that Arab states may attempt to achieve that type of weapon could lead Israel to try to have it in its arsenal as a deterrent.

Israeli planners may prefer to think of the use of nuclear weapons in tactical settings, but the population tended to see a reactive role for them (assuming Israel had such a capacity). Most Israelis perceived the use of nuclear weapons appropriate as a last resort following a nonconventional attack by another country. At a lower rate, about half supported the use of nuclear weapons in a desperate situation, or in order to save a large number of Israeli lives. At much lower levels was the support for using these weapons in more conventional military situations. This order was the same as 1986 and 1987, except that by 1991 the threshold of opposition to nuclear use had been lowered considerably.

Table 3.6. *Nuclear Weapons by Left-Right, 1987*

	Left 1	2	3	4	5	6	7 Right
Develop	58%	75%	79%	78%	79%	80%	84%
Justified to use	24%	48%	58%	57%	55%	57%	64%

Israelis perceived the use of nuclear weapons differently than did citizens of the United States or Western Europe during the cold war. The overwhelming response there and then was that nuclear weapons should be used only in total, global war and not in regional conflicts. Moreover, the use of these weapons of mass destruction were feared because of the implications of total annihilation. According to a 1984 poll, almost all (96%) Americans thought that a nuclear war was too dangerous, and 89 percent agreed that a nuclear world war would destroy mankind (Yankelovich and Doble 1984). Interestingly, the assessment of chances of a world war were identical (49%) among Israelis in 1987 and Americans at that time (Smith 1988).

Some Arab observers have argued that Israel's intentions were to use nuclear weapons in a strategic rather than a tactical manner, relating it to a Masada complex (Aronson 1984). There is some verification of this position in the responses to an open-ended question asked in 1988, in which the sample was asked why those who favored the use of nuclear weapons might take that position. The most frequent response, provided by a third of the sample, mentioned the experience of the Jews in the Holocaust and in World War II.

The moderate degree of politicization of the nuclear issue in Israel was evident when the left-right self placement (see Table 3.6) and party choice (not shown), were considered. Only for the extremes was there a clear connection. As one would expect from a nonpoliticized issue, the middle was undifferentiated and consensual. This is especially striking when compared to many other issues (see Chapter 4), and to other nations such as Germany (Rattinger 1987), New Zealand (Lamare 1989), and the United States (Gildemeister and Furth 1989). This is underscored by support of a nuclear-free Middle East by leaders of the right such as Ariel Sharon and the nuclear physicist–politician Yuval Ne'eman (Inbar 1986), and the championing of nuclear deterrence by leaders of the left (Feldman 1982).

Although relatively weak, the strongest correlation with demographic variables was for education; even then, the direction was opposite to the one generally found in other countries. In Israel, support for the use of nuclear weapons was *directly* related to level of education. Among those with only elementary school education, 68 percent in the 1987 survey supported the

development of nuclear weapons, and 41 percent thought there were conditions in which the use of such weapons would be justified. The parallel
numbers for the most highly educated were 81 percent and 61 percent,
respectively. Those who perceived a greater sense of threat from the Arabs
were more likely to support the development and use of these weapons.
Only the elderly (those over age 66) supported the development and use of
nuclear weapons compared with all other age groups.

The nuclear issue became hot in 1991, and was markedly affected by the
Gulf war. It represented the major threat expressed by the public; support
for the development and use of nuclear weapons grew, and the conditions
for use seemed to crystalize in the Israeli mind. Not only was there a
change over time in the position of the public regarding the development
and use of nuclear weapons, the public expressed its fear of these weapons
and the threat they posed (see Chapter 9).

WARS

Lebanon

On June 6, 1982, exactly 15 years after the start of the Six Days war, IDF
units crashed into Lebanon, "to push back the PLO [terrorists] to a distance of 40 km [25 miles] to the north," as Prime Minister Menachem
Begin assured President Ronald Reagan (see Schiff and Ya'ari 1984;
O'Brien 1986; Yaniv 1987b). By June 9 the Israeli Air Force had destroyed
the Syrian air-defense system and had shot down 25 planes without loss to
Israel, and by mid-June the IDF had entered East Beirut. The political
objectives of removing the PLO from Beirut and replacing Syrian hegemony over Lebanon with Israeli hegemony were more difficult to achieve.
Only at the end of August were the PLO and Syria ready to give up after
months of shelling and mediation.

As the PLO evacuation of Beirut was in progress in August, the
Maronite Bashir Gemayel was elected president of Lebanon, but instead of
embracing Israel, he tried to distance himself from it, and yet found it
difficult to establish his authority beyond his original political base. On
September 14, a bomb killed him when it destroyed the party headquarters
building at which he was speaking. Israel occupied West Beirut to prevent
any possible incident and to secure quiet.

Days later, the Maronite allies of Israel massacred hundreds of Palestinian
civilians, including women and children, at the refugee camps at Sabra and
Shatilla, in accordance with the practice of Lebanon's civil war (which had
been raging since the mid-1970s) of taking vengeance on any population

perceived as hostile. After the murder of the most popular Maronite leader, this action could be seen as predictable. Even more complicating for Israel, its minister of defense, Ariel Sharon, and its chief of staff, Rafael ("Raful") Eytan, had introduced the Maronite phalangists into the camps to clear out suspected nests of terrorists. Resisting calls for an inquiry, Begin made his revealing remark, "Goyim kill goyim, and they come to hang the Jews." By the end of the month, he had reversed himself, and the work of the Kahan Commission began. Ultimately, Sharon and Eytan and two others would be charged with indirect responsibility for the killings.

Withdrawal from Lebanon came because of the inconclusive political results, and because of the heavy toll taken by the action. By September 21, 1982, Israel had agreed to withdraw from Beirut under American pressure, and its army units were replaced by an international force of Americans, French, and Italians. This force left Beirut in February 1984 after suffering heavy casualties, including the death of 241 American marines when a suicide bomber drove a semi trailer loaded with dynamite into their barracks on October 23, 1983. Israel suffered a similar calamity the next month when 60 were killed and 43 were wounded, in an explosion of gas canisters at the military government headquarters in Tyre.

The "Peace for Galilee" operation, as the Lebanon war was officially called in Israel, provoked some of the most fractious manifestations of public opinion in Israel's history (Feldman and Rechnitz-Kijner 1984). As the war began, much of the Knesset and the public supported the limited goal of securing 40 kilometers, but when it was clear that Sharon and Eytan (and perhaps Begin) had more far-reaching plans, opinion split. On September 25, 1982, after the Sabra and Shatilla massacres, an enormous protest demonstration of 400,000 took place in Tel Aviv calling for a complete investigation and a withdrawal from Lebanon. In February 1983, at a demonstration of Peace Now in Jerusalem, a grenade was thrown into the crowd and a demonstrator, Emil Grunsweig, was killed. That type of violence, extremely rare in Israeli public life, indicates how fervent the public discourse was at that time.

The deep divisions well known in peacetime Israel had surfaced in wartime. A year after Sabra and Shatilla, in September 1983, Begin withdrew from politics, evidently feeling betrayed by Sharon, and the IDF began withdrawing from central Lebanon. Shamir replaced Begin, setting the stage for the bitter 1984 election, with its indecisive conclusion. The two large parties joined in a National Unity government, with a power-sharing arrangement. In January 1985, and as a result of the negotiations of the unity coalition, the Israeli government decided on withdrawal from Lebanon in three stages, leaving a security zone patrolled by a south Lebanese army and the IDF.

Public opinion generally supports military actions that are quick and successful (Mueller 1973). The typical reaction is rallying 'round the flag, and around the soldiers in the line of fire (Russett 1990). This was the Israeli pattern in the first stages of the war in 1982 as well; the country, including much of the opposition, supported the minimal goals stated by the government. But as the Peace for Galilee operation stretched out, and as international public opinion became more hostile, support splintered. By 1985, when the monitoring of public opinion in this series began, only a minority of the respondents (41%) took the Begin government's side in the debate, whether or not they saw the Lebanese action as a war of no choice, a war Israel had to fight against the PLO and Syrian forces in Lebanon to ensure its survival and security (Inbar 1989). Only 15 percent supported the actions taken in the Lebanese war, and an additional 60 percent thought that the IDF should have stopped at the 40–45 kilometer line, far away from Beirut. Another 25 percent said that the war should not have been fought at all. When asked a hypothetical question of whether a government in Israel is justified in going to war even if the citizenry objects, the sample split right down the middle.[3]

Some goals of the war had been achieved, according to those interviewed. The PLO had been weakened, and the threat to the settlements on the northern border had been lessened (see Figure 3.11). But the price paid was large: the image of Israel in the eyes of the world, Israeli democracy, the likelihood of peace, and the power of the IDF had all sustained relative losses.

Public reaction at the time of the war divided along political lines, and this was still true a few years later. In 1985, when the process of extricating the IDF from Lebanon was under way and with Shimon Peres as prime minister of the National Unity government, 27 percent thought that the Lebanese war had been worth the price paid by Israel in manpower, material, and tarnished international image. Two years later, and after Yitzhak Shamir had rotated into the prime ministry as the National Unity government agreement stipulated, the percentage replying that the Lebanese war had been worth it jumped 10 points to 37 (see Table 3.7). Contemplating the hypothetical situation of the terrorists again shelling settlements, the response pattern was quite similar between 1985 and 1987, although the option of using heavy artillery and airpower lost some of its appeal.

The chances that the IDF would have to reenter Lebanon were conceived as high by a third of the 1985 sample, as low by 57 percent, and as nonexistent by 11 percent. The preferred policy in Lebanon for this sample reflected the national mood at the time of the survey: 35 percent wanted the IDF out completely, and 1 percent wanted the IDF to get in and hold the country. The rest of the sample supported various versions of the

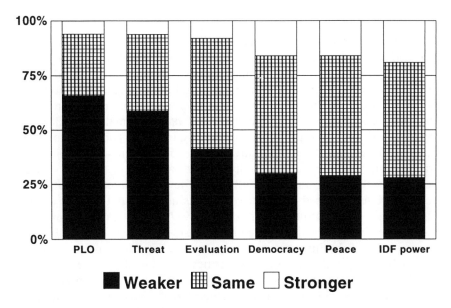

Figure 3.11. Effects of Lebanon war on threat and other factors (1985 survey). Variables: *threat* to settlements on northern border; *evaluation,* positive world opinion; *democracy* in Israel; and likelihood of *peace*.

Table 3.7. *Reactions to the 1982 War in Lebanon*

	1985	1987
Lebanese war was worth the price	27%	37%
Response if terrorists shell settlements again:		
Invade South Lebanon and hold territory	7%	7%
Heavy artillery and air bombardment	24%	18%
Limited military power to destroy bases	36%	44%
Pinpoint air raids against terrorist bases	26%	24%
Seek political solution	7%	7%

security zone option: a quarter saw a security zone controlled by the pro-Israel Lebanese units in the south of the country as the best solution; 28 percent wanted the security zone controlled by the southern Lebanese militia with the active support of the IDF, and another 10 percent wanted the zone under IDF control. The plurality position was the one adopted and the security zone has been controlled by the Lebanese units with active IDF support.

Intifada

The uprising in the territories, called *intifada* in Arabic, began in December 1987 and had a profound effect on Israeli public opinion (see Schiff and Ya'ari 1989; Freedman 1991; Shalev 1991; Goldberg, Barzilai, and Inbar 1991). It seemed to force the Israeli public and political leadership to think about the future of the territories in a more concrete and realistic manner than they had before.[4] It spotlighted for Israelis anomalies which were evident, and even written about, but largely ignored. The implication of making no decision about the future of the territories and their inhabitants was brought home more powerfully than it had been in the previous 20 years (Bar-Tal 1986; Barzilai 1990). A low-level, protracted situation of constant violence forced Israelis to confront issues many of them had conveniently pushed aside. In the years between 1987 and 1993, more than 1,200 Palestinians in the territories were killed by Israeli troops; some 150 Israelis were killed by Palestinian acts of terror; another 750 Palestinians suspected of collaborating with the Israeli authorities were killed by other Palestinians. Israelis had to judge the army and the role it was called upon to play as much of the world's mass media treated Israel's policy of attempting to suppress the intifada in a very negative manner.

The survey of 1990 focused on the intifada; in its third year, it was becoming very intense. By then, there were signs that more lethal weapons were being used by the Arabs. Murders of Jews by Arab attackers in Jerusalem and Jaffa brought a sense of urgency to the population which had been absent in earlier phases of the uprising. Even after the Iraqi invasion of Kuwait and the threats of Saddam Hussein against Israel, the public seemed more concerned with the threat of violence from Palestinian street action than from large-scale attack by Iraqi military forces – until SCUD rockets actually began falling on Tel Aviv and Haifa in January 1991. These fears reemerged soon after the Gulf war and seemed to become a permanent feature of Israeli life.

Using a nine-question battery to measure the generalized effect that the intifada had on the sample, only 5 percent reported that it had no effect on them or on the country. The eight questions were about changes brought about by the intifada regarding (1) personal mood, (2) national mood, (3) assessment of the election results, (4) voting intention, (5) political activity, (6) desire to live in Israel, (7) attitudes toward the Arabs, and (8) attitudes toward concessions to the Arabs. For most people an effect was reported, and the pattern generated was an inverse-U pattern: 8 percent reported change on one item, 12 percent on two, 14 percent on three, 19 percent on four, 20 percent on five, 16 percent on six, 6 percent on seven questions, and 3 percent on all eight. Moreover, reported attitude change regarding

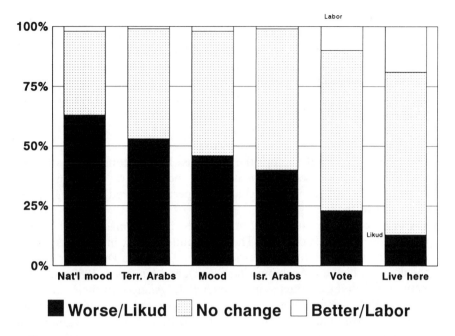

Figure 3.12. Effects of the intifada on national mood in Israel and on other factors (1990 survey).

the security issues was closely associated ($r = .32$) with change in vote intention (similar findings are reported in Jennings and Niemi 1981). This is especially revealing because there was almost no correlation between attitude change regarding security issues and change in other related topics, such as personal mood, willingness to live in Israel, and level of political activity.

The intifada had an impact on Israeli public opinion. Israelis said so quite clearly. In the 1990 survey, 53 percent reported that their opinions regarding security and politics had not changed as a result of the intifada. One in five respondents reported that their opinions had moderated as a result of the intifada, and an additional 28 percent said their opinions had hardened.[5] Other indications of the intifada's impact were clear in answers to questions about its effect, and these are portrayed in Figure 3.12.[6] As the numbers in that figure show, 63 percent thought that the national mood had become worse as a result of the intifada, and 46 percent reported that their own mood had soured. Only 2 and 1 percent, respectively, thought that the intifada improved the national mood and their own mood. Evaluations of Israeli Arabs and Arabs of the territories both became more negative as a result of the intifada. Sixty-eight percent said that the intifada did not change their desire to live in Israel, but 19 percent said it strengthened this desire, and 13 percent said that it decreased it.

In 1990, two-thirds thought that the intifada would not have an impact on their vote choice in future elections. The remaining third reported that the intifada had influenced their voting decision: 19 percent of the respondents who changed reported that they now planned to vote for the Likud and parties to the right of it, compared to 13 percent who said that their vote would now go to Labor and to parties to the left of it. The 1988 survey was conducted immediately before the elections. In that atmosphere, the impact of the intifada seemed greater, and the right was an even bigger winner: 48 percent reported no change, 31 percent moved to the right, and 17 percent to the left.

A more complete analysis of attitude change was made possible by a panel study of 416 respondents. These respondents were interviewed twice, once in the first wave of interviews conducted between December 9, 1987 (the day on which the Arab uprising began), and January 4, 1988; and then again in the survey conducted in October 1988. Analysis of their responses indicated three simultaneous processes operating on Israeli public opinion: (1) a generalized hardening of short-term positions since the beginning of the intifada; (2) a steady and increasing moderation of Israeli public opinion on certain long-term issues of security policy over the past few years; and (3) a growing polarization of attitude and political power between the more conciliatory left and the more hard-line right. A helpful distinction in ordering these apparent paradoxes was between short-term policy issues and long-term policy outcomes. The trends were of hardening on the first and slowly growing moderation on the second. Polarization resulted from processing of political events by individuals and political groups in different ways. This polarization, which characterized the electorate as well as the party system, is discussed in Chapter 5. The attitudes of the panel changed based on a composite measure to be presented in Chapter 4. Change was neither monotonic nor uniform. On the whole, the panel became more militant in the 10 months that passed, but the change was a matter of degree rather than a complete reversal.

As the intifada intensified, the intercommunal conflict became more impassioned, the difficulties that the army had in confronting a hostile civilian population became more prominent, and Israel's failure to reestablish law and order was more widely observed. The dilemmas of the situation sharpened. The Jewish public reassessed the threat which the Arabs posed, and the available options for the short run and the long run. In terms of long-term goals there seemed to be a trend toward greater moderation and compromise, yet in terms of short-term concerns, policies and means, Israelis remained as hawkish as ever or became even more hawkish, and supported a strong hand. There was willingness to forsake democratic norms such as the rule of law when these norms jeopardized security concerns, yet it came together with growing concern about the negative effect of the intifada on the army's fighting ethic (see Chapter 4).

The Gulf War

Go my people into your rooms, and close the doors behind you. Wait a short moment until the anger has passed. (Isaiah 26:20)

I will send to Babylon strangers. They will smite it and rend that land asunder. And they will surround it on the day of wickedness . . . . Spare not its young men; completely destroy its army. (Jeremiah 51:2–3)

The Gulf war, Saddam and his missiles, and threats to destroy the country represented for Israelis another chapter in the history of coping with challenges. The intertwining of death and life, grief and joy, is an everpresent fact with both existential and emotional consequences which, in Israel perhaps more than in other countries, it is impossible to avoid. Life and death come together in the culture, in the values, in the very ethos of the country. The intermingling of death and life is powerfully institutionalized in Israel by the sequencing of the days of mourning in memory of victims of the Holocaust and of Israel's fallen soldiers, immediately followed by Independence Day – creating an emotional and vivid juxtaposition of mourning for loved ones and affirming life.

Fear of one's own death – as well as fear of the death of loved ones – is generally accepted to be a natural, normal human emotion (Zilboorg 1943; Kastenbaum and Aisenberg 1972). During war, one is more consciously aware of this fear. Excessive preoccupation with fear of death is considered pathological (Feifel 1959; Templer 1972). While many, perhaps most, Israelis were afraid and anxious during the Gulf war, they nevertheless carried on with their lives and did not become preoccupied with death. In fact, one could almost say that over all, pathology was down in the country. Mental health clinics and private therapists reported a dramatic decline in the number of people who sought help. Psychologists were on duty at hospitals 24 hours a day – but almost no one came. Israelis were busy coping.

On the other hand, there were unobtrusive measures of the stress Israelis were under. First, heart attack rates increased dramatically, with the greatest increase reported for the Tel Aviv area, and somewhat lower rates of increase in Haifa and even lower rates for areas which had not experienced SCUD attacks. Second, Israelis had more problems sleeping than before the war. In addition, incidents of domestic violence and rape were up, with shelters for battered women filled to overflowing after the war. In the six weeks of the war, seven women were battered to death compared with a usual *annual* rate of three to four (Avgar 1991).

The Gulf war, as are all wars, was very difficult for Israelis – and with good cause. The missile attacks were designed to terrorize the civilian population and to involve Israel in the war. But the population was not terrorized. There was no collapse of civilian morale. And Israel did not get involved in the war.

In the 42 days of the war, 18 missile attacks were launched against Israel, for an average of one attack every two and one-half days. Forty missiles reached Israel: 26 fell in the Tel Aviv area, 6 in Haifa, 5 in the West Bank, and 3 in the south of the country. In two-thirds of the attacks (12 of 18), a lone missile arrived; in the other six incidents, 6 SCUDs landed. In the largest single attack of the war against Israel, 8 SCUD missiles arrived simultaneously. Once, 6 missiles were sent toward a single area in one attack.

It is notable how low the casualty rate was. As a direct result of the missiles, only 1 person was killed, and 230 were wounded, only 1 critically; the planning of the Israel Defense Forces anticipated an average of 3 to 5 deaths for each conventional missile (Ben-Meir 1991). Eleven people died indirectly from the missile attacks, 4 from heart attacks, and 7 from improper use of the gas masks which had been distributed to save lives. In addition, 226 people were injured for unnecessarily injecting themselves with Atropine, used to counteract the nerve gas that was not sent, and 539 cases of panic and anxiety were treated in hospitals. Only 60 people were actually hospitalized, and most of them only for a day or two.

While no damage was reported in 10 of the 18 attacks, on the whole property damage was relatively heavy, totaling several hundred million dollars. In Tel Aviv, 3,991 apartments were hit; 87 were destroyed and 869 were badly damaged. More than 100 public buildings and business structures were also hit. A total of 1,647 people were evacuated to hotels. The damage in the Tel Aviv suburb of Ramat Gan was similar: 3,742 apartments hit, 105 destroyed, 600 badly damaged, and 100 public buildings and business structures hit. Ramat Gan residents who were evacuated to hotels totaled 1,047.

Israel was under attack, but with all their experience, this war was different. Israel was not part of the coalition that fought against Iraq; there was no battlefront – only a home front. Israeli civilians instead of soldiers were the targets of missile attacks – and yet there was no military activity by Israel. This was a never-before-experienced first in Israel. The fear of chemical attack was ever present. The possibility of a gas attack prompted the authorities to institute a dramatic change in procedure. When the air-raid sirens sounded, Israelis grabbed their gas masks and ran to sealed rooms in their apartments, as Isaiah had counseled. The warning time was measured in seconds or a few minutes; use of communal air-raid shelters was not encouraged, partly because not enough had been prepared, and partly because too much time would elapse in collecting people there. Accordingly, unlike other wars in Israel, there was no sharing of time with neighbors, no alternative structures of social norms which emerged, no spontaneous leadership, group solidarity, and psychological and emotional support.

Most important, rather than being a nation-at-arms, Israel during the war was a nation-at-home. The economy slowed down almost to a standstill; schools were closed. There was no general call-up, so most fathers, husbands, sons, and brothers were present with their families, and as helpless as the other civilians usually thought of as weaker in war situations. Israelis living abroad did not return to join their army units since most of these units were not called up. The physical existence of Israelis at home had never seemed so threatened. There had been shelling of civilians previously, but the symbolism of death by gas made this situation different. Even the decision to station Patriot missiles with their American crews, while broadly supported, was a symbol of dependence and powerlessness. Day after day, as darkness approached and anxiety levels increased, Israelis came home and waited to be attacked. In Tel Aviv, the streets emptied by 4 p.m. Observers noted that while the history of the Jewish people had many examples of such behavior, the history of Israel did not. During the Gulf war, Israeli males were not warriors protecting their families, but citizens who were as helpless as their children. In many families, roles were reversed. It was the children who, having been drilled for weeks in their schools, showed their parents how to put on their gas masks and to seal the room.

In general, shifts in attitude are more likely to be gradual than sudden (McGuire 1985). Dramatic events are capable of stimulating attitude change precisely because a new definition and understanding of the situation are in place after the event. Attitude change is especially likely if the reinterpretation is echoed by opinion leaders, thus strengthening the new position and reinforcing the change (Mueller 1973; Keis 1975). But the evidence of change is not likely to be distinct or immediate. Most people continue to hold the attitudes they held, often using the event which just occurred to provide further justification for the position they held before the event.

The elements of the Gulf war situation created an ideal situation in which to search for attitude change. First, the time frame was very short. Although the crisis began with the Iraqi invasion of Kuwait in August, for most Israelis the real pressure began after the first missiles fell in the middle of January 1991. By the end of February, it was over. Second, the concentration on the war and its implications was almost total. The country closed down for the first five days, and then, for the next five weeks, concentrated almost solely on the war each evening and night. Third, almost all commentary reinforced the notion that this was a period of change. For Saddam Hussein, it was "the mother of all wars," but George Bush was equally flamboyant when he talked of "a new world order" and "a defining moment."

In Israel, it was clear that the Americans were calling the tune. Israel was told not to retaliate, and it did not. Officials turned to Washington for money to repair the economic damage done during the war. United States officials said very clearly that new patterns of behavior and relations would be expected in the Middle East after the war, and Israelis had no doubt that Americans included them in their expectations for creating a new era.

Israel's deterrent capability was not damaged by the war, according to 72 percent of the sample. Sixty-four percent saw the IDF as the source of Israeli deterrence, 18 percent thought nuclear weapons, 11 percent the United States, 6 percent God, and 1 percent the United Nations. The vast majority of Israelis – 85 percent – were satisfied or very satisfied with the government during the crisis.

Israelis said that the Gulf war had an impact on their opinions. When asked about it in the 1991 survey, 29 percent said that the war had changed their opinions regarding the security and political situations. Seventy-one percent indicated that their political positions had not changed as a result of the war. The *net* effect of the change, however, was not clear. Half of those who reported that they had changed (15% of the total sample) said they were *more* ready for compromise regarding the territories than before the war, but the other half (14%) said that they were *less* ready than before for compromise. To confound matters even more, 29 percent said that their attitude regarding the territories had changed because of the war; of those who reported change, 17 percent said they now thought that the territories are *more* important to Israel's security, and 12 percent said they were convinced by the war that the territories are *less* important than they thought before. These differences were not statistically significant; what was politically important was that change occurred in both directions and tended to cancel out each other (compare Barzilai and Inbar 1992).

The polarization which characterized Israeli politics in the 1980s was probably not changed by the war, but it was accelerated. Evidence of this polarization was seen clearly when the voting intention of those who reported that their attitudes changed was examined (see Table 3.8). The more extreme the party of choice, the more likely was the respondent to

Table 3.8. *Polarization and the Vote Choice, 1991*

A. "Did the Gulf war change or did it not change your opinion regarding the security and political situation? If it did, would you say you became more moderate or more militant?" (Effective N = 1,052)

	Left (8%)	Labor (20%)	Likud (36%)	Right (10%)	Religious (7%)	No decision (20%)
More moderate (15%)	18	22	15	11	3	14
No change (71%)	79	66	68	66	90	75
More militant (14%)	4	12	17	23	7	11

B. "And what about the importance of the territories for the country's security? Did the missiles fired from Iraq change or did they not change your opinion regarding the importance of the territories for the country's security? If they did, did you think the territories had become more important for the country's security, or did you think that they had become less important for Israel's security?" (Effective N = 1,049)

	Left (8%)	Labor (19%)	Likud (36%)	Right (10%)	Religious (6%)	No decision (20%)
More important (17%)	5	10	23	24	18	16
No change (71%)	76	71	67	70	76	73
Less important (12%)	19	19	11	7	6	11

report change in the direction of the pole of the chosen party. That is, those with a left-leaning orientation were more likely to report change in attitude as a result of the war, and that change was most likely to be in a conciliatory direction. Respondents on the right also changed, but in a more militant direction. There was much evidence that opinion was further polarized as a result of the war; there was little evidence that the war caused many to shift from one side to the other.

Some numbers will illustrate the point. For those who reported that the war changed their opinion and that they would vote for the left-of-center Citizens Rights movement, the ratio of change to a more moderate position compared to a more militant position was 12:1. For every Moledet (a right-wing party) voter who reported change in a moderate direction in the wake of the war, two Moledet voters said their attitudes were hardened on security and political matters as a result of the war. Labor voters who changed reported moving more in a conciliatory direction at a rate of 2:1.

Two groups changed in a balanced manner; that is, those who reported that their attitudes became more conciliatory as a result of the war were balanced in number by those who said that they became more militant. The two groups were those who reported Likud as their voter choice and the undecided. These are the two largest groups in the analysis (Likud 36%;

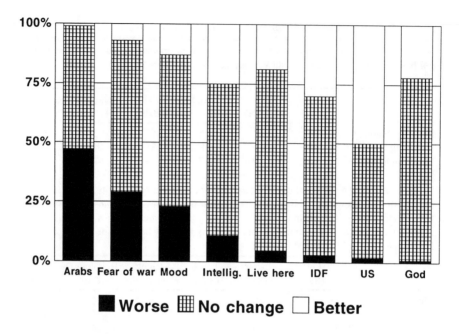

Figure 3.13. Effects of Gulf war on Israeli opinion of the United States and on other factors (1991 survey).

undecided 20%). Their decisions and the complexity of their patterns will likely have an important impact on the future of Israeli politics.

When asked directly whether opinion had changed about other subjects, change was measured (see Figure 3.13). Israelis' opinion of the United States improved dramatically after the war, with one of every two respondents expressing an improved assessment. The image of the IDF and the intelligence community also improved in the public eye as a result of the war. Belief in God and the desire to live in Israel also grew. Personal mood and the fear of war changed for the worse; the evaluation of Arabs (Israeli citizens, territories residents, and Arabs in general) deteriorated in a striking manner.

Although the Gulf war was relatively short, Israelis were certainly under stress. In a survey done during the war, two-thirds of those interviewed reported having more fear than before.[7] Women more than men, people with children, and not surprisingly, residents of the Tel Aviv area more than residents in the rest of the country expressed higher levels of fear and worse morale.[8] During the war, of those who said they felt "much more fear," 98 percent were women. In a survey done four weeks after the war,

78 percent reported having felt personally endangered and 70 percent reported having more anxiety than usual. Sixty-one percent of Israelis thought Saddam would use chemical weapons. And when asked if unconventional weapons in the hands of the Arab states represented a threat to them, three-quarters of Israelis responded "to a great extent" and another 20 percent responded "to a certain extent."

Reported behavior during the war was indicative of a group that felt very threatened. When asked if they went into their sealed rooms *and* wore their gas masks during the missile attacks, 65 percent said they always did and another 30 percent said they sometimes did.

Saddam kept insisting that he would destroy Israel. Did Israelis believe that he meant what he said? The great majority did. A month after the end of the war, Israelis reported that when the missiles started falling they believed that Saddam was out to get them. Two-thirds agreed "to a great extent" that Saddam was out to get them "as a Jew," and three-quarters believed both that he was out to get them "as an Israeli,", and "the Jewish people." Only a very small percentage did not think Saddam was out to get them as a Jew (11%), as an Israeli (5%), or the Jewish people (6%). More importantly, when asked to what extent they thought Saddam was out to get "you personally," 30 percent agreed "to a great extent," another 31 percent agreed – although with less intensity – and 38 percent responded "not at all." The "you personally" question generated a very different distribution from the others; considering the extreme nature of the question, this is a dramatic finding (see Figure 3.14). In addition, because it was distributed across the entire spectrum of Israeli society – men and women, religious and nonreligious, married and single, those living in Tel Aviv and those living elsewhere – it is even more noteworthy. The response to this question gives a strong sense of the stress Israelis were under during the Gulf war.

When missiles started falling on the Tel Aviv and Haifa areas, some in these areas left their homes. This was facilitated by the government's decision to close the schools and most of the economy. Estimates of the numbers of people who actually left varied widely, but based on the 1991 survey, fewer than 1 in 5 of those who were in dangerous areas reported that they left those areas because of the attacks, at least occasionally. A public uproar ensued when some, and especially Tel Aviv mayor Shlomo ("Chich") Lahat, a retired general, declared those who left town during the missile attacks "deserters." Later he hedged by exempting families with young children from that epithet. But the question of whether this judgmental standard should be applied to a civilian population under attack became a major topic of discussion for a population which had little else to do but to wait for the next attack. In fact, the large majority of Israelis rejected

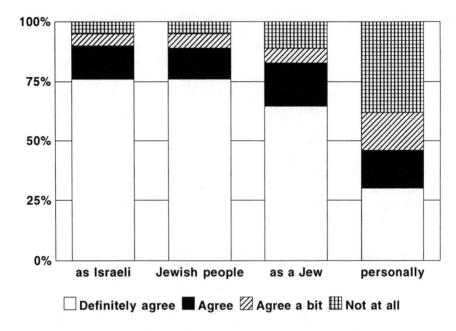

Figure 3.14. "Saddam is out to get you" (1991 survey).

the position. Seven out of 10 Israelis strongly disagreed with calling those
who left endangered areas "deserters," and another 12 percent disagreed to
a certain extent. Only 1 in 5 agreed or strongly agreed with the term.

The fact that the debate took place at all indicates the enormous emotional and existential impact that topics of war and peace have in Israel.
Each participant is part general, part soldier; part decision maker, part
citizen; part parent, part child.

The Peace Accord

Peace, cherished by all, did not come easily or without pain. Years passed
before an accord was signed, and once it was signed, waves of negotiations
and stalling and terror made it appear as if peace would never arrive. If
"euphoria" was ever an appropriate word in the Israeli context, it was
clearly not so when the 1994 survey was taken regarding the peace accord.

Those who had anticipated that peace would herald the marriage of two
peoples sharing the same territory were quickly disabused of that image.
More appropriately, after years of hateful marriage, a divorce was being
negotiated. And like many divorce negotiations, with children, property,

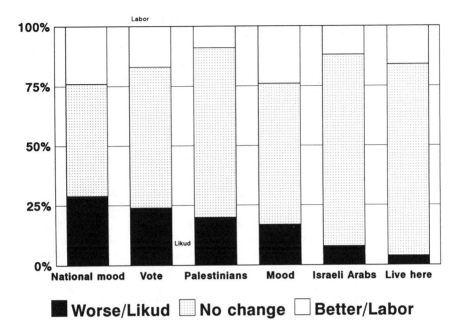

Figure 3.15. Effects of the Israeli-PLO peace accord on national mood and on other factors (1994 survey).

interests, pride, and the historical record at stake, the talks did not go smoothly. Some on each side feared (or hoped, depending on the point of departure) that the agreement would never be reached. The December 13, 1993, deadline for the signing of the detailed plans for the IDF pullback from the Gaza Strip and Jericho came and went. In February 1994, a right-wing Jewish doctor massacred some 30 Moslems while they were prostrate in prayer at the Cave of the Patriarchs in Hebron, a site holy to both Jews and Moslems. That furious and futile incident captured some of the hatred, frustration, danger, and threat felt by people on both sides.

When asked in 1994 (days before the Hebron slaughter) whether the peace accord with the PLO changed their assessment of the security and political situations, 69 percent said no, 19 percent said that it made them more ready for conciliatory moves, and 12 percent said it made them more supportive of militant positions. However, as seen in Figure 3.15, more respondents reported (1) that the national mood had soured rather than improved, (2) that it was more likely they would vote Likud rather than vote Labor, (3) that their assessment of the Palestinians was worse compared to those who said their assessment had improved. On the other hand, more reported that (1) their own mood had improved rather than worsened, (2) that their assessment of Israeli Arabs had become better compared with the number of those who said it had worsened, and (3) the desire to live in Israel was strengthened on the whole.

In sum, the prospects for peace increased over the years, and the likelihood of war declined. Israelis grappled with the implications of a new reality as peace became less of an abstraction and more a political risk. The IDF was respected, but not above criticism. To a certain degree, respondents proclaimed their readiness to make sacrifices for security, although they were anxious about their personal security and critical of the measures taken in the territories against terror. The nuclear issue was undeveloped in a political sense, but there was a persistent fear of nonconventional weapons.

There is a predisposition on the part of the population to support the government and its position in the initial stages of a security event, regardless of party in power. That support may fade, however, to be replaced by a polarization closely following the political contours of the public debate.

4

Change in Security Attitudes

ATTITUDES

It has been a truism of Israeli life since the Six Days war that the public was split between a more militant and a more conciliatory stand on the political and security issues that confront the state (Shamir 1986; Yishai 1987). But it was equally true that support for the more dovish positions grew over the years, especially after 1987. It is certain that this creeping conciliation coincided with the onset of the intifada and with the Gulf war, but it is not possible to prove that any single occurrence caused this trend. These events were evidently associated with surges in the attitudes of Israelis; acts of terror tended to stem the incremental change afoot in this period; most other events, however, accelerated moderating processes already under way.

Issues of national security are notoriously complex. On the enigmatic and emotion-laden issues of Israeli national security, and the territories and the inhabitants living there, it is probably accurate to point out that in addition to the Israeli polity being divided, Israelis within themselves are also conflicted. The issues are not simple and the ramifications are enormous. Hence, discrete questions often used to gauge the public's views on national security and the direction and extent of attitude change may be found lacking (Verba and Brody 1970). Single-variable indicators of attitudes and attitude shifts may give misleading indications of change (Converse 1964), since the underlying forces are likely to be much more intricate (Holsti and Rosenau 1984).

This caveat is important for any political system, but may be especially relevant when the political system is characterized by multipartyism and when centrifugal forces pull at the body politic (Sartori 1976, chapters 6 and 10). Then, the structure of opinion becomes an important political resource, and the more exact depiction of that structure takes on added significance. Because of the passion invested in political discourse, it is also likely that a process of simplification will occur, whereby observers and partisans collapse complex reality into imprecise renderings.

Israel in the second half of the 1980s was a good example of this. Not only did a government of national unity mask many of the fundamental differences between the parties, the intifada posed unprecedented challenges to the maintenance of order. Extreme multipartyism continued and was abated only somewhat by increasing the minimum percentage of the vote from 1.0 percent to 1.5 percent – 27 parties ran in the 1988 elections; 15 achieved the minimum 1 percent needed for representation; the corresponding figures for 1992 (after the minimum was raised to 1.5%) were 25 and 10, respectively. This multipartyism thrived on ideological distance and entrenched the polarization of opinion. In Israel, with a large number of parties and large ideological distances between them, centrifugal dynamics were evident. Anti-system parties on the extremes of the spectrum emerged and strengthened, and centripetal mechanisms reacted to the centrifugal tendencies of the party system (Linz and Stepan 1978). The phenomenon of national unity governments was best understood in terms of these factors, since public opinion and electoral processes were obviously closely related to policy outcomes.

While there was empirical validity to the widely accepted depiction of Israel moving to the right in the mid-1980s (Yishai 1987; Diskin 1991), that portrayal was partial, and might have been deluding to those who strove for an accurate picture of the attitude-policy nexus. Opinion was more complex. People seemed to differentiate their responses depending on the implied time-frame of the stimulus: on short-term issues, militant positions were taken; on long-term goals, more conciliatory stands were adopted. This is parallel to Yaniv's distinction (1987b, 140–7) between "basic security," that is, the ability to beat an enemy in war, and "current security," relating to day-to-day safety from subwar violence. In addition, a process of polarization of opinion was evident in this period.

To tap the more complex nature of security opinion, a scale composed of nine items was constructed. The coding of the questions gave the scale a range from 5 (hawkish) to 1 (dovish). The scale was not implemented in 1994 because many of the items used in the scale changed as a result of the peace accord signed with the PLO in September 1993. Scale scores decreased from the 3.1 range in the 1980s to 2.6 in 1993 as follows:

	1987	1988	1990	1991	1992	1993
Total	3.1	3.2	3.1	3.1	2.8	2.6

The scale was sensitive to the increased militancy of the late 1980s and the creeping conciliation of the early 1990s; the score peaked (was most hawkish) in 1988, a year after the intifada began. Sensitivity to war and conflict was also evident in the half-sample scores of 1990: after the invasion of Kuwait by Iraq the score was higher (3.1) than was the pre-invasion score (3.0). Even these slight variations are important because the scores were based on a series of identical questions over time, and the range of response was standardized. The dual conclusions were striking: creeping conciliation over time, growth of militancy in periods of tension.

The presentation and analysis of the component attitudes and the scale fit into the professional debate about stability and structure in public opinion. Converse (1964) argued that mass beliefs were largely characterized by random non-attitudes, which he contrasted with stable attitudes. Even when a panel design is used, in which the same individuals are reinterviewed, responses are found to change (Converse 1970). It followed that there was a low level of structure, or constraint, among attitudes for the mass public. The exception was for the "ideologues" who made up a small fraction of the public. These two issues, randomness of response and constraint of the belief system, became central topics in discussions of public opinion.

In the typical survey situation, in which a stranger asks the respondent to reply to many questions that he or she might never have thought of in just that way, the survey response may be more of a ritualistic answering of questions than an excercise in revealing preferences (Zaller and Feldman 1992), and the possibility of randomness in response is indeed great. That is why demographic questions, and queries about vote choice or degree of religious observance, show higher rates of stability than do most opinions (Inglehart 1990, chapter 3). But even if some answers are random and there is less than perfect stability at the individual level, appropriate sampling and polling techniques will still generate high levels of aggregate stability:

Collective measurements – averages (means or medians), majority or plurality choices, marginal frequencies of responses – will tend accurately to reflect the "true" underlying or long-term opinions of the individuals . . . . That is to say, even if individual opinions or survey responses are ill-informed, shallow, and fluctuating, collective opinion can be real, highly stable . . . and it can be measured with considerable accuracy by standard survey techniques. (Page and Shapiro 1992, 16–17)

Pursuing the same logic, it is preferable to use a set of questions, rather than a single one, to tap an underlying policy dimension. Any individual measure might miss the mark, but a series of questions will increase the probability of getting it right (Rokeach 1960).

NINE SECURITY ATTITUDES

The policy scale was composed of nine items relating to various aspects of the Arab-Israeli conflict and to Israel's security situation. After each item is treated individually, the scale will be discussed more fully. The wording of the individual questions and the results for each year are presented in Appendix II.

The items used in the policy scale were

1. the future of the territories acquired in the 1967 Six Days war;
2. civil rights to Palestinians were the territories to be annexed;
3. the establishment of a Palestinian state;
4. negotiations with the Palestine Liberation Organization;
5. encouraging Palestinians to leave ("transfer");
6. the use of military power versus negotiations;
7. participation in an international peace conference;
8. considerations of security versus the rule of law;
9. and the effect on Israel's army of keeping the territories.

Territories

The immediate focus of the efforts to solve the Arab-Israel crisis was the territories Israel occupied in the Six Days war of 1967. The two distinct options were to exchange these territories for peace, or to annex them to Israel. These polar options were widely discussed by the many politicians, diplomats, and individuals and groups who labored to solve the difficult emotional and political problems in which the region was embroiled. Some pointed out that the territories had been a cause of Arab animosity since 1967, but others countered that the enmity to Israel was evident well before the conquest of the territories in the Six Days war. Fearing that the Arabs were interested in the territories as a first step in their attempt to displace the Jews from Israel, the territories were seen by some as the symptom and not the malady. Others rejoindered with the call to seek a political solution which would be backed by the international community, so that Israel could live in recognized and secure borders, as mandated by United Nations Security Council resolutions 242 and 338, even if the territories were not included in those borders.

The debate enveloped the political system through the years. Politicians of all parties waxed eloquent, but when in power policy makers chose to ignore both alternatives and to muddle through without making any clear decision. Except for East Jerusalem, which was annexed in 1967, and the Golan, which was put under Israeli legal jurisdiction in 1981, the territories were ruled as occupied territory by the Israeli military. The argument against returning territories was bolstered by there being no recognized Arab authority with whom to negotiate, with the exceptions of Egypt in 1977 and the Lebanese for a number of weeks in 1983. The talks with Egypt ended with Israel returning the Sinai Peninsula. In 1991, another break-through occurred and in the fall of that year, the Madrid conference was convened and delegates from Syria and Jordan, as well as the Palestinians – none of whom had ever met in direct, formal peace negotiations with Israel before – effectively demolished the argument that there was no partner for peace talks. Israeli diplomats and decision makers were faced with the dilemma of decision more clearly than ever.

Since the political system was preoccupied by the dilemma, the issue obviously found its way into public opinion surveys. The results varied depending on the conditions which existed at the time of the survey, and the wording of the question. One widely applied form of the question asked respondents whether or not to return territories, and if so, how much. The data between 1973 and 1989 showed wide variation in opinion, but certain consistencies stood out (see Table 4.1). The overwhelming majority of Israeli Jews favored returning nothing or only a small part. Only a small minority consistently favored returning all or most of the territories.

The two periods in which the "return nothing" response was highest were times of severe security tension. The first, October 1973, was immediately after the outbreak of the Yom Kippur war; the second, September 1976, was soon after the hijacking of the Air France plane and the dramatic rescue at Entebbe airport. Similarly, the "no return" response was lowest in the spring of 1979, in the season of the Camp David meetings between President Sadat of Egypt and Prime Minister Menachem Begin of Israel, under the sponsorship of President Jimmy Carter of the United States. Another nadir of the "return nothing" category were the two measurements in 1975, a year in which public morale was at a depressing low as a result of the aftermath of the 1973 Yom Kippur war.

The temptation to find an explanation for each blip in the table is great but it must be resisted lest we begin predicting the past. The methods at our disposal simply do not warrant the attempt to "explain" the modifications in the array, for to do so would mean that we had extraordinary confidence that the percentages reported were precise, and that we had a theory to explain variation from one time period to another. We frankly possess neither the confidence nor the theory. We should recall that the numbers reported are estimates and must be understood in terms of a margin of error depending upon the size and the representativeness of the sample. Even if all the surveys were conducted according to all the rules of sampling and interviewer behavior, even if no secretarial or technical errors were present, even then we would be dealing with a margin of error of plus or minus 3 percent (or higher). The "return nothing" category for May 1989, reported as 41 percent, might "really" be 38 percent or 44 percent. The 38 percent figure for November 1989 might "actually" be 35 percent or 41 percent. In "reality," public opinion regarding not returning the territories in 1989 might have been identical at 41 percent in both time periods, or it might have been quite

Table 4.1. *Territories for Peace, 1973-1989*[a] *(in %)*

"In your opinion, are territorial concessions to be made or not to reach a peace agreement, and if so, what is the greatest concession that you would be willing to make?"

Date	Return all	Return most	Return a large part	Return a small part	Return nothing
10/73	5	4	16	11	64
12/73	8	8	24	13	47
7/74	5	9	27	19	40
1/75	12	17	27	14	31
10/75	5	8	31	19	37
3/76	14	8	29	12	38
9/76	5	8	18	12	56
1/77	5	7	26	21	42
11/77	8	7	24	19	42
1/78	11	7	21	11	50
9/78	9	8	27	17	38
1/79	11	7	21	11	50
3/79	7	12	32	23	27
4/79	6	9	35	22	28
9/79	9	5	24	14	48
3/81[b]	3	4	19	23	50
7/84[b]	8	6	23	21	42
2/86	5	10	21	18	45
8/86	6	9	21	17	47
3/87	5	8	23	18	45
2/88	4	9	27	17	43
6/88	8	11	26	17	39
8/88	7	10	26	14	39
1/89	6	11	31	17	35
5/89	8	10	27	13	41
11/89	5	8	32	17	38
1973-89 average	7.3	8.8	25.3	16.5	42.4

[a] Data collected by the Louis Guttman Israel Institute for Applied Social Research and supplied by Shlomit Levy and Hanna Levinsohn (1991), except where noted.
[b] From election study conducted by the author; survey conducted by Dahaf Research Institute.

different at 44 percent in May and 35 percent in November. We will never know for certain, but we must keep in mind that all opinion figures are approximations rather than exact renderings of reality.

Armored with an appropriate degree of cautious skepticism, two overall impressions in the data stand out. First is the overall stability of the distribution over time. Most people opposed giving back most of the territories all of the time. Second is the rhythm of variation which does seem to exist in the data. While we cannot explain each blip on the graph with equal conviction, we can point out that there were periods in which the magnitude of those refusing to return the territories lessened, and others in which it grew. A good example has to do with the distribution of opinion since the outbreak of the intifada in 1987. In the six readings taken after its beginning, the percentage of the samples preferring to return no territory was *below* the 17-year average. Perhaps the Israeli public learned from the intifida that the Palestinians were a negotiating partner; perhaps the costs of the uprising on Israeli soldiers and morale was deemed too dear; perhaps the reproach of world opinion for its handling of the uprising led to a reassessment of the value of keeping the territories. The mechanisms at work were very subtle and more complex than our theories allow us to understand at the moment, but it is also clear that something more than a random walk was at work.

That the fluctuation in opinion regarding the territories was patterned is evident when we consider a differently worded question used repeatedly since 1984. In this case, the attitude about the future of the territories was measured by asking the respondents two related questions which forced them to express an opinion, a technique used in ascertaining positions regarding complex issues. First, respondents were given a choice between (1) exchanging land for peace, (2) annexing the territories, or (3) leaving things as they are. For those who answered "leave things as they are," a second question was asked, in which respondents were forced to choose between returning and annexing (see Appendix II.1 and Figure 4.1).

Based on these questions, there was a steady increase in the percentage of respondents prepared to give up the territories for a peace treaty with appropriate security arrangements (compare Katz 1989). The population remained split, and the political system was unable decisively to solve the problem one way or the other, perhaps because of the intense but divided public. But the shift in public opinion was certainly noted by the major actors and it is likely that it had an impact on policy and policy makers. In 1986, using this wording, a little less than half of the population agreed to return the territories; by 1993, the number had risen to 60 percent.

There was fluctuation even within this period. The smooth swell of the response rate toward conciliation shown in Figure 4.1 hides the fact that before the August 2, 1990, Iraqi invasion of Kuwait, support for returning the territories had topped 50 percent; after the invasion and during the period of crisis before the Gulf war, support for returning fell back to 50 percent, to rise again after the war. Not surprisingly, for the sample of

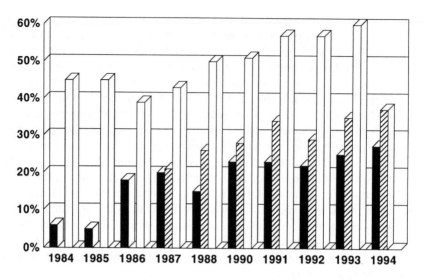

■ Rights and vote ▨ Palestine state ☐ Return territories

Figure 4.1. Changes in attitude toward return of territories and other factors, 1984–1994.

Israeli Jewish respondents living in the territories, support for returning the territories was always lower, with just under three-quarters of that sample favoring annexation.

A different version of this forced-choice question was employed in 1994. It began by presenting respondents with the same two basic choices of exchanging land for peace, and annexing the territories, but gave its interim alternative as autonomy for the Palestinians in the territories as provided for by the Camp David accords. Offering a middle position that was on the public agenda and being discussed by the representatives of Israel and the PLO had the effect of flattening the distribution by deflating the size of the other two options (see Appendix II.1a). The responses to this wording are used in the analyses for the 1994 data in Chapters 6 and 7.

Whether focusing on a final position as in the forced-choice question (see Appendix II.1) or stressing how much should be returned (see Table 4.1), support for moderate positions grew in public opinion over the years regarding possible solutions for the territories. We also see this when the rate of those ready to agree to a Palestinian state is monitored (see Figure 4.1 and Appendix II.3). Another example was the series of seven proposed

Table 4.2. *Proposed Solutions, 1990, 1993, and 1994*

	1990	1993	1994
Annexation and transfer	13%	13%	15%
Annexation, no transfer, no full rights for Arabs	20%	14%	15%
Annexation, no transfer, full rights for Arabs	8%	7%	5%
Status quo	9%	7%	a
Autonomy	24%	28%	36%
Return most of the territories to Jordan in peace agreement	19%	19%	14%
Palestinian state in territories as part of peace treaty	7%	7%	15%

ªNot asked.

solutions for the permanent status for the territories repeated for the 1990, 1993, and 1994 samples and reported in Table 4.2.

Proposals for autonomy and a Palestinian state generated more support in 1993 than they did in 1990, at the expense of annexing the territories without transferring Arabs, but also without providing them with full rights. The discrepancy between the percentages willing to have a Palestinian state in Figure 4.1 and in the results here is explained by presenting alternatives differently.

Differences in wording are enough to explain differing results in public opinion research (Mueller 1973; Schuman and Presser 1981). What is more, respondents may not be consistent in their responses when faced with questions worded differently in the *same* interview. An example from a question posed in 1991 is instructive. The solutions offered the respondents and the distribution of their choices were

Annexation and transfer	15%
Annexation, no transfer, not full rights for Arabs	16%
Annexation, no transfer, full rights for Arabs	5%
Status quo	12%
Autonomy	17%
Returning most of the territories as part of peace agreement	19%
Palestinian state in part of territories with security arrangements	11%
Palestinian state as part of peace agreement	5%

The highest total support was for annexation, but the rate of support for that solution fell between 1990 and 1994 from 41 percent to 35 percent. The largest increase was for the autonomy plan, from 24 percent in 1990, to 28 percent in 1993, to 36 percent in 1994. In a separate question in 1994, 71 percent said they favored autonomy for the territories.

Fifty percent chose solutions between annexation and a Palestinian state. Support for a Palestinian state doubled from 1993 to 1994, from 7 percent to 15 percent. By 1994, the status quo was gone and the thought of returning the territories to Jordan was less attractive.

In 1994, 35 percent called for annexation, 50 percent chose solutions somewhere between annexation and a Palestinian state, and 15 percent agreed to a Palestinian state. In sum, 65 percent favored solutions that involved returning the territories. The amount of overlap in the 1991 survey between the eight-option measure just cited above and the return/annex question of Appendix II.1 was a high .57 correlation. Still, it is striking that 58 percent favored return using one measure, and 35 percent using another.

One answer to this paradox is situational context. If alternatives are narrow, one choice is made; but if multiple options exist, other decisions seem appropriate. Another answer is inconsistency. Twelve percent of the 1991 respondents answered these two sets of questions inconsistently, that is, differently. This is especially striking because both sets of questions were very early in the interview, so fatigue and forgetting are unlikely explanations for the finding. But the error does not seem to be random: the incidence of the inconsistency tended to be in a hawkish direction. For each respondent who said "annex" on the forced-choice question and "return" on the multiple-options question, three respondents answered "return" on the forced choice question and "annex" on the eight-point question. From these data it is impossible to learn if the respondents were making subtle political points, if they were lying, or if they were simply confused. There seemed to be an underlying preference for keeping the territories if the situation were complex or confused enough to permit that and if that option were socially appropriate, but as the pressures for accommodation grew so did the social pressures, and led people at the end of the 1980s and beginning of the 1990s toward conciliatory positions.

We need few reminders of the delicate nature of interpreting survey results; but we should recall that the inconsistencies and incongruencies we might regard as a weakness are the stuff of what politicians use for their appeals. What seems as "noise" in public opinion data to us is an advantage for the politicians making difficult decisions, since many nuanced messages can be sent, and listeners may choose the ingredients of their choice, leaving the "real" meaning unclear.

Even for those Israelis who supported returning the territories, unilateral withdrawal from all the territories was out of the question, supported by only 8 percent of the 1993 sample. When applied to Gaza only, however, the rate of support for unilateral withdrawal shot up to 36 percent of the sample, although 54 percent rejected the notion totally even for Gaza. The response to the identical question in 1991 also had 8 percent willing to withdraw immediately, with 29 percent mentioning only the Gaza Strip, and 62 percent rejecting the notion completely.

Although the land mass is small, there are great differences in the way the Israeli public regards the territories under consideration. The West Bank, or Judea and Samaria, makes up the bulk of the area and is usually the focus of discussion. That area was appropriated by Jordan after the 1948 War of Independence although never recognized by the international community as part of the Kingdom of Jordan. In addition, there is the Gaza Strip, administered by Egypt until 1967, and the Golan Heights, claimed by Syria. The Sinai Peninsula and Sharm-el-Sheikh at its southernmost tip were important spoils of war because the peninsula's considerable land mass offered strategic depth, and its oil wells provided that much needed resource. But of all the real estate under discussion, it is Jerusalem which is the jewel in the crown, the pinnacle of aspiration, and which presents the thorniest of problems. The usual refrain from politicians and the public was that after all other obstacles to peace were removed, the negotiators would discuss Jerusalem, the most difficult issue on the agenda.

The Israeli public was sensitive to the differences between these territories. This was clear from a series of questions in the 1994 survey. In negotiating the permanent settlement with the PLO, the question will certainly surface about territories that Israel would relinquish. The range of opinion was extreme, from a high 84 percent for the Gaza Strip to a low 10 percent for East Jerusalem:

Gaza Strip	84%
Arab urban areas	42%
Western Samaria	30%
Jordan Valley	18%
Gush Etzion	14%
East Jerusalem	10%.

Table 4.3 presents data from the years 1968 to 1978 which record the rates of those who refused to return such real estate. The West Bank data were discussed regarding Table 4.1; a new data point is added for March 1975 and the low 36 percent rate for that month extends the anomaly for that year. For Gaza, there was a lower rate of refusal to return, but level of refusal was lower than for the West Bank, and over time, the trend was for less desire to retain.

The Golan Heights were considered nonnegotiable property by most respondents, not least because of their commanding position over the valley settlements of the northern Galilee. Between 1968 and 1978, the span of responses rejecting the notion of returning the Golan Heights ranged from 74 percent to 96 percent (see Table 4.3). In 1986, when asked if Israel should be willing to return the Heights to Syria in exchange for a peace treaty, 86 percent said no. As rumors persisted that the Israelis and Syrians were discussing the extent of Israeli withdrawal from the Heights in the

Table 4.3. *Return None or Only a Small Part of Territories, 1968-1978*
(in percentages)

	West Bank	Gaza	Golan	Sinai	Sharm-el-Sheikh
2/68	91	85	93	57	99
3/68	75	75	87	52	95
3-4/71	56	70	91	31	92
10-11/72	69	78	96	54	97
10/73	82	80	92	69	94
11/73	58	62	87	36	86
12/73	60	66	91	38	93
7/74	65	a	83	32	86
3/75	36	a	80	32	83
10/75	56	57	88	38	85
9/76	68	69	88	39	80
1/77	56	60	84	a	83
11/77	61	51	77	17	79
11-12/77	60	50	84	16	84
12/78	60	46	74	19	74

[a] Not asked.

Source: Guttman 1978, n. p.

Table 4.4

	9/1992	1993	1994
Unwilling to give back any of the Golan	49%	46%	46%
Willing to return a *small* part	33%	33%	33%
Willing to return a *large* part	12%	15%	14%
Willing to give up the *entire* Golan Heights	6%	6%	7%

peace talks, the future of the Golan Heights increasingly occupied Israeli public opinion. The size of the group opposed to any withdrawal remained very large. These were the responses to a question about the future of the Heights in conjunction with security arrangements acceptable to Israel and demilitarizing the relinquished territories in the 1993 and 1994 surveys, and in a Dahaf telephone survey in September 1992 ($N = 582$) (see Table 4.4). Using a three-alternatives question a few years earlier provided the distributions shown in Table 4.5.

The 1994 interview was in the field when the Geneva summit between U.S. President Clinton and Syrian President Assad took place in Geneva on January 16, 1994. A third of the interviews for the 1994 sample were

Table 4.5

	1987	1991	6/1992
Unwilling to give back any of the Golan	68%	64%	71%
Willing to return a *part*	26%	30%	22%
Willing to give up the *entire* Golan Heights	6%	6%	7%

Table 4.6

	Before or on 1/16/94	After 1/16/94
Unwilling to give back any of the Golan	42%	48%
Willing to return a *small* part	33%	33%
Willing to return a *large* part	18%	12%
Willing to give up the *entire* Golan Heights	7%	7%

conducted before or on January 16, and two-thirds afterward. If one of the summit's purposes was to soothe Israeli public opinion and prepare for an eventual withdrawal, it failed. In fact, there was evidence that it had the opposite effect (see Table 4.6).

That Clinton had to restate Assad's position to make it sound conciliatory, and that the Israeli leadership received Assad's remarks in a very cool manner, had a deflating effect on Israeli public opinion. That opinion started at a low point and showed no signs of being forthcoming to the Syrians. Respondents were asked whether or not Israel should be flexible in peace negotiations with the Syrians on each of the following, the reported percentage *opposed* (strongly oppose and oppose):

Limiting the freedom of movement of Israelis on the Golan Heights	81%
Control of water	80%
Syrian sovereignty over the Golan	78%
Removal of Israeli settlements from the Golan	71%
Leasing the Golan Heights from Syria for a number of years	56%
To U.S. military units between IDF and Syria	55%
Number of years for the complete implementation of the agreement	55%
Control the introduction of armed forces on both sides of the border	52%
Demilitarize the Golan; neither the IDF nor Syrian army will be there	52%
Joint supervision of nonconventional weapons (atomic, biological, chemical)	43%

After raising these issues with the respondent, the question of returning the Golan to Syria was again asked, this time with the wording "If Syria agrees to peace in every sense of that word, would you then be willing or not willing to return territory in the Golan Heights?" Mentioning various security arrangements and then repeating the question would provide an indirect measure of how flexible public opinion was on the issue and whether or not respondents would moderate their positions. The result was virtually no shift in position. If a referendum is eventually held regarding a peace treaty in exchange for the Golan Heights, it will be an uphill battle to win support for it.

Sharm-el-Sheikh and the Sinai are of special interest since these territories were actually returned to Egypt based on the peace treaty of 1979 worked out at Camp David. Sharm-el-Sheikh, a strategic asset and naval facility at the tip of the Sinai Peninsula controlling the Red Sea, was considered a permanent feature of Israel's new geography. Moshe Dayan went so far as to say that he would opt for retaining Sharm-el-Sheikh and not having peace, than for reaching peace without Sharm-el-Sheikh. The Israeli public thought so too, and the rates of refusal to return it were very high.

The reaction to returning the Sinai Peninsula was more variable. Israelis wanted to keep it most in October 1973 when the surprise attack by the Egyptian army threatened the loss of the peninsula to Egypt by war. In 1977, however, after Sadat's equally surprising visit to Jerusalem, the rate of refusal to return the Sinai plummeted to the teens. This rate seemed to stabilize after the return of the Sinai; when asked in the 1987 survey about the peace treaty with Egypt, 87 percent indicated support. Not only that, when asked in 1987 what the feeling was about the Egyptian treaty at the time of signing, 82 percent said that they were for it then.

The suggestion to redivide Jerusalem and return its eastern section to Arab jurisdiction was always very unpopular. In a time series between January 1975 and February 1988 in which they asked a question about Jerusalem 14 times, the Guttman Institute data show a range of 71 to 87 percent for leaving Jerusalem under sole Israeli rule under any condition, with 10 to 24 percent willing to establish the joint rule of Israel and Jordan over the city. When asked in 1993 if they would be willing to discuss the status of Jerusalem in the peace talks then under way, 83 percent of Israeli Jews said no. When asked in 1994 about the idea of allowing the Palestinians to have their capital in a unified Jerusalem which was the capital of Israel, 85 percent rejected the idea.

Citizen Rights for Palestinians in the Territories

Using the same question over the years, there has been a shift in support of civil and political rights for Arabs in the territories, were these to be annexed. Admittedly a hypothetical situation, this growth of support probably signifies a growth of salience of the issue for many Israeli Jews. The population in the territories could no longer be ignored or taken for granted, and as the intifada intensified, the residents of the territories became more human for Israeli Jews. And as that process advanced, solutions which would provide some or complete rights for these residents became more popular. Compared to 60 percent of the sample desiring to leave the situation as it was in 1984, in 1994 only 28 percent chose that option.

In contrast, granting more rights for Arabs of the territories if annexation took place won more support, including the right to vote in Knesset elections (see Figure 4.1 and Appendix II.2). Full political rights, including the right to vote, rose from 6 to 27 percent support. Those who wanted to annex generally did not want to give rights, and those who wanted to give rights preferred not to annex. The prospect of simultaneously doing both leads to deep philosophical – not to mention political – problems. One such problem is demographic in character. Adding a million Arab voters to an electorate of 2.5 million voters, of which about 17 percent is Arab, raises fundamental questions for Zionists about the Jewish nature of Israel.

A Palestinian State

The gradual trend in the direction of conciliation observed regarding the returning of territories and the issue of political rights was also evident regarding the establishment of a Palestinian state (see Figure 4.1 and Appendix II.3). The growth rate was steady and uniform. In 1987, about one in five respondents advanced the notion of a Palestinian state, while in 1994, the rate was 37 percent. The large majority of Israelis firmly rejected the notion, with 42 to 52 percent of the samples declaring that they *strongly* opposed the creation of a Palestinian state. Still, the increase in support was significant because the two large parties, the Likud and Labor, both spurned the idea. The overwhelming majority (83%) of Israeli Jews interviewed in the territories in 1990 rejected the idea of creating such a state.

Despite the opposition to the idea, the likelihood that a Palestinian state would be established in the territories in the next decades became more widespread in Israeli public opinion: in fact, that assessment doubled after 1990. In 1990, 37 percent thought a Palestinian state in the territories would eventually be established; in 1991, 48 percent, and in 1994, 74 percent!

The PLO

One of the most emotional issues in Israeli politics has been the proposal to negotiate directly with the Palestine Liberation Organization. Between

1986 and 1993 it was a crime for an Israeli citizen knowingly to have contact with a member of a terrorist organization; since the PLO was so identified by Israel, it was illegal for an Israeli to have contact with a PLO member. Still, there was strong evidence that the moderating trend in Israeli public opinion extended to that topic as well.

The Guttman Institute figures showed support for negotiating with the PLO at a low of 13–22 percent in their surveys of 1978, up to 34–37 percent in early 1990, and then down to 22–24 percent in late 1990 (Katz, Levinson, and Al-Haj 1991, 11). Hanoch Smith's time series showed that the acceptability of negotiations with the PLO, if it officially recognized Israel and ceased terrorist activity, moved from 43 percent in April 1987, through 53 percent in August 1988, to 58 percent in March 1989 (Brinkley 1989).

The 1987 and 1988 surveys in this study found that a third of the samples were prepared to enter into negotiations with the PLO "under the conditions that exist today," compared with 40 percent in 1990 (see Appendix II.4, 4A, and 4B). In 1991, after the war, the rate of support for entering into negotiations with the PLO fell slightly, to 29 percent. This rate was lower than the pre-intifada rate reported above and was not surprising, considering that the PLO openly sided during the Gulf war with Iraq's Saddam Hussein.

When confronted with a series of conditions in 1991, about half of the sample eventually agreed to negotiations with the PLO; 51 percent persisted in their opposition regardless of the conditions described. Eight percent were willing to enter negotiations with the PLO if it recognized Israel, an additional 8 percent if it recognized Israel and renounced terror. For 13 percent more, the PLO would have to recognize Israel, renounce terror, and stop the intifada. Twenty percent were willing to face the PLO in negotiations if it would recognize Israel, renounce terror, stop the intifada, and rescind the PLO charter.

By 1992, after the beginning of peace talks with a Palestine contingent in the Jordanian delegation certified not to be PLO, those willing to negotiate with the PLO rose to 43 percent, and by 1993 to 52 percent. Israel and the United States claimed that the PLO was not part of the negotiation process, although Palestinian interlocutors frequently consulted PLO leaders from and in Tunis, and the PLO itself reacted to developments as if it were at the table. Israeli public opinion became more comfortable with the idea of negotiating with the PLO, even though the Israeli leaders clung to the old formulas of excluding the organization.

On September 13, 1993, the joint recognition agreement between the PLO and Israel was signed in Washington, and the era of denying the

Table 4.7. *Support for Topics to Be Discussed in Talks with Palestinians 1990, 1993, and 1994*

	1990	1993	1994
Autonomy	61%	69%	[a]
A Jordanian-Palestinian federation	34%	48%	57%
Demilitarized areas evacuated by IDF	46%	55%	57%
A Palestinian state in some of the area with acceptable security arrangements for Israel	[a]	45%	51%
Removing Jewish settlements	32%	43%	50%
An independent Palestinian state	26%	30%	41%
East Jerusalem	13%	17%	14%
The right of return	9%	12%	14%

[a] Not asked.

legitimacy of the PLO reached a major junction. In the 1994 survey, 60 percent supported continuing the negotiations with the Palestine Liberation Organization. For years both major political parties and public opinion had rejected negotiations with that group. The shift in favor of negotiations was evident before the change in government policy. Once policy changed, the flow in that direction increased.

Respondents were not optimistic about the ability of the PLO to deliver. In 1994, only 35 percent thought that the PLO would be able to control terrorism after taking over; 6 percent thought the PLO definitely would be able to control terror, 29 percent thought so, 34 percent said no, and 31 percent said definitely not.

Further evidence of growing conciliation was the growth in the percentage of respondents prepared to talk about more things with the Palestinians (see Table 4.7). "What should be discussed in the negotiations with the Palestinians?" was asked in 1990, the period before any negotiations, in 1993, after the convening of the Madrid conference without the PLO, and then after the Israel-PLO accord in 1994. Policy change influenced public opinion: there were growing rates of readiness to negotiate each of the topics, except for East Jerusalem. Support for autonomy grew, and it was being discussed by 1994.

Israeli opinion in 1994 was more lenient toward the Palestinians than the Syrians (see Tables 4.4–4.6) regarding the appropriate negotiating stance. And still many opposed a pliant position. When asked in 1994 whether or not Israel should be flexible in peace negotiations with the Palestinians on each of the following, the reported percentage *opposed* (strongly oppose and oppose):

Limiting the freedom of movement of Israelis in the autonomous region	64%
Allowing the Palestinian police to have weapons	61%
Removal of Israeli settlements from the autonomous region	56%
Removing the IDF	41%

In 1994, the public seemed to be much less concerned with symbolic issues and much more concerned with security issues. When asked whether or not they agreed that these activities should take place in conjunction with the Palestinian autonomy, the following percentage *supported* (strongly support and support):

Issue money and postage stamps	67%
Run internal affairs	61%
Have international relations	55%
Be responsible for water, land, and natural resources	27%
Defend Jewish settlers	25%
Supervise border crossings	20%
Judge Jewish settlers accused of crimes	11%

Transfer

Transfer has become an important concept in the Israeli political lexicon in the last few decades. If two peoples cannot live in the same land, and if it is unacceptable to give up the land, then, the reasoning goes, the solution must be to transfer the other people from the land. Rabbi Meir Kahane's Kach movement espoused this concept, and the racist ideology in which this policy was couched led to its being disallowed to run in the 1988 and 1992 elections. Moledet, headed by Rehavam Zeevi ("Gandi"), also called for transfer of Arabs; the party won two seats in the 1988 elections and three in the 1992 elections; in 1991, Zeevi was made a minister in the government headed by Yitzhak Shamir. That government, and the Likud which headed it, formally rejected the notion of transfer, but accepted at least some of those who supported the idea.

Politicians were generally opposed to transfer, but Israelis were more evenly divided. When asked directly in 1991, 39 percent supported transfer: more than half of them (23 percent of the total sample) supported transfer for *both* Arabs of the territories and Israeli Arabs; 45 percent of those who favored transfer (16 percent of all respondents) favored it only for territories Arabs. When placed in terms of other political solutions, however, support for the idea was much lower. As already seen, when presented with political solutions in the surveys of 1990, 1991, and 1993, and of 1994, 13–15 percent selected annexation and transfer. An additional 21–28 percent called for solutions which included annexation, but not transfer (compare Katz 1988).

The proposal to transfer Arabs must be understood in terms of the political context. The more general the question, the higher the levels of support. For example, when asked whether the government should encourage Arabs to leave the country (the item used in the policy scale), 62 percent of the 1993 sample supported the idea, similar to the rates of support in the other years of the survey (see Appendix II.5). This wording tapped the predisposition of the respondent toward the Arabs without the complexities of the proposed solution, or the moral dilemmas of forcible transfer. Support for such encouragement varied over the years, and did not change much after the Gulf war; backing a government policy for having the Arabs leave the country won a bit more support after August 2, 1990, than before it.

A good example of the complexity of analyzing public opinion data comes from the intersection of those supporting transfer and those supporting annexation. As a policy option, the solution of transferring Arabs and annexing territories, taken together, was supported by 15 percent of the sample, as seen in Table 4.2. In 1991, about 40 percent were for transfer when asked about it alone and about 40 percent supported annexation by itself. The correlation between supporting transfer and supporting annexation was .38. This finding resonates with the fact that many leaders of Israel's right, including Likud leaders, supported annexation while objecting to transfer. Transferring and annexing are not interchangeable aspects of the ideology of the right: when the attitudes on these two matters were juxtaposed, it was found that three-quarters of those willing to return territories for peace were also opposed to transfer, and that two-thirds of those wanting annexation favored transfer. The surprising finding was that a quarter of those willing to return territories were also *for* transfer, and that a third of those who were for annexation were *against* transfer.

It may be that we should accept these findings at face value. While many subscribed to transfer and to annexation separately, the overlap in support was imperfect. The emotional or ideological bases from which these positions spring may be different. If that were the case, however, we might expect to find that when overlap did occur, it occurred throughout the population.

We found, however, that the degree of correlation between the two questions was clearly ordered by party vote, indicating that answers to the two questions go together better at the extremes of the left-right continuum than in the middle. The 1991 supporters of the extreme parties of Moledet and Tehiya on the right and Ratz on the left had the most consistent connection between their attitudes. Moledet and Tehiya voters almost universally wanted both annexation and transfer; almost all Ratz voters wanted neither.

The confounding of the connection between transfer and annexation was much more likely to take place in the middle segment of the party continuum. The pattern for the voters of other parties was not clear-cut. The dominant pattern for Labor and Shinui voters was to oppose both transfer and annexation. Tzomet and Mafdal on the whole supported both. Half of the undecided were against both transfer and annexation; the rest were divided equally among the categories of annex but no transfer, transfer but no annexation, and transfer and annexation. Voters for the Likud showed the largest spread. This heterogeneity in terms of policy positions afforded Likud politicians latitude in decision making. It also reinforced the intriguing possibility that respondents chose to give Likud their vote not because of the ideological clarity of its message, but because its message on these issues could be interpreted in many ways. These confounding or inconsistent aspects of the positions of some respondents indicate just how complex and unsettled public opinion is. This complexity sets the parameters within which politicians work, and these fluctuating parameters account for the possibilities and pitfalls facing decision makers (Feldman and Zaller 1992).

Talk or Fight

Even at independence, despite the almost universal agreement regarding the function of the army in preventing the destruction of the state, there were disagreements about the role that military force would play in Israel's attempt to ensure its continued existence. These disagreements surfaced in the early years of the state and were the background of the tense and difficult relations between two of the prominent leaders. David Ben-Gurion was the state's founding father and first prime minister and defense minister. Moshe Sharett was Israel's first foreign minister, and second prime minister. The differences can be summed up in one question: Can real security for Israel be achieved through military prowess, or, in the long run, is it better to rely on patience and pragmatic politics?

Sharett saw Israel as part of the Middle East and tried to understand the Arab point of view. In the long run Sharett saw the Arabs as partners in a nonviolent dialogue. Ben-Gurion, on the other hand, saw Israel as an extension of Europe in the midst of the Levant, which caused him to believe that no dialogue among equals could evolve; he therefore put his faith in military prowess as the only way to ensure the continued existence of the Jews in Israel (Bialer 1972; Pappe 1986). Ben-Gurion, the champion of the security-minded activists, won the argument, and his opinion forged Israeli policy from that time on.

If given the option between attempting to initiate peace negotiations and increasing military power, most Israelis would probably respond "both."

By forcing a choice, we get a better sense of priorities (see Appendix II.6). Between two-thirds and three-quarters of the general samples consistently espoused peace negotiations in each of the surveys until 1994. In that year, with negotiations under way, only 52 percent chose peace talks.

International Peace Conference

One of the most volatile of the issues included in the scale, this question has seen the most change in the conditions about which it asked. During the 1980s, an international peace conference was a shorthand for outside powers dictating terms of a settlement without the face-to-face negotiations which Israel always craved. In 1990, Israel's National Unity government broke up when Labor supported suggestions made by President Husni Mubarak of Egypt and U.S. Secretary of State James Baker to facilitate an international peace conference, and Shamir balked. Labor, led by Shimon Peres, was unable to win majority support in the Knesset for a Labor government. After Labor failed, the Likud led by Prime Minister Shamir succeeded. By 1991, however, Shamir accepted many of those same conditions and the conference was convened in Madrid.

Another important issue in the postwar preconference period was whether or not the United Nations would have a role in the conference. Given the extreme unpopularity of the United Nations in Israel, it was not surprising that the sample in 1991 gave more support to the idea of the conference being convened by the United States and the Soviet Union (before its breakup) than by the United Nations. The 1991 data in Appendix II.7 relate to the superpowers convening the conference; support for a conference convened by the United Nations was lower: 12 percent "definitely support," 39 percent "support," 26 percent "do not support," and 23 percent "definitely do not support." The superpower question was used in the policy scale for 1991.

Security versus the Rule of Law

The choice between the two polar extremes – security on the one hand, and the rule of law or other considerations on the other – was a stark one, and most situations allowed for more flexibility of definition and interpretation. But this dilemma characterized the public debate in Israel, especially in the 1980s (Negbi 1987, Hofnung 1991, Sprinzak 1991). In the face of the Lebanon campaign in 1982, and then with the onset of the intifada in 1987, the relations between the political and military spheres, and the manner in which the military operated within the framework of the rule of law, were scrutinized by the public. The issues were especially complex regarding the intifida, because the defense forces were not designed or trained for the type of police action which resulted from the low level of hostilities, almost always against stone-throwing demonstrators, that characterized the early stages of the uprising. The tactics used to repress and deter the Arab population called into question the commitment of the army and its civilian and military leadership to the rights of the demonstrators, and focused attention on the zealousness of certain officers and soldiers in interpreting the orders of commanders and political leaders.

Implementing the rule of law is often frustrating since what seems right and necessary must be deferred owing to abstract principle and legal maneuvering. Whether fighting crime, or fighting wars, the temptation to suspend the rule of law is always present. The samples were asked to rank their own opinion regarding the dilemma between security considerations on the one hand (rank 1) and the observance of the principles of the rule of law (rank 7) on the other (see Appendix II.8). In all six surveys the mean was on the security side of the midpoint, indicating a slight preference on the whole for security considerations. In 1993, for instance, 44 percent of the sample placed themselves in the first two ranks with a strong preference for security, while only 13 percent identified their positions strongly on the side of rule of law (ranks 6 or 7).

Effect on Israel Defense Forces

Respondents felt that the actions undertaken by the IDF in the territories were having a deleterious effect on its fighting ethic (see Appendix II.9). Using a seven-point scale, with 7 being a positive effect and 1 a negative effect, the mean scores for the two surveys before the intifada (1986 and 1987) were above the midpoint of 4, while the means since 1988 have been below 4. Even more indicative, the extreme negative rank (1) grew from 4 percent in 1986 to 19 percent in 1993.

THE POLICY SCALE

The policy scale was devised to yield a single score using a comprehensive measure which would permit comparison of the national mood over time. The answers to the nine questions, each weighted on a five-point array, formed the policy scale. The coding gave a score of 5 to the hawkish pole of the response and 1 to the dovish. The hard-line pole of the measure included support for annexing territories; denying civil rights to inhabitants of the territories; rejecting the establishment of a Palestinian state; opposing negotiations with the PLO; encouraging Palestinians to leave; choosing military power over negotiations; opposing participation in an international

Table 4.8. *The Policy Scale, 1987-1993*

	Standard Mean	Standardized deviation[a]	Effective alpha	N
1987	3.123	.850	.718	1,117
1988	3.193	.971	.799	873
1990	3.065	.914	.746	1,251
[before 8/2/90	3.006	.919	.740	689]
[8/2 and after	3.148	.906	.754	550]
1991	3.083	.870	.660	1,128
1992	2.805	.874	.741	1,191
1993	2.648	.912	.763	1,202

[a] The standardized alpha reliability coefficient is a measure of the degree to which the attitudes are interrelated; a coefficient at the levels reported indicates a high degree of clustering of the attitudes.

conference for peace chaired by the superpowers; preferring security interests over the rule of law; and assessing that army activities in the territories have a positive impact on its effectiveness.

Scale scores decreased from the 3.1 range in the 1980s to 2.6 in 1993. No score was calculated for the 1994 responses since the political issues had changed and some of the elements of the policy scale were no longer comparable. The 1986–93 scores were sensitive to changes because of war and conflict, as we have seen; another example is from the half-sample scores of 1990. After the invasion of Kuwait by Iraq the score was higher (3.1) than was the pre-invasion score (3.0). Applying the policy scale to independent samples between 1987 and 1993 generated a measure of attitude change based on the assumption of sampling theory that well-drawn samples of the same population will be equivalent within known bounds of probability. Using identical questions over time gave added confidence to the measurement, and strengthened the conclusion that during this time period there was a clear movement in the dovish direction. The scale scores, and the statistical evidence presented in Table 4.8, lead to the conclusion that the scale taps a general security policy dimension.[1]

Change in policy scores indicated shifts in the responses, which in turn reflected political and international developments. There was a clear movement in a more moderate direction for five of the nine items: the future of the territories, political rights of Arabs were the territories to be annexed, the establishment of a Palestinian state, willingness to involve PLO in peace negotiations, and participation in a peace conference. For the others, the movement was less sharp and decisive. The agreement to negotiate with the PLO and participation in the peace conference increased in the

1987–93 period but, as we shall see later in this chapter, there was fluctuation on these items during the period studied.

BACKGROUND VARIABLES

What drove the change in the mean score regarding the territories from 3.0 in 1984 through 3.1 in 1986 and 1987 to 2.4 in 1993? What factors correlated with the decrease in policy scale scores between 1987 to 1993 from 3.1 to 2.6? Two alternative paths could have brought about these oscillations: there might have been a large shift in the replies of certain groups, or the shift may have been occasioned by a more general movement by all or most groups. Was the conciliatory swing due to a change among one group, say the secular, or the older generation, or the ashkenazim? Or perhaps the religious, the young, or the sephardim became even more hawkish, and that had to be compensated for by very extreme dovish shifts by other groups. The possible roads to change for this type of composite score shift are many.[2]

The shift was not caused by a disproportionate movement of one group; rather, the pattern represented a rather consistent shift by all groups in the direction of conciliation. The swing of respondents with various social, economic, and political characteristics was uniform on the whole. Events and moods affected most of the groups, and in much the same manner (see Table 4.9). Over all, groups changed in the dovish direction, a considerable feat for both doves and hawks. In a sense the effort had to be greater for the already dovish since to move, say, from 2.0 to 1.8 represents a greater proportional distance than a movement from 3.2 to 3.0 for the hawks. In another sense, however, the attraction of the dovish pole was already in place for the former group, while for the latter group the natural pull was in the opposite direction.

Two aspects are important: background variables were helpful in predicting the original relative degree of dovishness or hawkishness; background variables made no difference in knowing the direction of change during the period under study. The finding of consistent movement in a conciliatory direction was remarkably stable in the data. As an example, consider the territories question for the 1984–93 period (see Table 4.9). The mean scores for the territories question (5 = annex; 1 = return) for the 1984–93 period are presented there by gender, age, education, continent of birth, religious observance, and vote decision. Illustrating with the continent of birth variable, the means for the territories question are presented in Figure 4.2. Continent of birth categorizes whether the respondent or the respondent's father was born in Europe or America (ashkenazi), both born in Israel, or one or the other born in Asia or Africa (sephardi).[3]

These data confirm the well-known finding that ashkenazim tend to be

Table 4.9. *Means for Territories by Background Variables, 1984-1993[a]*

	1984	1985	1986	1987	1988	1990	1991	1992	1993
Total	3.0	2.9	3.1	3.1	2.8	2.8	2.5	2.5	2.4
Male	2.9[b]	3.0[b]	3.0[b]	2.9	2.7[b]	2.7[b]	2.5[b]	2.4	2.5[b]
Female	3.0	2.9	3.2	3.3	2.8	2.9	2.5	2.6	2.4
Above 60 years	2.7	2.7	2.9	2.6	2.1	2.5	1.9	2.2	2.0
30 to 60 years	2.7	2.7	3.1	3.0	2.7	2.7	2.4	2.4	2.4
Below 30 years	3.2	3.2	3.3	3.3	3.0	3.0	2.7	2.7	2.6
Hi education	2.6	2.5	2.9	2.8	2.5	2.3	2.1	2.2	2.0
Mid education	3.0	3.0	3.1	3.2	2.8	3.1	2.6	2.6	2.7
Lo education	3.3	3.1	3.3	3.3	2.9	2.9	2.7	2.7	2.7
Ashkenazi	2.6	2.8	2.7	2.3	2.3	2.1	2.1	2.1	2.1
Israeli	2.9	3.0	2.9	3.3	2.9	2.8	2.1	2.3	2.2
Sephardi	3.4	3.3	3.4	3.3	3.0	3.2	2.9	2.9	2.7
Secular	2.4	2.7	2.8	2.5	2.1	2.2	1.8	1.9	1.9
Some religion	2.9	3.2	3.3	3.2	2.7	2.7	2.4	2.5	2.3
Much religion	3.4	[c]	[c]	3.5	3.2	3.4	3.0	3.1	3.2
Very religious	3.8	3.9	3.9	3.8	3.5	3.5	3.2	3.8	3.1
Left	1.3	1.5	1.9	1.7	1.3	1.3	1.3	1.1	1.1
Labor	2.0	2.2	2.4	2.5	1.5	1.8	1.6	1.5	1.7
Likud	3.8	3.8	3.7	3.7	3.5	3.7	3.0	3.4	3.3
Religious	4.0	3.8	3.7	3.3	3.2	3.0	3.8	2.9	2.9
Right	3.7	4.1	4.3	4.0	3.9	3.8	3.4	3.7	3.3

[a] The F ratio in the analysis of variance is statistically significant above .05 level for all cases except where noted.
[b] Not significant at .05 level.
[c] Religiosity measured using a three-response question: religious, traditional, secular.

more dovish than sephardim. The mean of the ashkenazi respondents was highest in 1986 at 2.8, and lowest in 1992 with 2.0; the highest mean for the Israel-born group was 3.3 in 1987, and its lowest was 2.1 in 1991; for the sephardim, the high of 3.4 was recorded in 1984 and 1986, and the low of 2.7 in 1993 (see Table 4.9 and Figure 4.2). All groups moved in a return territories direction, with the ashkenazim and the sephardim moving in tandem, and the pattern of the Israel-born more volatile. Taking these same data one step further, a trend line using the least-squares method was

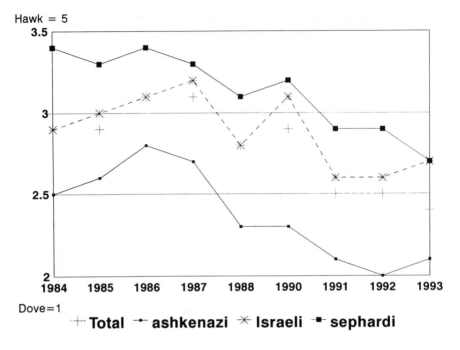

Figure 4.2. Attitude toward return of territories, by respondents' continent of birth group, 1984–1993. (Five-point scale: dove = 1, hawk = 5.)

employed to generate Figure 4.3. Observe the almost parallel movement of the total sample, the ashkenazim and the sephardim toward the return territories position, with the trend of the Israel-born moving in the same direction, but in a less pronounced manner. This finding is crucial for the future of Israeli politics since the second and third generations born in Israel with Israel-born parents were emerging as the dominant group before the mass immigration of the Jews from the former Soviet Union in the late 1980s and early 1990s. Although never exceeding more than 15 percent in these surveys, this Israel-nativist group will most likely remain the source of political, ideological, and intellectual leadership on matters of security policy in the foreseeable future.

An examination of Table 4.9 reveals that (1) all groups moved in the same direction from one point to another, and that (2) with the exception of gender, the differences among the means for the groups studied were statistically significant. The overall pattern seen in Figure 4.3 was the same for the other background variables as well.[4] The trend for age groups is displayed in Figure 4.4. The young were more hawkish than the old. The

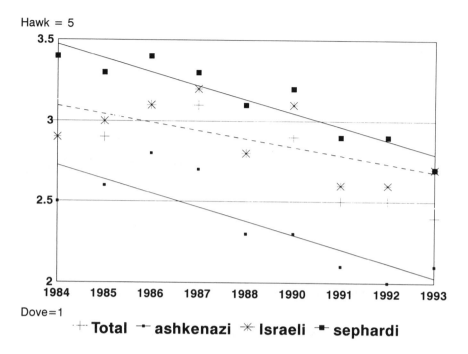

Figure 4.3. Attitude toward return of territories, by respondents' continent of birth group – trends, 1984–1993. (Five-point scale: dove = 1, hawk = 5.)

change in their positions over time, however, was roughly parallel. The young and the old both became more dovish over time. The pressures at work in the society on public opinion seemed to affect all groups in a similar manner.

These same patterns were evident for the policy scale scores (see Table 4.10). The hawks tended to be younger rather than older, have less education, were sephardi rather than ashkenazi, were religiously observant, and were likely to vote for parties of the right. These findings are familiar to all students of Israeli society and politics (Ben-Rafael and Sharot 1991). The surprise is in the consistent rate of change across groups. This pattern is revealed in Table 4.10; Figure 4.5 presents graphically the scale scores for the continent of birth groups and makes the same point visually. The finding argues for the emergence in Israel of a community politics above class-based or partisan considerations. This factor moderates the vocal polarization which sometimes is taken to represent politics in Israel. It may be that different processes are at work in different subcommunities to effectuate the universal shifts, but the end

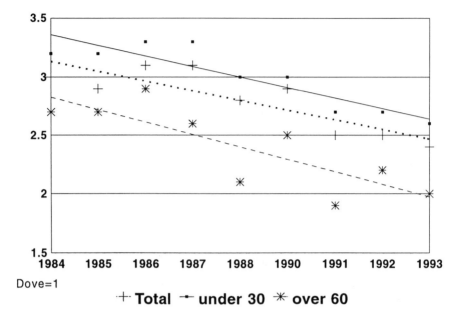

Figure 4.4. Attitude toward return of territories, by respondents' age – trends, 1984–1993. (Five-point scale: dove = 1, hawk = 5.)

result shows a striking homogeneity of swing. As will be shown in Chapter 5, demographic variables were less potent predictors of the vote than were issues. It is little wonder, then, that attitude change appears to occur in a generalized pattern.

Following this line of reasoning, it is no surprise that the policy scale score was related to the definition of the minimal conditions which would define a situation of peace, as discussed in Chapter 3. Breaking the policy scores into three categories, the most hawkish third had a widely distributed understanding of peace, while the dovish third and the third in the middle were both much more likely to define peace in terms of no war, and a peace treaty with security provisions. Regarding the way the respondents perceived the Arab definition of peace, almost half of the hawks thought that the Arabs did not want peace at all (see Figure 4.6). Those hawks who thought the Arabs did want peace again spread their choices of the conditions for peace, while the modal view of peace for the doves and those in the middle category was similar to their own preferences.

Table 4.10. *Means for Policy by Background Variables, 1987-1993*[a]

	1987-1993 Average	1987	1988	1990	1991	1992	1993
Total	*3.0*	3.1	3.2	3.1	3.1	2.8	2.6
Male	*3.0*	3.1[b]	3.2[b]	3.1[b]	3.2	2.8[b]	2.7[b]
Female	*3.0*	3.2	3.2	3.0	3.0	2.8	2.6
Above 60	*2.8*	2.9[b]	2.9	3.0	3.0[b]	2.7[b]	2.4
30 to 60	*3.0*	3.1	3.2	3.0	3.1	2.8	2.7
Below 30	*3.1*	3.2	3.2	3.2	3.1	2.9	2.7
Hi education	*2.8*	2.9	3.1	2.8	2.9	2.6	2.3
Mid education	*3.1*	3.2	3.2	3.2	3.1	2.9	2.8
Lo education	*3.2*	3.3	3.3	3.2	3.3	3.0	2.8
Ashkenazi	*2.8*	3.0	2.9	2.8	2.9	2.5	2.4
Israeli	*2.9*	3.1	3.2	2.9	2.9	2.7	2.5
Sephardi	*3.2*	3.3	3.4	3.3	3.3	3.0	2.9
Secular	*2.6*	2.7	2.7	2.7	2.6	2.4	2.2
Some religion	*3.0*	3.2	3.3	3.0	3.1	2.8	2.7
Much religion	*3.3*	3.4	3.4	3.4	3.4	3.2	3.1
Very religious	*3.5*	3.6	3.7	3.5	3.6	3.5	3.0
Left	*1.9*	2.0	2.0	2.0	2.0	1.7	1.5
Labor	*2.5*	2.8	2.4	2.5	2.6	2.3	2.2
Likud	*3.4*	3.5	3.6	3.4	3.4	3.3	3.2
Religious	*3.4*	3.5	3.6	3.5	3.5	3.5	2.9
Right	*3.7*	3.7	4.0	3.8	3.6	3.5	3.4

[a] The *F* ratio in the analysis of variance is statistically significant above .05 level for all cases except where noted.
[b] Within-group differences not significant at .05 level.

ATTITUDE CHANGE: A PANEL DESIGN

Attitude change over time is best studied using a panel design: asking respondents the same questions at different points in time. Data were available for this type of analysis for these samples: the attitudes of 416 respondents from the 1987 and 1988 samples were measured twice. The first wave of interviews was conducted between December 9, 1987 (the day on which the intifada, or Arab uprising, began) and January 4, 1988; the second was held in October 1988. In 1990, 213 of these same respondents were reinterviewed.

Hawk = 5

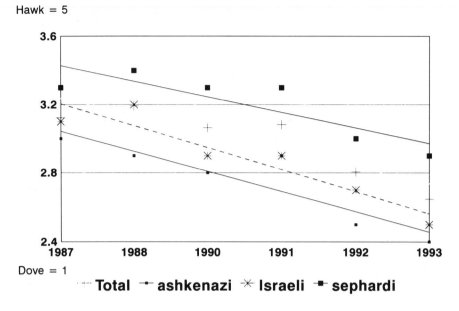

Dove = 1

Figure 4.5. Policy scale scores, by respondents' continent of birth group – trends, 1987–1993. (Five-point scale: dove = 1, hawk = 5.)

The respondents of the panel were presented with the policy scale questions in each interview situation. In the period between the interviews, the attitudes of the respondents changed in complex ways. There was no complete reversal of opinion, but there was definitely a tendency in a more militant direction. Based on the analysis of the first two stages, change occurred in both a more militant direction and in a more conciliatory direction, at the same time, across issues and across individuals.

Four of the questions occasioned aggregate change in a more dovish direction; four others, in a more hawkish direction. On one, respondents indicated greater preference for leaving things as they were. Those that changed in a more dovish direction included the major questions concerning possible long-term outcomes of the conflict: agreeing with the principle of exchanging land for peace versus annexation of the territories, attitudes toward the eventual establishment of a Palestinian state and toward encouraging Arabs to leave the country. These results concurred with those of several national cross-sectional surveys, which showed an increase in the number of those willing to consider compromise, to return territories, and to agree to an eventual Palestinian state (Katz 1989; Barzilai 1990). In

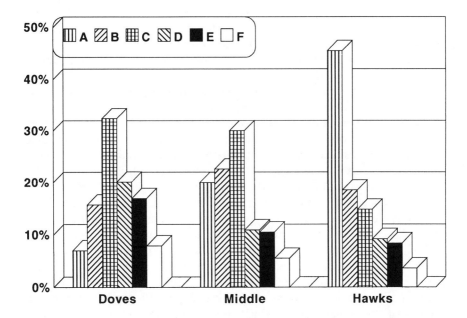

Figure 4.6. Perception of Arabs' peace attitudes, by respondents' policy scale scores. (Variables A-F refer to peace protocol listed under "Wanting Peace" in Chapter 3.)

addition, the assessment of the respondents of the effect that the army's presence in the territories had on its fighting ethic became much more negative over the 10 months of the intifada.

Regarding the question of the civil rights of Arabs were the territories to be annexed, fewer people agreed to increase civil rights in 1988 compared to 1987, yet most of those who changed their opinion preferred "to leave things as they are now" rather than decrease civil rights. The number of respondents choosing to decrease civil rights actually declined too. This hinted at the reluctance to change under pressure (Jervis 1976, Holsti and Rosenau 1984, Kegley 1986). During this period of crisis, many opted to retain the familiar rather than to experiment with new solutions on this issue which appeared problematic for both the right and the left.

Questions that generated a change in the hawkish direction concerned the forced choice the respondents were given between initiating peace negotiations and increasing Israel's military power as the best way to prevent war, and of whether security interests were more important than the rule of law when these two values were in conflict. This last question displayed the highest aggregate rate of change among all policy questions, followed by the question on the choice of negotiations versus increasing military power and the question about the effect on the army's ethic (see the last column in Table 4.11). Change in a more hawkish direction also included the idea of an international peace conference, and negotiations with the PLO. All of these questions referred to means and the short-term time frame rather than to long-term goals, although, of course, these distinctions are not clear-cut empirically (Shamir and Arian 1990).

On the questions of negotiations and the various formats for them, it was likely that some opposed negotiations during ongoing violence, and not necessarily because they had come to far-reaching decisions about the Palestinian cause. This is an example of the panel members "rallying around the flag" (Russett and DeLuca 1981; Flynn and Rattinger 1985; Holsti and Rosenau 1986a; Page, Shapiro, and Dempsey 1987), especially because the two major parties steadfastly opposed negotiations with the PLO, and those views were reiterated during the election campaign. The fact that the second wave of interviews was conducted shortly before the 1988 elections, a time when public debate and political awareness were most pronounced, may be a partial explanation for the incongruence of our results on the issue of negotiations with the PLO with the results of several ongoing surveys of the Jewish public, which showed an increase in willingness to enter negotiations with the PLO over time (Brinkley 1989).

Table 4.11 presents the change on individual policy questions, threat perception and respondents' vote intention (measured here dichotomously by political block: Labor and left versus Likud, right and religious parties), by descending order of attitude stability. Vote intention showed the most stability, with a total of 89 percent retaining their block voting intention for the year between the interviews, as shown by others.[5] This was followed by two central policy issues – the future of the territories and the idea of a Palestinian state. On these two issues, three important pieces of evidence stand out: (1) the degree of stability between the two interviews was higher than for any of the other issue questions; (2) the net change was in a dovish direction, although quite modest; and (3) the frequency distribution of these two questions was very different. On the question of the territories the sample split evenly, while on the question of a Palestinian state, a clear majority (about 75%) opposed it. These three patterns underscored the political importance of the shifts in public opinion during this period. The next item in terms of stability was the one referring to encouraging Arabs to leave the country, and on it, too, the trend was in the dovish direction. Another important policy question, regarding negotiations with the PLO, showed among the lowest levels of stability between the two interviews. People had less entrenched views on this issue, and they were evidently heavily influenced by ongoing developments and by the election campaign.

Table 4.11. *Stability and Change, 1987-1988 (N = 416)*

	Total % stable	Stable hawk %	Stable dove %	Change[a] to more hawkish	Change to more dovish	Net change[b]
Vote[c]	89	52	37	6	5	+1
Palestinian state	74	65	9	11	15	-4
Territories[d]	71	37	34	12	17	-5
Arabs leave	67	49	18	15	19	-4
International conference	65	23	42	22	14	+8
Negotiations/military	64	14	50	24	13	+11
Threat[e]	63	49	14	15	23	-8
Security/rule of law	50	36	8	36	15	+21
PLO[d]	49	22	18	29	22	+7
Civil rights[d]	47	6	28	29	25	+4
IDF[d]	43	14	15	23	35	-12

[a] For the questions asked, see Appendix II.

[b] Positive net change is in the hawkish direction; negative change is in the dovish direction.

[c] Respondents were divided into one of two categories: Labor and left; and Likud, right, and religious parties.

[d] Answers include a middle category which was not clearly hawk or dove. The "change to hawk" and "change to dove" categories include moves from and to this middle category.

[e] Threat was measured here by the assessment of Arab aspirations. These were listed as regaining some of the territories occupied in 1967, regaining all of them, conquering Israel, and conquering Israel and annihilating a large portion of the Jewish population in Israel. The last two responses were here considered hawkish.

The data presented in Table 4.11 show the complexity of public opinion change in two senses: (1) the different issue dimensions; and (2) the shifts of individuals on the issues in different directions. There was much more individual-level change than is evident in the net aggregate change figures; or in the words of Inglehart (1985; 1990, 106) regarding European data, "modest individual level stability together with remarkably high aggregate stability." Some people responded to the developments by changing to more hawkish views, whereas others moved in the more dovish direction. This was true with regard to all issues (see columns 4 and 5 in Table 4.11, and compare them to last column, which indicates aggregate net shift). Applying the policy scale at two points in time to the panel respondents gives us a summary of the scope and direction of change.[6] Table 4.12 presents the 1987 array of responses, used as the base for dividing the respondents into three groups of roughly equal size. The movement was complex but favored the hawkish end of the scale. The other movement which was significant was the depletion of the center. The middle position

Table 4.12. *Policy Scale Scores, 1987 and 1988*
(Total Table Percentages; N = 415[a])

| | Policy 1987 | | | |
Policy 1988	Dove	Middle	Hawk[b]	Total
Dove	19.3	7.0	5.1	31.3%
Middle	7.5	11.1	8.7	27.2%
Hawk	5.8	16.1	19.5	41.4%
Total	32.5	34.2	33.3	100%

[a] Apparent errors in addition are due to rounding.
[b] The hard-line pole of the scale includes support for annexing the territories, giving priority to increasing military power rather than entering peace negotiations, not participating in an international conference for peace chaired by the superpowers, preferring security interests over the rule of law, assessing that activities in the territories have a positive impact on the effectiveness of the army, opposing negotiations with the PLO, rejecting the establishment of a Palestinian state, denying civil rights to inhabitants of the territories, and encouraging Arabs to leave the country.

Table 4.13. *Change on Policy Scale Scores Between 1987 and 1988*

| | Policy 1987 | | | |
Policy 1988	Dove	Middle	Hawk	Total
Dove	19.3	7.0	5.1	31.3%
Middle	23.0	32.4	26.1	27.2%
Hawk	17.8	47.2	58.7	41.4%
N	135 (100%)	142 (100%)	138 (100%)	415

was contracted by a fifth between the two time periods, from 34 percent to 27 percent. The hawk pole grew from a third to 41 percent, while the dove pole retained its third of the sample.

The largest categories were of those who did not change between the two questioning periods; in all, half the respondents were in the same category in both time periods. Change was fairly symmetrical, with 5.1 and 5.8 percent, respectively, switching from the extreme hawk to the extreme dove position, and from the extreme dove to the extreme hawk categories. These patterns are displayed in an alternative manner in Table 4.13, in which the 1988 policy positions of the respondents are displayed by their 1987 positions.

The mean score on the 1987 policy scale was 3.10, and for 1988 it was 3.20; using the t-test difference of means measure, this difference was statistically significant. Several social categories were examined; in all of them there was a movement to the right using this summary scale.

The hawkish direction of change was statistically significant among respondents from Asian and African backgrounds, the religious, those above age 35, and men. Those under age 35 began more to the right than did the older group, but both groups shifted in that direction. So too with gender difference: women and men both moved toward the hawkish pole, with the women starting more to the right. Those closer to the hawkish position had less room for movement than those who began more to the left and moved in a rightist direction. Levels of education followed the pattern to the hawk pole, but none of the differences were statistically significant. Despite considerable speculation to the contrary, army service in the territories showed no discernible impact on attitudes (Jennings and Markus 1977; Horowitz 1982; Peri 1983; Arian et al. 1988).

It is clear from these panel data that much of the change in respondents' attitudes tended to be in the direction in which they were already leaning. This process is rooted in cognitive psychological mechanisms by which individuals interpret new realities according to stored knowledge and beliefs, among which political affiliations and ideologies are notable. Thus, a person who subscribed to the ideology of a greater Israel was likely to interpret the intifada differently compared with a respondent for whom democratic norms were critical (Fishbein and Ajzen 1975; Bar-Tal 1991). These psychological processes were further augmented through social and information networks of family, friends, and neighbors, as well as others significant to the individual, such as political commentators or leaders (Berelson, Lazarsfeld, and McPhee 1954; Katz and Lazarsfeld 1955; Huckfeldt 1983; MacKuen and Brown 1987). In Israel, there is much social overlap and differentiation along various lines, which is politically meaningful. The social networks – defined here largely by religiosity, ethnic origin, and class/education – reinforced this political cleavage rather than helped to dispel it. Kibbutzim and religious neighborhoods provide the most extreme examples. These other cleavages contribute to the political polarization.

The tendency toward polarization in the panel is also apparent when looking at individual items by different social groupings. For example, those from a European background and with higher education were more likely to vote for Labor and the parties of the left and to move in a dovish direction, especially regarding the issue of the territories. The opposite pattern is found for those born in Asia and Africa, and their Israel-born children; they tended to have lower levels of education, vote Likud, and moved more to the hawkish pole. This was true for Labor voters regarding the territories in both 1987 and 1988, and for the 1988 Labor voters about the establishment of a Palestinian state. The Likud voters, on the other hand, consistently moved in a hawkish direction regarding negotiations

Table 4.14. *Change on Policy Scores by Threat*

Threat	1987 Score	1988 Score	N	t-Value
High	3.31	3.64	183	5.31[a]
Middle	3.17	3.18	84	0.13
Low	2.77	2.57	128	-2.84[b]

[a] t-Test values of the differences between means significant at p < .001 level.
[b] t-Test values of the differences between means significant at p < .01 level.

with the PLO. Interestingly, however, they moderated their support regarding the idea of encouraging Arabs to leave the country as a solution to the political dilemma that Israel faced (see Chapter 5).

The respondents of the 1987 and 1988 panel who felt most threatened were least flexible regarding policy (see Table 4.14). The issues of the land and people of the territories were closely linked to feelings of being threatened: those most threatened were least flexible regarding the territories, as demonstrated in Chapter 2. Threat was also clearly associated with change in policy position: as threat rose, change toward the militant policy position increased (Birnbaum 1987). Those who perceived low threat had the lowest score on policy of any of the threat categories, and they were the only ones to change their policy positions in a dovish direction. The middle group barely changed at all.

In questions regarding Israel's greatest enemies, there was an interesting change related to ongoing developments: 11 percent more listed Iraq as Israel's second greatest enemy (after Syria) and 4 percent more listed the PLO. Between 1987 and 1988, with the war between Iraq and Iran ending and the intifada beginning, Israeli public opinion seemed to have responded.

In the spring and summer of 1990, a third wave of the panel study was undertaken. The number of successful third interviews was 213, more than half of the 416 who were interviewed in the first and second waves. While the problems of self-selection become more severe with each step, it is reassuring to note that the social and demographic characteristics of the three-wave panel sample corresponded closely to the general samples and to the population as a whole.

Among the respondents interviewed three times, the pattern of change with the onset of the intifada was similar to the one observed in the general samples. The means for the policy scale were 3.07, 3.22, and 3.09 for 1987, 1988, and 1990, respectively. Using a paired t-test, which compares the scores at each measurement point for the individual respondent, those seemingly slight differences were found to be very unlikely to have occurred by chance.

The largest categories were of those who did not change between the two time periods. Table 4.15 repeats for the three-wave panel the analysis of

Table 4.15. *Stability and Change, 1987 to 1988 to 1990 (N = 213)*

	Total % stable	Stable hawk %	Stable dove %	Change to more hawkish	Change to more dovish	Net change[a]
Vote[b]						
1987 to 1988	84	41	43	7	9	-2
1988 to 1990	88	41	47	4	7	-3
1987 to 1990	87	39	47	6	8	-2
Palestinian state						
1987 to 1988	78	69	9	9	13	-4
1988 to 1990	75	62	13	10	16	-6
1987 to 1990	71	62	9	9	20	-11
Territories[c]						
1987 to 1988	68	36	32	15	18	-3
1988 to 1990	69	35	34	16	15	+1
1987 to 1990	68	36	32	13	16	-3
Arabs leave						
1987 to 1988	67	47	20	18	15	+3
1988 to 1990	65	46	19	17	19	-2
1987 to 1990	63	46	17	19	18	+1
International conference						
1987 to 1988	63	23	40	25	13	+12
1988 to 1990	62	30	33	19	18	+1
1987 to 1990	60	22	38	27	13	+14
Negotiations/military						
1987 to 1988	60	11	49	26	14	+12
1988 to 1990	60	16	46	19	19	0
1987 to 1990	64	13	51	23	13	+10
Threat[d]						
1987 to 1988	65	51	14	16	19	-3
1988 to 1990	70	56	14	19	10	+10
1987 to 1990	70	57	13	18	12	+6
Security /rule of law[c]						
1987 to 1988	48	33	10	40	13	+27
1988 to 1990	56	45	7	17	27	-10
1987 to 1990	51	31	11	24	15	+9
PLO[c]						
1987 to 1988	53	24	18	29	18	+11
1988 to 1990	45	20	17	17	39	-21
1987 to 1990	43	14	20	24	34	-10

Table 4.15 *(Continued)*

	Total % stable	Stable hawk %	Stable dove %	Change to more hawkish	Change to more dovish	Net change[a]
Civil rights[c]						
1987 to 1988	60	32	28	25	15	+10
1988 to 1990	57	30	27	16	27	-11
1987 to 1990	61	27	34	18	20	-2
IDF[c]						
1987 to 1988	41	13	14	25	34	-9
1988 to 1990	45	9	19	23	32	-11
1987 to 1990	38	10	16	21	42	-21

[a] Positive net change is in the hawkish direction; negative change is in the dovish direction.
[b] Respondents were divided into one of two categories: Labor and left; and Likud, right, and religious parties.
[c] Answers include a middle category which was not clearly hawk or dove. The "change to hawk" and "change to dove" categories include moves from and to this middle category.
[d] Threat was measured here by the assessment of Arab aspirations. These were listed as regaining some of the territories occupied in 1967, regaining all of them, conquering Israel, and conquering Israel and annihilating a large portion of the Jewish population in Israel. The last two responses were here considered hawkish.

Table 4.11 and reveals similar patterns to those found before. The vote decision was very stable from one question period to another. The ranking of the variables of the policy scale was very similar to the one generated with the two-wave panel, with the exception that civil rights for Arabs of the territories was more stable than before. Positions regarding the international conference changed greatly because of changes in the political situation. The rush to the security pole of the security and rule-of-law issue was stemmed, and an adjustment of position seemed to be made. The assessment of the effect of the situation on the morale of the army was increasingly negative.

5

Politics

ELECTIONS

Policy is not made by public opinion; it is made by politicians elected to office. If the public participates in the election of leaders, and if the mechanisms used are open and fair, then the impact of public opinion on policy is through the selection process, in determining who is to decide. In a democratic setting, a proposition supported by a substantial portion of an articulate public is likely to attract the attention of the leadership.

Policy flows from election results because the elections empower those who make policy. Elections are the beginning of the process of setting policy for the nation, not the end of the process. Obviously, the phenomenon is cyclical since policy also interacts with later voting decisions, and decision makers keep at least one eye on the election calendar and one ear open to the musings of the media and the roar of the streets.

Because decisions are specific and elections diffuse, it is usually incorrect to view elections as a referendum on a given issue. Even in Israel, with the centrality of the security issue granted, and the salience of the territories obvious, both public opinion polls and election results are very imprecise predictors of future policy. In addition to the distribution of opinion and the intensity of the opinion holders, we must know which politicians assumed the important decision-making roles, and which nonelected public servants and advisors they appointed to decision-making positions. All of that, along with information about the international situation, the economy, the status of domestic issues, the control of the leadership of its own political party, and many other matters, will bring the observer closer to knowing about policy. Public opinion is in the equation, but it is certainly not the only part of it. Even if the demands of followers are precise, politicians prefer to be indeterminate and diffuse. Accordingly, it is very hard to know if policy follows opinion or makes it. It is easier to observe that leaders strive to give the impression of heeding public opinion because they hope that the electorate (or the party members or activists) will select or reelect them, and they wish to avoid the threat of being replaced because

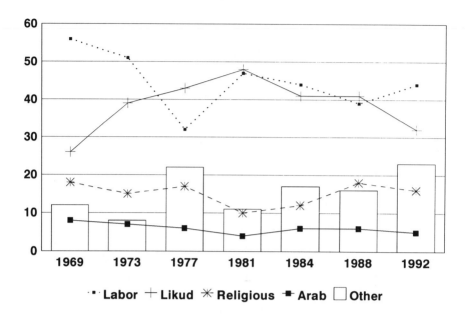

Figure 5.1. Changes in distribution of Knesset seats, 1969–1992.

of a gap between their positions and those of the public. Policy, in turn, affects public opinion in the sense that electorates often support the positions of statesmen (former politicians temporarily elevated to positions of power) at least until the next elections approach.

In the period between 1967 and 1994, as the debate over the territories raged and the difference between the parties seemed to crystallize, Israeli voters went to the polls seven times and registered a pattern of stability and of change (see Figure 5.1). The two major protagonists, Labor and Likud, transferred power to each other, Labor to Likud in 1977, and Likud to Labor in 1992, and even shared power between 1984 and 1990 in National Unity governments. Both parties transferred power from the founding to the second generation; both witnessed democratic innovations in the rules of leadership selection in their respective parties.

The religious parties had about as much parliamentary strength at the end of the period as they had at the beginning, although they had experienced periods of weakness, and the new parties of consequence in the religious camp had emerged. The number of Knesset members from Arab parties decreased from 1969 to 1992, even though in that period Arabs increased as a percentage of the electorate from about 12 to 17 percent.

Small changes in electoral politics can have enormous importance, but

Table 5.1. *Average Number of Knesset Seats in Four Periods, 1969-1992*

	1969 1973	1977	1981 1984 1988	1992
Labor	53.5	32	41.3	41
Likud	32.5	43	41.3	32
Religious	16.5	17	16.7	16
Arab	7.5	6	5.3	5

stable features are also important to note. The patterns generated by Labor and Likud in Figure 5.1 suggest the following periodization: (1) the pre-1977 period with Labor leading but in decline; (2) the 1977 reversal; (3) the three elections of close competitiveness of the 1980s; and (4) the 1992 reversal. The average number of seats using this periodization is presented in Table 5.1.

When the strength of the various groups was considered based on a calculation of each group's average number of Knesset seats in these periods, underlying trends become more obvious. Recall that the number of seats in the Knesset is only one measure of power, and does not take into account the potential support of parties which are ideologically adjacent and likely to be available in forming the governing coalition. After all, coalition formation is the vital skill in Israeli politics. The adjacent parties are presented in the "other" category of Figure 5.1. In years of reversal elections, these "other" parties did especially well: the Democratic Movement for Change (DMC) in 1977, and Meretz of the left and Tzomet of the right in 1992.

Labor weakened considerably during the period, and even its routing of the Likud in 1992 did not elevate it to the heights of its previous power. On the contrary, in 1992 Labor did only a little better than it had done on average in the three elections of the 1980s. The Likud was about as weak in the Knesset at the end of the period as it had been at the beginning. The successful periods for the Likud were 1977 and the 1980s. In the 1980s, Labor and the Likud registered the same average number of Knesset seats. Religious parties maintained their average strength throughout. Arab lists lost almost a third of their strength during this period.

This rendering of Israel's election results highlights points of volatility and lability. The detailed election results will determine the types of coalitions possible and the contours of the next coalition crisis, certain to come soon. The averages are revealing because they emphasize the typical, and by so doing provide a benchmark to study atypical reversal elections.

Table 5.2. *Votes and Seats, Labor and Likud, 1973-1977, 1988-1992*

A. 1973-1977	Valid votes	Labor	Likud[a]
1973	1,566,855	621,183	473,309
1977	1,747,820	430,023	583,968
% Increase over 1973	11.5	-30.8	23.4
		Labor seats	Likud seats
1973		51	39
1977		32	43
% Increase over 1973		-37.3	10.3
B. 1988-1992	Valid votes	Labor	Likud[a]
1988	2,283,123	685,363	709,305
1992	2,616,841	906,810	651,229
% Increase over 1988	14.6	32.3	-8.2
		Labor seats	Likud seats
1988		39	40
1992		44	32
% Increase over 1988		12.8	-20.0

[a] See note 1 in this chapter.

The first 30 years of Israel's independence were characterized by Labor party dominance. After eight elections won by Labor, the electorate changed the party in power at the polls twice, in 1977 and in 1992. The first time, the dominant Labor party lost power to the Likud as Labor hemorrhaged from self-inflicted wounds and lost votes to the reformist DMC, on the one hand, and to the Likud, on the other.[1] The 1992 shift was less complex and numerically smaller, as the Likud lost its 15-year lease on power to Labor.

In 1977, the Democratic Movement for Change took away so many votes from Labor that the Likud emerged as the largest party, ushering in an era dominated by Menachem Begin and Yitzhak Shamir, which lasted until 1992. Labor's loss of votes in 1977 (more than 30% of its 1973 total) was even larger than the Likud loss in 1992 (see Table 5.2). The Likud in 1977 increased its total vote over 1973 by almost a quarter. When the growth of the electorate is factored in, the Likud increased its proportion of the vote by 10 percent, while Labor's decreased by almost 40 percent.

Fifteen years after the defeat of 1977, and eight years after the stalemate of 1984, Labor returned to power in 1992 in a dramatic victory. Yitzhak

Rabin returned to the prime ministry he had left in 1977, with his two principal nemeses – Yitzhak Shamir of the Likud, and Shimon Peres of Labor – relegated to leader of the opposition and foreign minister, respectively, in Rabin's moment of victory. Rabin quickly formed a government in 1992, as Begin had in 1977, but the 1992 election results magnified comparatively modest changes in electoral behavior into shifts of power. Like the wave that grows as it becomes more distant from its source, either shift could have been enormous. Comparing the initial surges, however, the shift of 1977 was by far of greater magnitude. The reversal of 1992, although politically real, was electorally smaller.

In both 1977 and 1992, the combination of a ruling party in retreat and social and economic turmoil set the stage for the transfer of power. In both cases a significant number of voters abandoned the party in power, and these votes were dispersed to other parties on the same side of the political divide, or to parties in the other camp. Enormous numbers of new voters were added to the rolls through immigration in this period, and much of the electorate had been replaced through natural processes of aging and death.

The arithmetic of the elections indicates that there were some 330,000 valid votes more in 1992 compared with 1988, an increase of 14.6 percent (see Table 5.2A). In contrast to the large increase in the number of voters, the Likud vote decreased both in the relative and absolute senses. Compared with 1988, the Likud vote decreased by 8 percent, from 709,305 to 651,229 voters, reducing its parliamentary delegation from 40 seats in 1988 to 32 seats in 1992. Labor's delegation, on the other hand, grew from 39 to 44 seats, as its vote total swelled by a third, from 685,363 votes in 1988 to 906,810 votes in 1992. Labor's percentage of the vote grew faster than the swell of the electorate, as its percentage of the vote grew by 15 points between 1988 and 1992. The left-wing Meretz vote grew handsomely by almost 30 percent and its Knesset representation increased from 10 to 12 members. The total increase of votes for religious parties was only 3.2 percent because these parties were unable to make inroads with the new, secular immigrant voting stock. Tzomet of the right registered an amazing 265 percent increase compared with 1988 and had its delegation to the Knesset grow from 2 to 8 seats.

On the whole, the parties of the left outdid the parties of the right. Voters for left-wing parties (Labor, Meretz, and the Arab lists) totaled 1,284,992 voters. Parties of the right (Likud, Tzomet, Moledet, and three parties of the right that did not achieve the minimum 1.5 percent needed for representation) won 928,380 votes. Including in the "right" the National Religious party (first and foremost a religious party, which positioned itself to the right of the Likud), the total for the right would be 1,058,043 votes. Adding to this total the two ultra-Orthodox parties, we obtain 1,273,557 for the right-wing religious bloc combined, very close to the total left vote. More votes for parties which failed to win representation were registered for the right wing than for the left wing.

In terms of seats won, the left bloc had a slight edge of 61:59 over the right-wing/religious bloc. This hardly qualified as a landslide for the left or Labor. The previous Knesset, elected in 1988, had split 55:65. Labor with its 44 seats of 120 in 1992 was as large as it was in 1984, and 3 seats smaller than its 1981 strength. Furthermore, more Israeli Jews voted for the right-wing/religious bloc than for the left bloc. The total left was bigger than the right and religious only in conjunction with the votes of Israeli Arabs.

VOTING CHANGE

Public opinion sets the mood of the period in which the selected politicians are free to set policy; electoral change can be used as an important key to understanding that mood, and in unraveling the complexities of the opinion-election-policy nexus. One way to do this is by analyzing the patterns of respondents who switched their votes. For example, focusing on the Likud voters in 1988, how did they vote in 1992? Among them, who remained loyal and who deserted? In which direction did they go? What was their demographic profile? What position did they hold regarding the territories and the PLO? What influenced their vote? In parallel fashion, these questions can be asked for respondents who supported Labor in 1973: How did they vote in 1977? Who stayed with Labor and who left it? Where did they go? What was their attitude about the territories and the PLO? What affected their vote?

The analysis considers only those respondents who reported voting for Likud in 1988 and who said that they would vote for the right, the Likud, or Labor in 1992 (see Table 5.3), and those who voted Labor in 1973 and said they would vote for the Likud, Labor, or the DMC in 1977 (see Table 5.4). Those who had not made up their minds or gave no answer to the vote intention question were not included.[2]

When the sociodemographic profiles of the three 1992 groups are examined, it is clear that the predominant distinction among them was along the religiosity dimension. It is also the only statistically significant distinction. The largest differences both between 1992 Likud and Labor voters (34% to 14%) and among the three groups of voters were in the percent religious. Moving from the 1992 right voters through the 1992 Likud group to the 1992 Labor voters, the chances decrease that a respondent was religiously observant (45% to 34% to 14%).

In 1992, all three groups of 1988 Likud voters were overwhelmingly sephardim, explaining why there is no statistical difference among them.

Table 5.3. *Profile of 1988 Likud Voters*

| | 1988 vote Likud; 1992 vote: | | |
	Right	Likud	Labor
N (total = 310)	40	226	44
Demography (%)			
Religious	45[a]	34	14
Sephardim[b]	(78	70	64)
Under 30 years	(46	32	32)
Female	(60	52	43)
Attitudes (%)			
Opposed to returning territories[c]	67	66	24
Opposed to negotiating with PLO[d]	85	72	61
For Jewish religious law in Israeli public life[e]	38	41	21
Mentioning security/peace as most important issue	(59	54	41)
Preferring capitalism[f]	(60	58	59)
Vote motivated by (%):			
Party	22	43	23
Candidate	17	12	20
Issues	(61	45	57)
Vote choice affected by (%):			
Economic stand of parties	48	25	55
Territories stand of parties	(65	50	55)

[a] Using the chi-square test, differences are statistically significant above .05 level except for those in parentheses.
[b] Based on the background of whether respondent or father were born in (1) Asia or Africa (here labeled sephardim); or (2) Europe or America, or both born in Israel.
[c] Question described in Table 5.6, note d.
[d] Based on a yes-no question whether Israel should be willing to conduct negotiations with the PLO.
[e] Question described in Table 5.6, note f.
[f] Question described in Table 5.6, note e.

The figures range from 78 percent for those who shifted to the right, through 70 percent for those who stayed with the Likud, to 64 percent for those who shifted to Labor. Winning this nucleus of sephardim away from the Likud was crucial for Labor to succeed in 1992. Although Labor attracted them at lower rates than did the right or those who stayed with the Likud, the fact that Labor did it at all shows that the party was at least partially successful in changing its image from a party of ashkenazim with antipathy toward sephardim. Labor managed to retain

Table 5.4. *Profile of 1973 Labor Voters*

| | 1973 vote Labor; 1977 vote: | | |
	Likud	Labor	DMC
N (total = 382)	77	265	40
Demography (%)			
Religious	33[a]	17	10
Sephardim[b]	56	25	15
Under 30 years	35	14	30
Female	63	43	53
Attitudes (%)			
Opposed to returning territories[c]	53	27	27
Opposed to negotiating with PLO[d]	67	59	51
For Jewish religious law in Israeli public life[e]	(57	43	34)
Mentioning security/peace as most important issue	38	49	32
Preferring capitalism[f]	25	15	36
Vote motivated by (%):			
Party	(30	41	24)
Candidate	(19	15	19)
Issues	51	45	57
Vote choice affected by (%):			
Economic stand of parties	33	20	50
Territories stand of parties	40	25	22
Corruption	44	16	62

[a] Using the chi-square test, differences are statistically significant above .05 level except for those in parentheses.
[b] Based on the background of whether respondent or father were born in (1) Asia or Africa (here labeled sephardim); or (2) Europe or America, or both born in Israel.
[c] Question described in Table 5.6, note d.
[d] Based on a yes-no question whether Israel should be willing to conduct negotiations with the PLO.
[e] Question described in Table 5.6, note f.
[f] Question described in Table 5.6, note e.

sephardim in its ranks while simultaneously drawing away others from the Likud.[3]

The three groups of voters differed also on the other variables, but these differences were generally much smaller. This result is consistent with a high correlation between religiosity and the vote for all Likud and Labor voters (see Table 5.6) – the highest among the sociodemographic variables.

Regarding age – although the differences are not statistically significant –

it is interesting to note that there was no difference in the percent under age 30 among the Likud loyalists and the 1992 Labor voters (32%); in the past Likud was much more often the party of the young compared with Labor. Taken together with the small difference (6%) in the ethnic composition of these two groups of voters, we see the curbing of the two factors which were crucial in the 1977 turnabout and in voting patterns since. Age and ethnicity were still meaningful in distinguishing between Labor and Likud supporters, as 1992 cross-sectional correlations (see Table 5.6) showed, but their discriminating power was diminishing. The group that moved from the Likud to parties of the right had a much higher percentage of people under age 30 than the other two groups (46% compared to 32%). The higher preference of the young for the right – a pattern long established – continued in 1992. It is only in the comparison of the Likud loyalists with 1988 Likud voters who switched to Labor in 1992 that this relationship no longer holds.

The differences between the three groups of voters in their attitude toward the territories are the largest in Table 5.3. The group that shifted to Labor was much more conciliatory regarding the future of the territories than were the other groups. Those who shifted from the Likud to the right were as likely as Likud loyalists to oppose returning territories, but they were much more likely to oppose negotiations with the PLO.

On the question of state and religion, there were also clear differences: about 40 percent of the right and Likud groups supported the position that the government should see to it that public life be conducted according to religious tradition, compared with only 31 percent among those who switched to Labor. On the economic cleavage of capitalism and socialism there was no difference among the three groups of voters.

The 1977 picture was very different. Labor in 1977 lost a greater percentage of its previous vote than did the Likud of 1992, and many more of the 1973 Labor respondents were undecided or refused to tell how they would vote in 1977. The group of voters who selected Labor in 1973 and Likud in 1977 was almost twice as big as the one that went to the DMC (see Table 5.4). The 1992 shift was less along ethnic lines and more along issues, whereas the voters in 1977 who had chosen Labor in 1973 split by both ethnicity and policy. Most of those who left Labor for Likud in 1977 were sephardim (56%), while those who stayed with Labor and those who shifted to the DMC were predominantly ashkenazim (only 25 and 15 percent sephardi, respectively). Also, the age and gender differences among the groups were more pronounced in 1977 compared with 1992, as seen by their size and statistical significance. Those who moved either to the Likud or to the DMC in 1977 were more likely to be young and more likely to be female than those who remained with Labor.

The ones who moved from Labor to Likud were clearly different from those who stayed and from those who shifted to the DMC in their more hawkish policy stand regarding the territories and their greater affinity to religious observance (also in their preference for Jewish religious law in Israeli public life, although these differences were not statistically significant). The majority of all groups opposed dealing with the PLO, although this was much more prevalent among those who eventually voted Likud than among those who moved to the DMC. The switchers to the DMC supported capitalism more strongly; those who remained with Labor clung stubbornly to their socialism.

In 1977 the dynamic was driven much more by social factors, as judged by the size of differences among the three groups of voters, and in particular between Likud and Labor voters. Of the sociodemographic factors, ethnicity was the most important. Issues mattered as well. By 1992, the edge of the ethnic sword was deflected, while the ideological blade remained keen. Actually, of the demographic factors only religion remained a meaningful distinction in 1992, and the issue of the territories gained in strength over 1977. In 1977, the difference in the ethnic profile between Labor loyalists and deserters to the Likud was 31 percent; the difference between these two groups in their attitude toward the territories was 26 percent. In 1992, the comparable figures were 6 percent and 42 percent.

It is fascinating to note how similar the 1977 and 1992 patterns were for the samples when asked what factors determined their vote: identification with a certain party, the stands that a party takes on issues, the candidates offered, or whether a party is in government or in the opposition. In both cases, the parties' stands on issues were credited with determining the vote much more than the other factors, followed by party identification, and then the candidates; the opposition option was negligible. For those who were loyal to the same party in both periods, however, the rate of choosing the ideological factor was lowest compared to the other groups. Almost as high as the platform for the loyalists in both time periods was identification with the party. Ideology was flaunted by the changers; whether this was real or an artifact of the political culture was immaterial, what mattered was that the norm was to report that change of party tended to be driven by ideological reasons.

Considering the responses to questions in the two periods about whether various issues affect the vote decision of the respondents fortifies this analysis. Stands of parties on the territories or the economic issue were least important for the stayers and most important for the strayers. In 1992, the territories stand was important for at least half of each voting group, but least important for the loyalists. Economics in 1992 was much more important for those who left the Likud than for those who stayed with it. In 1977, a different dynamic was at work: the Likud voters who left Labor reported

Table 5.5. *Correlations[a] Among Voting Types,[b] Demographics and Issues[c]*
1977 (N = 382) and 1992 (N = 309)

| Survey | | | Demography | | | | | | Issues[d] | |
	Age	Gender	Den-sity	Educa-tion	Income	Reli-gion	Ethni-city	Terri-tories	Capit./ social.	State / religion
3/77	(-.03)	(-.02)	.15	.28	.12	.16	.24	-.12	-.20	.10
6/92	(.09)	(.09)	(.04)	(.01)	(.04)	.18	(.08)	-.29	(.02)	.16

[a] Pearson correlations, significant above the .05 level, except those in parentheses.
[b] Voters were divided into three categories: for 1992, respondents who had voted Likud in 1988 were categorized as either having switched to the right = 1, remained with the Likud = 2, or shifted to Labor = 3. For 1977, respondents who had voted for the Labor Alignment in 1973 were categorized as shifting to the Likud = 1, remaining with Labor = 2, or switching to the Democratic Movement for Change = 3.
[c] The coding for these correlations was: low scores indicate young age, female, sephardi, high density, low income, low education, high religiosity, willingness to concede territories for peace, favoring capitalism over socialism, and favoring public life in accordance with Jewish religious law, respectively.
[d] See Table 5.6, notes d, e, and f.

that they were affected by the territories issue, and the DMC voters, by the economic one.

The different dynamics of the two elections become clearer by considering the correlations of the vote with demographic variables and the policy issues, as presented in Table 5.6 for all Likud/Labor voters in the elections between 1969 and 1992. Table 5.5 presents the correlations for the voting groups just discussed. Those variables can be identified which discriminated among the 1988 Likud voters as they decided how to vote in 1992, and among 1973 Labor voters as they approached 1977. The sociodemographic variables of education, ethnicity, and social class (density and income) were related to that choice in 1977 for the three groups; these factors, however, lost their efficacy when applied to the three groups of 1988 Likud voters in 1992. Religiosity retained its potency in both periods, and the state-religion relations issue became more relevant to vote choice in 1992. The territories issue became sharper between 1977 and 1992. Interestingly, the classic social-economic ideological cleavage of socialism-capitalism had no significance at all for the 1988 Likud voters in their deciding whom to vote for in 1992. This contrasts to the 1973 Labor voters in 1977. For them this issue was associated with the vote – yet in the opposite direction than some Marxists would expect: those who shifted to the Likud, and who were of lower income, lower education, and lower standard of living tended to support the capitalistic point of view more strongly compared with those who remained loyal to Labor. This pattern is related to whether or not a voter belonged to the socialist-Zionist camp socially, politically, and culturally more than to ideological commitment to either socialism or capitalism.

In order to assess the relative importance of sociodemographics and issues when considered jointly, stepwise regression was used in the following way: two blocs of variables were defined, one including the sociodemographic variables, the other including the three issue-variables. Two stepwise regressions were then computed, entering once the sociodemographic bloc first, and once the issue bloc first, with the Likud/Labor vote as defined in Table 5.3.[4] The results complement the correlation analysis: demographic characteristics were dominant in 1977, issues more important in 1992. In the stepwise regressions for 1977, the bloc of sociodemographics accounted for 12 percent of the variance alone, issues added only 2 percent more when added next. By themselves, issues explained 6 percent of the vote variance when coming first in the regression. In 1992, issues and demographics "explained" together 10 percent of the variance; issues alone 8 percent, sociodemographics alone 5 percent. The only variable which was statistically significant in the full 1992 regression was the question of whether or not to return the territories. In the full 1977 regression equation, three variables were statistically significant: education, ethnic background, and the socialist-capitalist question. This last variable indicates a quite broad affiliation to the Labor camp, rather than to ideological statements. The results reinforce the interpretation of 1977 as a realignment grounded in demographics and establishing new and enduring election groupings. The year 1992 was predominantly issue-based, with the question of the territories looming large.

ISSUES AND DEMOGRAPHY

There has been a general decline in the importance of social cleavages for electoral behavior, and the simultaneous increase in issue voting in Israel and in other polities (Rose and McAllister 1986; Dalton 1988; Bartolini and Mair 1990; Franklin, Mackie, and Valen 1992). The grasp of social allegiance on voting patterns weakened in Israel, while the weight of issues in general and of the divisive issue of the territories as a factor in voting further increased. Placed in the broader perspective of postindustrial societies, Franklin et al. regard this as a developmental process, recognizing that it takes place in some countries later than in others. They also note that the decline in the structuring properties of the traditional social cleavages has not been balanced by increases in the structuring properties of new cleavages (chapters 19 and 20).

In most countries covered by Franklin et al., the amount of the vote variance explained by social structure and attitudinal variables has been reduced from the 1960s through the 1980s. This has not been the case in Israel. The difference lies in the nature of the issues which have captured the agenda. In most Western countries issues involving postbourgeois versus materialist values, gender issues, public versus private consumption, and state employment have gained ascendancy. While important, these issues energize certain publics and not others, and are not as central, critical, and engulfing as the major issue dimension in Israeli politics: the territories and the Israeli-Arab conflict. No wonder, then, that voting in Israel has become more structured, and that these issues have become a more important determinant of it over time.

The atomizing influences of advanced industrial societies are used to explain these changes and to suggest that the bases for electoral politics are changing. As a result of these processes, groups' cultural distinctiveness, social homogeneity, and organizational density are weakening, using Bartolini and Mair's (1990, chapter 9) terms. The more highly organized into exclusive and overlapping networks and associations whose internal structures are personalistic and hierarchical, the greater the group's political cohesion (Zuckerman 1982). As Zuckerman points out, such conditions are usually not prevalent, and postindustrial societies are even less likely to produce them. With increasing levels of urbanization, social and geographic mobility, growing heterogeneity, secularization and embourgeoisement, the revolutions in the mass media, in education and cognitive mobilization, changing organizational structures and ties, and the emergence of values and issues that are only weakly linked to specific demographic groups, issues and social bases are likely to become less coordinated.

The type of issue may generate different degrees and types of group loyalty. Some issues may be only weakly related to specific social groupings, as the postindustrial literature argues, but others can connect, and can reinforce existing cleavage structures by providing new reasons for the same people and groups to support the same parties (Franklin et al. 1992, 402). Ethnic grievances may have partly operated in this way in Israel in the 1980s. The complex issue of state-religion relations, which Israel has not yet resolved, is a good example of one that has gained in importance over time simultaneously with the social demographic characteristic of religiosity. Here we see a mutual reinforcement process between the issue and the groups, groups which are still quite clearly defined, and both socially and politically cohesive (in particular on the religious side). Thus the extent to which vote is related to sociodemographic characteristics of voters depends also on the nature of the issues on the agenda.

The changing bases of electoral behavior have been attributed with causing greater individual and aggregate level volatility in the vote (Dalton, Flanagan, and Beck 1984; Bartolini and Mair 1990). And as Franklin suggests, "a natural concomitant of this liberation (where it has occurred), is that the fortunes of individual political parties have become much less certain, and are dependent more largely on variations in leadership skills and other contingencies" (Franklin et al. 1992, 403). This generalization is certainly true of Israel. The 1992 elections, for instance, seemed to empower the electorate and the Labor party was called upon to lead for the next term, with the implicit threat that it too could be replaced in future elections.

The sources of electoral change can be sought in issues and sociodemographic factors (Dalton et al. 1984; Franklin et al. 1992). Political homogeneity of voting groups in Israel has increased from the 1970s through 1984 in terms of ethnicity, social class indicators, and religiosity, and this process was interpreted as a realignment in the electorate (Shamir 1986, 272–5). This same analysis also established the growing electoral importance of the territories issue over time. Extending the analysis to the 1988 and 1992 elections, it appears that the role of demographic factors has continued to recede since 1984 while the role of issues has further increased.

Table 5.6 presents the correlations between the Labor/Likud vote and various demographic and issue variables.[5] Inspecting that table along the columns, it is apparent that the twin issues of God and nationalism, always good predictors of the vote, have become more powerful over the years, and 1977 and 1992 do not stand out as critical years in the time series for these issues. On the state-religion issue, the trend of increasing correlations is smooth over time. The identification of Labor as an anticlerical party has strengthened, while the Likud has played to the traditional sympathies of much of its voting base, even though the origins and ideology of the Likud are very secular, as Liebman and Don-Yehiya (1983) have shown.

Issues and the Territories

In Chapter 4, the growth of those expressing readiness to return territories was documented. Extending that line back in time, the magnitude of the population refusing to return territories in 1992 was similar to the extent in the pre-1977 period (see Figure 5.2). The no-return figure is reported here because the format of the pre-1984 questions made that answer more comparable to the answers of the question available since 1984.[6] What is important to note is the manner in which the no-return curve follows the four-part periodization just discussed. In the period of Labor dominance, support for the no-return position was less than 40 percent of the samples; in the competitive 1980s the population split down the middle. The two reversal elections had a 42–45 percent rate for unwillingness to return.

Table 5.6. *Correlations[a] Between Likud and Labor, Demographics and Issues[b]*
1969-1992

Survey[c] (N)	Demography							Issues		
	Age	Gender	Den-sity	Educa-tion	Income	Reli-gion	Ethni-city	Terri-tories[d]	Capit./soc.[e]	State/religion[f]
10/69 (1017)	.17	(.05)	.07	(.00)	(-.04)	.08	.13	-.15	.23	.12
5/73 (1062)	.27	(.01)	.15	(-.02)	(-.01)	(.04)	.13	-.23	.17	g
3/77 (620)	.29	(-.03)	.18	(.01)	(.06)	.18	.32	-.28	.22	.17
3/81 (798)	.13	(.06)	.07	.09	(.00)	.19	.23	-.27	.16	.20
7/84 (807)	.20	(-.03)	.25	.22	.08	.37	.53	-.57	.32	g
10/88 (532)	.16	(.04)	.09	.15	(.01)	.27	.27	-.61	.30	.24
6/92 (657)	.10	(.07)	.13	.24	(-.02)	.40	.35	-.57	(.05)	.29

[a] Pearson correlations, significant above the .05 level, except for those in parentheses.

[b] The coding for these correlations was Likud = 1, Labor = 2. Low scores for the other variables indicate young age, female, sephardi, high density, low income, low education, high religiosity, willingness to concede territories for peace, favoring capitalism over socialism, and favoring public life in accordance with Jewish religious law, respectively.

[c] Preelection surveys used. In years for which multiple surveys were available, the one which contained the most variables used in the table was chosen.

[d] Before 1984, a question concerning the maximum amount of territory Israel should give up in order to achieve a peace settlement. In 1984 and after, constructed from two questions, the first asking preference between return of territories for peace, annexation, or status quo, and a follow-up question forcing a choice of those who chose the "status quo" option. See Chapter 4.

[e] The question asked about preference for the socialist or capitalist approach. The 1973 question asked if the Histadrut labor union should both own industries and represent workers.

[f] The question asked whether the government should see to it that public life in Israel be conducted according to the Jewish religious tradition.

[g] Not asked.

It is fascinating that the rate should be so similar despite the intense political and demographic changes between those two periods, and that the two reversals enhanced the political fortunes of parties supposedly at opposite ends of the ideological spectrum. The fact that the population split in this way at the time of reversal underscores the ambiguous link between public opinion and policy. After all, it was Labor which initiated settlements in the territories and used the weapon of expulsion to a great degree, and also projected a more moderate image, and it was why the Likud could enter into the Camp David agreements with its recognition of the "legitimate rights of the Palestine people" and inaugurate the Madrid conference in 1991 with all the implications for the future of the territories that such participation implied, despite its more hawkish image.

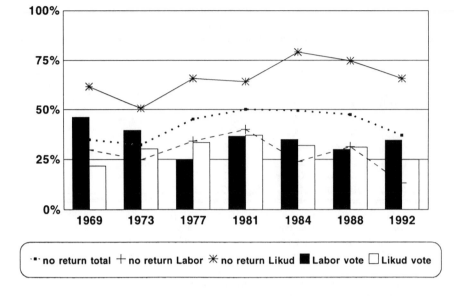

Figure 5.2. Refusal to return the territories, by vote, 1969–1992.

Election results provide mandates to make decisions, not prescriptions for policy.

Concentrating on the territories issue (see Table 5.6), the trend of growing correlations is less smooth, with the critical year being 1984, the election following the war in Lebanon, and the first one with Shamir replacing Begin as the head of the Likud. Since 1984, the correlations of the territories issue with the vote are very high and of similar magnitude. Over time, Labor has more unambiguously identified itself as the territories-for-peace party, and the platform of Labor has become less vague on this issue. The public perception of the difference between these two parties on the territories issue did not change much; almost two-thirds of the respondents in the 1981, 1984, and 1992 surveys thought these differences were big or very big. Yet 1992 was different from previous elections in that many more voters said that the territories would be an important consideration in their voting decision. In the 1992 sample, 52 percent said that the issue of the territories would very greatly influence their vote, compared with less than a third in previous elections. Adding the next category of response, 81 percent said in 1992 that it would influence them or greatly or very greatly, compared with 63 percent in previous elections.

The importance of the 1984 election – and evidently of the 1982 Lebanon war – is seen in the "no return Labor" and "no return Likud" curves in

Figure 5.2. For the bulge it generates in the otherwise smooth and parallel pattern, 1984 stands out. Likud and Labor voters diverged sharply, with Likud voters being very opposed to return, and the Labor voters unusually supportive of it. The trend in the following two elections was led by the Labor pattern, as the percentage of no-return Likud voters decreased, and the proportion of no-return Labor voters went down to its lowest level of the numbers recorded. Voters were never completely consistent with the reputed ideology of the parties they supported, but by 1992, a third of Likud supports and more than 8 in 10 Labor voters supported return.

The correlations between the vote and the classical economic cleavage between capitalism and socialism do not follow a clear pattern over time. They were strongest in 1984 and 1988. In 1992 there was no relationship whatsoever between voters' position on this question and their preference for Likud or Labor.

Demography and Ethnicity

The correlations in Table 5.6 provide important clues as to the nature of partisanship in Israel. Age has had a consistent relationship with vote, with the young somewhat more likely to vote Likud, and the old, Labor. This relationship has been generally regarded as indicating generation rather than life-cycle effects (Abramson 1990). Yet it is important to note that this correlation peaked in 1977 (and 1973) and reached its nadir in 1992. The first reversal was led by the young: youth abandoned Labor for the promises of the Likud or the DMC. In 1992, the Likud was forsaken by both the young and the old. Even though young voters were more attracted by the right, it is also true that Labor was more successful than in the past in attracting voters across generations. Gender has never been related to vote choice in Israeli surveys.

Class differences mattered to a degree, although the correlations were not consistent and not very strong. There was usually no relationship between the Likud-Labor vote and income, but the income variable is not the best measure of class in Israel, as it is the kind of topic an Israeli is unlikely to discuss in an open manner with an interviewer-stranger. Two other measures of class, living density (the number of persons per room) and education, tell a different story.

Class differences appeared with the reversal of 1977, with lower-class voters abandoning Labor in favor of the Likud. Education gained in importance after 1981, with the return to Labor of more highly educated voters who had deserted for the DMC in 1977. This process of class stratification continued in the 1980s and was still in evidence in 1992, although over time the education variable was stronger than the living density indicator. But based on the inconsistent and not too strong correlations of the vote with class indicators, combined with the pattern of correlations between the vote and the socialist versus capitalistic views, the class cleavage does not seem to be the driving force behind electoral choice and change in Israel. Note that in 1992 there is virtually no relationship between voters' preferences as to the structure of the economy and their vote, and in 1977 the correlation was of the same magnitude as throughout the 1970s. Moreover, the responses to this question are to be seen more as an indicator of whether or not a voter belongs to the camp of socialism-Zionism socially, politically, and culturally, rather than of ideological commitment. And class is not the most potent correlate of the vote in Israel.

Ethnicity and religiosity are much stronger correlates of the vote. The critical election year for both is 1977. Before that year, both dimensions barely distinguished Labor voters from Likud voters. In 1977, they both became important. Religiosity gained in importance over time, reaching an all-time high in the 1992 election. The relationship between ethnicity and the vote reached its highest point in the 1984 election, and has receded since.

For the two reversal elections, 1977 and 1992, both sociodemographic factors and issue concerns were important, but their impact was very different. To summarize their respective roles, multiple regressions were calculated for each year to explain the Likud-Labor vote with blocs of explanatory variables of sociodemographics and of issues (all appearing in Table 5.6), as was done above for the switchers. The stepwise regression was again used twice, entering once the sociodemographic bloc first, and once, the issue bloc first.

It was possible to account better for the vote in 1992 than in 1977 with these variables (the total R^2 for 1992 was .37 and for 1977 it was .22). But more important, issues were dominant in the explanation of the 1992 vote to a much greater degree than the sociodemographic characteristics of the votes. When coming first in the regression, issues "explained" 30 percent of the variance of the vote in 1992, compared to 18 percent for the sociodemographics when they came first. In the full regression, the territories question had the strongest impact as measured by beta (.46); the other variables that achieved statistical significance were age, ethnic background, religiosity, and whether the respondent supported socialism or capitalism, with beats which ranged between .09 and .19.

The 1977 results were exactly the opposite: the R^2 for the bloc of sociodemographics alone was .18, compared to .11 for issues alone. In 1977 demography carried the weight, although the additional effect of the territories issue cannot be denied. In the full 1977 regression, three variables were statistically significant, with age, territories, and ethnicity each having betas around .20.

Ethnicity has been a very important theme of the first two generations of Israeli independence and has occupied a major place in social science studies of Israeli society and politics (see Shamir and Arian 1982; Smooha 1987; Diskin 1991; Ben-Rafael and Sharot 1991). The 1977 reversal and the ascent of the Likud and the right in Israeli politics have been attributed by many to the ethnic cleavage. It is therefore relevant to expand on this theme.

The social and political tension between ashkenazim and sephardim referred to as the "ethnic issue" emerged from the imbalances occasioned by the dominant community of European background in newborn Israel absorbing hundreds of thousands of immigrants from Asia and Africa in the years after independence in 1948. The terms themselves are related to different ritual practices and usage adopted by scattered Jewish communities. The ashkenazi-sephardi terms are very problematic and imprecise. Thus, for example, many Jewish communities of southern Europe were sephardim, while communities in the eastern Mediterranean, India, Yemen, and Ethiopia could not appropriately be put in either category. Especially in the last half of the twentieth century, flourishing sephardi communities have been established in the Americas and especially in France. On the other hand, ashkenazim lived in Egypt and China. Regardless of the misleading inaccuracies incorporated in the terms, this sephardi-ashkenazi nomenclature became part of the political reality of Israel and has emerged as a major theme in Israeli politics.

The theme, however, while still important, has changed. To begin with, the proportions of the groups in the population have changed over time. In 1977, the majority of the electorate was ashkenazim (53%), 43 percent were sephardim, and 4 percent were Israel-born with fathers also born in Israel. In the 1988 election, for the first time the Jews of sephardi background outnumbered the Jews of ashkenazi background in the electorate. In 1992, with the mass immigration from the former Soviet Union, most of which was of ashkenazi origin, the proportions were 48 percent ashkenazim, 44 percent sephardim, and 8 percent Israel-born whose fathers were also born in Israel.[7] As a larger percentage of Israeli Jews were native-born, this cleavage became more distant. As indicators, consider that a majority of Israeli Jewish voters and 90 percent of Jewish children in Israeli elementary schools at the beginning of the 1990s were native-born. They were exposed to a culture which downplayed – if it did not successfully alleviate the disparities – of these ethnic distinctions. The rate at which a member of one group married a member of the other group was a high and constant 20 percent. The number of children from these "mixed marriages" grew and the blurring of the term's clear meaning was heightened.

Beyond the label is the question of social and political meaning. Although fading, the labels are still of enormous importance. The major political parties vie to recruit politicians who could be presented as authentic leaders of these groups, and by 1992 the lists of both Labor and the Likud featured impressive and almost equal numbers of sephardi politicians. And yet, in spite of significant headway achieved by sephardim in and through politics, equality in terms of actual power was not achieved.

Two telling incidents involving the ethnic theme occurred during the 1992 campaign. One involved David Levy, then foreign minister in the Likud government. As the convention of his party determined their candidates for the Knesset and their positions on the Likud list, Levy did poorly in this preelection politicking. He contended ethnic discrimination and threatened to withdraw from the Likud and run on a separate list which would appeal to Likud voters of Moroccan descent. He was ultimately placated by being granted various concessions and promises, and he remained on the Likud list, but the incident rekindled the animosities common to Israeli politics in the 1980s and raised the question whether ethnicity had faded as an issue.

The second episode took place in the non-Zionist ultra-Orthodox haredi community. A venerated spiritual leader well into his 90s, Rabbi Eliezer Shach, pronounced that it was desirable to vote for the haredi-ashkenazi United Torah list rather than for the haredi-sephardi Shas list, because sephardi leaders had not yet developed sufficiently to be entrusted with political power. Incensed, many of the devout sephardi followers abandoned their rebbe and voted Shas, a list which met their desire to vote for an ultra-Orthodox party and satisfied their desire to identify with their slurred ethnic group. Perhaps Rabbi Shach had a correct theological point to make; his understanding of the social psychological correlates of electoral behavior in Israel, however, was imperfect.

Ethnicity matters in Israeli politics, just as it does in social spheres. Politicians of sephardi background are more obvious in both big parties, although often in places lower on the electoral lists submitted by the parties, and not in top positions. Ashkenazim still dominate much of the economy and bureaucracy, and while sephardim are abundant in numbers, on the whole they are in positions of lower status. Stubborn facts of the reality of Israel in the early 1990s were that ashkenazim continue to dominate in the two major parties and in the smaller parties of both right and left, and more broadly, in other social institutions such as the media, the armed forces, and the universities, while Jews in Israeli jails are still overwhelmingly sephardim, mostly North African, and especially Moroccans.

The ethnic cleavage manifested itself in voting behavior dramatically in the 1977 election when many voters abandoned their long-standing practice of supporting Labor. But they shifted largely along ethnic lines. Sephardim gravitated to the Likud, and ashkenazim to the DMC. These two defections so weakened Labor that the Likud could take over the reins of power, resulting in the beginning of the Likud era of Israeli politics. In 1981 and 1984 many of the ashkenazim were back with Labor, the campaigns were especially bitter and focused on the feelings of exploitation toward Labor felt by many sephardim. The ethnic vote was most pronounced in the 1984 elections, although the 1981 election campaign was most taken up with the ethnic cleavage.

As the proportion of sephardim grew in the electorate, it was clear that Labor would always have an uphill battle regaining power until it could increase its share of the sephardi vote. That shift occurred in 1992. The trend was not overwhelming, but the movement of sephardim to Labor was substantial enough to provide the bounce which Labor needed to regain power. This transformation worked only because it occurred in conjunction with two other things: the movement of other former supporters away from the Likud to parties of the right, and the impetus given Labor by the new Soviet immigrants who supported it.

The ethnic bounce which Labor received in 1992 is depicted in Table 5.7. Of those born in Asia and Africa or whose fathers were born there, 26 percent reported that they had decided to vote Labor in 1992. This was slightly lower than the 1977 rate (29%), but the sheer numerical increase of the sephardi population made the net electoral increase dramatic. At the same time, the Likud's share of this group was falling from 53 percent to 41 percent. So while it is accurate to report that the Likud did much better among sephardim than Labor did in 1992, the relative and absolute successes of Labor within this group must be considered to complete the picture. If we consider only Likud and Labor voters, Labor's share of the two party vote in 1992 was higher than in 1977. Moreover, the comparison between 1977 and 1992 is incomplete in another sense as well. In all the elections since 1977 the share of the Labor vote among sephardim continually decreased; only in 1992 did this share increase.

The group born in Israel whose fathers were also born in Israel is another important indicator of the fortunes of the parties. Likud was 20 percentage points less successful with these voters in 1992 compared with 1977, while Labor's draw was 9 points higher. To calculate the political significance of these figures, recall that the size of this group in the sample doubled in the course of the 15 years. Labor in 1992 did best among the shrinking group of ashkenazim (those who were born or whose fathers were born in Europe and America) at the rate of 47 percent of their vote, but Likud's support was minuscule at 16 percent.

Looked at the other way by considering the contribution of each group to the electoral fortunes of the parties (see Table 5.7B), a fascinating picture

Table 5.7. *Ethnicity and Voting Behavior 1977 and 1992*

			Respondent or father born in:		
			Asia-Africa	Europe-America	Both in Israel
A. % Voting for (ethnicity by vote; other vote choices not reported):					
Likud	1977		53	20	44
	1992		41	16	24
Labor	1977		29	40	26
	1992		26	47	37
DMC	1977		12	26	20
Meretz	1992		6	20	18
Right	1992		19	10	13
Religious	1977		5	11	9
	1992		8	8	8
B. Contribution of group to (vote by ethnicity; percentages sum horizontally):					
Likud	1977	($N = 305$)	52	38	10
	1992	($N = 297$)	68	21	11
Labor	1977	($N = 337$)	26	69	5
	1992	($N = 356$)	35	50	15
DMC	1977	($N = 202$)	18	75	6
Meretz	1992	($N = 129$)	23	57	19
Right	1992	($N = 148$)	64	24	12
Religious	1977	($N = 83$)	17	76	7
	1992	($N = 81$)	51	36	14

emerges. Likud in 1992 was more heavily sephardi than in 1977, with two-thirds of its votes coming from that group in 1992 compared with about half in 1977; Labor was much more balanced, with half its voters ashkenazim, a third sephardim, and the rest second-generation Israelis. The Likud came close to being left only with its hard-core supporters, while Labor in 1992 was able to enlarge the circle of its voters.

The conclusions regarding other parties confirm many of the trends just discussed. Meretz did more than three times better among ashkenazim and second-generation Israelis than among sephardim, and the parties of the right were twice as popular among sephardim than they were among ashkenazim. The religious parties drew equally from all ethnic groups in 1992, very different from their 1977 pattern, which showed strong support among ashkenazim.

Most of Meretz's support came from ashkenazim, similar to the 3 out of 4 rate of the DMC in 1977. Two-thirds of the voters for the parties of the right in 1992 were sephardim. The most notable shift was for the religious parties. They successfully adapted to the demographic shifts in Israel after

1977. From a situation in which three quarters of their vote came from ashkenazim, in 1992 half their vote was sephardi, one-third ashkenazi, and 1 in 7 was a second-generation Israeli. The pattern of their support was almost identical to the distribution in the general population. This is a political achievement of enormous magnitude; had one of the large parties been able to achieve such a distribution of appeal at a high level, its electoral victory would have been massive.

An important determinant of the 1992 election result was the blunting of the high degree of support that sephardim gave the Likud. As seen in Table 5.6, the correlation between ethnicity and the Likud-Labor vote was still high in 1992 at .35, although lower than the peak 1984 correlation of .54. It was enough for certain slippage to take place; coupled with the flow of Likud supporters to the right and the influx of Labor supporters from the new immigrants, the added support for Labor was sufficient.

VALENCE, POSITION, AND WEDGE ISSUES

Candidates in democracies often couch policy in a vague manner, partly because future conditions can only be estimated, and partly because being overly specific may antagonize potential supporters. They would prefer to stress valence issues, but campaigns sometimes force them to deal with position issues; the former is related to high levels of agreement, the latter to conflict (Stokes 1963). Peace and unemployment are classic valence issues: all agree that it is good to have the former, bad to have the latter. Party strategists prefer to stress valence issues so as not to alienate important segments of the electorate. In such cases the contest is over images, over which party or leader is perceived to be better able to achieve the desired value, such as peace or prosperity.

Elections are sometimes portrayed as a contest over position issues, and the 1992 election is a good example. It was seen by many observers as a referendum over the future of the territories, and its results as a rebuttal of the not-one-inch position of the greater Israel ideology. This reading is inappropriate for two reasons. First, it ignores the one-vote many-issues dilemma, in which a voter is called on to assess all of public policy, and the future of the country, and the ability of the leadership, among other things, all with one vote. Why assume that it is this one issue, important though it admittedly is, which drives every vote? Second, it accepts the central assumption of the spatial theory of voting, an assumption which is seriously flawed. The spatial theory holds that voters are located at some point in a hypothetical policy space, that these voters can identify where the candidates or competing parties are in terms of that space, and that the voters choose the candidate or party closest to their positions. More likely, many voters fail to see issues in a sharp positional manner, and perceive them policy options in a diffuse, emotionally laden, symbolic manner (Rabinowitz and MacDonald 1989; Rabinowitz, MacDonald, and Listhaug 1991).

The proximity assumption of the spatial model indicates that one will vote for the candidate or party whose opinion is closest to that of the voter's. The directional model posits that most people have a diffuse preference for a certain direction of policy making and that people vary in the intensity with which they hold those preferences. As if writing about the Israeli case (their work is actually about American politics), Rabinowitz and MacDonald conclude that a democratic system can allow for almost random turnover of policy because of a paradox of democratic political systems. Mass publics fail to control policy because of the lack of issue voting, thus giving the elite latitude in decision making. Yet policy making tends to follow mass policy preferences. How does this relationship come about?

The directional model resolves this apparent paradox. Directional theory predicts no policy control when the electorate is evenly divided. Under that circumstance successful candidates can favor a wide range of policies. However, when there is a clear majority preferring an option, a politician favoring that preference will be advantaged. Thus directional theory predicts considerable control by the mass under certain circumstances and absolute lack of control in other circumstances.

Rather ironically, mass control does not require high levels of issue voting. Issue voting occurs when politicians present different issue directions with sufficient intensity. An evenly divided and highly polarized electorate is the condition that should generate the most issue voting and the least real control of policy. Under this condition elections are virtual lotteries because the two sides cancel each other out, yet the policy consequences of the outcome are likely to be substantial. The election thus legitimates an "experiment" in a certain public policy. (1991, 115)

How accurate a description of the Israeli system! The vote is the important ingredient in determining who will decide, but not in determining the direction policy will take.

There was increased issue voting in Israel, as evidenced by the growth in the correlation between the territories issue and the vote for Likud-Labor between 1969 and 1992. But that does not necessarily imply that the salience of the territories issue was always the important factor in each of the elections. There were elections in which the electorate perceived internal rather than security considerations as the major driver of the campaign (see Figure 5.3). The 1981 and 1984 elections focused on domestic issues and were charged with ethnic overtones. They coincided with the pre-Lebanon and pre-intifada periods, respectively, and reflected the period in which Israeli security policy seemed most arrogant and cocky.

The open-ended question asked was "What is the most important problem facing the government?" and respondents gave a range of answers, here recoded as security- and peace-related, on the one hand, and related to

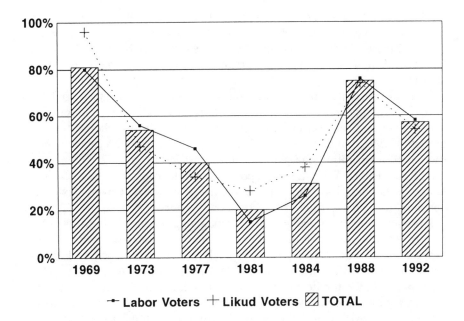

Figure 5.3. Security versus peace as major vote issue, 1969–1992.

domestic issues, on the other. These questions, asked shortly before the upcoming elections, provide a sense of the issues on the mind of the electorate. What is fascinating to note is the universal impact of the mood of the times on the voters of the two largest parties. Coming from the same political environment, these voters basically reacted in the same manner. One could imagine Likud voters being much more security-conscious, for example, and Labor party voters stressing a domestic agenda. But this did not happen. The striking feature of Figure 5.3 is that both groups shifted together over time. Likud voters were more likely than Labor supporters to mention domestic issues in the 1973 and 1977 elections before the Likud came to power, and they were more likely than Labor voters to mention security and peace issues in 1981 and 1984, years in which the Likud was in power. But what is even more arresting is that the swing of the curves was simultaneous, indicating strong societal forces at work rather than partisan, parochial ones.

While analysts can categorize issues as being valence or position, party strategists are anxious to find issues – wedge issues – which will split the opposing camp and make at least some former supporters of the other side amenable to appeals to change their vote. The wedge issue has a time-honored placed in political thought and practice. James Madison (1792) wrote that parties seek "to weaken their opponents by reviving exploded parties, and taking advantage of all prejudices, local, political, and occupational, that may prevent or disturb a general coalition of sentiments." Schattschneider (1975, 67) caught the same spirit when he observed, "The effort in all political struggle is to exploit cracks in the opposition while attempting to consolidate one's own side."

Such wedge issues may be crosscutting position issues which split the opponent's supporters, an example of which would be the relations between state and religion in Israeli politics. Labor did not choose this approach in 1992, but Tzomet did. Wedge issues may also be valence issues, such as the corruption charges leveled against Labor in 1977, and against the Likud in 1992. Whether using position or valence issues, the tactic is to place the issue high enough on the public agenda that it overrides other concerns for at least some of the opponent's voters.

Another strategy of wedge issue campaigning relates to priorities. One may try to lure voters on the basis of a different priority set rather than a different issue position or party image. Labor took this tack in 1992 by emphasizing its different order of priorities, denouncing the Likud's settlement policy in the territories on the basis of allocating too much of Israel's limited resources to the wrong target, rather than attacking the merits of retaining the territories. Contrasting its program with the Likud's policies of pouring resources into the West Bank and Gaza settlements, Labor promised to invest in infrastructure, education, welfare, and creating jobs within Israel. This line of argument could appeal not only to Likud voters with more conciliatory attitudes toward the territories, but also to hard-line voters who were not willing to give up territories but who felt that their direct concerns of employment and opportunity were being neglected because of the Likud government's order of priorities.

Wedge issues may be defined by differences in the direction and intensity of electoral behavior and attitudes for various voting groups. One aspect of this can be ascertained by asking whether or not a series of items affected the vote decision.[8] Items are ranked on this dimension in Table 5.8 in descending order for the total sample, and then for four groups of voters: those who voted for Labor in both 1988 and 1992, those who chose Likud in 1988 and Labor in 1992, Likud twice, and Likud in 1988 to parties of the right in 1992. Of the eight issues, the differences among the voting groups were statistically significant only for three.

Wedge issues appeal disproportionately to one group but not to others. Those 1988 Likud voters who switched to Labor mentioned the Likud's settlement policy and the intifada more often as a factor in their vote decision than other groups of voters, and these were major wedge issues in Labor's campaign strategy. The intifada was dealt with indirectly, in valence terms, by reference to "personal security," which under the Likud had seemed to

Table 5.8. *Influence of Issues on the 1992 Vote (in %)*

Issues	Total population (N = 1,192)	Labor88 Labor92 (N = 227)	Likud88 Labor92 (1) (N = 44)	Likud88 Likud92 (2) (N = 227)	Likud88 Right92 (N = 40)	Spread (1 minus 2)
Intifada	86	(90[a]	96	85	94)	11
Unemployment	81	(86	84	78	81)	3
Handling of peace talks	78	(84	84	83	86)	1
Beginning of peace talks	74	(80	73	83	83)	-10
Corruption	74	81	91	68	61	23
Likud settlement policy	72	79	84	67	72	17
Immigrant absorption	69	(76	68	69	72)	-1
Relations with U.S.A.	62	74	63	59	39	4

[a] Using the chi-square test, differences are statistically significant above .05 level except for those in parentheses.

deteriorate. The settlements, too, were attacked not directly but, rather, in terms of the Likud's distorted order of priorities. Regardless of Labor's strategy to frame these themes in terms of a valence issue or in terms of priorities, the position element could not be taken out. On the basis of the question reported in Table 5.8 it is not possible to distinguish among these various aspects. The intifada and the settlements issues worked on both position and valence levels. Jewish Israelis wanted to see an end to the intifada, and wanted more money spent on such things as education, health, and jobs within Israel. Yet by the very mention of these issues, one was likely to elicit a position preference as well regarding the territories.

Displeasure with immigrant absorption and with relations with the United States were two other valence issues of the campaign. Yet on the basis of the importance attached to them by the different voting groups, they should not be considered wedge issues in 1992. About 70 percent of the sample said that the question of immigrant absorption had had an effect on their vote, but there were almost no differences among the voting groups. As to the state of the relations with the United States, the picture was somewhat more complex. Shamir and the Likud had refused American requests to halt settlement construction in the territories, and Washington countered by refusing to grant guarantees for the $10 billion loans which Israel wished to take for the absorption of the Soviet immigrants. This item discriminated best among former Likud voters who went to the right, for whom the issue was not important, and other former Likud voters. It was most important for loyal Labor voters. The issue was not at all potent in luring Likud supporters to Labor; it did not distinguish between 1988 Likud voters who stayed with Likud and those who moved to Labor.

Corruption was the best example of a wedge issue in the 1992 election if judged by the size of the difference in importance attached to it. Generally speaking, the corruption issue operates in this manner in elections in many countries and is a wedge issue that the opposition tries to use against the party in government. Before the 1992 elections, the state controller issued a series of scathing attacks on government ministries and the corruption issue played a prominent role in the campaign against the Likud. Two-thirds of those who voted Likud in 1988 and chose Likud again, and 61 percent who moved to the right in 1992, said that the corruption issue had influenced their choice. But for those who moved from Likud to Labor, 91 percent mentioned corruption as an influence, compared with 81 percent who chose Labor both times. The differential between Likud loyalists and voters who switched to Labor on this item is the largest (23 points). The corruption issue was significant in prying voters away from the Likud and to Labor, according to their own account. This is an echo of the 1977 race in which a very high 62 percent of DMC voters who had voted Labor in 1973, and 44 percent of the 1977 Likud voters who chose Labor in 1973, said that corruption had affected their choice, compared with only 16 percent among Labor loyalists (see Table 5.4).

To provide information on the direction of preference and to distinguish between valence or position or priority considerations, respondents were asked another series of questions about whether the government should spend more, less, or about the same as it does for each of several topics.[9] For two of the most important areas of the Likud coalition – religious institutions and yeshivot, and the settlements in the territories – the expenditures were seen as undesirable (see Table 5.9). Jobs, education, and health, on the other hand, were very popular. The public wanted a new ordering of priorities, which Labor represented well in its campaign strategy.

It is clear from Table 5.9 that the settlements were the major wedge issue of the 1992 elections. The differential score of 75 is huge, and this is the only issue area on which one side (1992 Labor voters) as a group wanted less spending and the other side (1992 Likud-right voters) wanted more spending. This trade-off between spending in the territories and spending on other domestic matters was raised by Labor and the left in previous elections, but not as a major theme. It only caught fire in the 1992 campaign, and it did make a difference. Recalling that the disparity in the position issue of territorial concessions between 1992 Labor and Likud voters who voted Likud in 1988 was 42 points (see Table 5.3), it would seem that the practical matter of expenditures in the territories made a difference

Table 5.9. *Differences Between "Spend More" and "Spend Less," 1992*

Issues	Total population ($N = 1,192$)	Labor88 Labor92 ($N = 227$)	Likud88 Labor92 (1) ($N = 44$)	Likud88 Likud92 (2) ($N = 227$)	Likud88 Right92 ($N = 40$)	Spread (1 minus 2)
New jobs	89[a]	(90[b]	96	88	86)	8
Education	83	90	82	75	75	7
Health	75	81	84	76	60	8
Security	60	(61	73	70	70)	3
Immigrant absorption	34	(40	34	21	39)	13
Unemployed	33	22	36	41	34	-5
Ecology	20	42	11	-3	10	14
Settlements	-29	-70	-59	16	25	-75
Religious institutions and yeshivot	-61	-87	-84	-44	-50	-40

[a] The numbers reported are the results of subtracting the percent saying "spend more" from the percent saying "spend less." The statistical significance of the differences was tested using the chi-square test on the basic cross-tabulations. Differences were statistically significant above .05 level except for those in parentheses. The spread is the gap between these results for groups (1) and (2).

[b] Using the chi-square test, differences are statistically significant above .05 level except for those in parentheses.

beyond the position issue of the territories. This notion was tested using the same method introduced before to assess the relative impact of issues and sociodemographics. Two stepwise regressions were run on the Likud-Labor vote, using as predictors positions on the territories and desirable level of expenditure for the settlements.[10] Using both the R^2s and the beta measures from the regression with both predictors, it was found that policy positions were clearly more important than the priorities question in the total population, although priorities made a significant additional contribution. Among 1988 Likud voters, both variables had a similar effect on the vote. These results support the supposition that the question of expenditures on settlements mattered beyond the issue of the future of the territories and operated as a wedge issue in the 1992 election.

Expenditures for religious institutions and yeshivot were found to be another wedge issue in 1992. The differential score of 40 points was also very high. Using the same stepwise regression analysis just described, the expenditures and the policy questions had similar-sized effects on the vote in the general sample, with the former somewhat stronger. Among Likud voters, level of expenditure for religious institutions was more important than the attitude on the issue.[11]

PARTY IMAGES AND CANDIDATES

Issues were found to be central to the 1977 and 1992 turnovers, in particular the issue of the territories. The relevance of issue positions and the potency of priorities relating to these positions will be developed in Chapter 8. Another key aspect of voting behavior involves prospective evaluations of the competing parties – the answer to the question "Who can deliver?" (Fiorina 1981; Miller and Wattenberg 1985).

Prospective evaluations have been found to be very important in explaining both the 1988 and 1992 election results in other multivariate analyses (Shamir and Arian 1990; Shachar and Shamir 1995). The analysis of the 1988 elections sorted out short-term (intifada related) from long-term (the future of the territories) aspects, and pointed to the latter as the more potent one for voting behavior. The analysis regarding 1992 distinguished between the security aspect and the economic one and showed the former as the crucial one. Taking all these analyses together, it is clear that the images of the parties in terms of their ability to achieve goals that are generally favored by the electorate are significant factors in voting behavior. The dimension which mattered related to the Israeli-Arab conflict and the future of the territories, as seen by the items of putting an end to the intifada and striving for peace. Prospective evaluations – primarily but not only in areas relating to the future of the territories – were a significant factor in the 1992 voting patterns. They complemented other issue considerations such as the positions held by voters on whether to compromise or not on the territories, and their priorities in budget allocations in the territories rather than within Israel. All these concerns taken together present a picture of an electorate which is very much issue-driven.

Respondents have been asked over the years to evaluate which political party (Labor or Likud) would best be able to achieve different goals. Such questions are, of course, heavily loaded with party identification, and can only be meaningfully analyzed in multivariate analysis or comparatively across groups of voters and across items. The array based on the 1994 survey is presented in Figure 5.4. In the 1992, 1993, and 1994 surveys, Labor was perceived as better able than the Likud to secure true peace, and democracy. The Likud was perceived as better able than Labor to secure a Jewish majority, land and peace, and quiet and order in the territories. These were dramatic changes from the 1988, 1990, and 1991 surveys in which the Likud led in all categories.

Evaluations relating to the securing of true peace and the preservation of democracy were the elements that have changed the most since 1988, to the detriment of the Likud. This gives us a measure of changing mood in the country, and also attests to the issues which swayed many of the switchers during this period. The bold prominence of the bars in Figure 5.5

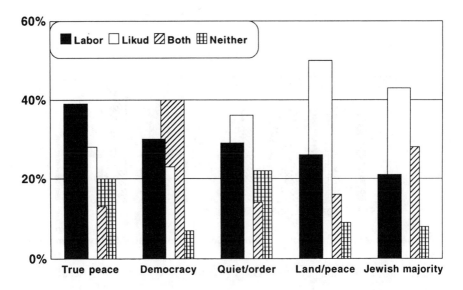

Figure 5.4. Party images, 1994. ("Which party will better secure true peace . . . ?")

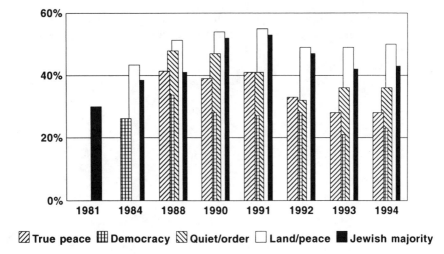

Figure 5.5. Likud image, 1981–1994. ("Which party will better secure true peace . . . ?")

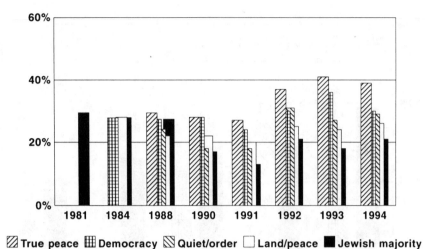

Figure 5.6. Labor image, 1981–1994. ("Which party will better secure true peace . . . ?")

provide a symbolic referent of the Likud image in those years. By contrast, the bars for Labor on the same scale seemed shrinking and meek (see Figure 5.6). Only toward the end of the period, in 1992, 1993, and 1994, was there an upward slope in the pattern. But the overall impression was that the resurgence of Labor was tenuous and could quickly be reversed.

6

A People Apart

The onus of Israel's security position was obvious. The country faced the seemingly undying enmity of most of its neighbors, prepared for and fought war after war, devoted a very large part of its population and financial resources to the imperatives of security (Brecher 1972; Horowitz 1982; Peri 1983). Geography and demography produced a very difficult security posture. The perception of threat was very real.

The reality of the Israeli situation – and certainly its rhetoric – was of a nation threatened. The clear feeling of basic mistrust regarding the international environment is a basic feature of the foreign and security policy of Israel. There is a fundamental belief that in the final analysis the world will do nothing to protect Jews, as individuals, as a collectivity, as a state. This is why the Holocaust was possible and why, if it depended on the world at large, the Holocaust could happen again. The fact that 82 percent of the 1986 sample expressed the opinion that a Holocaust is again unlikely seemed to be related to their faith in the Israel Defense Forces and not to their belief that the Gentiles had changed.

Early political leaders set the tone. While making enormous achievements in social and economic spheres in prestate Palestine, the Zionist leadership appeared stuck on the observation that the major actors in the international arena seemed to react to the Jews in a manner similar to what Jews had experienced elsewhere and before. For the Jews who had come from Europe, the only difference seemed to be that the enemy was now Arab-Muslim instead of European-Christian; for those who came from Muslim lands, the behavior of the local Arabs seemed consistent with the distance they had often experienced in the lands they left. The high hopes of the early years of settlement vanished, and by the 1930s an immediate physical threat was felt by Jews in both Europe and Palestine. The new motif, which has become a lasting element in the Zionist ideology since that time, was the basic similarity in the security threat faced by Jews everywhere, whether in their sovereign state of Israel or in the Diaspora.

In her autobiography, Golda Meir relates her fears as a child of a pogrom in her native Kiev – a pogrom which in the end did not take place. She felt that her conclusions based on that distant non-happening were relevant at all times and places: "That pogrom did not take place at all, but to this day I remember how frightened I was and how angry I was that the only thing my father could do to protect me as I waited for the bullies to come was to nail some planks on the door. And more than anything else I remember the feeling that this is happening to me only because I am Jewish. . . . That was a feeling which I felt many times in my life – the fear, the feeling of being downcast, the awareness of being different and the deep instinctive belief that a person who wants to stay alive had better do something about it" (Meir 1975, 11).

When David Ben-Gurion resigned as prime minister in 1953 he made a speech which stressed the total and constant hostility of the outside world: "We took upon ourselves a mighty three-pronged struggle: a struggle with ourselves, with our Diaspora mentality, unworthy habits and a weak structure of life of a nation without a homeland, scattered and dependent on the favors of others; a struggle with the nature of the land, its desolation, its poverty and its ruins by the hand of man and of God; a struggle against forces of evil and hatred in the world, far and near, that did not understand and did not want to understand the uniqueness and the wondrous mission of our nation since we stepped onto the stage of history in ancient times until these very days" (Ben-Gurion 1965, 11).

Abba Eban – known as one of Israel's more moderate and less emotional leaders – describes the condition of Israel on the eve of the 1967 Six Days war as follows: "The chilling wind of vulnerability penetrated to every corner of the Israeli consciousness. When we looked out at the world we saw it divided between those who wanted to see us destroyed and those who would not raise a finger to prevent it from happening" (Eban 1972, 180). This from a man who knew well the diplomatic stage and its major actors, who could not be accused of chronic xenophobia or deep fear of the Gentile. We get a glimpse through Eban of the depth of the feelings of threat and persecution in the worldview of the Israeli.

Even Meir Yaari, a leader of Mapam (a left-wing socialist party), whose platform called for coexistence with the Arabs, admitted that at least some Arabs were not interested in the continued existence of the State of Israel. In his book *Tests of Our Time* he writes, "The Arab reactionaries in neighboring countries never accepted the existence of the state of Israel, just as they had never accepted the immigration of Jews to the country. . . . I repeat: none of us disagrees that the state of Israel is surrounded in the present, just as it has been surrounded during all the years of its existence, with provocations and aggressive schemes on the part of the ruling groups in the neighboring countries" (1957, 116, 121).

Central to the ideology of groups on the right of the political spectrum was the role played by the Holocaust and the light it shed on the nature of man in general and the treatment which Jews in particular could expect from the Gentiles. In his book *The Revolt*, Menachem Begin writes: "Ask the Jews: Is it possible to destroy a people? Is it possible to annihilate millions of people in the twentieth century? And what will the 'world' say? The innocent ones! It is hard to believe, but even in the twentieth century it is possible to destroy an entire people; and if the annihilated people happens to be Jewish, the world will be silent and will behave as it usually behaves" (1950, 36). The operative conclusion based on this description is clear: "The world does not pity the victims; it respects the warriors. Good or bad – that is how it is" (p. 50). The motif of the Holocaust continued to play a central role in the conception and rhetoric of Menachem Begin, of the Herut party which he founded and led, and of the Likud governments which he and Yitzhak Shamir headed.[1]

Threat is not an abstract conception; it is anchored in specific political situations. But the mind-set of being a people apart, of going it alone – relying on oneself, on the military strength of Israel, on the Jewish people, and on God – was central in explaining the relations between perceived threat and policy position. By exploring these interrelationships, it will be shown that the ideology of going it alone was directly related to policy, and that it tended to drive those who perceived threat to an inflexible policy position.

PATTERNS OF THOUGHT AND BELIEF

Rationality

The schism which has characterized Israeli politics since the Six Days war is one of worldview and mind-set as much as it is one of policy and social class. The confounding feature of the situation is that these factors penetrate one another and so far have prevented the emergence of a leadership which can claim the allegiance of both sides of the camp. One side's rationality is the other side's foolhardiness or cowardice; the abstract notions used in the debate feed both points of view.

The truth of the matter is that the Jewish population shared many values and most policy positions. Divisions also existed, and they were real; moveover, it was reasonable for politicians, journalists, and observers to focus on them, but this focus overlooked the overarching agreement – the ideological glue – which permitted the system to move ahead. Only by recalling that most politicians operated in the ooze of the accepted values can we understand how political change could have occurred during the period.

The complex psychological backdrop to the prolonged conflict characterizing the Israeli experience was a set of widely shared values which will be identified as the People Apart Syndrome. It identified and sanctified Israel as a people with unique challenges and opportunities. It was a secular nationalist extension of the biblical covenant of the notion of the chosen people. This People Apart Syndrome is the catechism of Israel's religion of security, itself a major element of the country's political culture (Herman 1977; Liebman and Don-Yehiya 1983).

Religion often flourishes in periods of uncertainty; as the vision of the future is upsetting, people turn to a superior force for comfort. The defense future of Israel is uncertain enough to warrant a restless search for assurance from natural – or even supernatural – sources to aid in grappling with it. A solution to a mystery is sought.

Israel's security is such a pervasive preoccupation in the country and the resources that it demands are so large, it is not surprising that the Israeli public has developed unique ways of dealing with it. On the symbolic and psychological levels, there are the Almighty and the Jewish people; on the level of rationality and professionalism, there are the Israel Defense Forces, the Mossad, the Shin Bet (General Security Service), and Israel's other security institutions. Together they make up a complex mosaic which is at the heart of the religion of security.

This religion of security is based on deep-seated core beliefs about the nature and destiny of Israel and the Jewish people. These values are at the heart of the Israelis' orientation to security. The organization of attitudes incorporates elements which have an instrumental orientation with those which have a mystical one. There seems to be a basic coexistence between a rational model of security policy which posits predictable relations between means and ends, on the one hand, and beliefs which deny basic tenets of instrumental rationality, on the other (Mannheim 1949; Richards 1971; Ryan 1972; Lukes 1974; Weber 1978; Majtabai 1986). Many Israelis seem to blend these two kinds of beliefs: about making definable efforts and thereby achieving observed ends, and about divine intervention and historical determinism.

Israel's religion of security is a mix of deeply held beliefs based on nationalist and religious symbolism, on the one hand, and rational and professional considerations on the other. Rationality in the sense used here has to do with a realistic probability calculation based on available data; irrationality would be characterized by an unrealistic probability estimate

(Simon 1985). This implies that the rational determination will employ rules of evidence and inference while the irrational one will employ other means to reach conclusions (Jervis 1976, 119). The religion has its dogmas, its scripture, its priests, its festivals, its processions, and its ceremonial garb. These are manifested in the doctrines and orders, the generals, parades, and uniforms of the Israeli army. Many of these are typical of all armies, but for the Jewish army they also relay the messages of the horror of the Holocaust, the mysteries of Masada, and messianism. The entire nation participates, as when the air-raid sirens become audible memorials on days of mourning to the victims of World War II and Israeli soldiers and civilians killed in the line of duty. The lines between emotion and goal-oriented function seem to blur when the sirens blare.

For all the fireworks that opposing political positions inspired, the intriguing finding was that almost half (47%) of Israelis[2] thought that Israel's policies were always or generally rational, as opposed to irrational. In the questionnaire, rationality was defined as policy guided by logic, and irrationality as policy guided by feeling and belief. Another large group (42%) answered that the policy was sometimes rational and sometimes irrational. Only 11 percent felt that Israeli policy was always or almost always irrational. When the same concepts were applied to Arab states, 23 percent felt that they were always or generally rational, 37 thought that they were sometimes rational and sometimes irrational, and 40 percent declared them always or generally irrational. The correlation between the two was .15 and was statistically significant above the .001 level.

Threat was related to thinking the Arabs states irrational, dovishness to the feeling that it was the Israeli government that pursued irrational policy. This is an important finding, because it also means that those with low threat more likely considered the policies of Arab states rational, while the hawks of 1987 thought of Israel's policies as rational. Threat impacted on perceptions of the rationality of the enemy, policy position on the assessment of Israel's rationality. None of the correlations was very high, but the two which were statistically significant above the .001 level were between the threat score and the rationality of the Arab states (.17), and between the policy score (low score means a dovish position) and Israel's rationality (−.12) When the survey was conducted in 1987 the National Unity government reigned, and Yitzhak Shamir of the Likud was prime minister. Accordingly, the correlation between the rationality questions and the vote was very low. Voters of the Likud, Labor, and many on the right graded Israel's policy as rational because all of these parties were represented in the government. Threat perceptions were significantly related to feelings that the Arab states were irrational, but much more weakly related to assessments that Israel's policy was rational. Policy scale score and vote decision were related to the evaluation that Israel's policy was rational, but much less associated with the judgment that the policies of the Arab states were irrational.

Religion

It would be natural to point to religious thought as the antithesis of rational thought. Based on belief and transcendental sources, a pattern of religious thought would stress hierarchy, authority, and revelation. The distinction is important, but unfortunately we are dealing with imperfect measures of rational and religious thought. In the last section, rationality was measured by assessment of policies; religion will be measured in this section by observance and policy preference, not by the manner in which a nonrational thought process deals with reality. Religion will be used as the antipode of rationality. In both cases, the measurements are close to the concepts under study; not perfect, but the best available.

Religion in Israel is highly politicized in Israel and must be considered in three separate spheres, the cultural, the personal, and the political:

1. At the *cultural* level, Israel is a Jewish state. Whatever that means to different actors and parties, a basic fact of Israeli life is that the Bible, the Hebrew language and calendar, the geography of Israel, and Jewish holy days play a central role in the shared culture for religious, secular, and those in between.
2. *Personal* religious observance does not necessarily lead to a political conclusion, although empirically, religious observance is more closely related to opinions supporting the establishment of religion as a public influence, to hawkishness, and to voting for parties of the right. Still, being the Great Book that it is, the Bible is replete with quotations which can justify many political conclusions, and levels of religious observance (public or private) are to be found in every camp.
3. In a *political* sense, support for applying Jewish law as a guide for Israeli public life is an important dimension of the role of religion in the state. Since "Jewish law" means *halacha* (Orthodox rabbinical law), it is not surprising that support for its promulgation is strongest among the observant.

Israeli public life is governed by a "status quo" agreement worked out at the time of independence and still in effect. In reality the interpretation of the status quo fluctuates depending on the bargaining strengths of the parties. Politically, Jewish Orthodox religious parties have always been included in government coalitions and, because of their pivotal role between the two large parties, their political power has generally been perceived to be greater than the size of their delegation in the Knesset.

The delegation of many aspects of personal and public life to the control of religious rules and rabbinical regulators was decided upon by the secular Knesset; these practices are reinforced by cultural norms and by habit. These areas of control include marriage and divorce, rest days (Sabbath

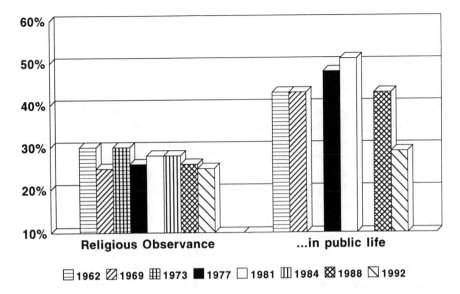

Figure 6.1. Religion: Personal observance compared to public conception, 1962–1992.

and holy days), and the observance of dietary laws in facilities supported by public funds.

During the decades under study, from the 1960s into the 1990s, the shared cultural dimension and the degree of personal religious observance in the country appear to be remarkably stable. On the public level, by contrast, variation is the rule and it seems to reflect a desire not to allow either the religious or the seculars to have a clear advantage. Thus, for example, seculars perceived that the power of religious parties increased during that period, and the degree of support for instituting Jewish law in public life declined.

The stability of the rate of personal observance and the volatility of the public aspect of religion are shown in Figure 6.1. Between 1962 and 1992, despite enormous change along most dimensions of Israel's existence, the rate of those responding that they observe "all" or "most" of Jewish religious law is amazingly stable at 25–30 percent. The other responses provided were "some" and "none." These numbers are consistent with the estimate that about a quarter of Israelis are observant in an Orthodox sense or even beyond that, including 6–10 percent haredi, or ultra-Orthodox; that about 40 percent are determinedly secular; and that the rest are somewhere between those poles. Also important to note is that about 15 percent of Israeli voters select Jewish Orthodox parties, and about a quarter of Jewish school children are enrolled in state-financed religious schools.

By contrast, support for having the government see to it that public life in Israel be administered in accordance with Jewish religious law oscillated from a high of 51 percent in 1981 to a low of 29 percent in 1992, with an average of 41.[3] The 1981 election was the first that both sides thought the other had a chance of winning. In 1977, Labor was on the ropes, but the Likud victory came as a total surprise to many. By 1981, the stakes were perceived to be very high because the race seemed to be a toss-up, and the campaign polarized the electorate. In fact, 1981 led to the highest total number of seats for the two biggest parties (95 of 120; 48 for Likud, 47 for Labor) ever achieved in Israeli political history. These elections were highlighted by nasty confrontation with ethnic overtones. In the public mind (fortified by survey research results), sephardim supported the Likud and religion, and ashkenazim were more likely for Labor and a secular style of life.

By 1992, a more generalized anti-Likud mood had set in. The Likud-right-religious government which followed the collapse of the National Unity government in 1990 was considered as extreme right-wing as any Israel ever had. Religious parties and their demands evidently merged in the minds of many voters with frustration with the limping economy, the failure to absorb the immigrants streaming in from the Soviet Union, the tensions with the United States over settlement policy and loan guarantees, the continuing Arab uprising, and feelings of lowered personal security.

MECHANISMS FACILITATING TENACITY

How do Israelis persevere in a mental frame that contains feelings of threat and confidence in overcoming? What mechanisms are used to facilitate holding these two sets of beliefs? How are these belief patterns distributed within various sectors of Israeli society?

Israelis have been able to achieve cognitive harmony between feelings of being threatened and of believing in the country's ability to overcome (Festinger 1957; Heider 1958; McGuire 1985). Four operative mechanisms seem to be dominant: perceived success, denial, differentiation, and a belief system called here the People Apart Syndrome.

Perceived Success: The Importance of U.S. Aid

The Israeli record, it could be argued, is a record of success; therefore no dissonance is perceived between threat and the ability to overcome. That Israelis feel secure in a very threatening situation is the heart of the duality which exists in Israel. They have withstood more than 45 years of military, economic, and political challenge, and they have posted an impressive array of victories. Not only that, since the middle 1970s, the United States has been a generous and consistent patron, supplying about $3 billion yearly.

After a period in the 1950s in which there was some indecision regarding the side Israel should be on in the cold war, siding with the West was considered understandable in terms of the Soviet Union's very cool treatment of Israel and in light of the economic and political support of the United States and American Jewry, and Israeli commitment to Western-style democracy. Israel's participation in the defense arrangements which the United States was setting up in the region was rejected, as much because the Americans did not want to strain their relations with the Arab states of the region – who were seen as important American assets – as because of Israeli reasons. Israel then sought relations with Europe, and primarily with France, who was a staunch ally and a supplier of military equipment from the 1950s until the middle of the 1960s, when de Gaulle closed the supply lines because of disapproval of Israeli policy.

The post-1967 period brought close relations with the United States, which reached a pinnacle during the Yom Kippur war when the American airlift provided needed material to the Israeli army. Although there have been periodic crises in the bilateral relations, the basic theme of Israeli foreign affairs since 1967 has been to maintain close relations with the United States government, regardless which party was in power in Washington or in Jerusalem.

The obverse of the warm relations toward the West was the very cold relations with the Soviet Union. This distance was primarily a reflection of the negative role, from Israel's point of view, which the Kremlin played in the Middle East. On the eve of the Six Days war, Eban (1972, 146) felt that the "Moscow-Damascus equation was the heart of the Israeli dilemma. The most wild and aggressive enemies of Israel operated under the giant shadow of Soviet defense." It was agreed that the Soviet Union under Gorbachev would be a co-sponsor of the Madrid peace talks; soon after, the Soviet Union no longer existed and Russia remained in that capacity. Normal relations were renewed.

Israelis expressed very high levels of support for the United States and believed in its continued commitment to Israel. This was especially noteworthy because of the cynicism and skepticism which are important features of Israel's political culture. Relations between the two states were seen as extremely favorable in the 1987 survey, with more than 8 in 10 reporting a very good or good opinion of the United States, and the relations between the United States and Israel were perceived as very good or good. Seventy-three percent were convinced that Israel could rely on the United States to continue to supply arms.

Table 6.1

	1990	1991	1993
US-Israel relations very good or good	60%	82%	71%
US security commitments reliable	54%	64%	56%

These figures regarding the United States were strikingly positive compared with rates in the countries of Western Europe (Rabier, Riffault, and Inglehart 1986). This was not a self-evident finding since the American investment and commitment to these other countries was also very great. The Spanish and Italian samples had the next highest rates of very good feeling after the Israelis, but at a third of the Israeli magnitude. Most samples, with the exception of Greece, reported moderately good feelings regarding the United States. When asked about the relations between their countries, again the Israelis stood out, with 31 percent giving relations a grade of very good, followed by the British and the Italians.

This boon appears to be accepted as a thing which Israel richly deserves, and therefore will continue. Whether or not it will is, of course, a political decision, and the debate continues (see Organski 1990). Adversity stimulates reactions of anger and interpretations of antisemitism, but success is embraced without hesitation or qualification.

The perception of the United States continued to be good over the years, but lower than the rate achieved in the wake of the Gulf war. United States security commitments were deemed credible by a majority of the respondents (see Table 6.1).

The United States sees Israel as a strategic asset and that is the main reason it supports Israel, according to 50 percent of the sample in 1993, and 60 percent in 1991. An additional quarter in both years thought that support derived from the shared values of democracy and freedom, while 23 percent in 1993 attributed the backing to the influence of American Jews, compared to 13 percent in 1991.

The role of the United States in the peace process was seen as a mediator and guarantor by 7 out of 10 respondents in 1994, and as a power which would impose an agreement only by 23 percent. Eight percent thought there would be no peace agreement. The respective rates in 1993 were 75, 20, and 5 percent.

Regarding American Jews, 72 percent of the 1991 Israeli sample thought that they support Israel government policy very strongly or strongly, compared to 58 percent in 1990. But if there was a serious policy conflict, U.S. Jews would side with Israel according to 59 percent of these respondents in 1991, and 52 percent in 1990. Fifty percent in 1991 and 1990 thought that American Jews could influence U.S. policy regarding the Arab-Israel conflict.

In the waning days of the Soviet Union in 1991, only 19 percent had a positive evaluation of the Soviet Union, although 75 percent thought there was a change for the better recently in that country's orientation toward the Arab-Israel conflict. A third thought the Soviet Union can have a major impact on the search for peace. According to 60 percent of the sample, the Soviet Union is active in the Arab-Israel conflict because it wants to reestablish its influence in the Middle East, another 15 percent because it wants to achieve peace, and 12 percent see it as a way of cooperating with the United States.

Denial

A second mechanism of balancing dissonance is denial. Variations of this are at work in Israel: one example is that of the "no choice" syndrome in which dissonance-generating elements are denied or ignored under the excuse of continuing with a policy "because there is no other alternative." This slogan encourages heroic effort and improvisation, on the one hand, and is used to excuse shoddy planning and poor execution, on the other. The effectiveness of the phrase wore thin as first Egypt and then other Arab states opened peace talks with Israel. There has also developed a mass form of selective perception encouraged by the production and consumption patterns of the Israeli media. Although Israelis produce and consume communications related to the military and political situation at a very high level, information which is harmful to the prevailing myths is often effectively screened out. This is done partially (although rarely) through military censorship and more often through a process of self-censorship imposed by editors and reporters and gratefully accepted by the reading and viewing publics. As the media became more varied and competitive in Israel, the scope of available opinion became broader, but the habit of self-imposed censorship is a strong one and obviously serves important functions for the difficult balancing acts between threat and optimism in which many Israelis engage.

A third form is the refusal to reexamine basic ideological positions, at least until political considerations force revision. For a long time, Israelis denied the nationhood of the Palestinians, for example. This position was articulated most forcefully by Golda Meir of the Labor party, although Menachem Begin of the Likud retreated from it at Camp David. In the 1980s, all mainstream Israeli parties rejected the possibility of negotiating with the PLO and of creating a Palestinian state. As the uprising of Arabs in the territories continued, it was clear that these bastions might fall, and that indeed happened in the summer of 1993 for the Labor party and the government it headed. But until then, by viewing the problem of the uprising in terms of the immediacy of military tactics instead of long-term political strategy, tunnel vision was encouraged.

The primacy of the military in Israeli everyday experience and in its society has conditioned its citizens to focus on a military perspective, often at the expense of a broader political one. Using the example of the territories, if there is no political problem (either because there is no one to talk to or because the land belongs to Israel) then dissonance between perceptions of threat and between belief in ability to overcome is erased; in its place are left the tactical problems of how to organize the army and the country in order to achieve law and order, and questions about the appropriate media policy in order to get a better press or at least not a bad one. It is in this light that the 1993 decision to recognize the PLO and to engage it in political negotiation must be assessed. This was a watershed, not only for what it meant for Israeli policy, but also for the challenge it posed to the political psychology of Israelis.

Differentiation

One major challenge of the peace process was the need for the Israeli public to find a new mechanism to relate to the changing political circumstances in which it found itself. After all, the old enemy, the PLO, was suddenly the partner at the negotiation table and the authority in control of the Palestinian police force; the villain of old, Yasir Arafat, was now seen shaking hands, and more, with Israel's leaders.

The enemy had to be humanized in some way, or at least de-demonized. One way to do that was to differentiate the former enemy from other elements of the non-Jewish, non-Israeli world, reminiscent of the manner in which many Israeli children overcome the dilemma by distinguishing between "good Arabs" and "bad Arabs." The PLO had become good, or at least possibly good, and therefore worthy partners at the negotiation table; they had recognized Israel's right of existence and had denounced terror. The fundamentalist Hamas, which had not done these things, retained the title of "bad Arabs." The categories did not change, only the designation of the roles various groups played had changed.

The political discourse quickly centered on which groups and individuals among the traditional enemies of Israel were now entitled to bear the title "good," whether they really meant it, and how could we know that they could be trusted in the future. For extremist right-wing Jewish fundamentalist groups such as Kach and Kahane Chai, the answers were that no Arab can be trusted, and from that position many grotesque conclusions could be drawn, including massacre at the extreme, or at least transfer (Sprinzak 1991). Other positions were less extreme in their prescriptions, but equally bleak in their diagnosis. At the other end of the continuum were those who believed in the basic goodness of all people, and those who would judge the deeds of the individual rather than the rhetoric of the group to which one belongs.

The confidence building measures often called for in order to deepen the peace process attempted to foster this device of differentiation. At the beginning of the peace process in 1994, it was evident that there was still much confidence building to be done. When asked whether the signing of peace agreements with appropriate security arrangements would mean the end of the Arab-Israeli conflict, for example, 47 percent said no, and 53 percent said yes, almost identical to the distribution in 1993 (48% no), before the agreement with the PLO was signed.

Fostering the process of differentiation is probably the most important function of the political leadership regarding public opinion. Highlighting the subtle distinctions which constitute complex political situations is a thing leaders can choose to do, or select to ignore. Public opinion is often predisposed to simple and simplistic renditions, and when not aided by legitimate and authoritative persons in power, the public is likely to take the path of least resistance and to adopt a position which is not complex. The shift in opinion regarding the PLO was aided by the Likud and Labor governments' unsuccessful search for negotiation partners among the Palestinians in the territories; when the Rabin government finally chose to recognize the PLO because no other interlocutor could be found, the transition for public opinion was less difficult. Another example was the movement in public opinion regarding the West Bank and the Palestinians, on the one hand, and the stubborn resistance of public opinion to a possible agreement involving the return of the Golan Heights to Syria. In the first case, the leadership worked hard at changing images and differentiating between Palestinians interested in seeking peace and those opposed; lacking a parallel assessment and announcement regarding Syria, there was no reason to believe that public opinion would shift. The dilemma for the political leadership was that such an effort was a necessary condition of opinion change, but by no means a sufficient condition.

THE PEOPLE APART SYNDROME

Two Constructs: God-and-Us and Go-It-Alone

The most pervasive mechanism for overcoming the anxieties of the security situation in Israel was the People Apart Syndrome. The set of values

Table 6.2. *The People Apart Syndrome*
Constructs, Agreement Rates, and Factor Loadings, 1987

A. God-and-us Construct:		
	% Agree	Loading
1. Masada will not fall again	85	.762
2. The God of Israel will not lie (Isaiah 15:29)	75	.702
3. The guardian of Israel will neither slumber nor sleep (Psalms 121:4)	90	.686
4. It is good to die for our country	68	.614
5. If one rises to kill you, kill him first	90	.399

Standardized alpha reliability coefficient: .769

B. Go-it-alone Construct:		
	% Agree	Loading
1. World criticism of Israeli policy stems mainly from antisemitism	68	.614
2. To prevent a war with the Arab countries, Israel must increase military power	32	.570
3. The whole world is against us	51	.536
4. Not to return territories of the Land of Israel is a principle not to be challenged under any circumstances	46	.531
5. Israel is and will continue to be "A people dwelling alone" (Numbers 23:9)	69	.520
6. Right to the land	45	.413

Standardized alpha reliability coefficient: .688

depicted as the People Apart Syndrome was an articulated belief system which served as a catalyst in processing policy options and as a binder in strengthening political positions (Converse 1964; Arian 1968).

The People Apart Syndrome was made up of two constructs that emerged from a factor analysis of attitudinal measures used in the 1987 survey (see Table 6.2).[4] These constructs – the God-and-us construct and the go-it-alone construct – together identified Israelis as a people apart. The two constructs of the People Apart Syndrome were widely advanced by Israelis, with the God-and-us construct statements supported by more than two-thirds of the 1987 respondents, and the statements of the go-it-alone construct by about half. There was much overlap between the two measures: when the God-and-us and go-it-alone constructs were divided by their median scores, the consistency ratio was 2:1. As is later demonstrated in Table 6.6, two-thirds of the 1987 sample scored high or low on both the God-and-us and on the go-it-alone constructs (gamma = .6). The 1994 picture was almost identical, and the correlation of the two constructs in the 1994 survey was also .6.

The results for the God-and-us construct were quite stable as well, lending credence to the claim that these are basic values, underpinning attitudes even as situations change. The consistency in relative order and magnitude are important to note. The God-and-us elements had the following percentages of agreement in 1990, 1991, and 1994, respectively: Masada will not fall – 85, 90, 82; God will not lie – 80, 86, 79; guardian of Israel – 91, 92, 89; good to die for one's country – 69, 70, 62; if one rises to kill you – 91, 95, 86. The slight increases in 1991 may be attributed to the effects of the Gulf war; the decreases in 1994, to the accelerating peace negotiations with Arab neighbors.

The go-it-alone elements showed a higher degree of variation although they, too, retained familiar patterns. The following were the percentages of agreement in 1990, 1991, and 1994, respectively: world criticism – 61, 68, 50; increase military power – 40, 29, 48; world against us – 46, 43, 35; not to return territories principle – 51, 43, 41; a people dwelling alone – 69, 68, 54; right to the land – 36, 33, 36. As the peace negotiations proceeded, a change in assessing the world's reaction, the sense of isolation, and the importance of the territories seemed to be taking place.[5]

The constructs were closely interrelated and tapped separate but related dimensions of the Israeli public's mind-set, as their content indicates and as the Pearson correlations (see Table 6.4) demonstrate. The first related to the special, mystical relation perceived by many among God, Israel, and Jewish history; the second, to feelings of isolation and to the belief that ultimately Jewish destiny depends on the Jews. In two speeches Yitzhak Rabin, the only native-born prime minister of Israel, depicted the difficulty in weaning oneself from the ideas dominant in the culture (Haberman 1993). In his inaugural speech to the Knesset upon becoming Israel's prime minister in July 1992, Rabin declared that Israelis must stop thinking that "the whole world is against us." But in commemorating the fiftieth anniversary of the uprising against the Nazis by Jews in the Warsaw Ghetto in April 1993, he spoke of what was to be learned of the Holocaust:

What will we learn? We will learn to believe in a better world. But most important, we will not trust in others any longer, generous as they may be: only us, only ourselves. We will protect ourselves.

All politicians have one speech for domestic circumstances, and a second for foreign audiences. Most politicians would select the conciliatory speech for the foreign occasion, and the more militant for the domestic one. In Rabin's case, the exact opposite took place. Perhaps at home he was trying

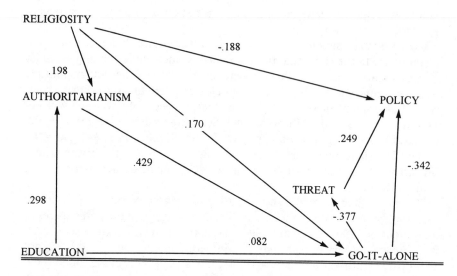

Figure 6.2. Path analysis of a People Apart, 1987. (Meaning of low scores: *policy* – more moderate, conciliatory attitude toward territories; *go-it-alone* – Israel must ultimately rely on itself; *authoritarian* – closed-minded, clear-cut solution sought; *education* – none through 8 years; *religiosity* – high degree of observance.)

to educate, and abroad to reflect. In any event, for an Israeli, going it alone, even if others be "generous," was not an easy thought to shake.

Interrelations

The impact of these attitudes and beliefs on policy preferences are reported in Figures 6.2 and 6.3 and will be investigated using five elements: (1) policy preferences regarding the territories and other security issues. For the 1987 sample, the full policy scale[6] will be used; by 1994, since the policy scale and some of the elements constituting it had taken on different meanings, only the territories question (see Chapter 4 and Appendix II.1A) is used in the analysis; (2) the People Apart Syndrome comprising attitudes about the nature of the State of Israel, the Jewish people, and its history; (3) a personality scale measuring authoritarianism (see Table 6.3); (4) an assessment of the degree of threat[7] Israel faces; and (5) demographic variables.

The relations between the attitude clusters (policy, God-and-us, go-it-alone, authoritarianism, overcome, and threat) displayed in Table 6.4, generated a matrix in which 14 of the 15 correlations in 1987, and 11 of the 15 in 1994, were statistically significant. The weakest correlations were with the overcome construct, and as noted in Chapter 2, the variance for the

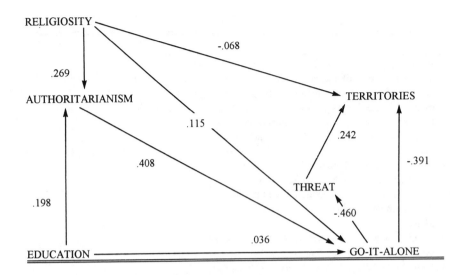

Figure 6.3 Path analysis of a People Apart, 1994. (Meaning of low scores: *territories* – willing to return territories for peace; *go-it-alone* – Israel must ultimately rely on itself; *authoritarian* – closed-minded, clear-cut solution sought; *threat* – hope for peace greater than threat of war; *education* – none through 8 years; *religiosity* – high degree of observance.)

questions which make up this score was limited. The God-and-us, the go-it-alone, and the authoritarian constructs showed very high levels of correlation (above .47) among themselves for both time periods. The highest levels of correlation and significance throughout were demonstrated by the God-and-us and go-it-alone constructs. Also, the policy score for 1987 and the territories response for 1994, with the threat constructs, showed high levels of interrelationship with the other constructs.

The policy scale for the 1987 sample, and the territories question in 1994, were significantly related to other constructs; specifically, for respondents in the 1987 survey, those who preferred more conciliatory policy positions regarding the Arabs and the territories had high negative correlations with the God-and-us construct (−.40), the go-it-alone construct (−.55) and a high positive correlations with the threat construct (.43). The same trends repeated themselves for the territories question in 1994. Conciliatory policy was related to hope for peace and assessing as unlikely the outbreak of war.

The fascinating part of the Israeli case is not only that these psychological factors are so powerful (Flynn and Rattinger 1985), but also that the demographic variables usually associated with these kinds of attitudes were less

Table 6.3. *The Authoritarianism Scale, 1987 and 1994 (% Agree)*[a]

	1987	1994
1. In the long run, it is best to choose friends whose ideas and tastes are similar to your own	54	58
2. A group that allows too many disagreements among its members cannot last for long	54	56
3. Compromise with political enemies is dangerous because it generally means being unfaithful to basic values	43	46
4. Views in the world are divided into two groups: those which are right and those which are wrong. Accordingly, people also are divided into two groups: those who have right ideas and those who have wrong ideas	40	41
5. From among all of the views that exist in the world it seems there is only one that is correct	38	32
6. God will watch over us, if we are deserving of it, even if we are not prepared for the next war	38	37
7. Most people do not know what is best for them	38	43
8. Most ideas thought up today are not worth the paper they are written on	36	45

[a] All statements (except 5 and 6) were presented as five-choice Likert scale questions, with an "uncertain" midpoint; statements 5 and 6 offered four choices. The percentages reported are "certainly agree" and "agree" responses.

related (see Table 6.5.) Gender had no impact whatsoever and is not reported; age had almost no bearing on the pattern of responses, and social class – as measured by living density, the number of persons per room in a household – had only a moderate impact. Education and religiosity were more closely related to these variables; those with low levels of education and high levels of religious observance were most likely to support nonconciliatory policy positions and to score highest on the People Apart constructs.

Arraying Israel's many political parties along a right-left continuum provided a high degree of correlation with policy position, with the People Apart Syndrome, and the perception of threat (see Table 6.5). Authoritarianism was also related, but at a lower rate of association. The fact that the 1994 correlation between territories and vote choice was lower than the parallel coefficient for 1987 must be judged cautiously since the measure of policy used was different in the two periods. Using identical questions for the other correlations (those between vote choice and the constructs of the

Table 6.4. *Policy and Attitude Constructs[a] Correlations,[b] 1987 and 1994*

	1987				
	2	3	4	5	6
1. Policy	-.40	-.55	-.27	-.12	.43
2. God-and-us		.49	.47	.17	-.21
3. Go-it-alone			.57	.11	-.39
4. Authoritarianism				-.01[c]	-.12
5. Overcome					.10[d]
6. Threat					

	1994				
	2	3	4	5	6
1. Territories	-.33	-.55	-.33	-.03[c]	.47
2. God-and-us		.60	.47	.05[c]	-.40
3. Go-it-alone			.64	.07[c]	-.60
4. Authoritarianism				-.03[c]	-.36
5. Overcome					-.06[e]
6. Threat					

[a] Meaning of low scores:

    1. Policy: more moderate, conciliatory attitude toward territories; for 1994 territories -- willing to return territories for peace and security (see Chapter 4).

    2. God-and-us: unique relationship between God and Israel

    3. Go-it-alone: Israel must ultimately rely on itself

    4. Authoritarian: closed-minded; clear-cut solutions sought

    5. Overcome: Israel will be able to deal with threats

    6. Threat: hope for peace greater than threat of war.

[b] Pearson correlations significant at $p < .001$ level unless otherwise noted.

[c] Correlation not significant.

[d] Significant at $p < .01$.

[e] Significant at $p < .05$.

People Apart Syndrome, and threat perception, and authoritarianism) generated higher correlations between 1987 and 1994. The explanation must be sought in the political context. During the 1987 survey, the National Unity government included most of the major parties, the policy was one of no movement, and clear policy alternatives were not evident. In fact, it could be argued that the National Unity government ultimately adopted positions which closely resembled the minimal positions of the right and the Likud. The political and military frustration which accompanied the prolonged demonstrations and riots of the Arabs in the territories – and to a lesser extent of Israeli Arabs as well – was an additional push in the direction of the right. Regardless of wish or fantasy, and because there was no moderate

Table 6.5 *Constructs[a] and Demography Correlations,[b] 1987 and 1994*

	Vote choice	Age	Education	Religiosity	Living density
			1987		
Policy	.58	-.07[d]	-.15	-.33	-.14
God-and-us	-.32	.05[c]	.26	.30	.24
Go-it-alone	-.36	.01[c]	.26	.30	.09[d]
Authoritarianism	-.25	.02[c]	.33	.26	.20
Overcome	-.06[e]	-.11	.03[c]	.08[e]	-.06[c]
Threat	.28	-.03[c]	-.13	-.10[d]	-.09[d]
			1994		
	Vote choice	Age	Education	Religiosity	Living density
Territories	.51	-.04[c]	-.18	-.24	-.13
God-and-us	-.44	-.03[c]	.21	.32	.13
Go-it-alone	-.59	.03[c]	.25	.39	.11[d]
Authoritarianism	-.41	-.03[c]	.25	.39	.11
Overcome	-.04[c]	-.09[d]	.03[c]	.08[e]	.02[c]
Threat	.51	-.02[c]	-.13	-.25	-.12

[a] Meaning of low scores:
  1. Policy: more moderate, conciliatory attitude toward territories; for 1994 territories - willing to return territories for peace and security (see Chapter 4).
  2. God-and-us: unique relationship between God and Israel
  3. Go-it-alone: Israel must ultimately rely on itself
  4. Authoritarian: closed-minded; clear-cut solutions sought
  5. Overcome: Israel will be able to deal with threats
  6. Threat: hope for peace greater than threat of war.
  Vote choice: range of five groups from left (1), through Labor, religious, Likud, and right (5).
[b] Pearson correlations significant at p < .001 level unless otherwise noted.
[c] Correlation not significant.
[d] Significant at p < .01.
[e] Significant at p < .05.

interlocutor in 1987, the only realistic policy in the minds of many Israelis was a policy of holding on. And that was the posture facilitated by the People Alone Syndrome. By 1994, the political agenda of the Labor party was in play, and people assessed the situation in a more partisan manner.

Table 6.6 explores the interconnections between God-and-us and go-it-alone and reiterates the overlap between God-and-us and go-it-alone, when the respondents were dichotomized into nearly equal groups: the

Table 6.6. *The People Apart Construct[a] and Policy Score Means*
(Total Table Percentages)

| God-and-us | Go-it-Alone | | | | | |
| | 1987 (N = 887) | | | 1994 (N = 967) | | |
	Low	High	Total	Low	High	Total
Low	36%	18%	54%	41%	17%	58%
High	15%	31%	46%	13%	29%	42%
Total	51%	49%	100%	54%	46%	100%

[a] Meaning of low scores:
  God-and-us: unique relationship between God and Israel
  Go-it-alone: Israel must ultimately rely on itself
  Policy: more moderate, conciliatory attitude toward territories.

Table 6.7. *Policy Score Means for the People Apart Cells, 1987*

| God-and-us | Go-it-alone[a] | | |
	Low	High	Total
Low	1.73	1.41	
High	1.72	1.21	
Total			1.51

[a] For size of cells, see Table 6.6.

low-low and high-high cells were the most populous, giving substance to the high correlations between the two reported in Table 6.4 (in 1987 it was .49, and in 1994 .60).

Table 6.7 presents the mean scores for the policy construct in 1987 for the four groups of the God-and-us and go-it-alone intersection. In this examination, an important difference emerges: those who accepted the propositions of the go-it-alone construct were little influenced by the God-and-us construct in determining their policy positions. Conversely, the God-and-us construct became important for those who rejected the go-it-alone arguments. Those who rejected both sets of statements were most likely to be conciliatory regarding policy toward the territories and the Arabs, followed by those who accepted God-and-us but rejected go-it-alone. Those who accepted go-it-alone were the least conciliatory on policy regardless of their God-and-us score.

Path Analyses

An explanatory model of the major relationships is presented in Figures 6.2 and 6.3 using path analysis (Duncan 1966; Blalock 1970). The model conceived of policy toward the territories and the Arab inhabitants as being dependent on an individual's perception of threat, the go-it-alone construct, and religiosity. Go-it-alone in turn was affected by authoritarianism, education, and religiosity. (In the path analysis, only the go-it-alone construct was used since it discriminated more effectively on the policy scale score used for 1987, and the territories response used for the 1994 path analysis.) Both education and religiosity were connected with authoritarianism. These core values and background characteristics are at the base of an Israeli's orientation to national security issues. The results of the path analyses showed that high levels of religiosity and low levels of education are both related to authoritarianism, and to go-it-alone.

The path analysis revealed the important role of the go-it-alone construct in transforming the authoritarianism of low education and highly religious sentiments into nonconciliatory policy positions. Threatened authoritarians tended to hostility.

Authoritarianism had a tremendous impact on go-it-alone, but almost none on perceived threat (except through go-it-alone). Threat was a shared communal experience, not limited to a certain social class, religious sect, or personality type. It had a strong correlation with policy (correlation of .43 in 1987, .47 in 1949; see Table 6.4), but it was not affected by demographic factors.

It is clear that the People Apart Syndrome, and especially the go-it-alone construct, was important in explaining a conciliatory or unyielding policy position. Again, demographic variables were less powerful in this explanatory model. It is the effect of the go-it-alone construct, especially in tandem with the perception of threat, which explained policy. These analyses provided powerful evidence of two central characteristics of Israel: first, the importance of the feelings of aloneness and self-reliance which characterize Israelis, and second, the generalized distribution of these convictions, regardless of class, education, and age.

THE INTERSECTION OF MIND-SETS

The People Apart Syndrome was noteworthy because it was not the exclusive dominion of one segment of the Israeli population. Israelis were sharply divided about many things, but the People Apart Syndrome captured much of the tone of Israeli political discourse and the mind-set of a large portion of the population. A better understanding of its distribution within Israeli society can be had if one considers the constructs of the People Apart Syndrome by religious observance. While these were related, the association was not perfect. There were obviously some who scored high on the syndrome but were not religious, and religious persons who did

Table 6.8. *People Apart Construct Means[a] by Religious Observance*

Religious observance[b]	1987 (N = 1,040)		1994 (N = 1,103)	
	God-and-us	Go-it-alone	God-and-us	Go-it-alone
Very high	1.59	1.44	1.67	1.38
High	1.73	1.67	1.78	1.58
Some	1.82	1.81	2.12	1.93
None	2.22	2.10	2.43	2.31
Total (100%)	1.90	1.84	2.10	1.91

[a] Meaning of low scores:
  God-and-us: unique relationship between God and Israel
  Go-it-alone: Israel must ultimately rely on itself
  Policy: more moderate, conciliatory attitude toward territories.
[b] The distribution of the religious observance categories were 9, 17, 45, and 29 percent in 1987, and 9, 18, 47, and 26 percent in 1994.

not score high. The People Apart Syndrome is replete with allusions to the Bible and to Jewish history, and while all Israeli Jews share this heritage, religious Jews are probably more exposed to it than others. Accordingly, it is instructive to portray the distribution between the constructs and religious belief more fully.

The mean scores on the People Apart constructs by degrees of religious observance are presented in Table 6.8. As religiosity increased, support for the positions of the constructs grew steadily. When studied another way (not shown in the tables), the group which was both religiously observant and scored highest on the God-and-us and go-it-alone scales was found to be somewhat smaller than the group which was both nonreligious and scored lowest. The size of the deviant groups (scoring low on one and high on the other in 1987) was identical within each of the People Apart Syndrome constructs: for the God-and-us scale it was 5 percent of the total sample in each group, and for the go-it-alone construct it was 4 percent.

Agreement with the People Apart principles carried over beyond the group that was religious to a larger extent than opposition to the statements carried over beyond the nonreligious. This was the basis of the ideological and political strength of the People Apart mentality. The People Apart message was a pervasive one and was absorbed by a wider array of individuals than was the opposite message. The rejection of the statements was more likely to be concentrated among those who were not religiously observant. The spread of religious behavior for those who agreed with the People Apart statements was greater than for those who disagreed and were not religious.

Additional insight is available by studying the correlation between the

Table 6.9. *People Apart Constructs[a] and Religiosity by Ethnic Background[b]*
(Pearson Correlations[c])

	1987		1994	
	God-and-us	Go-it-alone	God-and-us	Go-it-alone
Asian-African	.15	.23	.20	.28
	(*N* = 489)	(*N* = 452)	(*N* = 475)	(*N* = 423)
European-American	.31	.29	.29	.28
	(*N* = 366)	(*N* = 324)	(*N* = 472)	(*N* = 429)
Israel	.35	.46	.17	.29
	(*N* = 103)	(*N* = 98)	(*N* = 151)	(*N* = 140)
Total	.30	.30	.28	.33
	(*N* = 962)	(*N* = 878)	(*N* = 1,103)	(*N* = 996)

[a] Meaning of low scores:
   God-and-us: unique relationship between God and Israel
   Go-it-alone: Israel must ultimately rely on itself
   Policy: more moderate, conciliatory attitude toward territories.
[b] Asian-African includes Israel-born whose fathers Asian- or African-born; European-American includes Israel-born whose fathers European- or American-born; Israel includes Israel-born whose fathers Israel-born.
[c] All correlations significant at $p < .001$ level.

People Apart Syndrome constructs and religious observance by continent of birth (see Table 6.9). Respondents born in Asia and Africa, and those born in Israel whose fathers were born in Asia or Africa, had the lowest correlation between God-and-us and religiosity and a moderate one between go-it-alone and religious behavior compared with the other groups. This indicates their more general acceptance of the statements of the syndrome regardless of extent of religious observance. In addition to the cells of high agreement and much religious observance, the Asia-Africa group was very evident among those in the "middle" categories of the constructs and in the "some" categories of religious observance. This spread is what accounted for their generating the lowest correlation between religiosity and God-and-us.

For the Europe-America group, a reverse but parallel pattern held. They were very strong in disagree categories for the constructs and nonobservance and, to a lesser extent, in their adjacent cells, resulting in a higher correlation for God-and-us and religiosity. Those born in Europe and America and Israel-born whose fathers were born in Europe or America, tended more to disagree with the syndrome statements *and* to be nonobservant. Their greater consistency compared with the Asian-African group resulted in a much higher correlation coefficient.

The second-generation Israel-born group had the highest correlation between religiosity and the constructs in 1987, and it was reasonable to assess that the generalized spread of the People Apart constructs, regardless of religiosity, may have been contracting. However, by 1994, with the correlations lower, it was increasingly likely that a more complex reality was emerging. The patterns for this group are crucial for their numbers are growing fastest in the population and their attitude structure will likely be dominant in the next generation. In 1987, these Israel-born of Israel-born fathers were overwhelmingly of European extraction. By 1994, a higher proportion of that group was of Asian-African background, and the correlation for the Israel-born group was much lower than for the 1987 sample. Evidently, as children from the Asian-African born group joined this cohort, they brought with them their more generalized support for the People Apart constructs and, coupled with the more secular Israel-born of European extraction, had the effect of decreasing the size of the correlation.

The second-generation group will increasingly be an amalgam of respondents who trace their roots back to one of the other two groups, as was evident in the 1994 patterns. Although the members of this group share a common educational and national existence, they also have cultural baggage which may lead to a more consistently crystallized pattern of cleavages of attitudes and behavior. They carry the seed of the future, but that future is ambiguous. It could lead to a greater degree of consensus because those born in Israel of Israeli fathers will probably distribute themselves throughout the spectrum, as seen in the progression from 1987 to 1994. On the other hand, the amalgam may break up into distinct ethnic-cultural parts, increasing the levels of consistency within each group, which could lead to ever more tense relations between two mind-sets. Whichever scenario plays itself out, Israelis are likely to remain a people apart. The question is whether those distinct mind-sets will be reinforced by other cleavages such as political ideology, social class, and economic position. To date, the correspondence among these categories is only partial. That, too, has allowed fluidity of position and malleability of opinion.

The protracted conflict in which Israel finds itself has activated mechanisms of group solidarity and ideological consensus which have contributed to the ability of the nation to persist. Whether this is conducive to long-term security or not is a matter of political debate, but there is no doubt that Israelis have managed to resolve the inconsistency of perceiving threat and believing in their ability to overcome.

It is a basic tenet of Israel's political culture to feature identification with the People Apart Syndrome. The builders of national myths from biblical times to the present would endorse such an endeavor. The beliefs of the People Apart Syndrome are widely supported by Israelis, with the God-

and-us construct statements supported by more than two-thirds of the respondents, and the statements of the go-it-alone construct agreed to at a lower rate.

Both constructs are closely related to policy preferences; the interrelations among a hard-line policy, support for the People Apart Syndrome, and authoritarianism were very high. A substantial portion of Israelis, although not all, saw policy through the perspective of the syndrome and were guided by these precepts. These values penetrated at all age levels, making it unlikely that cohort replacement will generate change in the attitude structures of Israelis. Religious observance and low education levels were more closely related to these opinions.

The structure of the ideology within the society and the attitudes which constitute it are well designed to withstand long periods of frustration and stubborn resistance. This is a key factor in how such a small community can withstand so many pressures for such a long time.

The People Apart Syndrome establishes identity by excluding the outsider. It is important to note that Israeli Jews are extremely confident in overcoming both "external" and "internal" threats; by "external" they seem to mean anything that must be faced with force (whether Arab states, Palestinian terrorists, or dissident Israeli Arabs); an "internal" problem has to do with political maneuverings, and that might relate to coalition formation, religious parties, or Jewish settlers. This distinction will be explored in the next chapter. When the territories are discussed as a security issue, they are regarded as an "external" matter. This allows the acceptance of noncompromising policies toward the territories and their inhabitants in a polity otherwise characterized by a democratic ethos.

The People Apart Syndrome permits rejecting the outsider and thereby increases solidarity within the community by casting together the lot of all. This is a tremendous strength for defining the community of the Jewish state of Israel. It facilitates the ignoring (or worse) of the Arabs, and it ties with bonds of community other Jews who accept the premises of the People Apart Syndrome, even if they disagree on the specifics of policy. Disagreement regarding the syndrome is a more serious matter, and it is often portrayed as close to treachery. In these senses the People Apart Syndrome serves as a beacon and as a crutch – and as a self-fulfilling prophecy.

7

Threat and Policy

Threat is related to policy choices; the greater the threat perceived, the lower the risk an individual is willing to take (Rokeach 1960). Threat is the perceived intent and ability of something or someone to inflict harm or to block the attainment of a goal.[1] Still, to explain why one policy choice is chosen over another, or what connections are made between desired goals and the means to achieve those goals (Simon 1985), we need more information.

We should know, for example, whether a perceived threat corresponds to an objective threat. In addition, it is important to know whether a threat is perceived that way. Whatever the intention of the sender of the message, to be acted upon threat must be perceived. Threats can be intentional and actual in which case the situation includes both a sender and an intended receiver, but threats can also be unintended and yet perceived. "Perceived" can have the meaning of "received," implying a sender, and it can also mean "imaginary." Sometimes, even though no threat is sent one can feel very threatened and can react in a negative and hostile fashion to what or to whom we perceive as the origin of the threat. Foa, Steketee, and Olasov-Rothbaum (1989) developed a model of the development of post-traumatic stress disorder based on the finding that perceived threat is a better predictor of the disorder than objective threat. Their theory incorporates the concept of generalization of the strongly emotional event which originally threatened to a wide variety of stimuli which include the cognitive interpretation of events. Thus, although no threat was sent, one may perceive a threat, and behave accordingly.

An example of a threat that was perceived although none was sent is cited by Cohen and Kelman (1977, 185–6). They relate that during a problem-solving workshop between Palestinians and Israelis, the following incident took place. During one of the breaks between sessions, a Palestinian participant drew on the blackboard a symbol consisting of a cross, a crescent, and a Star of David. This symbol represented his vision of a future Palestine in which Christians, Moslems, and Jews would live together in peace and harmony. He was totally unprepared for the reaction of the Israelis upon their return to the room. They described the symbol, in tones of somewhat amused resignation, as further confirmation of what the Palestinians had in mind for Israel. As they saw it, the symbol represented Israel (the Star of David), encircled by the Arab world (the crescent), with a dagger (the cross) piercing its heart. The parties in conflict obviously had very different perceptions of the same symbols; the intentions of a message or an act can have one meaning to the sender and another to the receiver.

In assessing the role of threat perception for an individual determining a position in a policy domain, the answers to three questions are vital: (1) Regarding the policy domain, is the proposed outcome supported or opposed? (2) How threatening is the proposed policy outcome to the individual? (3) How likely does the individual think it is that this outcome will come to pass?

Knowing the degree of threat and assessment of likelihood that the event will occur, can we specify the conditions under which an individual would take a conciliatory position rather than a militant one? Rational choice theory provides us with a possible model; that theory considers expected utility models for decision making under risk. Applying its principles, the theory assumes that respondents attempt to maximize values deemed important to them by behaving in a manner which would produce the greatest likelihood of achieving those values (Raiffa 1968; Abelson and Levi 1985). If that were the case, the rate of support for returning the territories should be highest for those not threatened by that hypothetical eventuality and who thought the outcome not imminent (see Table 7.1). The rational actor who felt threatened and who predicted that the return of the territories was likely should have the lowest rate of support for the policy. According to the rational choice model, actors are risk-averse. Accordingly, perception of threat will be a more powerful driver than the likelihood issue. Put differently, the primary ordering will be driven by threat, the secondary categorization will be along the dimension of likelihood.

The expected ranking of the respondents in terms of these dimensions is given in Table 7.1. Individuals who felt threatened should have lower rates of support for returning the territories than respondents not threatened. Likelihood assessments should work differently among the threatened and not threatened. Among the threatened, high likelihood of occurrence will magnify the threat already perceived, while among those not threatened the respondents who see the return of the territories as likely will have the highest support rate.

Table 7.1. *Policy Preference, Threat, and Likelihood: A Model*

Threat	Outcome	Response rank for policy
No	Likely	Highest
No	Unlikely	High
Yes	Unlikely	Low
Yes	Likely	Lowest

Security

Applying these considerations to the issue of returning the territories, we observe a confounding picture: 58 percent of the 1992 sample said they were willing to return the territories for peace; 68 percent reported being threatened by the possibility of the territories being returned; 45 percent thought it likely that they would be returned. It was fascinating that the percent willing to support the proposal of return was greater than the percent of those who thought the outcome likely, but smaller than that of those who were threatened by the plan.[2] The correlations – all statistically significant – among the three variables were: (1) threat and returning −.51 (threat was a good predictor of not wanting to return); threat and likelihood −.19 (at a weak level, the higher the threat, the *less* likely return was); and return and likely .24 (those supporting return thought it likely that it would happen).[3]

The appropriate questions to apply the model were available in the 1992 and 1994 surveys. When testing the model, some expectations were fulfilled, but others were not (see Table 7.2). The prediction about the relations between threat and policy was clearly correct. Equating perceived threat with risk, those who felt that there was little to risk were much more inclined to the moderate position of being willing to return the territories. For those for whom the risk (threat) was greater, the rate of support to return the territories was lower. The second finding, however, was inconsistent with the prediction of the rational actor model. While threat discriminated as anticipated, the likelihood question did not. For those not threatened, the prediction succeeded: those who thought return likely supported return at a higher rate than those who thought return unlikely. But for the threatened, the likelihood question had an opposite effect from the one predicted. Those who were threatened and who thought it likely that the territories would be returned, had a *higher* rate of support for returning them than did those who thought the outcome was unlikely.

Table 7.2. *Return Territories*[a] *by Perceived Threat and Likelihood*
1992 and 1994

Threat	Outcome	Return 1992	Return 1994
No	Likely	94% ($N = 204$)	78% ($N = 370$)
No	Unlikely	81% ($N = 141$)	54% ($N = 48$)
Yes	Unlikely	36% ($N = 450$)	25% ($N = 225$)
Yes	Likely	55% ($N = 286$)	38% ($N = 541$)

[a] The territories measure for 1992 was based on a two-question battery with choices of return for peace, leave as is, and annex; for those answering leave as is there was a follow-up question forcing choice between return for peace and annex. The percentage reported for 1992 is those who ultimately chose return for peace. For 1994, the same procedure was followed except that the choices were return for peace, autonomy, and annex, with the forced choice for those who chose autonomy. The changed wording explains the different magnitude of the results. See discussion in Chapter 4, and results in Appendix II.

The order of the percentages for those threatened deviated from expectation. Using the 1992 numbers, the order of 36 percent and 55 percent was the inverse of the predicted one. Why would those threatened and who thought the outcome more likely have a higher rate of support for the policy than those threatened and who thought the return of the territories unlikely? A possible answer is the "get it over with" effect. Since what is being discussed is likely to happen whether or not it is seen as threatening, it is better that it should take place quickly; and if supporting the proposition will make it happen more quickly, then I will offer my support. Thus, if the territories are going to be returned eventually no matter what I prefer, and there are costs to holding on to them, best get rid of them sooner rather than later, and at least cut down the transition costs, no matter the level of threat perceived. While this makes some sense, the explanation flies in the face of the usual Israeli pattern of behavior and of the Middle East perception of time. More usual is the atmosphere of an Eastern market, where many have firm opinions until the next bargaining position is adopted and a new firm view is taken, to be held staunchly until the new position is embraced, and on and on. Time is often seen as a resource to be cherished, and as such it is not to be squandered because of anything as unreliable as an assessment of the probability that a distant event might occur. Buying time is the norm until a decision is forced. And during the process, it is

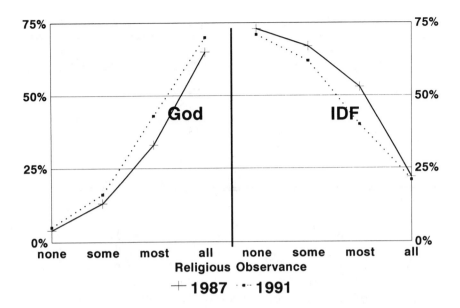

Figure 7.1. Identity of the guardian of Israel, 1987 and 1991.

hoped that some development will occur which will make the situation more favorable and that ultimately there will be more to gain from the decision or unnecessary altogether.

The "get it over with" type of reasoning is closer to the predictions of prospect theory than to the rational actor model. Prospect theory uses a descriptive psychological analysis of judgment and choice that departs from rational theory. It takes into account factors such as emotions and desires, and information necessary to make decisions, realizing that thought processes are bounded by limitations on memory and computational capabilities (Kahneman and Tversky 1979; Kahneman and Tversky 1984).

While rational choice theory predicts risk aversion independent of the reference point, prospect theory predicts risk aversion in the domain of gains, and risk seeking in the domain of losses, and a greater sensitivity to losses than to gains. "A person is risk-averse if he or she prefers a sure outcome over a risky prospect that has an equal or greater expected value" (Quattrone and Tversky 1988, 721). By contrast, one is loss-averse if losses loom larger than the corresponding gains. Holding on to the territories is costly and the expense in lives, money, and moral standards is eroding the society. Hence, cut losses.

Another possibility is that the model presented in Table 7.1 does not

Table 7.3. *Likelihood by Perceived Threat and Return Territories*[a]

Return	Threatened	Outcome likely 1992	Outcome likely 1994
Yes	No	63%	92%
		($N = 305$)	($N = 314$)
Yes	Yes	49%	78%
		($N = 319$)	($N = 259$)
No	No	33%	79%
		($N = 40$)	($N = 104$)
No	Yes	31%	67%
		($N = 417$)	($N = 507$)

[a] See note a, Table 7.2.

adequately portray the dilemma of reality. We who do this kind of research – and maybe those who read the results as well – are naturally attracted to the bottom line: the answer to the question of how many support returning the territories, and how many oppose it. Other factors, such as threat perception, likelihood of occurrence, vote, level of education, and so on, influence the decision which we regard as the dependent variable – the one to be explained. But perhaps in the real world, identifying the policy response as the dependent variable is misleading. It may be that what varies is the assessment of the likely occurrence of a phenomenon, and that policy choice and threat together predict differences in assessments of the likelihood of the outcome (Heller, Saltzstein, and Caspe 1992). Those who do not want to return territories and who are afraid of doing so may think that returning them is most unlikely. And those who want to return them and are not threatened by that eventuality may be most likely to assess that returning the territories will happen. Fears and policy positions might drive the assessment of the likely outcome.

That seems to be the case, at least for the extreme cells (see Table 7.3). The highest rate in 1992, at 63 percent, of those thinking it likely that the territories will be returned was for those who agreed to return them and who said they were not threatened by that outcome. The lowest assessment of likelihood was 31 percent of the respondents who did not want the territories returned and who were threatened by that eventuality. But the combination of return and threat was only partially successful in differentiating between levels of assessed outcome. For those who agreed to return, the rate of those who thought that return was likely was higher for those not threatened (63%) than for those who were (49%). However, this combination did not differentiate between levels of threat for those who opposed returning; that rate was at 33 percent for those not threatened, almost the same as the 31 percent of those who opposed returning and who were threatened. In other words, the return-threatened combination was effective in differentiating among those who thought the outcome likely only for those who wanted to return the territories.

Using the 1994 data, after the PLO-Israel agreement made the assessment of return more appropriate, the numbers soared, but the patterns remained. Again, the combination of readiness to return and low threat generated the highest rate of likelihood assessment (92%), and the rejection of return and the perception of threat was associated with the lowest rate of those who thought the likelihood high (67%). The categories of return-threat, and no return–no threat generated similar levels of outcome likelihood (78–79%).

It is also possible, of course, that the interaction between preferred policy position and assessment of the likelihood of outcome determines level of threat. This type of argumentation is often heard: I support holding on to the territories, but the government is going to give them away anyway and that frightens me. Or conversely, that I want to return the territories but the leadership will hold on to them and that will be bad. I am scared. Are differences in levels of threat knowable having information on policy and likelihood assessment of outcome?

Yes and no. Threat and policy preference overwhelmed the role of the assessed likely outcome in this case. In the 1992 data set, 91 percent of those not wanting to return territories for peace reported feeling threatened by their return, whether or not they thought the outcome likely. The discriminating effect of the likelihood of the outcome variable was better in predicting the rate of perceived threat among those willing to return the territories. Almost 60 percent of those who thought the outcome unlikely and wanted to return the territories felt threatened, compared with 45 percent perceiving threat among those ready to return the territories and who rated that outcome as likely. The same pattern held in 1994, although the numbers were different, of course.

A good test for the power of the threat variable as a predictor would be its ability to discriminate among more finely calibrated levels of threat perception and the interaction between likelihood assessment and policy preference. This test was possible because the question about perception of threat in both 1992 and 1994 used a four-category response; in the analyses above these four responses were collapsed into two – threatened and not threatened. But using the original four categories of response with its more finely adjusted measure of threat, we could know more about the effect of threat in the model. This test lent credence to the proposed model; we find that hawkishness was very strongly related to the most threatened category, regardless of level of assessment of likelihood, and much more weakly

Table 7.4. *Mean Score for Chances of War[a] by Perceived Threat
and Likelihood of Returning Territories, 1994 Survey*

Threat	Outcome	To Jordan	Autonomy	Palestinian state	Annexation
No	Likely	1.9	2.5	3.0	5.0
No	Unlikely	2.7	3.3	3.8	4.1
Yes	Unlikely	3.2	3.6	4.8	3.7
Yes	Likely	2.9	3.6	4.7	4.2
Total		2.7	3.3	4.2	4.4

[a] 7 = war very likely; 1 = almost no chance of war.

related to the three other levels of threat perception. Those who said they
were very threatened in 1992 were disproportionately found in the two 91
percent cells; the very threatened made up two-thirds of those who fell in
the 91 percent cells, although they represented less than 40 percent of the
total sample. In other words, hawkishness and a high level of threat were
closely bonded, and level of threat nicely predicted extreme policy position. The higher the threat, the more likely that an extreme policy position
would be taken.

The political psychology of Israelis facing ongoing threat to their personal and national existence can be tested in yet another way. Threat
perception and the assessment of likelihood of an event occurring should
be connected in a regular manner with estimations of the chances of war.
Assuming that war is universally threatening, the strength of the feeling
about the probabilities of war could provide an unobtrusive measure of the
mechanism through which threat and probabilities are processed. Returning to the basic model, we may assume that threatened respondents will
perceive war as more likely than those not threatened and, again, that
likelihood assessments will have different effects for the threatened and not
threatened. Among the threatened, high likelihood of occurrence will magnify the perception of the likelihood of war, while among those not threatened the respondents who see the return of the territories as unlikely will
have the lowest assessment of the likelihood of war.

These speculations are tested in the data presented in Table 7.4. The
mean score of the chances of war (see Chapter 3) were calculated for the
four threat-likelihood types. The data again point to the anomaly evident
in the earlier discussion. The order hypothesized among the four categories
is not evident in the empirical data, although for two of the tests – the
chances of war if there will be autonomy or if there will be a Palestinian
state – the means are very similar for all those who reported threat percep-

tion, regardless of the likelihood of the occurrence. For the other two contingencies – returning the territories to Jordan or annexation – those who perceive threat and see the outcome unlikely show highest assessments of war were the territories returned to Jordan, and lowest were the territories annexed.

The data underscore the role that reality plays in structuring political attitudes. Neither the Jordanian option nor annexation were very likely when the poll was taken. The Israeli government and the PLO were engaged in negotiating autonomy arrangements, and some feared – or hoped – that those arrangements would eventually lead to a Palestinian state. For autonomy and the Palestinian state – both on the public agenda – outcome assessments were overpowered by threat perception. For the other two options, distant and unlikely, outcome assessments were potent in combination with threat perception in ordering the probability estimates of the likelihood of war. There is an important hint in these data about the processes at work, and it has to do with the reality of the options. When faced with unfolding events, denial and get-it-over-with are replaced by more powerful drivers – threat and fear.

Religion

To see how generalized these patterns were, the model was also applied to a domestic conflict – the one between religious and secular Jewish Israelis. They are also involved in an intense conflict, yet obviously not nearly as life-threatening or violent as the security issue. These two conflicts have alternately simmered and raged for decades and seem to be related to each other for Israeli Jews. When conflict with the Arabs is dormant and the perception of threat from them is low, the conflict between religious and secular Jews seems most intense. The rule in group dynamics that external threat is a good way to create internal group solidarity plays an important role in this interchange. Internal conflicts between Jews emerge especially when external threats from the Arabs are inactive. It is almost as if there were a quotient of threat and anxiety in the society, and that the Arabs have first call on filling that quotient. If there is surplus, then domestic tensions emerge. In the context of the hierarchy of needs and threats, it is only when safety needs are not threatened by the Arabs that esteem needs can emerge.

This conceptualization follows Maslow (1954), who posited a theory of human motivation which assumed a universal hierarchy of basic needs with six levels. The appearance of each succeeding level was contingent upon the satiation of the lower levels. It is only when lower levels are extensively gratified that higher level needs may appear. "Physiological needs" (such as hunger and thirst) are at the base of the hierarchy. If these needs are not met, they dominate all behavior. "Safety needs" are the next level and are directly seen in infants, reactions to strangers, sudden noises, and the threat of being dropped. In adults they are seen mainly in situations such as wars and natural disasters. The next level consists of "belongingness" and "love needs," which appear only when physiological and safety needs are relatively satisfied. The fourth level is conceptualized as "esteem needs" and includes (but is not limited to) the desire for strength, dominance, recognition, mastery, and the need for independence and freedom. The fifth level is "cognitive" and "aesthetic needs" and the highest level of the hierarchy is the need for "self-actualization."

Threats can also be conceptualized in an order that parallels Maslow's hierarchy of basic needs and prioritizes both the order, and perhaps the strength, with which we react to them. So, for example, a belief that life is threatened (safety need) may motivate a stronger, more consistent reaction than a belief that style of life is threatened (esteem need). Threat derives from the balance between feelings of vulnerability, on the one hand, and judgments regarding the capacity to overcome challenges, on the other.

The conflict between religious and secular Jews in Israel, while it can be very bitter and intense, relates to a different level of existence from the Arab-Israeli conflict. Extremists on both sides would prefer to have the opposing group disappear, but the means chosen to achieve extreme goals are more moderate in the domestic setting than in the anarchic international one. Jews have often regarded solidarity as a moral and existential value, perhaps because of their historical dispersal and weakness, perhaps because of their sorry lot when unity was not achieved, and maybe for both reasons. Yet the secular-religious conflict between Jews in Israel often belies this strong need.

The roots of the conflict between religious and secular Jews in Israel go back to the birth of the idea of political Zionism in Eastern Europe. There it developed as a secular, nationalist movement which was opposed by most of the Orthodox establishment. As is clear for much of the world in the unsecularizing post-cold-war era, nationalism and religious fundamentalism are still forces of tremendous potency, and their competing demands lead to great tension and even violence (Juergensmeyer 1992).

One of the most violent periods between religious and secular Jews occurred in the mid-1980s, just before the outbreak of the intifada. Israel was enjoying a period of unprecedented quiet with the Arabs, the peace treaty had been signed with Egypt, de facto peace existed with Jordan, a cease-fire held with Syria, and a security zone had been established in southern Lebanon after the withdrawal of most IDF troops.

The political power and influence of the religious grew – and especially the ultra-Orthodox – and in the 1988 elections they scored an increase of four Knesset seats (see Figure 5.1). This increase of four out of a total of 120 seats shocked much of the secular community. It was perceived as an enormous increase and created strong feelings of panic and siege. In truth, the number of seats in 1988 for religious parties was not more than they had in the past; but the intensity of the conflict and the fact that they were joined in coalition with the sympathetic Likud of the right, heightened the sense of threat. Moreover, the increase of power was for the non-Zionist ultra-Orthodox parties, and not for the familiar National Religious party. The NRP, which embraced both Zionism and Orthodox Judaism, and had instituted many of the provisions of the status quo, was in decline.

In the mid-1980s, incidents increased as some ultra-Orthodox attempted to prevent secular Israelis from committing acts which the religious thought of as desecrations of the Sabbath. For example, they threw stones at secular motorists who were driving on the Sabbath; patrons in pubs on the Sabbath were attacked; demonstrators disturbed movies being shown on the Sabbath.

Some seculars reacted. In 1986 there was a series of violent, ugly antireligious incidents. In one, a group of furious secular Jews burned a synagogue in Tel Aviv – along with prayer books and Torah scrolls. During that same period bus shelters in Jerusalem which had bathing suit advertisements deemed lewd were destroyed by a group of ultra-Orthodox. In another incident swastikas were painted on the wall of the Great Synagogue in Tel Aviv by secularists, and an 11-year-old boy from Mea Shearim – an ultra-Orthodox religious enclave in Jerusalem – was briefly kidnapped by a secular who shaved off the boy's sidelocks. The behavior on both sides inevitably brought up horrible memories of diaspora pogroms.

As noted in Chapter 6, the degree of religious observance has been very stable for the last 30 years in Israeli society, while support for having the government see to it that public life be administered in accordance with Jewish religious law has varied depending on the political circumstances (see Figure 6.1). Respondents were also asked whether the separation of religion and the state threatened them, and how likely they thought it was that the separation would come about. With these questions we can replicate the model used above for the territories to the realm of the religious conflict.

For the 1994 sample, 61 percent were opposed to having public life in Israel administered in accordance with Jewish religious law; 35 percent reported feeling threatened by the possibility of the separation of religion and state, but only 15 percent thought it likely that this separation would take place; the comparable numbers for 1992 were 70, 42, and 19 percent, respectively. For the religious issue, the same pattern of correlations was

Table 7.5. *Public Life by Perceived Threat and Likelihood[a]*
1992 and 1994

Threat	Outcome	Opposed 1992	Opposed 1994
No	Likely	84%	71%
		(N = 110)	(N = 115)
No	Unlikely	83%	76%
		(N = 555)	(N = 655)
Yes	Unlikely	51%	35%
		(N = 375)	(N = 343)
Yes	Likely	60%	42%
		(N = 106)	(N = 65)

[a] Percentage is those opposing having public life in Israel administered in accordance with Jewish religious law.

generated as in the security domain, but at lower levels of association: .44 for the relationship between the policy question and threat, and nonsignificant correlations for the other two associations in 1994; the 1992 correlation between separation and threat was .37, the other two were .05. Feeling threatened in one domain was associated with being threatened in the other (.35), and those who wanted to return territories tended to oppose having public life regulated by Jewish law. Likelihood responses were not related with each other or with any of the other measures.

The data in Table 7.5 are to be compared with those in Table 7.2; in both cases a "yes" response meant changing the status quo: returning the territories, or not having public life run by Jewish religious law. Regarding religious policy, threat was again a good predictor of policy position: support for having public life run by religious law was highest among those threatened by the separation of religion and state. The model successfully predicted the differences within the threatened group with those who thought the occurrence likely generating the highest levels of support for the policy; however, the likelihood of occurrence did not discriminate among response rates of those not threatened.

Both threat and likelihood worked together in predicting the rate of support for the policy proposition. The higher the rate of threat, the lower the support; among the threatened, the more likely the occurrence, the higher the rate of support. Replicating the observations used for the security domain for religion, the policy and threat questions were not effective in predicting rates of likelihood. A much better combination was policy and outcome: they predicted level of threat very well. The progression of categories was from those most threatened who do not want public life run in accordance with Jewish religious law but who think it likely that this situation will come about (70% in 1992), to those (at a rate of 66% threatened) who opposed the idea and thought it unlikely to happen, followed by those who supported public life according to Jewish law and thought it likely to happen (41%), and then opposers who thought it unlikely and they were least threatened (29%).

There is an intriguing regularity in the consistent failure of the model to predict the ranking of responses. The fact that the threatened were most resistant to change was expected, but the fact that among the threatened those who thought the event likely advanced the change more supports the notion of prospect theory that people tend to be risk seekers in the domain of losses. This empirical support for prospect theory has implications for leaders intent on leading an anxious population in new directions. For those already convinced of the cause, the emphasis should be on averting future dangers (such as war and terror, or civil war); for the hesitant and fearful, stressing the fact that the conclusion is inevitable (returning the territories, for example) can focus the mind of the threatened on cutting down potential loss from international sanctions or isolation. Projecting a dual message is dangerous for any leadership because audiences cannot be selected as easily as messages can. The threatened may be listening when the nonthreatened are addressed. The leader runs the risk of being accused on inconsistency. But running the risk may be worth the cause which the leader is trying to espouse. This dual response to threatening situations is a key which can harness the threat undeniably perceived and turn it in the policy direction of peace, or of war.

THREATS COMPARED

Perceptions of threat, intense policies, and intolerant attitudes toward the threatening group function to prevent resolution of conflict. As Marcus, Sullivan, and Theiss-Morse wrote, "when [an] emotional trigger is threatening, people react with intolerance. When emotions are not aroused, people are more tolerant" (1990, 31). These characteristics were found in both the security and the religious domains.

Perceived threat in a prolonged conflict is used to maintain and enhance the conflict by justifying negative stereotypes of the "other" group, and to transform the other from one with a normal range of positive and negative characteristics into one whose qualities are only negative. In Chapter 2, the perception of respondents regarding the hostile and threatening aspirations of Arabs was documented. Unfortunately, no parallel data regarding the perceptions of Arabs were available.

There is asymmetry in the religious-secular conflict. Gordon (1989, 649–50) found that "the secular viewed the religious significantly more negatively than the religious viewed the secular. . . . Negative stereotyping by the secular appears to be typical . . . [while] negative stereotyping by the religious is infrequent. For the secular, the more interaction they had with the religious, the more negatively they evaluated it. This was much less true of the religious."

No directly comparable measures of threat in the two domains were available because the nature of the conflicts are so different. Nonetheless, finding approximate equivalents is worthwhile because of the light it may shed on the way threat interacts with policy choices. Security threat was measured here as the sum of responses to the questions regarding the possibility of peace between Israel and the Arab countries in the near future, and the assessment of Arab aspirations.[4] These questions were replicated for the religious-secular conflict: all respondents were asked about coexistence between religious and secular; religious were asked what the goals of the secular were (from leaving things as they are to making the state completely secular), and the secular were queried about the goals of the religious (from leaving things as they are to making the state conform with Jewish religious law).

Each of the three threat measures (security, religious, and secular) had a range from 2 to 8 points, with the higher score indicating more threat. Using this comparison of domains, the security issue was found to be most threatening: the mean for the entire sample was 5.2. For secular respondents, the mean of the threat from the religious was 4.9, and the mean threat score from the seculars for religious respondents was 4.3. This finding closely follows Maslow's expectations of a hierarchy of needs and, by extension, of threats.

Differences between policy choices existed for those who were threatened and not threatened. This finding was foreshadowed in Chapter 2, and it is reiterated in Table 7.6. As level of threat decreased, the propensity to support a more extreme position declined. Thus, in the security domain, willingness to return territories increased as threat receded. For the secular, the same pattern pertained: as threat declined, the willingness to have public life run in accordance with Jewish religious law increased. The exception to this pattern was for the religious whose pattern of support was not related to the degree of threat they perceived generated from the secular.

Those who were threatened – regardless of whether they were religious or secular – were more intense in their public policy preferences. The differences reported here in the whole population for security, and for the secular regarding religion, were consistent and significant. Threat affected

Table 7.6. *Policy and Levels of Threat (1991 Survey)*

Return territories for peace (1 = yes; 5 = no)

Level of threat	N	Mean[a]
High	482	2.9
Middle	271	2.5
Low	310	1.9
Total	1,063	2.5

Public life according to Jewish religious law (1 = yes; 4 = no)
For seculars:

Level of threat	N	Mean[a]
High	244	3.3
Middle	232	3.1
Low	290	2.9
Total	766	3.1

Public life according to Jewish religious law (1 = yes; 4 = no)
For religious:

Level of threat	N	Mean[b]
High	63	2.3
Middle	133	2.0
Low	97	2.2
Total	293	2.1

[a] The F ratio in the analysis of variance was statistically significant above .000 level.
[b] Not significant.

the policy preferences of respondents in both domains, but because the religious conflict was at the level of esteem needs and the security issue at the level of safety needs, the potency of threat in the religious domain was weaker. Nevertheless, in both areas there were real differences between the policy choices of the threatened compared with the nonthreatened.

Perceived threat was related to policy choices and this increased the polarization between the two groups. The higher the perceived threat, the more negative stereotyping; the more negative the characterological judgments made, the more one viewed the relationship with hostility (Gordon 1992). The data in Table 7.7 show percentage of respondents who supported the notion that public life in Israel should be conducted according to Jewish religious law, by religious observance and by whether or not the respondent felt threatened by the other group. The most intense positions were taken by those who felt threatened: 90 percent of the religious who

Table 7.7. *Religious Observance, Threat, and Policy (1991 Survey)*

Religious/ secular	Threatened by *other* group (N)		% Agreed that public life should be according to Jewish religious law
Religious	Yes	(50)	90
Religious	No	(48)	64
Secular	No	(87)	38
Secular	Yes	(269)	26

felt threatened by the secular supported the public life proposition, and only 26 percent of the secular who felt threatened by the religious supported the plan. Those who reported not being threatened by members of the other group had less intense rates of support.

Threat perceptions enhance solidarity by castigating negative aspersions on the other group. This process is all the more notorious because the negative qualities of the other group may be well earned. Mediators and international relations experts are partial to confidence-building measures as a means to allay fears and risks. This is good technique if the motivations of the other group are indeed benign. But if their goals are hostile, accurate perceptions of threat are very functional and in place. The difficult problem is how to avoid misconstruing the motivations and goals of the other group. When the secular (or the Arabs) change their stripes and their aspirations alter, how are the religious (or Israeli Jews) to know that? The same for the other group. The task is most complex because there is no single authoritative indication, and those seeking to avoid change can always point to extreme expressions of some on the other side. It is precisely at this moment that leadership must be brought to bear; to probe meaning on the part of the adversary, and to educate members of the collectivity.

An alternative to developing comparable measures of threat for the two domains is to assess the intensity of perceived threat using a common thermometer of threat across various spheres. To that end, respondents were presented with issues and asked to indicate the degree they felt threatened by each, using a four-point Likert scale ranging from very threatened to not at all threatened. The percentages feeling *very* threatened, the most extreme of the four categories, are presented in Table 7.8.

A number of points are of interest in this list. First, the stability of the response rate is striking. The three measurements were conducted at very different times in Israel's political and security realities: the first in 1991 immediately after the Gulf war, the second after the opening of the Madrid peace conference and just before the 1992 national elections, and then in

Table 7.8. *Topics Identified as "Very Threatening," 1991, 1992, and 1994*

	1991	1992	1994
Nonconventional weapons in the hands of the Arabs	76%	70%	67%
A nondemocratic regime in Israel	66%	63%	65%
An equal number of Arabs and Jews in the country	58%	53%	a
Another war with the Arabs	55%	71%	a
A Palestinian state	51%	50%	37%
The cessation of United States aid	49%	48%	a
A state based on Jewish religious law	43%	43%	a
Returning the territories	36%	36%	33%
Separating state and religion	12%	20%	17%
Mass Jewish immigration from the Soviet Union	8%	a	a

[a] Not asked.

the 1994 survey after the signing of the PLO-Israel peace accord. Although the times and the respondents were different, the rankings for the various items, and sometimes even the percentage mentioning the item as very threatening, were almost identical. The only item whose relative rank changed between the points in time was fear of another war with the Arabs, and that number grew from 55 percent to 71 percent. This is further evidence for the argument made in Chapter 3 that the Gulf war increased the sense of foreboding about a future war with the Arabs, especially since the threat of nonconventional weapons had been added to the equation; that fear, while still very high, seemed to shrink over time.

Fascinating also was the recorded fear that a nondemocratic regime would emerge in Israel. For all the blemishes of the Israeli political system, widely discussed at that time, respondents appeared very aware of the possibility that their democratic form would be lost, and they were not sanguine about that eventuality; additional confirmation of that point is presented in Chapter 9. Because there were strong and intense feelings about many matters, the threat of losing the right to speak freely and to fight for these opinions was evidently seen as a menace.

After the threat of war and the loss of democracy, there were fears generated by issues relating to the Arabs and the territories. The specter of the United States ceasing its aid of Israel was also very threatening. Religious tensions seemed to be of lesser magnitude in comparison to the threats posed by war, the loss of democracy, and security issues. The religious issues, while always near the surface of conflict in Israeli domestic political life, were constrained by other pressing events. Least threatening was the daunting prospect of absorbing the immigrants from the Soviet Union.

Table 7.9. *Threat* by Religious Observance (1991 Survey)

	Secular (N = 779)	Religious (N = 298)	t-Value[b]
A nondemocratic regime in Israel	3.6	3.3	-4.09
Another war with the Arabs	3.4	3.3	-2.20[c]
A state based on Jewish religious law	3.2	1.3	-10.94
A Palestinian state	3.1	3.4	4.75
Returning the territories	2.8	3.2	6.19
Separating state and religion	1.8	2.4	8.83
Security threat[d]	5.1	5.7	7.11

[a] Means of 4-point Likert scale in response to the question: "To what extent do each of the following pose a threat to you?" Answers ranged from 4 = "a great extent" to 1 = "none at all"; thus the higher the score, the higher the threat.
[b] t-Test differences significant at p < .001 level, except where noted.
[c] t-Test differences significant at p < .02 level.
[d] The sum of the responses to the questions regarding the possibility of peace between Israel and the Arab countries in the near future, and the assessment of Arab aspirations, ranging from 8 to 2.

Threat perceptions were distributed differently among the secular and religious based on the 1991 data (see Table 7.9). Differences between secular and religious were statistically significant except for these four items: nonconventional weapons in the hands of the Arabs, an equal number of Arabs and Jews in the country, the cessation of United States aid, and mass Jewish immigration from the Soviet Union. For three of the items, the secular were more likely to be threatened than the religious. The largest difference was on a state based on Jewish religious law; this threatened the secular of course much more than the religious. Regarding another war with the Arabs there were very small, although significant, differences. On the nondemocratic regime there were also differences, with the secular evidently seeing the regime as a protection of its freedom. The religious expressed more threat than did the secular on the two security-related issues on which there were significant differences – a Palestinian state and returning the territories. Also, using a composite measure of security threat, the religious generated higher threat than did the secular.

For the two security issues on which there were differences, the religious perceived more threat than the secular, but the issue which generated the greatest degree of difference between the religious and the secular had to do with religious matters. That was the issue of separating state and religion; obviously the religious expressed more threat than the secular. This was an issue which had polarized Israeli society for years. In 1969, 49 percent were for separation to a very great degree (36%) or to a great degree (13%), and 51 percent were somewhat opposed (13%) or were completely opposed (38%). In 1981, the pattern of the distribution was similar, with a slight shift in the direction of opposition to separation. The split in 1981 was 45:55. Before the 1992 elections the issue caused a furor when the Labor party convention approved a platform plank calling for the removal of political influence from religious life. The implications of such a plan were clear and far-reaching and caused enormous threat among religious parties, and among secular parties (including Labor) that had plans of forming their coalition after the next elections with religious parties. Accordingly, the leaders of the Labor party reconvened the convention that had made the decision, organized in a more controlled and thorough fashion, and had the plank withdrawn.

BELIEF UNDER STRESS: THE GULF WAR

There are processes that work at the collective level to enhance the ability of Israelis to face difficult and ongoing security threats. Some of these were discussed as the People Apart Syndrome in Chapter 6. Another aspect of this topic has to do with beliefs during times of crisis.

The notion that many people turn to God in moments of extreme anxiety is an old one, well documented in anecdotes, in literature, and by social scientists. On a related topic, there is a relationship between secure feelings of attachment – a strong permanent bond – between oneself and another, and the diminishment of the fear of personal death. People who are secure, as opposed to those who are insecure, tend to be less fearful of danger because they do not feel alone in the existential reality of smallness, finitude, and helplessness (Mikulincer, Florian, and Tolmacz 1990). It is not difficult to extend this argument to the relationship between man and God.

There was evidence of a turn to religion in one form or another on the part of some Israelis during the Gulf war. Two weeks after the war, 70 percent of respondents agreed that the low rate of casualties was a miracle, 38 percent certainly agreed, and 32 percent agreed.[5] And when asked if, as a result of what they went through they became more believing or more religious, 10 percent said they became much more, and another 17 percent said a little more. About their belief in God, 22 percent reported that it became stronger. Six weeks after the war, in answer to the same question, the results were almost the same, with 19 percent reporting that belief in God became stronger as a result of the crisis. For religious respondents, the low rate of casualties was strongly associated with a miraculous event.

Ninety percent of observant Jews agreed that the low rate of casualties

Table 7.10. *The Guardian of Israel, 1986, 1987, 1991*

	1986	1987	1991
Israel Defense Forces (IDF)	57%	61%	56%
God	15%	19%	23%
Jewish people/State of Israel	23%	13%	15%
U.S.A.	2%	4%	1%
Each person must watch out for himself	2%	2%	5%

was a miracle. The mix between the holy and mundane, with somewhat different proportions, was evident for the secular as well. When non-observant Jews were asked to what extent they agreed that the low rate of casualties was a miracle, 65 percent did so. And the rate of support for the statement "God will take care of us, if we are deserving, even if we are not prepared for the next war" was up to 45 percent in 1991, from 40 percent in 1990, and 37 in 1987 and 1986.

The boundaries that Israelis place on the relationship between the sacred and the profane have been explored by a series of questions, and respondents have been regularly asked about the guardian of Israel. In 1991, 92 percent agreed that "the guardian of Israel would not slumber nor sleep," up from 90 percent in 1990 and 1987, and 79 percent in 1986. The distribution of the identity of the guardian of Israel was proved, and the results are presented in Table 7.10.

Half of the religious respondents identified God as the guardian, 33 percent of them replied that it was the IDF. Only 12 percent of the nonreligious named God as the guardian of Israel, and 65 percent of the secular chose the IDF. The more observant one was, the higher the percentage who named God as the guardian of Israel and vice versa for the IDF. This general pattern has persisted since the question was asked first in 1987; all groups generated an increase in the percentage answering God and a decrease in those responding the IDF in 1991 (see Figure 7.1 on p. 191). Perhaps the decrease in the percentage of those who selected the IDF was due to the intifada, and to the difficult situation the army found itself in while trying to cope with the Arab uprising, and to the trauma of the Gulf war.

Five weeks into the war, Israelis were asked whether they have more private prayers today than before the war. Thirty-five percent of all respondents replied yes – itself an impressive finding. Half of the religious reported an increase in private prayer, but what is far more interesting is the fact that a third of the nonreligious reported an increase in private prayer. Breaking the sample down by gender, 37 percent of women and 30 percent of men reported an increase. Having children did not make a difference: 36 percent of those with and 34 percent without children reported an increase. Nor did living in Tel Aviv or Haifa or elsewhere make much of a difference.

Israelis were also asked whether during the time of the crisis they observed more of the tradition. Were they, for example, lighting candles or blessing the wine before the Sabbath more than before the war? Eighteen percent of the sample replied that they were. When the responses were broken down, 39 percent of the religious and 15 percent of the secular said they observed more of the tradition during the crisis, 22 percent of females and 12 percent of males, 19 percent of those with children and 17 percent of those without, and 18 percent of those living in the Tel Aviv area, 11 percent of those living in Haifa, and 21 percent of those living in the rest of the country replied that they were observing more of the tradition.

Not all of those who reported an increase in observance also reported an increase in private prayer. More than a third of those who reported an increase in religious observance did not report an increase in their private prayers. Combining the results of both questions, 42 percent of the sample reported an increase either in private prayer or traditional observance, or in both. And breaking that number down, two-thirds of the religious and a bit more than one-third of the secular reported some form of increase.

One possible reason Israelis are very good at living with clear danger is their ability to deny and push away fear and anxiety. Data from the three surveys during the Gulf war provide a convincing demonstration of this ability. In the survey done during the war, 12 percent reported having much more fear. In the survey done two weeks after the war, 22 percent reported having had much more anxiety. In the survey done six weeks after the war, 33 percent reported having had much more anxiety. The question used during the war asked about "fear" and the question in the later surveys asked about "anxiety," but even so the results are striking. Even if we consider only the results of the two surveys after the war which used the identical question, the increase was substantial and provided an important contrast to the consistency of the results over time regarding the question of increase in belief. During the crisis it was most important to have as positive an attitude as possible and to go on with life as normally as possible. This notion was an important norm into which children in Israel are socialized at an early age; in addition, it is usually good psychological advice. Keeping busy gives one less time to concentrate on feelings. Behaving as normally as possible helps one feel as normal as possible – instead of feeling afraid. When the crisis ended, with more and more distance from the event, and when life returned to normal, Israelis allowed themselves to know how they really felt during the war.

A consistent relationship between level of fear or anxiety and religious behavior was observed. During the war, of those who reported having much more fear, 50 percent reported an increase in private prayer and almost a third told of an increase in religious behavior. Of those who reported feeling no fear, a third reported an increase in private prayer and 12 percent reported an increase in religious behavior. Four weeks after the war, of those who felt much more anxiety, 36 percent reported that they became more religious; of those who felt more anxiety, 28 percent became more religious, and of those who reported no change in anxiety, only 16 percent became more religious. The number who agreed that the low number of casualties was a miracle went up as the level of anxiety went up.

Six weeks after the war, of those who felt personally endangered to a great degree during the war, a quarter reported stronger belief in God, of those who felt in danger to a certain degree, 19 percent reported stronger belief, and of those who did not feel in personal danger at all, only 10 percent reported an increase in belief. Although the percentages varied from question to question, the overall relationship between higher levels of fear or anxiety and an increase in belief and religious behavior was clear.

The higher one's anxiety during the Gulf war, the more likely one was to feel threatened both by nonconventional weapons in the hands of the Arabs and another war with them.[6] Anxiety was not related to any of the other issues. More interesting was the relationship between some of these issues and strength of belief that peace was possible in the near future. The more likely the belief that peace was possible in the near future, the more threatened by a nondemocratic regime in Israel, another war with the Arabs, the thought of nonconventional weapons in the hands of the Arabs (the respective correlations were .14, .11, and .11, and statistically significant); and the less threatened by the thought of a Palestinian state and returning the territories (the correlations were both $-.15$ and statistically significant).

Threat perceptions are always an important ingredient in conflict, no less so in the security and religion domains in Israel considered here. Important functions are fulfilled by perceiving threat, such as enhancing group solidarity and facilitating the ability to cope with dangers that evoke great anxiety. The dilemma for the society and the individual is that these learned patterns of perceiving threat will ossify and will prevent the flexibility needed to perceive that the nature of the threat may have altered.

8

Values

Competing values is the stuff of politics. Psychologists see values as central to the cognitive organization of the individual and as a basis for the formation of attitudes, beliefs, and opinions (see Rokeach 1970; Rokeach and Ball-Rokeach 1989). In recent years, the overarching concept of right and left, sometimes referred to as the conservative-liberal continuum, which was at the heart of political mass belief systems research (Converse 1964) has been largely replaced by the notion of diverse values. Regarding values as "conceptions of the desirable means and ends of action" (Kluckhohn 1951, 395), the crux of the shift from the point of view adopted here is that there may be various sources for structuring political attitudes. This variety allows for much individual level variance in the structure, constraint, and content of mass belief systems, which has been the focus of most current research in this field. This line of research suggests that mass policy preferences are significantly structured by basic or central values (see Hurwitz and Peffley 1987; Feldman 1988).

The notion of diverse values compels attention to value conflict, as cherished values compete in real-life situations. Concentrating on various values instead of one overall ideology represents simultaneously a more simplistic and a more complex view of belief systems. It is simpler in the sense that it does not expect or require people to develop one compound, sophisticated, and integrated system of beliefs. Instead the focus is on discrete values which, like ideology, may provide the vehicle to explain reality and to posit standards of desirability. These values serve as shortcuts or heuristics to guide people's interpretation of a complex and changing world, but they may or may not be connected, integrated, or coherent.

This view is at the same time more complex because it allows for different value components to be at odds, and it suggests the need for trade-offs among values and the setting of priorities. This is the basic view of values taken by psychologists who tend to conceptualize values as inherently comparative and competitive, and measured by ranking methods rather than by ratings (Rokeach 1970; Rokeach 1973; Rokeach 1979; Rokeach and Ball-Rokeach 1989; Tetlock 1986; Tetlock 1989; Alwin and Krosnick 1985; Krosnick and Alwin 1988).

Approaching values as a hierarchical system recommends itself for two major reasons. First, values in political situations often conflict. Trade-offs are required and are explicitly stated in court rulings. They are implicit in policy decisions, even if politicians try to hide and obscure them for political and electoral reasons. Value contention and trade-offs arise when opinions are to be established on various issues on the public agenda. Second, many societal values are consensual, that is, supported by almost all members of a society or at least by a large majority. For such values, meaningful variance will not be in how many people support them, or in how much people support them, but in other ways. Stokes (1963) distinguishes between valence and position dimensions of politics, and discusses one way such "valence" dimensions enter politics, namely, through party images. Conflict and variance center on the question of which political party or leader will succeed in creating an image of being best able to achieve this value. Another way people vary on such a "valence" value is in how they rank it when it is in conflict with other cherished values. In such situations, the order of priorities may become the bone of contention and be politicized. These value hierarchies may then be of interest in themselves, and in their consequences for policy.

The fact that basic values in Israeli political culture and its Zionist roots are in tension has been discussed extensively by observers of the Israeli political scene (Cohen 1989a, Cohen 1989b, Smooha 1990). The basic tenets which relate to the discussion are: (1) Israel as a Jewish state; (2) Eretz (the land of) Israel; (3) democracy; (4) peace. Each of these may be an end in itself, or may be a means to achieve other ends. In principle, for example, most Israeli Jews might support a value if it were cost-free, but in reality trade-offs must be made. Thus, for many on the right and among religious Jews (but not only them), greater Israel is an end in itself. For others, it is a means for achieving peace and security, or for absorbing more immigrants. Each of the values considered may be instrumental for some, serving as a means for achieving another value, or it may be an ultimate value, an end in itself, for others.

These four values are enunciated in Israel's declaration of independence, which embeds the basic values of Israeli society. While not legally binding, the constitution has great symbolic importance (Rubinstein 1991). The right of the Jewish people to its homeland embodies the Zionist justification for the establishment of the State of Israel. This value of Israel as a Jewish state is the most pervasive one in the culture.[1] Eretz Israel is referred to in the opening section of the declaration, thus binding the notion of the national home closely to the land, and is a value deeply ingrained in the Zionist ethos of national revival.

Democracy in the broadest sense of equality of political rights is also generally supported, at least in the abstract, with the courts bolstering these rights in principle and in practice over the years.[2] Peace is a common aspiration, reiterated by politicians, sung about in popular songs. Being accepted among the nations of the world, and in particular by states of the region, was always one of the major goals of Zionism and of Israeli policy, and an important dimension of Israel's national interest (Harkabi 1988). After four and one-half decades of independence, peace seemed progressively more feasible.

The issue of the territories has become the basic bone of contention in contemporary Israeli politics only because of the trade-offs it involves. If it were not for the indigenous Palestinian population (the "demographic problem") and international pressure, and if holding on to the territories were not perceived as an obstacle to peace, most Israeli Jews would prefer a greater Israel (the post-1967 war boundaries) to the smaller Israel which was militarily more vulnerable. If Israel could keep these territories with no price attached, just about every Israeli Jew would support that situation.

If the country opts for greater Israel, it must either restrict the political rights of the Arabs of the territories or face the possibility of a country without a Jewish majority, or perhaps raise the probability of war. If it decides to prefer a democratic state with a Jewish majority, then the notion of keeping the territories becomes less attractive. If one wants a greater Israel with a Jewish majority, the demographic imbalance between the Jewish and Arab populations will have to be redressed. Some support the notion of transfer, others think denying civil and political rights to the Arabs of the territories makes the issue moot, while others believe that large Jewish immigration will solve the problem.

Peace, some on the left tell us, is possible only with returning the territories and avoiding the need to deal with the 1.6 million Arabs under Israel's military rule. Activists on the right argue that the strategic depth provided by the territories, coupled with massive Jewish immigration, will strengthen the state, will offset the demographic advantage of the Arabs in the territories, and will be the best recipe for a low probability of hostilities. The permutations are many, and the substance of these trade-offs is the stuff of contemporary Israeli politics.

The tensions and dilemmas around these values are not new; they have accompanied Zionism from the onset (Horowitz and Lissak 1978, 1987; Kimmerling 1983; Gorny 1987). But they were contentious only when political reality disturbed their status as valence dimensions about which all could agree, and forced politicians and the public to take sides. After the conquests in the Six Days war, these dilemmas became pertinent again, although it took years for the conflict over these competing values to dominate the public agenda. In this vein, Tetlock emphasizes how value conflict and the trade-offs they require are unpleasant (1986, p. 819). On the psychological level they are unpleasant for cognitive, motivational, and affective reasons. Politically they are unappealing in that the compromises they demand are difficult to justify to the public and to political activists, in particular to those whose value priorities have been forsaken.

Here we examine the value priorities of Israeli Jews in the late 1980s, as well as their impact on policy positions with respect to the Israeli-Arab conflict. The four values just described will be considered; most Israeli Jews would be happy to achieve each one of them, if they did not conflict with achieving other goals. Were they to be observed in a political vacuum, one would learn little; much more will be understood by considering them in terms of competing values in specific contexts.

VALUE PRIORITIES AND CHANGE

The data come from the 1987, 1988 and 1990 surveys, in order to take advantage of the reinterviewed panel respondents. The value ranking task was first presented to respondents in the 1988 survey and repeated in 1990. The following question was posed: "In thinking about the various paths along which Israel can develop, there seem to be four important values which clash to some extent, and which are important to different degrees to various people: Israel with a Jewish majority, greater Israel, a democratic state (with equal political rights to all), and peace (that is, a low probability of war). Among these four values, which is the most important to you?"

The "Jewish majority" was presented since it seemed closest to the original Zionist idea, as well as to common usage in Israel, although competing specifications of a Jewish state, such as a state where Jewish culture and tradition are dominant, or a theocratic state where the Torah is the law of the land, are also possible. The Hebrew term for greater Israel is commonly recognized and widely used in political discourse. Democracy was conceived of as equal political rights for all, including the franchise to Arabs under Israel's jurisdiction. Peace was explained as a situation in which there was a low probability of war, so as to set it clearly apart from more formal aspects of peace agreements. The respondents were asked to rank all four values, and they had no apparent problem with the task.

Recent analyses of Israeli society and culture have emphasized the shift from universal principles toward particularistic, more traditional, tribal and primordial emphases, often related to religion and to the land at the expense of a secular civil culture. For example, Kimmerling (1985b, 272) suggests that "from the time of the 1977 change in government [the ascent of the right-wing Likud to power], Israeli leaders began to utilize the concept of 'Eretz Israel,' for two principal reasons . . . to demarcate the new physical boundaries of the collectivity . . . and to define the collectivity's identity as 'Eretz Israel' . . . [as] a moral community based upon primordial symbols and ties." Similarly, Shafir (1991, 52) writes that "the post-1967 era in Israel was mainly of cultural transformation, aimed at generating what political sociologists call a legitimation shift. This shift resulted from efforts by the supporters of territorial expansion to find a popularly acceptable replacement for the demographic calculus deeply ingrained in most Israelis."

Based on these writings and the utterances of participants and observers of the Israeli political scene, one would expect Jewishness to be the major value priority of the respondents, and greater Israel to be of considerable importance as well; democracy should rank lower. The value priorities of Israeli Jews as measured by the ranking task only partially conform to these expectations.

Two values – Jewish majority and peace – were ranked high by a vast majority of the population, and the two other values – greater Israel and democracy – ranked generally low. The same overall pattern existed in 1988 and in 1990: in 1988, peace was mentioned first by 34 percent of the sample, with a Jewish majority close behind at 33 percent (see Figures 8.1 and 8.2). In 1990, the order of these two values was reversed, although the percentage mentioning them was similar: Jewish majority received 39 percent of the first-place mentions, and peace 35 percent.

Equally important was the consistent low ranking for the other two values in both time periods: in 1988, greater Israel and democracy were mentioned as the first priority by 19 percent and 15 percent, respectively; and by 14 percent and 12 percent, respectively, in 1990. Both of these lower ranking values were directly related to the political disposition of the territories – greater Israel related to the land, democracy related to the citizen rights of the people on the land. Forced to choose among the four goals, greater Israel was not the priority value for most of the respondents.

Figures 8.1 and 8.2 show the full rankings and provide a more detailed picture of those values which are more, and those which are less important – and therefore potentially more divisive. The results for the two time periods are again consistent, although not identical.

The Jewish majority value yielded the greatest consensus in its highest overall ranking and the lowest variance.[3] Israeli Jews ranked it as most important (taking the full ranking into account) and they varied least with respect to the ranking of it, compared to the other values. Particularly impressive was the small number of respondents who ranked it last in each

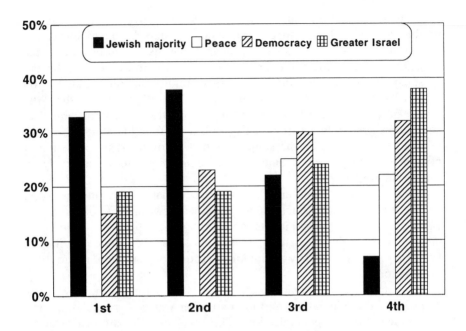

Figure 8.1. Value choices – ranking Jewish majority, peace, democracy, and greater Israel, 1988.

of the interviews. The least frequently mentioned value as a first choice was democracy; but it was mentioned more often in second and third place. Greater Israel was close behind democracy in its low number of first choices, but it was most often the lowest-ranked value. The demographic consideration seemed to be in the backs of the minds of many respondents, while the territorial instinct was much weaker. The notion of the right of the Jews to Eretz Israel may have gained acceptance and legitimacy, but when choices had to be made, most Israelis opted for a Jewish majority rather than for a greater Israel.

When the respondents' first and second priorities are counted together, the results for 1988 and 1990 are very similar. About 70 percent of the samples ranked Jewish majority as either first or second; 52 percent in 1988 and 60 percent in 1990 ranked peace first or second. Close to 40 percent in each year included democracy among the first or second ranked values, with a similar number for greater Israel.

These results accentuate how superficial it is to portray politics in Israel as a struggle between the camp that wants to keep the territories, and the camp that is willing to give them up if it would lead to a secure Jewish state.

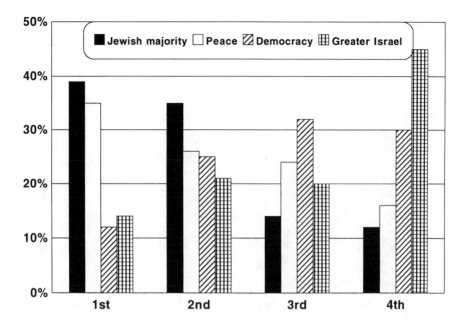

Figure 8.2. Value choices – ranking Jewish majority, peace, democracy, and greater Israel, 1990.

The picture that emerges is of a population firmly supporting a Jewish majority in their state, with a very strong desire for peace. Keeping Israel Jewish by maintaining in it a Jewish majority is undoubtedly a valence dimension in Israeli politics. Peace is too, though to a lesser extent. The values of land and democracy are less important. While there is consensus regarding democracy as an abstract principle, and greater Israel could also be an agreed-upon goal, their collective lower priority and contemporary political circumstances make them the substance of debate and conflict. Indeed, they have been transposed into divisive position issues in Israeli politics. The distinction between valence and position dimensions is thus not clear-cut; these are not inherent qualities, but instead depend on the political context.[4]

The individual level ranking of the two values which are less important to the group as a whole – greater Israel and democracy – is much more stable over time than the rank ordering of the two more mentioned values.[5] Consensus is associated with a generalized acceptance which implies that a value will retain a high ranking, although its order may change. On the other hand, a value which is conflictual, and hence political, maintains a

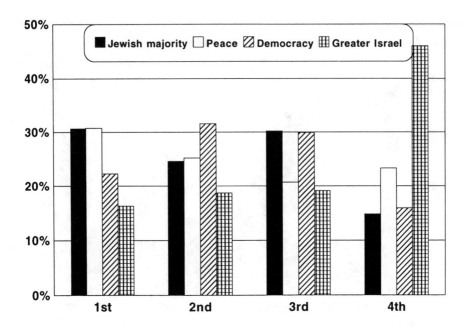

Figure 8.3. Value choices – ranking Jewish majority, peace, democracy, and greater Israel, 1994.

relatively more stable order over time. These same patterns were found again in later surveys as well, with slight differences of emphasis. The distribution for 1994 is presented in Figure 8.3.

POLITICAL AND IDEOLOGICAL STRUCTURE
OF VALUE PRIORITIES

The distribution of the value priorities was not random. Rather, they were placed in tandem with the respondents' political and ideological worldview, as measured by their right-left self-placement.[6] The highest absolute value correlation of the right-left continuum was with the rank ordering of greater Israel. This correlation was − .43 in 1988, and − .40 in 1990. Democracy and right-left were correlated at .33 in 1988, and .29 in 1990; peace and right-left at .28 in 1988, and .24 in 1990.[7] By far the lowest correlations were between right-left and the rank order of Jewish majority, (− .16 in both years).[8]

This correlation pattern establishes greater Israel as the most partisan and conflictual dimension, since its correlation with the right-left continuum is the highest. On the other hand, having and keeping a Jewish majority in the state has a very low correlation with the political continuum, which means that it does not differentiate well between left and right. This result again supports the depiction of it as a valence dimension in Israeli politics. Peace is closer to Jewish majority in the size of its correlations; it does a better job than Jewish majority in differentiating right from left, but is a much weaker indicator compared to greater Israel and democracy. Democracy is closer to greater Israel in its partisan quality. In terms of the size of the correlations, democracy and peace fall in between the two extremes.

Higher preferences for democracy and peace tended to be associated with the left; higher support for greater Israel, with the right. Preference for a Jewish majority, the most strongly supported value, was very weakly related to the left-right continuum, with a slight tendency to go with the right. Another perspective on the same issue is given by the correlations among the four values. Those are quite similar at the two time points, and in the general and panel samples. One should keep in mind that measuring the values by way of the respondents' ranking builds in negative correlations among them, as the sum of the rankings for each respondent is constant (Cattell 1944; Clemans 1966; Alwin and Krosnick 1985). These correlations are presented in Table 8.1 in the first three columns.

First, there is an extremely low relationship between the preference for a Jewish state and for greater Israel. The correlation between the two is virtually zero, which means that those for whom the Jewishness of the state is the most important value do not come from the group of people who cherish a greater Israel, any more than from those who do not value a greater Israel. This result, together with the relatively low preference for greater Israel discussed in the preceding section, suggest that while the "primordial" land-oriented aspects of Jewish identity may be on the rise, when forced to choose priorities, land is still low and unrelated to the preference for a Jewish state.

Also, the correlation between democracy and peace is very low. All the other value preferences generated high correlations. Highest were the correlations between greater Israel and both peace and democracy, and the correlation between a Jewish majority and peace. People who ranked greater Israel high tended to rank peace and democracy low. People who ranked a Jewish majority high, tended to rank peace low. There was also a tendency for people who ranked a Jewish majority high to rank democracy low, but this negative relationship was weaker.

It is thus not the clash between Israel as a Jewish state and Israel as a democratic state – a combination which Meir Kahane (1987) so fervently denounced – that stands out in these public opinion data, but rather the

Table 8.1. *Combinations of Values: General and Panel Samples*

Value (1st/2nd choice)	Correlations[a]			% Panel		
	1988	1990	Panel[b]	1988	1990	Stable
Jewish majority/Greater Israel Greater Israel/Jewish majority	-.05[c]	-.07	-.03[c]	26	33	56
Democracy/Peace Peace/Democracy	-.16	-.10	-.08[c]	18	14	34
Jewish majority/Democracy Democracy/Jewish majority	-.38	-.35	-.29	18	19	30
Jewish majority/Peace Peace/Jewish majority	-.39	-.51	-.49	30	26	28
Greater Israel/Peace Peace/Greater Israel	-.53	-.46	-.48	5	7	9
Greater Israel/Democracy Democracy/Greater Israel	-.43	-.51	-.57	2	2	0
Total				100	100	

[a] The correlations are cross-sectional correlations between each pair of value rankings, for the 1988 general sample, for the 1990 general sample, and for the 1988 panel. For example, -.16 in the second row is the correlation between the rankings of democracy and peace obtained in the 1988 general sample.
[b] The correlations are for the preferences given in 1988 by the panel respondents. The correlations for their 1990 rankings were very similar.
[c] Not significant at .05 level.

competition between the value of greater Israel and the values of peace and democracy, and between peace and a Jewish state.

Still another way of looking at political and ideological constraints is to examine the mixture of choices made by the respondents. Given four values, there are twelve possible permutations for combining the first and second choices. In fact, six combinations were sufficient for more than three-quarters of the samples (see Table 8.2). The six pairs most often used were the two combining peace and a Jewish majority, the two containing a Jewish majority and greater Israel, and the combinations of peace with democracy, and of Jewish majority with democracy.

The combinations of the first two values mentioned are arrayed along a right to left self-placement continuum in Table 8.2. Toward the top of the

Table 8.2. *Ranking Values, 1988 and 1990*

	1st Choice	2nd Choice	% of Respondents	Right-left means[a]
1988				
1.	Greater Israel	Jewish majority	14.3	2.2
2.	Greater Israel	Peace	2.7	2.3
3.	Jewish majority	Greater Israel	12.7	2.4
4.	Democracy	Greater Israel	3.7	2.5
5.	Peace	Greater Israel	3.3	2.7
6.	Greater Israel	Democracy	1.6	3.1
7.	Democracy	Jewish majority	6.4	3.5
8.	Peace	Jewish majority	17.4	3.5
9.	Jewish majority	Peace	10.5	3.7
10.	Jewish majority	Democracy	9.3	3.9
11.	Peace	Democracy	13.2	4.8
12.	Democracy	Peace	5.0	5.0
1990				
1.	Greater Israel	Jewish majority	7.9	2.3
2.	Jewish majority	Greater Israel	15.8	2.6
3.	Greater Israel	Peace	3.7	2.6
4.	Greater Israel	Democracy	2.2	2.6
5.	Peace	Greater Israel	5.8	2.9
6.	Democracy	Greater Israel	0.8	3.1
7.	Jewish majority	Democracy	9.8	3.4
8.	Jewish majority	Peace	13.5	3.5
9.	Peace	Jewish majority	16.1	3.5
10.	Democracy	Jewish majority	3.9	4.1
11.	Peace	Democracy	12.9	4.3
12.	Democracy	Peace	7.6	4.6

[a] The right-left self-placement continuum is a seven-point scale with 1 right, and 7 left; the mean was 3.4 for both the 1988 general sample (N = 735) and the 1990 general sample (N = 1,204).

list, the right end of the political spectrum, the value of greater Israel dominates, while at the bottom (left), democracy is often in evidence. The combination with the most extreme right-wing placement (place 1) was greater Israel and a Jewish majority; the most extreme left-wing placements (places 11 and 12) comprised democracy and peace. The Jewish majority and peace values were scattered more widely throughout the list. The left was thus characterized by placing a high value on peace and democracy, and the right on greater Israel and Jewishness. This pattern illustrates the claim that opposing political groups have ideologies and

Table 8.3. *Stability and Change in Value Rankings (Panel Sample)[a]*

	Mean 1988	Mean 1990	Mean difference	t-Value	Significance
Jewish majority	3.07	3.24	+.17	2.18	.030
Peace	2.75	2.54	-.21	-2.15	.032
Greater Israel	2.07	2.15	+.08	0.95	.345
Democracy	2.12	2.14	+.02	0.16	.871

[a] Value rankings are measured from 1 (lowest ranking) to 4 (highest ranking). Effective sample size between 194 and 200.

labels which are not necessarily arrayed along one dimension, but may have different concerns, definitions, and priorities (Conover and Feldman 1981; Kerlinger 1984; Huber 1989; Ventura and Shamir 1992).

When the level of consistency in the rankings across the two time periods is examined, two interesting patterns are found. First, the ends of the scale based on the right-left continuum were very similar in both 1988 and 1990. The ordering of most other combinations for the two years was not the same; four of the value combinations moved one ranking, two combinations moved two rankings, and two moved three scale positions. Second, and more interesting, the changes of the value combinations' rankings along the left-right continuum make sense ideologically and politically. Those value mixtures which changed rankings (with one exception) had "conflicting" values, that is, one value which "goes" with the right, and one which "goes" with the left. Again, with one minor exception, they all moved in the "correct" direction – in the direction of the value which was the first priority. So, for example, Jewish majority and democracy moved up toward the right end (from rank 10 to rank 7); Jewish majority and peace similarly relocated toward the right (from rank 9 to rank 8); peace and Jewish majority shifted toward the left (from rank 8 to rank 9); democracy and Jewish majority moved from rank 7 to rank 10, also in the direction of the left.

Similar results were obtained from an examination of individual-level stability of the first and second choices of the panel respondents. Overall, about 35 percent gave the same two values as most preferred at the two points in time (not necessarily in the same order). The "right-left mean" column in Table 8.1 presents these stability rates for the different combinations of values. Most impressive is the close correspondence to the patterns generated by the cross-sectional correlations between the pairs of values already discussed. The pairs of values in Table 8.3 are ordered by descending order of stability, and they correspond almost perfectly to the increasing negative correlations among the values constituting each pair. The less compatible the values are, the less often do the respondents repeat these combinations.

Most consistent or stable were the respondents for whom a Jewish majority and greater Israel were most important: among them, 56 percent repeated the same choice two years later. Least stable were respondents who combined greater Israel either with democracy or with peace. There were relatively few respondents who made these choices in each survey (see Table 8.2 for the general samples, and columns 4 and 5 in Table 8.1 for the panel sample), but among them only one respondent repeated the same choice twice. The stability scores for the other value combinations fell in between.

These data, analyzed cross-sectionally and over time in different ways, show that the values and value combinations were not randomly selected by the respondents. The correlations of the value rankings with the right-left continuum provide a good indication of their political and ideological connotation. The value of keeping Israel Jewish, the basic Zionist rationale for the establishment of the state, came out as a clear and strong valence dimension in Israeli politics. It was the most important value for Israeli Jews and related least to partisan political debates, despite attempts to politicize it. The Likud in particular, and other right-wing parties more generally, adopted the motto throughout the 1980s of being "the national bloc," implying that being a Jewish nationalist (i.e., a true Zionist) meant belonging to the right. This tactic was an example of clever campaigning, aimed at mobilizing and legitimizing one side while delegitimizing the other. As a valence dimension, the notion of a Jewish state is appropriate for a party that wishes to be perceived as centrist and to mobilize supporters across the board. But the data show that the Likud and the right were not successful in monopolizing this value. Being a highly valued valence dimension, this basic Zionist value has never been seriously challenged; rather, it kept off the agenda altogether certain policy options, such as a binational state of Jews and Arabs, or the PLO program for a secular democratic state.

Peace, too, though to a lesser degree than the value of a Jewish majority, was highly important for Israelis. Its correlation with the right-left continuum was the lowest after a Jewish majority. The attempt by Labor and the left to appropriate this value by identifying themselves as the peace camp was again smart packaging because it had very broad appeal, but in a political sense it did not mean much. In fact, it was Begin's Likud government in 1979 that signed the peace agreement with Egypt, and Shamir's Likud government in 1991 that led the country to the international peace conference in Madrid.[9]

People's rankings of democracy and greater Israel had stronger correlations with the political continuum, which indicates that they are politicized. It is interesting to note that an attempt to account for the variance in the value rankings by sociodemographic and other attitudinal variables was more successful with these two values and least successful with the Jewish majority and peace values. The highest R^2s were for greater Israel, followed by democracy, peace, and Jewish majority, exactly the order of these values in most of the analyses.

Certain values hung well together but did not bond with others. Greater Israel in particular did not seem to go well with democracy or peace. Few respondents chose those combinations as their first and second priorities (see Tables 8.1 and 8.2); the negative correlations between these values were the highest, and respondents who chose such combinations did not tend to repeat them.

The value combination packages are represented in the political arena by political parties, which actively promote them and mobilize the public using them.[10] The extreme left parties adhered to the combination of democracy and peace, and the extreme right, to the values of Jewishness and greater Israel. These were the most congruent packages according to the data. The messages of other parties, in particular the large Likud and Labor parties, were more blurred and their supporters endorsed several value packages. In the charged political atmosphere of Israel of the 1980s, it was not surprising that extreme parties grew electorally at the expense of the center since they presented more consistent packages (Shamir 1986; Arian et al. 1992).

The distinction in terms of value priorities between the political extremes was sharp, but when the full spectrum was considered (see Table 8.2), the picture was more mixed and blurred. When considered by voting intention, differences were evident between the Labor and left bloc, on the one hand, and the Likud and right bloc, on the other. But voters of the right and voters of the left had more in common with each other in their priorities of values than they had differences. In both cases, a Jewish majority and peace were the two highest values. For voters of the Likud and right a Jewish majority and peace were ranked first and second, followed by greater Israel (see Figure 8.4). Voters for Labor and the left set as their first priority peace, followed by a Jewish majority, and then democracy (see Figure 8.5).

Priorities overlapped quite considerably in terms of the two most important values, notwithstanding the rhetoric of the politicians. Differences between the right and the left were more evident regarding the values of democracy and greater Israel. Those were the less important values to respondents on the whole, and also to the respondents belonging to each of the two blocs. But many more on the right named greater Israel as first or second choice than on the left, and more on the left mentioned democracy.

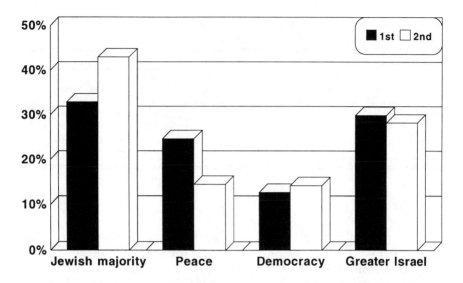

Figure 8.4. Value choices as they apply to Likud and right voters, 1988 (*N* = 395).

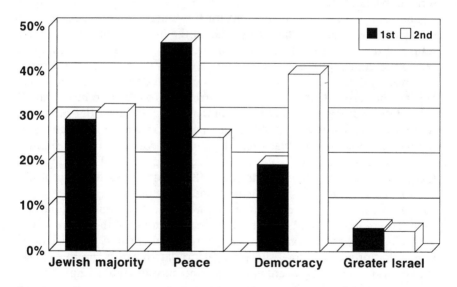

Figure 8.5. Value choices as they apply to Labor and left voters, 1988 (*N* = 271).

Table 8.4. *Correlations Between Value Rankings and Policy Preferences*
(Panel and General Samples)

| | Panel | | | | General | | | |
| | Policy scale | | Territories | | Policy scale | | Territories | |
	1988	1990	1988	1990	1988	1990	1988	1990
Greater Israel	.50	.43	.53	.51	.45	.41	.42	.44
Democracy	-.44	-.30	-.41	-.31	-.45	-.36	-.39	-.29
Peace	-.35	-.35	-.29	-.28	-.26	-.26	-.16	-.27
Jewish majority	.27	.27	.17	.10	.23	.22	.13	.12

VALUE PRIORITIES AND POLICY PREFERENCES

To have political credence, value priorities must be related to policy preferences. To examine these relations the simple correlations between the separate value rankings and policy preferences were generated. Two policy measures were used throughout the analysis. The first related to the future of the territories question and the second was the policy scale, both described in Chapter 4.[11]

Table 8.4 presents the correlations for the general samples between the four value rankings and the policy scale in the first two columns, and the future of the territories question in the next two. The next four columns repeat the same information in the same order for the panel respondents.[12] It is evident that value priorities were indeed related to the policy positions held by the respondents. Most of the correlations were quite high, and all were statistically significant at the commonly used .05 level. Furthermore, when the correlations for the different value rankings across the years and samples were compared, the general pattern of correlations was similar.

The values appear in Table 8.4 in descending order of their average (absolute value) correlation with policy. This order holds for each of the eight columns, with very minor exceptions.[13] The order corresponds completely to the pattern of correlations between the value rankings and the right-left continuum, and reinforces the interpretation of the values in the preceding sections. The value ranking most closely related to policy position is that of greater Israel; its average correlation across the row is .44. While it is the least important value, it is the most discriminating. A small minority of Israelis rank it as most important to them, and its average ranking is the lowest, similar to that of democracy; but the relative preference for it is the most potent predictor of willingness to return territories versus annexation and security policy more generally. The more one espouses greater Israel over the other values, the more likely one is to oppose the return of the territories and adopt hawkish positions more generally.

The other important finding consistent with the conception of the role of values is that the relative importance one attaches to keeping Israel a Jewish state was only weakly related to policy positions; its average row correlation of .20 was by far the lowest among the four values. Those who attached more importance to this value were slightly more likely to be hawkish and support annexation, but this tendency was weak. To put it differently: knowing the importance of a Jewish state for a respondent provided the least indication of the stand taken on policy items on the public agenda. Indeed, as has been seen, this value was the most highly prized by the samples, and it also had the least variance in people's ranking of it. This is the clearest example of a valence issue, and as such it related least to the conflictual issues on the agenda. It is important to note that this result is not an artifact of the ranking's lowest variance.

Next in importance after greater Israel in terms of the strength of the correlations with policy came democracy, with an average row correlation of −.34. Democracy as a value was ranked low by Israeli Jews among the four values, and, like the other low-ranking value of greater Israel, it was a conflictual value. The average correlation of peace with policy was −.28, which put it in the third place, before Jewish majority and after democracy. Respondents who ranked peace or democracy higher were more likely to adopt dovish positions, compared to respondents who cared less about these two values. The values of Jewish majority and peace, ranked high by the samples when value choices had to be made, were the weakest predictors of policy positions. Greater Israel and democracy, on the other hand, which were ranked lower, were more political and conflictual and therefore more closely related to policy positions.

Simple correlations are, of course, not enough to establish the importance and the impact of values on policy attitudes. Multivariate analysis is required to demonstrate the influence of values when other factors are controlled for. And some analysis of change is called for to bolster the causal interpretation that values affect attitudes. These analyses are undertaken here using regression techniques.

The focus is on the values as a whole, for two major reasons. First, it is important to substantiate the claim that value rankings matter, and not simply that each value has a separate impact. Second, there is a technical problem involved in the estimation of the unique effect of each of the four value rankings, as there is a linear dependency among the ranked items in the set. Three of the four value rankings determine uniquely the fourth. Thus all four values cannot be included in one regression equation as they would produce perfect multicollinearity. More crucially, the partial regression coefficients do not provide appropriate measures of the impact of the values, since they indicate the unique effect of each variable, holding all other variables constant – including the other value rankings. In any case, information about the joint effect of the value rankings is fully contained in three of the rankings.

For each of the two dependent policy variables, two stepwise multiple regressions in three steps were performed, with the blocs defined a priori. The first regression entered the three value rankings in the first stage, other attitudinal determinants of policy position in the second stage, and psychological and sociodemographic variables in the third stage. In the second stepwise regression the order of the first two stages was reversed: first, all attitudinal variables except the value rankings were entered; next the value rankings; and finally, the psychological and sociodemographic variables. This design allowed the assessment of the impact of the value rankings in two ways. The R^2 from the first stepwise regression estimated the contribution of the full set of value ranking on policy positions without taking into account any other attitudinal variables. The R^2 from the second stepwise regression provided a minimum estimate of the contribution of the values, in that it tells what the information about the full set of value rankings adds to an understanding of policy attitudes above and beyond other attitudinal factors.[14]

Only in the 1990 survey were all the appropriate questions asked to estimate the full models. The value ranking task was introduced only in the 1988 survey, and was not available for the 1987 sample. In 1988, some of the other attitudinal questions were not asked. But the panel design allows the extension of the analysis over time. For panel respondents, the estimate of the full model can be made at three time points. This requires use of the 1988 values measure as an indicator for the 1987 values orientation of the panel respondents in the equations predicting their 1987 policy attitudes, and to use the 1987 God-and-us and go-it-alone scales in the 1988 equations.[15]

Table 8.5 presents the summary results of these regression analyses with the policy scale and the territories question as dependent variables, for the general 1990 sample, and for the panel sample, on the 1987, 1988, and 1990 policy scores. The results obtained using the smaller panel data set need to be approached with caution; thus it is reassuring to find that they are consistent with the general sample results. The lowest contribution of values is in the magnitude of 6 percent of the policy score's variance, the highest contribution is 37 percent. The numbers for the two dependent variables are quite similar. On the average, value rankings when they come first explain 23 percent of the variance of policy; when value rankings come after all the other attitudinal variables, they still add to the "explanation" of policy on the average around 11 percent. By all standards, this is impressive.[16]

Table 8.5. *Summary Statistics for Stepwise Regressions on Policy[a]*

	Policy scale				Territories			
	1990 Sample	1987	1988 Panel	1990	1990 Sample	1987	1988 Panel	1990
Total R^2	.42	.44	.61	.46	.26	.24	.46	.37
R^2 values first	.23	.18	.37	.21	.20	.08	.30	.29
R^2 change; values second bloc[b]	.06	.11	.15	.07	.10	.06	.14	.19
$N =$	647	138	136	145	643	134	133	149

[a] Regressions include as predictors three of the value rankings (Jewish majority, democracy, and greater Israel), scales measuring other attitudinal constructs found to affect policy positions including threat, go-it-alone, God-and-us, and overcome; the dogmatism scale, and all important socio-economic variables. These included a dummy variable for ethnic background, income, education, density of living conditions, religiosity, age, and sex.
[b] Values inserted after other attitudinal predictors.

Value rankings matter and have a significant effect on policy. Yet, all of the tests to this point were cross-sectional. To strengthen the argument further, the panel data has been employed to show that value rankings affect change in policy attitudes.

We have so far shown that value rankings do matter and have a significant effect on policy. Yet, all of our tests were cross-sectional. To make the case stronger, we will use the panel data to show that value rankings affect change in policy attitudes.

To do so, respondents' policy scores (at time t) were regressed on their past policy positions (at t−1) and on the basic attitudinal positions they held at time t. Policy attitudes as a function of the position the respondents held on that issue in the past, but also of where they stand now in terms of threat perception, on the God-and-us, go-it-alone, and overcome constructs, and in terms of their value rankings, all of which are assumed to structure their specific attitudes (eight independent variables in all) were specified. By including the lagged dependent variable in the model as predictor, the impact of these basic attitudinal variables on the changes in policy attitudes can be estimated by holding initial policy attitudes constant. At the same time, the problems inherent in analyzing change scores can be avoided, and it is possible to control for any initial differences in policy positions (Markus 1979; Kessler and Greenberg 1981).

For such panel models, ordinary least-squares is usually not appropriate and results in biased estimators, since the disturbance term in the equation will be correlated with one of the regressors – the lagged dependent variable. Instead, two-stage least-squares was used.[17] The results of this

Table 8.6. *Dynamic Regressions on Policy Positions^a: Panel Data*

| | Policy scale | | Territories | |
	1988	1990	1988	1990
$N =$	115	125	114	128
R^2	.54	.40	.39	.33
Stepwise results				
Stage I: Yt -1^b R^2	.26	.23	.13	.23
Values in Stage II R^2 change	.15	.06	.19	.08
Values in Stage III				
(after Yt -1 and other attitudinal predictors)				
R^2 change	.08	.03	.12	.07

^{a} Regressions included eight predictor variables: the lagged dependent variable, three value rankings, God-and-us, go-it-alone, threat, and overcome.

^{b} Yt -1 is the dependent variable lagged, e.g., in the regression where the dependent variable is the 1988 policy scale, Yt -1 is each respondent's 1987 policy scale score. The estimation technique involves the use of instrumental variables in a two-stage least-squares estimation procedure.

dynamic analysis are presented in Table 8.6. The first two columns provide the results for the policy scale. The first regression is that of the 1988 policy scale scores on the 1987 policy scale scores, the 1988 value rankings and other 1988 attitudinal variables.[18] The second regression is that of the 1990 policy scores on the 1988 scores and the 1990 attitudinal variables. The next two columns provide the results for similar regressions on the territories question.

These results show that the value rankings had an effect on changes in policy position and not only on them at the same point in time. In 1988, value rankings "explained" 15 and 19 percent of the change in policy positions from 1987, when coming first; and add 8 and 12 percent to the "explanation" of the change in policy above and beyond the other attitudinal variables. In 1990 the corresponding numbers were lower: values explained 6 and 8 percent when coming first and 3 and 7 percent beyond the other attitudinal variables.[19]

To the burgeoning literature which argues that the mass public is less "innocent" ideologically than previously suggested, it is important to add that when values are in conflict, people's value hierarchies structure their policy preferences to a significant degree. Moreover, value priorities are not random but are politically and ideologically structured, and certain value combinations are more prevalent and more enduring than others. An impressive amount of the variance of policy positions relating to the Israeli-Arab conflict was explained by people's value priorities among peace, greater Israel, democracy, and Jewish majority. These value priorities accounted for significant portions of the variance of policy positions as well as changes in policy position; they did so on their own and also beyond other attitudinal predictors.

The data presented here explore the conditions under which value hierarchies matter more and less. The first wave of the panel was in the field in December 1987, just as the intifada started and before its meaning was grasped by either the Israeli public or policy makers. The 1988 and 1990 data were collected well into the first and third years of the intifada, the 1988 survey coinciding with the election campaign. The intifada had a great impact on Israeli public opinion (Arian et al. 1992). A major result was that the conflict among the values became more pronounced and more articulate. Under such circumstances, value rankings became more strongly related to the attitudes to which they were pertinent. With greater awareness of the value trade-offs, the ranking became more consistent with policy options one supported; rankings became less general and abstract, and therefore more highly related to specific attitudes (Ajzen and Fishbein 1977; Ajzen 1989).

Table 8.4 demonstrated that value rankings had more influence on people's attitudes toward the territories in 1988 and 1990 than in 1987, but this pattern did not hold for the policy scale. However when the distinction is made between the politically involved and the noninvolved, the same pattern as for the territories question was found among the former, but not among the latter. Issues regarding the territories may be more directly related to the values than are other, more general positions on foreign and security affairs. Therefore those who are less attentive and less sophisticated politically may not have made these connections, resulting in greater congruity with the simpler territories question, but not the more general and complicated security policy syndrome. Sniderman and Tetlock (1986, 75) indeed suggest that "the less aware [people are politically], the more likely a connection is to be made with an immediately relevant and relatively specific idea; the more aware they are, the more likely it is to be made with a relatively removed, and comparatively abstract idea." While they have in mind the connection between policy preference and more proximal or distal values or ideas, the same logic applies here.

The intifada seems to have increased the role of value rankings in structuring people's policy positions. In a similar vein, the 1988 election campaign seems to have increased the relation between people's value hierarchy and policy positions (as suggested in Tables 8.5 and 8.6). Election campaigns provide political stimuli that seem to strengthen the relationship between value preferences and policy: they sensitize people to their value priorities and to conflicts among values as well as among values and issue positions, resulting in more constraint. This analysis points in the direction of political contexts which accentuate value conflict, such as the intifada and election campaigns; but such circumstances are varied and many.

The dilemma facing Israel is to order the values of a Jewish state, democracy and equality for all, peace and the land of Israel, in a manner which will preserve consensus in the polity. It has been shown that the Jewish majority and peace values were ranked high by a vast majority of the population and provide the consensual basis of the political discourse. The values of greater Israel and democracy were less important and conflictual; they exhibited more individual level stability, and were more strongly correlated with policy attitudes and the right-to-left self-placement. Toward the right end of the political spectrum, the value of greater Israel dominated, while at the left, democracy was dominant. The value of Israel as a Jewish state was shown to be a clear valence dimension in Israeli politics. Despite attempts to politicize it, most Israeli Jews supported the value regardless of party identification.

9

Democracy

One of Israel's most impressive achievements has been to maintain the level of sacrifice and alertness necessary to handle its security problems, while sustaining a democratic political system. Just as features of Israeli democracy are often criticized by observers and participants, so too is the fit imperfect between security-related issues and democratic practices. Tensions between the two were often near the surface. Israel's short history has been replete with dilemmas concerning the rule of law, censorship, freedom of organization, the politicization of the military, and the multiplicity of roles played by the military (Negbi 1987; Hofnung 1991; Kremnitzer 1993). As Yaniv (1993, 227) put it, "The most fundamental flaws of Israeli democracy are revealed . . . when the system is evaluated against the universal standard of the rule of law."

Most Israelis who were born abroad and not in Israel came from non-democratic countries; most born in Israel lived only under democratic government. As a native-born generation becomes more dominant, the bulk of the population will have grown up under democratic government. But, of course, it will have been an experience of growing up under Israeli democracy, with that peculiar blend of Eastern European factionalism and Jewish communal focus. The individualism and emphasis on civil liberties which characterize many Western, postindustrial regimes were never important features of Israeli democracy, although recent trends have highlighted that direction.

Israeli democracy provides a mixture of great attention to formal matters such as majority rule and elections, but more cavalier concern for the underpinning values of democratic life such as civil liberties and minority rights. While a vocal and growing segment of the public stresses these values, they seem to be pursued and tolerated by the powers-that-be until other interests, such as security demands or coalition convenience, overwhelm them. Still, the maintenance of democratic government throughout Israel's history must be considered as one of its finest achievements, even

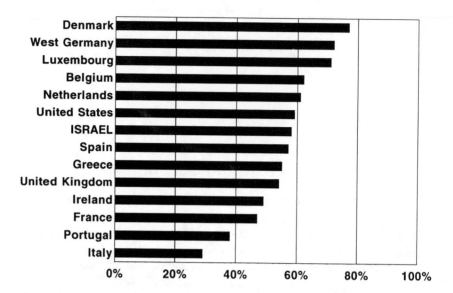

Figure 9.1. Public satisfaction with democracy in Israel and in other democratic countries. (Data: 1987 for Israel, 1985 for other countries.)

though it is a democracy which keeps nuclear preparations (or the lack of them) under a thick veil of secrecy, one in which a foremost jurist agreed that the security services were allowed to apply "mild physical pressure" in interrogations (Kremnitzer 1993), and in which press censorship has been always present even if it is often self-imposed (Lahav 1993).

No less important, Israelis seemed satisfied with their democracy. When asked about it in 1987, almost 60 percent expressed their contentment with the regime. This was almost precisely the rate of Americans who expressed that opinion and put Israel squarely in the middle of the range of satisfaction with their democratic governments compared to Western European and North American populations (see Figure 9.1; Rabier et al. 1986; Janda, Berry, and Goldman 1993, 56). Israel placed between the more gratified respondents of countries of northern Europe and the less fulfilled citizens of southern Europe. Since that question was asked in 1987, a number of steps have been taken to further democratize the Israeli system, such as the introduction of primaries in the selection procedures of the two major parties, and the provision that the prime minister will be directly elected. Time will tell whether or not Israelis find that these reforms add to their satisfaction with democracy.

Israelis were not unanimous in their positive evaluation of democracy, but on the whole their assessment over time was approving. The number in Figure 9.1 is based on the question asked in 1987, to which 58 percent said that they were pleased (50%) or very pleased (8%) with the functioning of Israeli democracy, compared with 42 percent who were somewhat (33%) or very displeased (9%) with it. When asked in 1990 whether or not the political system of Israel was too democratic, 52 percent responded that it was just right, 34 percent said it was too democratic to a very large (7%) or certain extent (27%), and another 14 percent thought that it was not democratic enough to a very large (2%) or certain (12%) extent.

As in other democratic countries, civil rights were upheld by Israeli public opinion, especially in their abstract form (Shamir and Sullivan 1983). As these principles became more concrete, support for them dwindled. For example, whereas 87 percent of the 1988 sample acknowledged democracy to be the best form of government, 24 percent accepted the statement that under certain conditions it is best to take the law into your own hands. Another instance: 66 percent agreed with the principle that "everyone must have the same rights before the law regardless of their political views," but only 41 percent of that same sample disagreed with the statement that "Jews who commit illegal acts against Arabs should be punished less severely than Arabs who commit illegal acts against Jews." Put more clearly, 59 percent thought that Jews should get special treatment from their democratic state.

The question discussed in Chapter 4 about the degree of civil rights to be extended to the residents of the territories should they be annexed to Israel is relevant here (see Appendix II.2). The public's opinion changed over time regarding the civil rights which should be extended to the residents of the territories in a very liberal direction. From about 1 in 5 favoring some or all rights in 1984, by 1994 more than 1 in 4 supported granting these Arabs full rights, including the right to vote in Knesset elections. An additional third was for extending civil rights but not the right to vote for members of the Knesset in 1993. Leaving the situation as it was at the time of the interview fell to 28 percent in 1994 from 60 percent in 1984. The percentage favoring a decrease in rights was more stable. Aggregate support for rights increased, although there was evidence of individual change in a less supportive direction; among panel respondents who were asked the question twice within a period of a year, willingness to extend rights decreased as the intifada continued (see Chapter 4). Advancing rights was a tough measure of the willingness to support democratic principles in a very difficult situation, and Israelis interviewed, on the whole, came through the test well.

The possibility of annexing the territories posed a stark dilemma for Israelis who thought about civil rights. In 1986, the territories were administered by military authorities and civil rights were accordingly curtailed. Arab inhabitants of the territories did not enjoy the political and civil rights which are part and parcel of modern democratic regimes. They could not vote for the Knesset, and much of their personal and communal activity was regulated by administrators of the Israeli civil and military authorities. Since they were under Israeli jurisdiction, the inhabitants of the territories did have the right to apply to Israel's Supreme Court which serves as the country's High Court of Justice. The dilemma was that if the territories were turned over to some other jurisdiction (such as Jordan), civil rights for the inhabitants might not be the new regime's top priority. For civil rights to be achieved, perhaps, paradoxically the answer was annexation; but that would have to be at the expense of Palestinian self-determination.

The choice between the two polar extremes – security on the one hand, and the rule of law on the other – was a stark one, and most situations allowed for obfuscation and interpretation so that a clear choice between two extremes was unnecessary. This dilemma characterized the public debate in Israel, especially in the 1980s and 1990s. In the face of the Lebanon campaign in 1982, and then with the onset of the intifada in 1987, the relations between the political and military spheres, and the manner in which the military operated within the framework of the rule of law, were closely scrutinized by the public (Negbi 1987; Sprinzak 1991). The issues were especially complex regarding the intifada, because the defense forces were not designed or trained for the type of police action which resulted from the low level of hostilities, almost always against stone-throwing demonstrators, that characterized the early stages of the uprising. The tactics used to repress and deter the Arab population called into question the commitment of the army to the rights of the demonstrators, and focused attention on the zealousness of certain officers and soldiers in interpreting the orders of commanders and political leaders.

Implementing the rule of law is often frustrating since what seems right and necessary at the moment must be deferred owing to abstract principle and legal maneuvering. Whether fighting crime or fighting wars, the temptation to suspend the rule of law is always present. The samples were asked to rank their own opinion regarding the dilemma between security considerations on the one hand (rank 1) and the observance of the principles of the rule of law (rank 7) on the other. The results show that the population always favored the security side of the equation, and over the years this trend seemed to strengthen; the mean for the 1987 survey was 3.6, and it declined as time went on, reaching the point closest to the security pole and farthest from the rule of law pole at 3.0 in 1988, and 3.1 in 1993. Compared to 28 percent who placed themselves in the first two ranks at the security end of the continuum in 1987, 37 percent did so in 1994; the percent who chose ranks 6 and 7, at the opposite end of the proposition, fell from 16 percent in 1987 to 15 percent in 1994 (see Appendix II.8).

The perception in public opinion was that the actions which the IDF was called upon to undertake in the territories was having a deleterious effect on its fighting ethic. Using a seven-point scale, with 7 being a positive effect and 1 a negative effect, the mean score of the samples between 1986 and 1990 fell from survey to survey from 4.2 to 3.6, then vacillated in later surveys, reaching a low point of 3.2 in 1992 (see Appendix II.9).

A third reading of the priorities of the Israeli population was provided by the respondents' placing themselves on a seven-point scale that ranged between the opinion that security must always be above all other considerations (rank 1), and the proposition that always preferring security considerations above social and economic ones may be more harmful than helpful in the long run (rank 7). The mean rankings in each of the surveys was near 3.0 on the seven-point scale, again indicating a leaning toward the security proposition. In 1990, 45 percent of the respondents placed themselves in the first and second ranks, strongly supporting the security position, compared with only 7 percent in ranks 6 and 7.

These attitudes were weakly related to social class variables, such as education, and more strongly related to political attitudes and the reported vote (Arian et al. 1988, chapter 6). These findings reinforce the basic finding that Israeli public opinion is malleable on security matters and bears the potential for change. Public opinion is not blocked by immutable bonds to social class or ethnic background. It is the political system and its leadership which hold the keys for opinion change and for policy change – or lack of change. Voters of the Likud and the right, and voters of the religious parties, were much more likely to be near the security pole than were voters of Labor and the left. But the results must be understood in a relative manner; while it was true that the left was farther away from the security pole, it was also important to point out that the score of Labor-left on the security–rule of law question was 3.7 in 1988 and 4.0 in 1992. The midpoint of the seven-point scale is 4. So while the left in Israel was more "liberal" than the voters of the right and the religious party supporters, using this measure it was very close to the center in a more absolute sense, and moving closer to it.

Not only did they choose security, Israelis interviewed in 1987 thought that the political leadership preferred security over the rule of law by a 2:1 ratio; however, this was a more "democratic" rate than the respondents gave the founding fathers of the country. When asked about the leaders at the time of independence, the respondents' assessment, at a 3:1 rate, was that those leaders favored security over the rule of law. The following question was presented: "To what extent does the present political leadership give preference to security interests as opposed to the principle of the rule of law, or on the contrary, do they more prefer the rule of law to security interests?" Thirty-six percent responded that the leader preferred the rule of law always (6%) and usually (30%), and 64 percent thought they preferred security interests usually (54%) and always (10%). When asked "about the political leadership at the time of independence," the respondents indicated that they thought that decisions were even more security-oriented in the past than they were at the time of the 1987 poll. A very high 76 percent thought that in the independence era security interests were given primacy always (28%) or usually (48%), compared with only 24 percent who thought that rule of law issues were always (3%) or usually (21%) preferred.

During the late 1980s the activities of the Shin Bet and the Mossad were more widely discussed and became more public than had been the case before. A quarter of the 1987 sample thought there was insufficient supervision of these organizations, while another quarter said there was too much oversight; half said that the amount of control was just right.

This ability to give a tough-minded evaluation of the security situation is an important characteristic of Israeli public opinion. And turnabout is fair play. A good example of that was evident regarding a set of questions asked in 1987 about spies and spying. In the period before the fieldwork, Jonathan Pollard, an American Jew working for the U. S. Navy, had been convicted of spying for Israel. The sample was asked whether it was "justifiable for Israel to spy on the United States in order to procure information vital for Israel's security." Forty percent of the sample thought that this was very (11%) or somewhat (29%) acceptable, with 60 percent rejecting the notion somewhat (35%) or completely (25%). It is fascinating that this distribution is almost identical to the responses for a second question: whether it is "justifiable for the United States to spy on Israel in order to procure information vital for America's security." In response to that question, 36 percent responded affirmatively as opposed to 64 percent who disagreed.

LEADERSHIP AND LEADERS

Israelis put great stock in the defense of the country, and they were respectful of the security establishment, but the cynicism that characterized the society was not far from the surface. For the most part, Israelis reported that they trusted the statements of their leadership regarding security. Between 70 and 80 percent said they completely trusted these statements in various surveys, with 20 to 30 percent more reticent to do so. However, in the more politicized atmosphere of the negotiations under way in 1994, the sample was almost evenly split regarding the credibility of the government's explanations of its intentions in the political negotiations: 19 percent thought they were very credible, 35 percent said credible, 22 percent thought barely credible, and 25 percent not credible at all.

The motivations of the leadership when making decisions in the security sphere, however, were viewed with a jaundiced eye by the Israeli public. When asked whether the country's elected leaders made their decisions regarding security solely on the basis of objective and relevant considerations, or whether other considerations also played a role, a third reported that objective considerations guided their decisions, and two-thirds thought that extra-security considerations also played a role. When the same question was asked regarding the IDF's senior commanders, the view was less skeptical, but still far from trusting. Fewer than half of the respondents thought that the decisions of the army commanders were always motivated only by professional and relevant considerations, and a little more than half thought that other considerations also came into play. The questions regarding the political and military leadership were asked in both 1986 and 1987, and the response rates were almost identical.

The support for democratic norms notwithstanding, there is a stubborn respect for the strong personality in Israeli politics, up to a point. This is part of the explanation of the enormous popularity of leaders like Ben-Gurion and Begin. The notion of a strong leader superseding the rule of law has long been supported by Israeli public opinion. In 1969, 64 percent preferred strong leadership to "all the debates and laws," and by 1981 the number was 72 percent. In 1984, just after Begin's resignation, it was down to 50 percent, and rose to 56 percent in 1988. In a 1990 question, the same issue was sharpened by a bolder question, and then the public proved reticent to replace democracy with a strong leader. The question was whether one agreed or disagreed, "given the present situation in the country, to declare a state of emergency and to give up the democratic frameworks provided by the Knesset and the cabinet, and to have a strong head of government with unlimited powers to deal with the situation." Seventy-one percent disagreed, 26 percent agreed, and 3 percent agreed to the arrangement for a limited amount of time.

Begin and Ben-Gurion were considered Israel's "best" prime ministers by far. Of the eight persons who held that position starting in 1948, the two shared almost 80 percent of the 1990 survey and 72 percent of the mentions in 1994. Begin led in 1990 with 41 percent, followed by Ben-Gurion with 38 percent; by 1994 the gap had widened, with Begin receiving 44 percent and Ben-Gurion 28 percent. Proximity in time was certainly related to this, because almost 30 years had passed since Ben-Gurion left office when the question was posed in 1990, compared to 7 for Begin. Nonetheless, the two

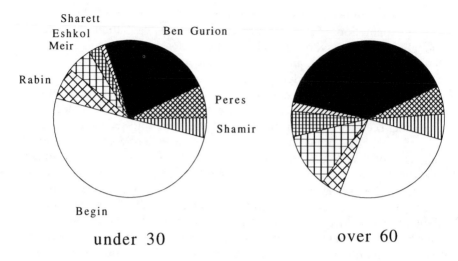

Figure 9.2. Ranking of "best" prime minister, by respondents' age (1994 survey).

of them were clearly the stars; none of the other six prime ministers received more than 8 percent (see Table 9.1, column 1). The generational cleavage in Israeli politics is clearly indicated; when the mean ages of those making each choice were calculated, the Ben-Gurion choosers were seven to ten years older than those who chose Begin, on average. The mean age of those choosing Ben-Gurion in 1990 was 44, while for Begin's choosers it was 34.6, the youngest of any of them. Another way of making the same point is to isolate the young (under 30) and the old (over 60) and see the patterns of their choices. That calculation is displayed in Figure 9.2. Begin was clearly the choice of the young, Ben-Gurion of the old.

The second generation of Israel tended to be Begin, Likud, territories, young, sephardi, religious; just as the first had been Ben-Gurion, Labor, kibbutz, now older, ashkenazi, secular. Some of these generalizations were developed in earlier chapters; others are evident in Table 9.1. A majority of those who chose Begin and Rabin as best prime minister were sephardi; this was also true of those who selected Shamir in 1994. Rabin's success with this substantial part of the population is important, because Labor has had difficulty penetrating this ethnic group. This underscores the finding presented in Chapter 5 that it was Rabin's broad electoral appeal that accounted in part for the 1992 reversal. Eshkol, Meir, and Peres, on the other hand, received much less proportional support from sephardim.

Regarding education, those who chose Shamir in both 1990 and 1994 had the lowest average number of years of education; those who chose Moshe

Table 9.1. *Best Prime Minister by Demography and Issues,[a] 1990 and 1994*

	Total %	% Sephardim	Mean age	Years of education	Religious observance	Left-right	Policy score
1990 Survey							
David Ben-Gurion	38	40	44.0	12.9	2.0	4.1	2.8
Moshe Sharett	1	33	38.4	13.9	1.6	4.1	2.6
Levi Eshkol	6	28	46.2	13.7	1.8	3.7	2.7
Golda Meir	5	30	39.4	13.3	1.8	4.2	3.0
Yitzhak Rabin	3	54	35.5	12.6	1.8	3.6	2.9
Menachem Begin	41	70	34.6	11.9	2.3	5.4	3.4
Yitzhak Shamir	3	44	35.9	11.6	2.3	5.2	3.5
Shimon Peres	3	31	42.6	13.6	1.9	3.3	2.4
Total	100	52	39.4	12.5	2.1	4.6	3.1
1994 Survey							
David Ben-Gurion	28	38	44.1	13.4	2.0	3.9	[b]
Moshe Sharett	1	38	43.1	15.1	1.4	3.9	
Levi Eshkol	3	26	45.2	13.7	1.6	3.9	
Golda Meir	8	23	44.3	14.0	1.9	4.3	
Yitzhak Rabin	6	51	38.2	13.1	1.8	2.6	
Menachem Begin	44	67	37.4	12.3	2.4	5.1	
Yitzhak Shamir	3	57	38.8	11.3	2.4	5.6	
Shimon Peres	7	28	39.8	14.0	1.6	2.8	
Total	100	50	40.0	13.0	2.1	4.4	

[a] Low scores for these variables indicate young age, lower education, no religious observance, and left respectively. For the 1990 policy scale, more conciliatory position.
[b] Not calculated for 1994, as explained in Chapter 4.

Sharett, the highest. Eshkol, Meir, and Peres were also chosen by those with a higher mean education level, while Begin, the other Likud prime minister in the list in addition to Shamir, was selected by those whose mean education was lower. Those who selected Begin and Shamir were much more religiously observant on average than the rest; Sharett was chosen by those who were most secular. It is interesting that the mean religious observance score for Ben-Gurion was in the middle; in fact, Ben-Gurion was a devout secularist but one who was identified with the establishment of the status quo in religious affairs.

On policy issues, the Likud-Labor distinction was firmly in place, as is appropriate when choosing among politicians. Those who chose Begin and Shamir placed themselves much more to the right than did the population as a whole; Peres and Rabin were the choice of those farthest to the left.

Regarding policy in 1990, Begin and Shamir were chosen by those with militant attitudes; with the exception of Peres, who was clearly favored by conciliators, the mean policy score of those who chose the others was in the middle. Those who chose Ben-Gurion and Sharett were quite dovish. This is fascinating because much is made of the policy debates between the two, and although conditions and problems were very different, Ben-Gurion was generally considered much more hard-line than Sharett (Sharett 1978). The comparison between the two is relative to the debates within the Labor party in the 1950s. When the comparison is made to the more right-wing Likud leaders, Begin and Shamir, the distinction between Ben-Gurion and Sharett remains, but it is put in its proper perspective: the Ben-Gurion choosers' mean policy score was 2.8, Sharett's group's a more dovish 2.6. Peres's group was most dovish at 2.4; those of Begin (3.4) and Shamir (3.5) most hawkish.

Since politicians make policy, and the public has a role in choosing the politicians, the public's preference is important. As in other countries, Israelis rally 'round their prime ministers in wartime, and incumbents are generally more popular than alternative candidates. These two generalizations stand out when survey results of the 1973–81 period are considered (see Table 9.2). Golda Meir was in semiretirement before being called to the prime ministry by her party upon Levi Eshkol's death in 1968, but in November 1973, a month after the Yom Kippur war which would eventually bring about her downfall, she was still the plurality choice of the respondents. Prime Minister Rabin outpolled Peres by 10 points in March 1977, but by May of that year, after Rabin removed himself from the top of the Labor list because of foreign currency improprieties, Peres was 11 points ahead. Begin, head of the opposition in March and May, scored about 20 points in both time periods; the same Begin was prime minister a month later and polled 47 percentage points.

Table 9.2 offers some interesting marginal notes regarding the fortunes of political actors of the period. During the Yom Kippur war, it was suggested by many that Golda would go. Allon and Dayan were considered by many as her heirs apparent, although they came, respectively, from Ahdut Haavoda and Rafi, factions of the Labor party outside the mainstream Mapai. The men whose intense competition would bedevil the party for the next two decades and more, Rabin and Peres, were not even mentioned in November 1973. Yadin's name emerged with the DMC in 1977, and Dayan's reemerged when he was defense minister in 1973 in the Labor government, and in 1981 when he was foreign minister in the Likud government. Weizman served in that same Likud government as defense minister. Sharon, Levy, and Shamir were mentioned for years in the Likud, but Sharon's and Levy's candidacies really never took off; Eban faced the same fate in Labor.

Table 9.2. *Choice for Prime Minister,[a] 1973-1981 (%)*

	11/73	3/77	5/77	6/77	3/81	4/81	5/81
Golda Meir	35	3	1	2	[b]	[b]	[b]
Yitzhak Rabin	[b]	28	13	11	20	20	22
Shimon Peres	[b]	18	24	13	24	22	18
Menachem Begin	19	19	21	47	28	33	41
Yigal Allon	17	1	1	1	[b]	[b]	[b]
Moshe Dayan	10	[b]	[b]	[b]	9	6	5
Yigael Yadin	[b]	12	8	11	[b]	[b]	[b]
Ariel Sharon	[b]	5	1	0	4	2	1
Ezer Weizman	[b]	[b]	[b]	[b]	6	5	4
Abba Eban	4	1	1	1	0	3	2
Yitzhak Shamir	[b]	[b]	[b]	[b]	2	2	1
David Levy	[b]	[b]	[b]	[b]	2	1	1

[a] Incumbent prime minister at time of survey italicized.

[b] Categories not shown are other candidates and no answer; total equals 100%.

We turn to the 1981 campaign, the most bitter, violent, and unsavory one in Israel's history. It was the first election in which the outcome was unclear in the public mind, since the reversal in the 1977 elections had been a surprise. The polls in March showed Labor winning handily; the actual results led to the largest concentration of votes for the two biggest parties and a virtual tie, with 48 Knesset seats for the Likud and 47 seats for the Labor-Mapam alignment. The personalities of the two candidates, their styles, and the public's images of them, indicate that an end had come to the politics-of-the-middle period. With the emergence of Begin and Shamir, on the one hand, and of Peres on the other, the era dominated by politicians generally accepted had passed; the period of division and polarization had begun. The center was evacuated, to be replaced by a shriller type of leader, and a more vitriolic brand of competitive politics.

Two months before the 1981 elections, before the parties' lists were in place, the people's choice for prime minister was split among Begin, Peres, and Rabin. Peres successfully fought off Rabin's challenge for first place in the party in the party convention, but the stinging attacks which featured the intrafaction fighting in Labor weakened his candidacy, and Begin successfully fought off the Labor challenge led by Peres. By the end of the campaign, Labor's two candidates still had about 40 percent between them, but Begin as the choice for prime minister climbed from 28 to 41 percent.

The battle between left and right, return and annex, ashkenazim and sephardim, was highlighted in the 1981 elections. Labor was confident that the 1977 reversal was a temporary mood-swing on the part of the electorate, and that its deserved dominance would be returned to it. Begin and the

Likud fought hard, pointing to the peace treaty with Egypt, and Finance Minister Aridor instituted economic policies which made consumer goods very affordable before the elections, and which made the rate of inflation soar afterward. Religious and ethnic symbols were brandished by the Likud, and Labor, preoccupied with its internal struggle, reacted poorly. As never before, the campaign was a fight over images of parties and leaders (discussed also in Chapter 5 and Arian 1989a, chapter 8).

How the two leaders were perceived became crucial to the campaign. Begin had entered office with the image of an unyielding hawk, and had managed to compromise his way to a peace treaty with Egypt. Peres had been in the public eye for years, but never as prime minister. To win, he would have to project a very positive image. But he was only partially successful. Consider four traits that voters everywhere would admire, and certainly voters in a country such as Israel, beset with challenges of survival (see Figure 9.3). The figure is arranged in a high-low and average format. Each bar represents the mean scores given the relevant leader on the trait mentioned. The high point of the bar is the mean score on a six-point scale for that trait for those in agreement with the position of the candidate regarding the territories (for Begin unwilling to return, for Peres willing to return). The low point is the mean for the group opposing the position taken by the candidate, and the "total" tick is the mean for the whole sample. This manner of display allows us to assess visually the means of the groups, and the spread of the difference between the two groups. Return territories was chosen because most respondents answered the question, and the population split about evenly. Using only Likud and Labor voters would have limited the number of respondents available since many chose other parties or had not yet decided how to vote, and it would have reiterated the relationship between party choice and candidate image.

We begin with the trait of being a strong leader. Figure 9.3 indicates that overall, Begin was considered to be stronger than Peres (tick marks), but that the differences were not great. Those who favored keeping the territories gave Begin a higher mark for strength than those who supported returning them gave Peres. In other words, people on Begin's side were more confident in their candidate on that score than were those on Peres's side. Those who disagreed with the political positions of each of the other candidates, though, gave the opposing candidates identical scores for strength; that is seen by observing that the low points for both candidates are identical.

Honesty was another matter entirely. There was simply so contest; Begin was perceived as being much more honest than Peres. Not coincidentally, many of the attacks on Peres from within his own party during the fight for the first place on the list focused on his alleged duplicity and deception. Whatever the reason, the differences between the two on this dimension

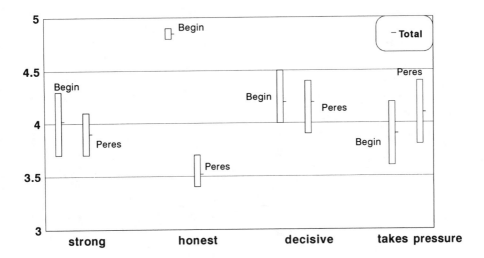

Figure 9.3. Begin and Peres: Comparison of personal images, 1981. (Six-point scale: 6 = strong, honest, decisive, takes pressure; 1 = weak, dishonest, indecisive, cannot take pressure. A high score for Begin indicates hawks and for Peres, doves.)

were dramatic. The mean score regarding Begin's honesty was much above that of Peres's. No less important, the range of opinion concerning Begin was very small – both those who agreed with his position on the territories and those who did not perceived Begin as very honest. The perception about Peres was very different.

Much less divergent was the public's perception regarding the decisiveness of the two candidates. Begin did slightly better, but the patterns were very similar. Regarding the ability to stand up to pressure, Peres did better than Begin. Begin had been through the Camp David agreements and had been under much pressure, especially from Jimmy Carter, the American president (Dayan 1981; Weizman 1981; Touval 1982; Quandt 1986). Evidently the public took the accusations of some of his detractors to heart. But when these perceptions were translated in the vote after a grueling campaign, it was Begin who squeezed out the victory.

This same technique of presenting the data is used for assessing the public's feeling regarding the trio that dominated Israeli politics in the 1980s – Shamir, Rabin, and Peres (see Figure 9.4). These politicians were evaluated with a love-hate thermometer measure, a technique often used in political polls. Respondents are asked to gauge their feelings toward the candidate on a 10-point scale, from 10 if they feel close (love), and a 1 if they feel repulsed (hate), or any position in between. Figure 9.4 is again

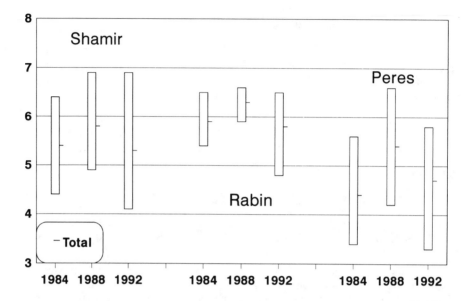

Figure 9.4. Shamir, Rabin, and Peres: Comparison of changes in respondents' love-hate attitudes, 1984, 1988, 1992. (Ten-point scale: 10 = love, 1 = hate. A high score for Shamir indicates hawks and a low score, doves; for Rabin and Peres, a high score indicates doves and a low score, hawks.)

arrayed with the tick mark being the overall score, the high point of the bar for Shamir being for those who wanted to retain the territories, and the low point for those who preferred to return them; for Rabin and Peres, the high point of the bar is for those willing to return territories, and the low point for those who wanted them held.

The most striking feature of the figure is the wide range of scores consistently generated by Shamir and Peres, and the much more compressed range for Rabin. Perceived to be more of a hawk than Peres, but more of a dove than Shamir, Rabin was in a less polarizing position. Peres is seen to suffer from a very negative profile. He has been probably the most stigmatized leader ever to reach the top of the Israeli political pyramid. Those who wanted to keep the territories disliked Peres much more than those who wanted to return them disliked Shamir (compare the bottom points of the various bars). Conversely, those who wanted to retain the territories liked Shamir more than those who wanted to return them liked Peres (compare the top points of the bars).

Personality clashes and nasty competition were not the province of Labor alone; they were evident in the Likud as well. In the post-Begin era,

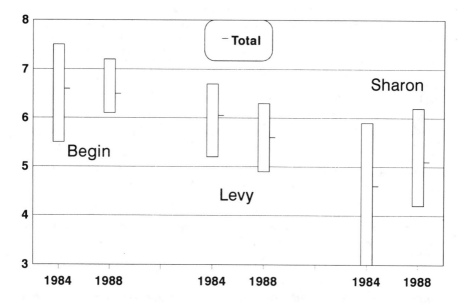

Figure 9.5. Begin, Levy, and Sharon: Comparison of changes in respondents' love-hate attitudes, 1984 and 1988. (Ten-point scale: 10 = love, 1 = hate. A high score indicates hawks and a low score, doves.)

the major antagonists were Yitzhak Shamir, David Levy, and Ariel Sharon – all contenders in the 1980s. In the 1990s, new names such as Binyamin "Bibi" Netanyahu and Benny Begin (Menachem's son) also emerged. It is revealing to compare the thermometer score which Begin registered in 1984 and 1988 with Levy's and Sharon's in those years (see Figure 9.5), and with those already discussed for Shamir, Rabin, and Peres from Figure 9.4. Begin was far and away the most popular of the six. His two average scores were about 6.5; of the others, only Rabin approached that in 1988. And even among those who agreed with his position about keeping the territories, Begin's approval was unparalleled compared to the scores of other politicians: he was the only politician to have any reading above 7.0, which he scored for both measurement periods among those who wanted to retain the territories. For others who wanted to keep the territories, Sharon, the super-hawk, scored about 6.5.

Sharon was the most reviled of the politicians, scoring a 3.0 on the thermometer in 1984 among those who disagree with him and were willing to return the territories. This was after the Lebanese war which Sharon had engineered, and he was highly unpopular; his pattern in that year was similar to the ones generated by Peres in 1984 and 1992. Their spreads were

Table 9.3. *Choice for Prime Minister,*[a] *1994*

	Total sample	Labor voters	Labor voters; party members	Likud voters	Likud voters; party members
N =	1,239	328	25	308	41
Labor (%)					
Rabin	28	62	68	b	b
Peres	14	29	32	b	b
Likud (%)					
Netanyahu	21	b	b	51	63
Sharon	10	b	b	15	15
Benny Begin	9	b	b	18	7
Levy	2	b	b	4	2
Tzomet (%)					
"Raful" Eytan	13	2	b	7	2

[a] Other candidates not reported, hence totals do not equal 100%.

[b] Not relevant.

wide, and their total ratings were low. Shamir also had a large spread, but his averages were higher. Levy's pattern in his camp was similar to Rabin's in his, with narrow spreads and respectable averages.

The next generation of Likud leadership was introduced after the resounding defeat the party suffered in the 1992 elections. Shamir and Moshe Arens stepped aside and younger men competed in the 1993 primaries. As the primaries approached, Netanyahu emerged as a strong contender, even outstripping Prime Minister Rabin in the prime minister choice question in the 1993 survey. By 1994, Rabin had outrun Netanyahu, with other candidates also having substantial support (see Table 9.3). Primaries in both Labor and Likud have been closed to party members only; Table 9.3 presents the survey results, first for the entire sample, then for those who reported they would vote Labor or Likud if the elections were held that day, and then for those who would vote Labor or Likud and who reported that they were a member of a political party. The assumption was that this last combination would participate in either the Labor or the Likud primary. Both front-runners did better among their party's members than they did among their party's voters.

DOING DEMOCRACY

National security issues are very salient to Israelis. They are exposed to these matters from an early age, and society reinforces this exposure; political socialization in Israel is coextensive with an introduction into matters of national security. This has been true throughout Israel's history: fathers, teachers, big brothers, boyfriends, and uncles have gone off to the army, to military reserve service, and to war; an important element in the status system of adolescents is the army unit to which they aspire, and the one into which they are finally accepted (Arian et al. 1988, chapter 5).

These patterns were underscored during the 1991 Gulf war, in which the home front became the battlefield. Everyone – including infants and children – wore uniforms (gas masks), and all were recruited for active service, as schools and nurseries closed for weeks. Television had special war-related news programs for children, and the war built to a crescendo just as the Jewish holiday of Purim (a joyous festival, especially for children, celebrating the defeat of the biblical Haman with masquerading and reveling) was observed. There can be no doubt of the salience of national security issues in Israeli life.

Salience, however, is not the same as impact. That there is an unusually high degree of awareness of national security issues does not in and of itself explain how these issues affect the course of Israeli politics, how public opinion impinges on the direction of national security, nor indeed, how the simultaneous championing of security matters and a democratic political system is effectuated (Zaller 1992; Nincic 1992).

The expectation is that members of a democratic public should be informed and interested about policy and that they should participate in politics; students of the American scene are divided about how influential the public is, but agree that the data clearly show low rates of information, interest, and participation. The case in Israel can be summarized as follows: Israelis are prolific consumers of the news media and they are attentive to security issues, they are knowledgeable about security matters, and yet they are tentative about their security attitudes and feel they have little influence on security matters. They believe they must be supportive of government and obey orders, even though they are skeptical about politicians and even army chiefs.

Israelis are known to be immense consumers of news (Katz and Gurevitch 1976). In both the 1988 and 1992 surveys more than half the respondents reported reading at least one newspaper a day. The mass media received mixed reviews, however, regarding the degree of their responsibility in reporting security matters. Fifty-seven percent thought they were very responsible (12%) or responsible (45%) in 1993, compared with 45 percent (4% and 41%, respectively) in 1987, and 67 percent (11% and 56%, respectively) in 1986.

Israelis are very well informed about security issues. Two questions regarding the status of the Arabs in the territories were applied in 1986 and in 1987 to test the level of information about relevant matters. Most Israeli

Table 9.4. *Political Knowledge,*[a] *1986 and 1987*

	1986		1987	
	High Court of Justice	Vote	High Court of Justice	Vote
Do Arabs in the territories have the right to ____?		?		
Definitely	*31%*	5%	*27%*	6%
I think so	29	17	29	11
I don't think so	22	19	24	20
Definitely not	18	*59*	21	*63*
Correct answers (%)	*60*	78	*56*	83
Two correct answers (%)		*45*		*52*

[a] Correct responses italicized.

Jews have no meaningful social contact with Arabs, so it was felt that these questions would identify those who had made an effort to gain and retain information on subjects of importance to the national security debate. The two questions asked were "Do the Arabs of Judea, Samaria, and the Gaza Strip have the right to apply to the High Court of Justice?" and "Do the Arabs of Judea, Samaria and the Gaza Strip have the right to vote in Knesset elections?" The correct answer for the first question was yes and for the second no (see Table 9.4). More than 55 percent answered the first question correctly in each survey, and more than three of four answered the second one correctly. Moreover, more than half got each of the answers right.

In 1987, respondents were also asked a series of questions relating to security matters such as armaments, prisoner exchanges, foreign aid, and the military budget (see Table 9.5). A very high 45 percent of the sample gave four or five correct answers to the questions.

Compare these levels to the 46 percent of Americans who could name their representative in Congress, and to the 30 percent who knew that the term of a U.S. House member is two years. Only 38 percent knew in 1964 that the Soviet Union was not a member of NATO, and only 23 percent in 1979 knew that the United States and the Soviet Union were the two nations involved in the SALT talks. In 1987, at the height of the Iran-Contra scandal, only half knew that the United States was supporting the rebels rather than the government in Nicaragua (Page and Shapiro 1992, 9–11).

There were only slight differences in the distribution of opinion when considered by various background factors. For example, respondents born

Table 9.5. *Security Knowledge,*[a] *1987*

Who makes the F-16?	Israel has submarines	Number of terrorists in 1985 exchange		U.S. military aid to Israel in 1987	Defense as % of government budget	
Israel 7%	*Yes* 62%	58	4%	< $1 billion 6%	< 10%	3%
France 6	Maybe 27	140	9	*$1-3 billion 53*	*10-40%*	47
U.S.A. *85*	Maybe not 9	485	18	$3-5 billion 32	40-75%	42
England 2	No 2	*1,150*	*61*	> $5 billion 9	> 75%	8
		3,900	8			

Correct Answers: 5 - 18%; 4 - 27%; 3 - 28%; 2 - 19%; 1 - 8%.

[a] Correct responses italicized.

in Asian and African countries and children of fathers born in those countries had a lower level of two correct answers to the political knowledge question (about 40%) than did their counterparts from Europe or America and second-generation Israelis (about 50% each). Security knowledge was related to both higher levels of education and lower perceptions of threat. This is consistent with Rokeach's (1960, 68) notion that beliefs fulfill two needs: they provide a cognitive framework in order to know and understand the world, but they are also used to deal with threatening aspects of reality. As the need to ward off threat becomes stronger, the cognitive need to know becomes weaker. Both needs can work together, but high levels of threat can lead to dogmatism or closed-mindedness (compare Tetlock 1983). These data offer no basis for declaring the less knowledgeable dogmatic, but the interactive impact of both high education and low threat on security information indicates that direction.

Despite high levels of knowledge, only 26 percent of the 1986 respondents felt they understood enough to express an opinion about security matters. Two things are important here: first, the rate of people who regularly express opinions on security matters (32%) was higher than those who felt they understood enough to express an opinion. Second, the difference between the low rate of confidence in themselves and the high rate of confidence in the leadership (82% say they can rely on the statements of the country's leaders concerning security issues) represents the deference which public opinion grants the leadership as it aligns itself with government policy.

Social and political differences were only weakly related to variations in attitude and to behavior patterns. Those who supported Likud positions on defense policy in the 1986 survey were stronger in their support of the government during crisis than were Alignment supporters (90% vs. 84%), and they tended to express opinions more often (34% vs. 28%). On the other hand, supporters of the Alignment defense position thought the media treated the security issue in a responsible way compared to the Likud supporters (74% vs. 60%), and they had a higher rate of correct answers to the political questions (48% vs. 42%). There were almost no differences between the two groups about whether they understood enough about security issues to express an opinion or whether they can influence security policy.

Israelis placed great importance on consensus during times of national security stress. The view that one must support the government in times of crisis, such as war, even if one differed with the government's policies, was agreed to by 83 percent of the sample in 1993, by 81 percent in 1988, and by 87 percent in 1986. When asked if criticism was permitted under these circumstances, more than a third said no, only 9 percent said that even vocal and strenuous opposition was permitted, with more than half of the sample allowing criticism, but of a subdued and restrained manner.

There was a good deal of readiness to obey authorities, even if one disagreed with these orders. The problem of conscientious objection, while a very visible issue in the 1990s, was relatively marginal in the early decades of statehood. Those who chose not to serve were rarely mentioned. Some probably left the country in order not to serve; others who were deferred, or excused for whatever reasons, generally chose not to advertise the fact. The special arrangements by which certain yeshiva students did not serve were widely seen as a necessity of the political parties for coalition purposes, but it was understood that they were exceptions to the norm, rather than the establishment of a new norm. Even after Lebanon and the onset of the intifada, army service and obeying orders were still clearly the societal norms. In the 1990 survey, for example, only 16 percent justified conscientious objection in any form.

When asked in 1990 about one's own hypothetical behavior, specifically relating to service in the territories, 83 percent reported that they would obey orders, 8 percent answered that they would serve in the territories but would request not to have any assignment related to putting down the uprising, 7 percent said that they would request service outside of the territories, and only 2 percent of the sample said that they would refuse the order to serve in the territories.

Refusing orders was generally considered an inappropriate pattern of behavior. In the 1987 survey, less than two years after the withdrawal from Lebanon, the respondents were asked about the correctness of certain types of behavior on the part of an officer who was in disagreement with government policy. Most respondents (about 70%) approved of the officer's speaking to his superiors about his disagreements with the policy, and asking to be relieved of his command. A third of the sample condoned the officer's communicating his attitudes in the mass media or his writing an anonymous letter expressing his position. Fifteen percent of the respondents thought it was permissible for the officer to disobey the orders given him.

In the 1994 survey, there were signs that this pattern was changing as issues regarding the future of the territories became more salient. Respondents were asked if they thought that a soldier was permitted to refuse to obey an order to remove Jewish settlers: 32 percent said the soldier could refuse such a command, and 68 percent said that the soldier could not refuse. When asked if they personally would obey such a command, 62 percent said yes and 38 percent said no. This rate of hypothetical refusal was high compared with previous hypothetical situations asked about in these surveys.

The situation in 1994 seemed to be at a different level. It might have been that there was a greater sense of national security in the country, but political anxiety was on the rise. A third of the sample seemed to be aware of the explosive nature of the situation the country faced. When asked to assess the chances of civil war as a result of the agreements that were being negotiated, 9 percent thought the chances were very high, and 24 percent thought the chances were high, compared with two-thirds who thought the chances were low (34%) or very low (33%).

The anxiety stemmed from the emergence of political friction among Jews in Israel. Israelis had long been accustomed to religious fractionalism and security solidarity. Now this familiar pattern was breaking down. The most obvious reminder of the breakdown was the 1994 Purim day massacre of Moslems at prayer in Hebron. A fanatic Jewish settler had undertaken the act, but the fear prevailed that others, especially Jewish settlers in the territories, might undertake other awful acts. In any event, there was no doubt that the settlements would be difficult to defend in an autonomous Palestinian enclave, and that the settlements would become a difficult point in negotiation with the PLO.

The Likud government's settlement policy had played an important role in the 1992 elections, and the call for a change in national priorities and U.S. pressure not to spend the aid money it provided Israel in the territories helped bring about the political reversal which catapulted Labor to power. Labor had cut back support for settlements, and there was much anxiety among the settlers about the future. In public opinion, there was virtually no change regarding the Jewish settlements in the territories since the 1992 elections. About a third supported them, a quarter opposed them, and the balance was ready to support them for security reasons (see Table 9.6). This was the crucial middle group that would be needed to win a majority for retaining or removing the settlements.

Table 9.6. *Support for Settlements in the Territories*
1992, 1993, and 1994

	1992	1993	1994
Completely support	30%	31%	32%
Only for security reasons	42%	40%	44%
Completely oppose	28%	29%	24%
Total	100%	100%	100%

Most respondents (55%) opposed removing the settlements in the permanent agreement – 34 percent very strongly, 21 percent somewhat opposed. The other 45 percent was composed of 15 percent very much in favor, and 29 percent somewhat in favor. There was overwhelming support (87%) in favor of financial support to those who might be forced to move because of the political agreements reached.

The response to the question about obeying orders was related to political opinions and to vote preference; the correlation with one's opinion about settlements, for example, was .33. The question about civil war probably tapped other anxieties in addition to political ones. Thus the correlations were lower between assessment of civil war and position regarding the settlements (.13), on the one hand, and a soldier's obligation to obey orders and the likelihood of civil war (.09).

The connection between demographic variables and these three questions revealed much of what has been documented here about patterns of attitudes in Israeli politics. Educational level, religious practice, and ethnic background are more closely related to politics and political matters; age and gender much less so. So too here: educational level, religious practice, and ethnic background were each related to one's position regarding the settlements, related but at lower levels to army obedience, and related even more weakly to the perceived likelihood of civil war. Age and gender showed no clear pattern at all. Figure 9.6 reports the rates of agreement with each of the questions for each educational level.

The generally high level of support for government and its treatment of security was especially fascinating in light of the low levels of influence Israelis believed they had over security and defense matters. Only 2 percent said that they and their friends could influence decision making on security issues to a great extent, with another 14 percent reporting that they could do so to a certain extent; 62 percent, however, reported they could not do so at all. When asked about specific issue-areas, such as the defense budget and the release of terrorists, the pattern remained about the same.

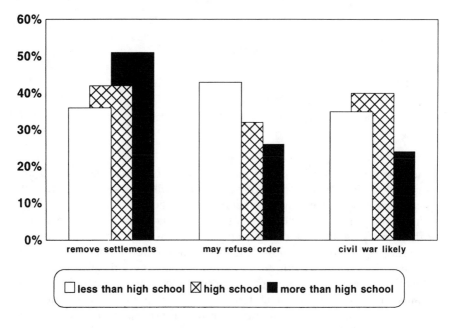

Figure 9.6. Attitude toward settlement in the territories, by respondents' education (1994 survey).

The other side of following orders is the level of trust generated by the leadership. Paradoxically, although the norm to follow orders was firm, the degree of trust in the leaders was lower. When asked in 1986 whether the army chiefs made security decisions based only on professional and relevant considerations, only 47 percent agreed. Not surprisingly, political leaders got lower grades than the army command regarding the professional nature of their decisions about security. Only 32 percent said that the political leaders' decisions regarding security were based on professional considerations. What is surprising, in light of the prevalent myth about the importance of security and the uniqueness of the army, is that both groups received such low assessments. When asked from whom to take advice regarding the future of the territories, the generals were mentioned by half the respondents in 1986 and 1987, and politicians by 17 percent. Political science professors were alluded to by 8 percent, higher than rabbis, who were mentioned by only 2 percent. After the generals, the public seemed to trust itself: about a quarter mentioned public opinion as the appropriate guide to setting policy. Not an unhealthy indicator in a democracy.

10

Conclusions

The best metaphor I know for the experience of observing political and security opinion in Israel is a long, extended roller-coaster ride. The ride goes along smoothly enough and then, quite without warning, the car takes a headlong plunge into the unknown, a dive which may be experienced as either terrifying or exhilarating, depending on one's point of view. Unlike an amusement park ride, however, this form of entertainment seems endless, with no finale leading to a smooth and soothing finish. In the past there has been one important regularity: that after an initial surge of change, things settle down and revert to familiar patterns with altered expectations for the next plummet. But there is no assurance that the jaunt will not spin out of control, and that after the next plunge the conductor (government) will not be able to assert authority as in the past, and will no longer take proud responsibility for the last surprise, or be in a position to exhort the public to prepare itself for future nasty turns.

The security debate in Israel surges and ebbs, twists and turns, pulsates and relaxes. These spasms often occur during and immediately after traumatic security or political events: a terrorist attack, a concession in peace talks, a war, a diplomatic breakthrough, a confrontation between Jewish settlers and the IDF. During these intense periods of articulation, the public absorbs the disputation and begins processing the content of the disputation. These are powerful stimuli and they are widely covered by the news media; they dominate public discourse and private conversation.

Organized expression of opinion is also widely covered but is obviously related to ongoing events. Politicians draw red lines beyond which the country cannot go; other politicians deplore these red lines. Rabbis offer their own advice to decision makers and soldiers based on holy sources; they are disputed by other rabbis and by politicians. Soldiers imply willingness to disobey orders; retired officers band together in support or denunciation of a policy move or a reaction to a given event. The results of a public opinion poll relating to policy and security are published. High school students write letters, partly reasoned, always emotional, explaining their support of or opposition to policy. These letters might declare opposition to being conscripted or the students' determination to disobey certain orders in the army, or they may express the opposite sentiments. Others express their opposition to those who wrote the original letters. Whatever the content, there are those who read into such missives much about the future generation.

As important as these expressions of opinion are in the political and media life of a nation, they are likely to raise more questions than answers, to provide more heat than light, to reinforce the already convinced, to cause further consternation in the minds of the perplexed. Are the declarations of Arab states and the pledges of nations of the world strong enough guarantees for relinquishing strategic territory and resources? Can Israel's continuing security be achieved by military means in the face of a hostile indigenous Arab population, growing in numbers and expressing more and more enmity toward Israel's continued occupation? Does liberal, humanist education lead to pacifist tendencies and defeatist attitudes? Does the national-religious curriculum of the Orthodox Zionist parties lead to extreme chauvinism and disregard to the rights of non-Jews? Which rabbis are right, those who interpret the scripture as forbidding the relinquishing of territories of the land of Israel, or those who claim that preserving life is of a higher priority, and hence the relinquishing of territories in which life is endangered is permitted. Is there one law for all, or is there a sense in which Jewish life, rights, and affliction have superior status in the religion, norms, and culture? Is Israel really at the brink of disaster and civil war, with a split army, a divided polity, and struggle between synagogue and state reminiscent of the Dark Ages of Europe?

These are some of the major questions of Israeli politics, and most of them demand interpretation of facts, appreciation of historical developments, or expertise in rabbinic literature. Answers given often justify and reinforce positions already held. These expressions are very different from the types of conclusions to be drawn from the public opinion surveys used in this study. The passion of politics and the urgency of organization are absent in the polite and detached demeanor in which a survey research unit collects the responses to questions in attitude studies.

This distinction between the way public opinion is perceived and the manner in which it is manufactured is the dilemma of whether public opinion is discovered or created, as discussed in Chapter 1. The argument developed here is that public opinion is never spontaneous in either its generation or its application; it is "out there" when one wishes to use it – either to influence policy based on a claim of having "discovered" it, or when it is tapped by some type of systematic method, such as a public opinion survey. Organizational leaders try to persuade that they represent the masses and their opinions, but most decision makers discount these claims. The implicit model employed by decision makers seems to be that the attitudes of "public opinion" are generally labile, out there but unexpressed; nonetheless, they are to be respected since they have great potential if transformed into votes or protest. Public opinion is usually in resident mode, dormant but available, setting the mood but not necessarily the agenda, as scenery aids the plot but generally does not determine it.

The support of public opinion is often a necessary, but not sufficient, condition for the setting of policy. Peace treaties do not flow from a receptive public opinion; a reluctant public is a resource to be molded, or an obstacle to be overcome; reported opposition by mass opinion to a policy is not necessarily a dead end for the leader pursuing his course. A peace treaty, like prosperity, comes at the end of the process of preparing for peace or prosperity, rather than at the beginning of the debates about them. Public opinion is never the agent which brings about peace; at best, public opinion can signal that the appropriate attitudes are in place once the appropriate details of a peace deal are worked out. The predisposition can be learned from public opinion surveys, the disposition must come from the politicians. That is the most important division of labor in democratic politics.

Public opinion in the past decades in Israel has won an unearned reputation as equally split, demographically divided, and spawning policy stasis and paralysis. While there is some truth in each characterization, there is more implied in these descriptions that is false. Let us consider each of these claims.

First, that opinion was equally split. In Israel of the 1980s and 1990s, there were two powerful opposing tendencies in Israeli public opinion, one more militant, one more conciliatory. But there was a third, middle ground group, which was the key for coalition building and policy formation. It is hard to give precise estimates of the size of these groups, but it is more useful in the understanding of Israeli politics of thinking of this division as 30–40–30. About a third of the population was convinced of the correctness of the militant position, another third, of the conciliatory stand, with the rest of the population somewhere in the middle.

The message conveyed by this division is more important than the precision of the numbers used in the approximation. A majority of the population – although split between the two opposing poles – had strong and relatively set positions, but neither pole could win a majority without the pivotal middle group. This middle group was just as informed and interested as the polar groups, but attitudes for that group seemed less set and less committed. For much of the period, the middle group was divided almost evenly between the two polar camps, but this middle group was mobile, and since it was less intense, committed, or set than the polar groups, it could be moved if the political or security situation warranted.

Because the middle group was needed for a winning strategy, each extreme group had to restrain its policies if it wanted to secure majority support. For although the invective generated by the competition broadcast by both parties seemed extreme, neither party in power turned out to be as radical as portrayed by its opponent. Part of this was a result of Israel's coalition system; part was a result of parties' generally being cautious. Neither party was quite as horrid as the opposing party predicted during the election campaign. The Likud did not annex the territories, despite calls to do so, and Labor negotiators were not the easy pushovers for the first Arab who came to a table professing to seek peace, as some opposing politicians predicted they would be.

The part of the spectrum in opposition, which by definition did not need to form coalitions with the middle since it had no chance of securing a majority, was not under pressure to moderate the expression of its policy preference until (and if) it was elevated to power.

More was shared by the two polar camps than divided them, and this was certainly true in the realm of security. But it is in the nature of politics to exaggerate conflict and difference, rather than to celebrate cooperation and similarity. That the two sides were not as far apart as was sometimes portrayed was evident in the shared values throughout the society and in the fact that for about a third of the period between 1967 and 1994, Israel was ruled by a series of National Unity governments which featured the joint rule of the two major contenders to power, Labor and the Likud. Between 1967 and 1970, and then again between 1984 to 1990, the leaders of the two parties shared power and responsibility. One unprecedented arrangement even had the Labor's Shimon Peres and the Likud's Yitzhak Shamir rotate the prime ministry among themselves without having new elections called.

The standoff between the two parties gave the politicians of the victorious one enormous power. There seemed to be only a narrow cushion between the two camps; although the 40 percent might be movable again at a different stage, at the moment of victory most voters seemed committed to one worldview or the other. Accordingly, the politician could conduct policy consistent or inconsistent with the professed program. There was no alternative which could immediately replace the policy offered, nor any credible punishment for following a contested policy. That lesson remains firmly in place. Public opinion is not about to dictate policy; public opinion comes into play twice, once when it provides the backdrop for the choice of leader and leadership group and, next, when it judges the policies made by the politician.

Second, that opinion was closely related to – if not predetermined – by demography. It was true that an individual's original position regarding the territories – and on many other political and security issues as well – was often related to ethnicity, education, religious observance, and other socio-demographic characteristics, with the ashkenazim, more educated, more secular Israelis apt to agree to give up the territories for peace, and the other group opposed. This split has been especially sharp since the 1977 reversal which brought the Likud to power for the first time in Israeli history, and over the years the split has seemed to take on an air of natural permanence.

The split gave the appearance of a people divided; but the swing from conciliation to pugnacity and back again was a universal swing, and not one that was predictable knowing demographic characteristics alone. In other words, the demographics of the citizenry provided the original orientation, but the shifts tended to cut into each of these groups. This is important because it highlights the fact that public opinion was not frozen. On the contrary, the Israeli population was alert, responsive, and malleable. Public opinion, while originally structured along social class lines, was not set in a firm and final manner. And when it moved, it responded to cues that were effective on most strata of the society, and affected all of them in similar ways. Given the proper conditions, then, the potential flexibility of public opinion was great.

The years under discussion witnessed the increasing inclusion in the mainstream of Israeli society of the native-born Israeli children of the sephardi immigrants who had peopled the country during the strivings and achievements of independence and nation building. Although the sephardim grew to make up more than half of the Jewish population of the country by the 1990s, dominance in most domains was retained by the ashkenazim and their children. In the first decades of the state, most sephardim, like most of every other group, supported the dominant party and its leaders, then called Mapai and led most prominently by David Ben-Gurion. It was only after the 1973 Yom Kippur war that this emerging sephardi group altered its allegiance to the parties of the right and religion in a disproportionate share. The moment of their growing ethnic identification coincided with a hardening of the political debate in the country about the future of the territories, and the end of the euphoria of the post–Six Days war period with the clash of arms on Yom Kippur 1973. The social tensions and the political division fed off each other. The groups crystallized into two different camps: the secular, better educated, higher-class, Labor- and left-voting doves who were predominantly ashkenazim; and the more religious, less educated, lower-class, Likud- and right-voting hawks who were sephardim by and large. But there was no genetic determinant at work that made sephardim hawks, and no innate inclination of hawks to be sephardim, just as there were no natural rules which made doves of ashkenazim, or ashkenazim of doves.

The confluence of forces in the last quarter century overlaid the ethnic, religious, social, and political cleavages in Israel in an unusually sharp fashion. This crystallization was reinforced by contentious electoral campaigns in which the flames of ethnic and religious divisions were fanned; if the division was spawned by ideology, interest, and worldview, it was sustained by invective, ethnic hostility, and negative stereotyping.

It is not that demographic division was absent; it is that the use of the concept of demographic cleavage desensitizes the observer to aspects of unity and uniformity, and hence to a less complete understanding of the country's reality. Observers of the Israeli scene, used to the stable cleavages of the last quarter century, tended to downplay the broad-based, almost universal shifts to the right or to the left which affected all groups regardless of where they began. The percentage that responded that Israel had a "right to the land" dropped steadily between 1986 and 1993 in all demographic categories; there was also a uniform increase in the percentage of those willing to return the territories for peace and security in all demographic categories. Moreover, even those who retained their view about Israel's "right to the land" generated a growing rate of readiness to return territories over the years. Something systemic was going on, quite different from explanations stemming from changing demography or polarization. Other examples of this same phenomenon were the universal hardening of opinion in 1988 immediately after the onset of the intifada, and the uniform spurt in conciliation among all groups after the Gulf war.

Choice and options characterized certain aspects of political life as well. Israelis always had the opportunity to choose among many parties, but they had little control about the goings-on within the parties. In the 1990s, party primaries became fashionable, and the law governing the elections planned for 1996 had the prime minister elected directly by the voters, and not by the politicians in the back corridors of power. Changes in the incentive structure of the parties reflected the shift of Israel from a society which was relatively structured and hierarchical to one groping toward a new diversity and a more open structure.

Third, that the split in public opinion spawned stasis and policy paralysis. In fact, politicians chose policies which could be characterized as paralyzed or immobile for their own political purposes, or because of their assessment of the politically feasible, although they often found it convenient to blame public opinion for inaction. Public opinion and election results were obviously related, and it is noteworthy that the 1981, 1984, and 1988 elections generated results in which the two big parties were virtually tied, and had to rely even more heavily than usual on coalition partners to prevent the other party from taking power, on the one hand, and to pass their own policies, on the other. The Begin government of 1977 and the Rabin government of 1992 faced only one of these problems: they needed coalition support for their policies, but they were free from the anxiety of the opposition party's easily forming an alternative coalition.

Neither public opinion nor policy has been static over the decades. In fact, there has been constant variation in the distribution of opinion. In the post–Six Days war period and until the Yom Kippur war, the fraction of the population willing to make the sacrifice of territories for peace was about as high as it was in the early 1990s, reaching almost 60 percent by 1993. In the second half of the 1970s and through the 1980s the conciliation fraction shrank to a much smaller magnitude. Acceptance of the PLO and a Palestinian state also grew in the late 1980s and early 1990s, although both positions were strenuously opposed by both major parties, and by every government Israel had until 1993.

Israeli public opinion is structured primarily along political lines rather than class ones. It follows that the social institutions which might mediate in the process of forming the public's views are less important in the Israeli case than is the role of political institutions, such as the party and the leader. The appeal of the party or a leadership group could bring about change in the public stand regarding security and defense policy. This is more likely, it seems, than the possibility of class or group interests emerging to redefine public policy. While there is no necessary contradiction between the two, public opinion in Israel will likely follow a political route rather than a social one.

And leaders, once selected, used their party platforms much in the manner train riders use station platforms: more to get in on than to go anywhere with. These leaders seemed to be free to do almost anything they wished because they were able to mold public opinion to policies very different from their stated programs. In fact, it was under Rabin's first stewardship as prime minister in the 1970s that Jewish settlement in the territories was undertaken. The Begin who worked out the scheme which led to a peace treaty with Egypt did so at the cost of the Sinai Peninsula and the Jewish settlements there; but he could also invade Lebanon in a vain attempt to wipe the PLO off the list of Israel's adversaries. Shamir's Likud government, whose coalition was as far to the right as any in Israeli history, worked out the rules for the peace negotiations which opened in Madrid in 1991. The Rabin who expelled 400 Hamas activists could be prepared to make concessions rejected by other Israeli leaders in the past. Each of these zigs can be explained away by the zags of internal politics and international pressure, yet that each of the politicians "got away with it" in terms of local politics is noteworthy.

Analysis of Israeli public opinion is confounded by the increasing diversity and alternatives available in the society. While communal, ethnic, and religious ties remain central for many, there has also developed an overlay of consumer-oriented, individualistic, atomized cultural elements. Structural developments highlighted the relaxation of the norms of similarity and uniformity. Privatization and competition are the slogans of governments controlled by parties of the right or the left. Increasingly, many aspects of private life are affected by these principles, including health delivery systems and education, with the emergence of private clinics and universities. International travel is more widely available, aided by the lifting of the travel tax; local newspapers and radio stations have provided different messages to different audiences; widespread availability of the VCR, a second television channel, and cable television broke the long domination of the government-related channel. One set of numbers makes the point vividly: in the early 1980s, 95 percent of all television viewers watched the evening news on the government authority's station; in 1994, the parallel figure was 30 percent. It was not that Israelis were less interested or less informed, it was that they now had a choice about what and how to consume their news.

The serious nature of the challenges Israel confronted, coupled with their immediacy, magnified the extent of public debate. There was much to talk about, and security and the political issues related to it generally topped the list of public topics. There were high levels of knowledge about security and political matters; people were involved in more active ways as well, including service in the army and voting.

There was an enormous increase in the use of polls and surveying in Israel during the years under consideration. The mass media commissioned surveys and published results regularly. Telephone interviews and talk shows proliferated, and assertive members of an already loquacious nation found additional avenues of discourse and expression. Israel was never a debating club with restricting rules of interaction; proponents came out hitting hard, usually only verbally, as demonstrated by the volume of discourse in radio and television talk shows, in coffeehouses, and on the floor of the Knesset. Face-to-face interviews with representative national samples of the Jewish population were a major expression of public opinion, and the only one considered in this book, but certainly not the only way public opinion found expression. Demonstrations, opinion leaders, editorials, to name a few, were other ways.

The mood of the country and the tone and content of the discussion were different at the end of the period under consideration here. When the first of the studies reported here was conducted, in 1962, Israel was a small country at war with all of its neighbors, struggling with economic, social, and security challenges, and about to become part of the cold war. Its economy was weak but growing, its army the envy of the region and the object of sacrifice by the country's population. Thirty-three years later, when the last interviews were done in 1994, Israel had been at peace for 15 years with Egypt, its largest neighbor, and it was negotiating with its other Arab neighbors and the PLO its withdrawal from territories it had captured and held for more than 25 years in exchange for formal peace. The cold war had ended with a shattered East, but with the United States, Israel's chief ally, left with a weakened economy. Israel's economy had expanded and strengthened at a much faster rate than the other states of the area; its army remained one of the most formidable in the region. Its people were veterans of the long war and showed some signs of fatigue and fewer signs of the vigor and confidence that had characterized the earlier period.

The weakening of confidence applied mostly to the assessment of the nation's future; at a personal level, things were as good as ever, and they were expected to get even better. Although Israelis have been known to have exaggerated reactions, being too elated in times of joy, and too depressed in moments of peril, what they seemed to have lost in the intervening years was the propensity to see in national betterment the reward for personal restraint. There developed a "me" generation in Israel as steadily as in the rest of the world; "all of us for the nation" seemed to be replaced by "me, and now."

This shift did not parallel a lessening of military tension or a solution to the international problems Israel faced. Conceding territories was but one element of the policy complex that Israelis faced. Israelis were prepared to risk much to avoid war, and supported peace, especially if that could come about on Israel's terms. They perceived Arabs as much less peace-loving. But, not surprisingly, there was also evidence of inconsistencies in responses, partly because alternative scenarios regarding the dilemmas of security were so numerous and unclear, and partly because for most of the surveys discussed here no actual agenda item was on the negotiating table. Israelis were neither maximalist nor minimalist in defining peace; the peace with Egypt, so often criticized by Israeli officialdom for its incomplete "cold" nature, exceeded the population's minimal definition. The threat of nonconventional weapons introduced terrifying nightmares of widespread death and destruction. Although never processed by the political parties, the specter of nuclear, chemical, and biological weapons was a dark apparition which terrified Israelis. They had faced armed threats by Arab nations; it was the intransigence of the problems associated with the occupation of the territories taken in the 1967 war which seemed to fatigue the body politic.

The acrimony of Israeli politics played out against a backdrop of shared dread and anxiety. Security tensions and fear of personal safety were permanent features of the lives of Israelis, as was the set of mechanisms which Israelis marshaled, despite their politics, to overcome these fears. Shared values and myths buttressed a covenant of national security and military strength. Biblical allusions, memories of the Holocaust, and thoughts of those who had sacrificed their lives fighting terror and wars, provided instances of national solidarity and bonding. A sense of being a people apart – yet together – somehow special even if besieged, was widely accepted by members of a society that internalized these values by virtue of a wide variety of formal and less formal socializing settings. This successful socialization was all the more impressive because of the relentless toll constant vigilance demanded, and because it coincided with far-reaching social change.

Change in public opinion was affected by ongoing events. A good example of this was the 1982 Lebanon war, which initially enjoyed broad support. This support was in tune with the perceived short-term threat posed by the PLO in Lebanon. Short-term threats are grasped in a similar manner by most Israelis, while long-term matters are more amenable to political and factional interpretation. Originally supported by most of the population, the Lebanon war became divisive only when it was clear that the government's long-term plan went beyond the one originally announced. Then it became a cause of intense political and factional debate.

The intifada provided another instance of mass opinion's being sensitive to developments. The Arab uprising shocked the Israeli public and made it more aware of the implications of the policies of occupying the territories over a long period of time. The reaction for most of the public seemed to be twofold: to tighten the grip and to be harsh in the short term, but to find a long-term solution which would extricate Israel from the dilemmas of the territories. Concurrent with the growing support for returning territories for peace, respondents overwhelmingly favored the death penalty for terrorists and were in favor of a tougher policy to restore quiet in the territories. This tough-minded stance of the public did not ignore shortcomings of the IDF, or the politicization of the security issue by military and political leaders. The public held the military leaders in higher esteem than their political leaders.

The perceived prospects for peace between Israel and its Arab neighbors increased as the Gulf war ended, as negotiations with the Arab states in Madrid began, and when the PLO and Israel reached a joint recognition agreement. In contrast to the previous 45 years of enmity and hostility, chances for peace seemed reasonable when the talks began in October 1991. The Soviet Union, which had armed many of Israel's enemies, was collapsing; the United States, flush from its Gulf war victory, was anxious to get the talks under way, and the Democrat Bill Clinton, who was about to be inaugurated as the new American president, also seemed committed to them. In September 1993, when Yitzhak Rabin signed the document of principles with PLO head Yasir Arafat, chances for peace seemed very good; the Labor party's Rabin had been prime minister for more than a year, having won election on a tough short-term–conciliatory long-term platform. The mood in Israel was as ready for concessions as it had been for at least a quarter century, and while there were serious obstacles to overcome, the region seemed poised on the brink of a new era.

But the short term kept getting in the way of the long term. Fanatics on both sides used terror to incite anger and fear in an attempt to derail any deal. Acrimony between the sides grew as terror on Israeli streets led to the deportation of more than 400 Hamas activists in December 1992, and after various postponements, the Madrid talks resumed only to continue in their stalemated pattern.

Other anguishing turns of events tore at the social and political consensus in Israel, slowed the movement toward peace, and even threatened civil war. An example of this was the February 1994 carnage by Dr. Baruch Goldstein, perpetrated just after the last survey reported in this volume was completed. He slaughtered 29 Moslems prostrate in prayer at the Cave of the Patriarchs in Hebron. Goldstein was immediately overpowered and killed by other Moslem worshipers in the midst of the massacre. His action was clearly outside the realm of accepted behavior in Israeli society; most mainstream politicians and opinion leaders condemned his act in the most severe language. There were others, however, who were more equivocal. At his funeral his actions were applauded and he was revered as a saint. Many of those who honored him belonged to Kach and Kahane Chai, extreme right-wing groups that were banned after the massacre by government decision under an Israeli law which allows banning an organization on the grounds that it fosters hatred and racism.

Evidence of support for Goldstein's atrocity continued to surface. One rabbi's statement, which seemed to lend religious authority to the action, was circulated. High school students were quoted as saying that it was time the Palestinians understood that innocent Arabs could be gunned down just as terrorists gun down innocent Jews. One student told a television audience that his class had stood at attention in memory of the martyred Goldstein. A panelist reacted in horror, stating that the class's teacher should be fired, the principal should be disciplined, and the education minister should commit suicide. The dictum of Rabbi Meir Kahane (assassinated founder of the racist Kach movement) hung in the air: "I say what the rest of you think." Prime Minister Rabin admitted to being surprised by the extent of support for Goldstein's act and spoke of his fear of the rise of Jewish racism.

Beyond the policy showdown, there seemed to be a division in the country driven by two types of thought patterns: on the one hand, the rational camp, assessing and acting on the assumed interrelations between means and ends, seeking pragmatic solutions to difficult problems; and on the other hand, the irrational, or at best extrarational, camp, whose modes of thought stemmed from emotional and mystical sources, motivated by religion and revelation, convinced that truth resided in their formulations even if those were inaccessible to the uninitiated, beyond empirical evidence or hardheaded analysis. Sequences such as the Hebron massacre of 1994 and the support Goldstein's action drew, afforded one reason to assess that the mind-set demonstrated by these Israelis was not that different from the ones associated with the fanaticism of the revolutionary regime in Iran.

These two mind-sets were not new features of Jewish history, and they had been evident in the recent past. The surge of the radical right in Israel in the 1980s, and especially the support won by Kahane in the 1984 elections, were the clearest manifestation of this.

The implications of this extrarational ideology for the continuing existence of a democratic regime were troubling; the effect of these developments on Israeli politics was not positive. Citizens of a democracy are called upon to exhibit a high degree of tolerance, but they must also be able to secure themselves from the excesses of the fringes. When the two mind-sets clashed in the security debates over the future of the territories, the integrity of the rules of the democratic game was severely threatened. The clash of ideologies also affected official policy and added to the fury of public debate and exhortation. Jews and Arabs, certainly those in the territories, were treated differently by the authorities. Calls were made encouraging soldiers to refuse orders: in the 1980s, certain fringe groups called on soldiers not to serve in the territories. In 1994, for the first time, a number of prominent rabbis of the right-wing settler community ruled that soldiers should not obey commands to remove Jewish settlers from their homes in the land of Israel, even if those commands were given the army by the legally constituted government. These are very serious matters indeed.

They widened the divide among the parties on the policy debate and fostered the sense of a deeply split society. Yet mass opinion generated only partial overlap between policy positions and the two mind-sets explored here, although the distinctions seemed clearer at the edges. The nationalist rabbis and the radical right provided much of the script of the discourse, but its application varied widely throughout the population. Statements proclaiming a unique relationship between Israel and God, or announcing that Israel would ultimately have to rely on itself for its security, were widely supported in the society but were imperfect predictors of policy position. A strong and recurring relationship was found between a hawkish policy position and agreement with a series of statements supportive of the spirit of nationalism and extrarational interpretation of events. But division between the two camps was imperfect, with only partial overlap in the population between support for these statements and policy positions.

Personality type and threat perception were at least as influential in determining one's policy position. That policies were not clearly identified with mind-sets did not defuse the political tension, it only meant that the divisions had imperfectly permeated the public mind. Religion, or at least religious symbols, were involved in this connection, and religious observance was found to be a good predictor of hawkishness, extrarationality, and threat perception. At the organizational level, not all religious groups of individuals supported these expressions, let alone the extreme positions of the radical right. Religious parties, and especially those wedded to pioneering Zionism, such as the National Religious party, agonized over the conflict between religious dictates and the laws of the state, but other parties, such as the Aguda and Shas – no less orthodox but much less nationalist – were less conflicted by the searing conflict between two cherished principles. Most Israelis, not religious in an Orthodox sense, accepted many of the dictates of the traditions without accepting the spiritual authority of the rabbis.

There remained more open questions than answers. Will a forthcoming event reinforce the nationalist values of those who supported Goldstein and his ilk? Or perhaps the fact that racist opinions were almost universally condemned as unacceptable would lead to the strengthening of the camp which opposed racism. Would a climate of opinion emerge as a result of the peace talks with the PLO which could provide enough assurances so that most Israelis could relax their suspicions and apprehensions regarding Arabs, or would vengeance for the massacre further stifle hopes for a reasonable settlement of the 100-year dispute? What was the scope of support for racist, anti-Arab positions? No precise number can be offered, although we know that membership in organizations with that type of ideology number a few hundred. Are intolerant attitudes, based on either fear or hate, the exclusive province of the militant right? Hardly. Would perceived threat always lead to the same extreme conclusions? Certainly not. While it is reasonable to suggest that support for the racist position would be more concentrated in the 30 percent militant camp, it must be quickly noted that not all of that camp would support those views, just as not all conciliators would support unilateral withdrawal from the territories or the evacuation of that part of Jerusalem which was governed by Jordan before the 1967 war.

Perceived threat was shown to be a good predictor of a more militant position, lower levels of threat a good indicator of a more conciliatory position. Hostile Arab aspirations and a low probability of peace were the definition of perceived threat. Threat was found to be closely linked both with policy positions and with background variables. Threat perceptions were also part of the political debate, probably learned by members of both sides, and adopted to fit the political message.

Israel's situation was intrinsically threatening and one's personality predisposed one to higher or lower levels of threat perception; in addition, one seemed metaphorically to receive a measure of threat perception when one adopted one or the other of the two dominant political packages available in Israel. The more hawkish, in addition to the background variables already mentioned, were meted out a larger measure of perceived threat than were their dovish counterparts. The essence of the qualities seemed more concentrated the more elements of the package one had. Education, or religious observance, or age were each related to both policy position and threat perceptions. These relations to policy position and threat perceptions became stronger when controlling for religious observance, for instance. Each added element reinforced other facets of the total package. Yet the relations between ethnicity and authoritarianism were not found to be high until the political element of refusing to return the territories was added to the equation. The confluence of all these elements provided the richness of the political reality in which people operated, and gave a deeper color to the assessment that opposing camps were facing off over an unbridgeable divide.

Threat was very effective in predicting an individual's willingness to risk returning the territories for peace (or, in a related test, to conduct public life in Israel according to Jewish religious law). The threatened were most reluctant to change the status quo. However, no parallel regularity was discovered regarding the assessment of the likelihood that the event would occur, although it seemed reasonable to predict it would. Two different processes seemed to be at work in each domain considered. In both the security domain and the religion domain, threat differentiated, but likelihood of the event's occurrence worked only among those who were threatened; members of this group were found to be risk seekers when it came to losses. This implied that leaders intent on taking an uneasy people forward to a new policy would be well advised to divide their message. For the unconcerned, risk seeking can be broached openly; but for the threatened, risk aversion should be formulated in terms of avoiding further losses.

The public seemed to realize that trade-offs had to be made to attain security or to reach peace; respondents showed willingness to sacrifice, to a degree. More taxes and more military service were tolerated, if not enthusiastically embraced; most understood that security and peace would mean giving up cherished values. When the trade-off among competing values was explored, it was found that certain values hung well together but did not bond with others. The two values of a Jewish majority and peace were widely accepted, while the values of democracy and greater Israel were divisive. Democracy was a code word for rights to Arabs, and greater Israel meant preferring territories over Arab rights. A Jewish majority and peace were valence issues and were desired by most respondents, while democracy was especially acceptable to those on the left, and greater Israel to those on the right.

When a trade-off between values is mandated, as they were during the years under study, people's value hierarchies structure their policy preferences to a significant degree. Value priorities were shown to be not random but politically and ideologically structured, and certain value combinations were more prevalent and more enduring than others. Much of one's policy preferences relating to the Israeli-Arab conflict, as well as changes in policy position, was explained by people's value priorities.

The value combination packages were represented in the political arena by political parties which actively promoted them and mobilized the public by communicating their messages in terms of these packages. The extreme left parties adhered to the combination of democracy and peace, and the extreme right, to the values of Jewishness and greater Israel. The messages of other parties, in particular the large Likud and Labor parties, were more blurred and their supporters endorsed several value packages. In the charged political atmosphere of Israel of the 1980s, it was not surprising that extreme parties grew electorally at the expense of the center since they presented more consistent packages.

But in spite of the bitter contest among values, parties, and politicians, it would be a mistake to overlook the basic fact that voters of the right and voters of the left had more in common with each other in their priorities of values than they had differences. In both cases, a Jewish majority and peace were the two prized values. For voters of the Likud and right a Jewish majority and peace were ranked first and second, followed by greater Israel. Voters for Labor and the left set as their first priority peace, followed by a Jewish majority, and then democracy.

And so we are left with politics. One's message, one's image, one's credibility, all are important in determining the vote. Likud in 1977 was successful in weaning many sephardim from Labor; Labor in 1992 won enough of their children back to return to power. But like many things in a dynamic country, no simple formulation captures the complexity of public opinion or its role in the political process. The political system of Israel has been notably opened in the last years, with the introduction of primaries by party members to select candidates for high office, and with the new constitutional provision for the direct election of the prime minister. Whether these changes pander to populist rumblings, as some critics would have it, or increase access to the public at the expense of oligarchical and stagnated political parties, as others perceive it, there is no doubt that politicians have their eyes and ears open, and their pollsters working, as never before.

There are swings in public opinion, but these can be mainly overlooked by the policy maker. Confidence may sink before a war and rise after it, but variation on the basic issues is slower to come about and more resilient once the change takes place. More crucial to the voter and to public opinion are issues very close to home: personal safety and economic performance. Governments of both parties have declared their intention to enhance these, but voters assess the successes of these parties in terms of their own lives. They seem to judge the incumbent party retrospectively (what have you done for me lately?) and the competing party prospectively (what are you likely to do for me?). If the retrospective judgment is satisfactory, then there is no reason to switch leadership. If the retrospective grade is only fair, then a voter might consider whether the promised performance of the second party will be far superior to the familiar performance of the incumbent. Only then might there be a reversal and change in the governing party. The 1992 reversal is explained by almost all respondents being anxious about their safety and that of their families, being convinced that measures used in the territories to put down terror were too soft, and being sure that the government was jeopardizing too much by insisting on settlements even though that would cost the country the American loan guarantees. It was a time of growing conciliation and increased readiness to negotiate withdrawal from territories for peace agreements. Public opinion wanted personal safety and economic well-being, and was willing to suffer withdrawal from territories if that was the price it took to achieve those goals. This nuance is crucial to understanding how the big issues on which the media focus are important, but not the complete picture. The smaller details of day-to-day life are ultimately crucial because in the end they will influence the voters who in turn will select the leaders who will make the big decisions.

The immediate tendency to follow the leadership gives politicians enormous leverage. They can change policy, if they so decide, secure in the knowledge that they will be able to swing public opinion to their position if they properly present it; in short, if they lead. No less important, they can retain the status quo, if they deem that international considerations allow this, or even turn policy around completely. This is especially true when opinion is informed and involved, and evenly split, as it is in Israel. The system is not frozen, and a divided public opinion is not a harbinger of no change in policy. The 1980s saw an almost even division in public opinion and in political power between the two major camps in Israeli politics. But that was an exception in Israeli history and in the experience of most nations. As the 1992 elections showed, that paralysis did not last. And it was *political* factors that brought about the downfall of the Likud and the reassertion of Labor in those elections, just as political factors led to the 1977 reversal that removed Labor and installed the Likud; those factors coincided with shifts in both policy and opinion.

Political change drives and is driven by public opinion. There are large swings in mood or orientation which set the possibilities for the moment, and these seem to affect the entire polity in an almost universal manner. The perception of high degrees of threat, the preponderance of myths of dominance, chosen-ness, or vulnerability, and the leaders who are selected to lead – to translate and transform opinion into policy – all of these are mediated by public opinion. The issues of policy – of territories and rights, of withdrawal and Jerusalem – seem too intense, too big, too fateful, to be the stuff of political change. Political change in a democratic system comes about as a result of more mundane things – personalities, campaigns, wedge issues. A relatively small number of voters switching from one party to another, or one party managing to lose its momentum, or another changing its image, is enough to transfer power, and with the transfer of power goes the right to set policy. Marginal changes in voting behavior against the backdrop of the mood or orientation of public opinion provide the backdrop for this change in personnel at the top levels of government, and for major shifts in policy.

In very close order, the observer of Israeli politics and security can conclude that things have never been better – or worse. Perhaps that is the moment to recall the aphorism that in the Middle East things are never quite as good nor quite as bad as they first appear. Israel in 1994 signed a peace treaty with Jordan and seemed on the brink of other arrangements which could change the face of the region; its military security had never been better, and its record of economic growth and diplomatic achievement were impressive. However, it was certain that extremists on both sides would continue to attempt to block further progress in the peace talks, and that their chances of success were at least reasonable, considering the mayhem that they could wreak. Israel's domestic strength was being severely tested by compromises already agreed to and by those that would be called for in the near future; destabilizing processes could be triggered because of disobeyed military orders, civil disobedience, bitter denunciations of leaders, and threats of civil war. No democratic leadership could go unscathed in this type of atmosphere.

Most of the Israeli population were anxious and interested observers in the political drama, but not active participants. Most would support the government and would continue to obey military orders in a showdown, and most would be loyalists in a civil war, but that was not the point. The fact that significant groups with a substantial number of followers challenged the legitimacy of the government had never happened since the founding of the state. The government would probably win the showdown, but the showdown itself would damage the fragile fabric of Israeli democracy.

Appendix I: The Samples

This book is a product of the surveys carried out under the auspices of the National Security and Public Opinion Project of the Jaffee Center for Strategic Studies at Tel Aviv University, of which the author is director. The project, initiated in 1984, monitors Israeli public opinion on issues related to national security.

The questionnaires were composed by project researchers, and data were analyzed by them; the fieldwork, including pretesting and sampling, was done by the Dahaf Research Institute, headed by Dr. Mina Zemach. The 1988 and 1992 surveys were also supported by a grant to Michal Shamir from the Sapir Center for Development of Tel Aviv University. The Department of Political Science of the University of Haifa provided support for the 1992 survey.

The surveys were based (unless otherwise noted) on samples representing the adult Jewish population of Israel. These did not include individuals from kibbutzim or from the territories occupied by Israel after the Six Days war of 1967. An exception to this rule was the special supplementary sample of 119 West Bank residents conducted in 1990. Use was also made of a special sample of 300 kibbutz members collected in 1962. These special samples were analyzed separately and not comingled with the national samples.

The dates of the project's surveys were: (1) June 1985; (2) January 1986; (3) December 9, 1987–January 4, 1988; (4) October 1988; (5) March–October 1990; (6) March 16–31, 1991; (7) June 1–21, 1992; (8) January 1–15, 1993 and (9) January 11–February 9, 1994. Sample sizes were 1,171 in 1985; 1,172 in 1986; 1,116 in 1987; 873 in 1988; 1,251 in 1990; 1,131 in 1991; 1,192 in 1992; 1,139 in 1993; and 1,239 in 1994.

Earlier attitude and election surveys going back to 1962 were also used. An attitude survey in 1962 undertaken by Aaron Antonovsky of the Louis Guttman Israel Institute of Applied Social Research was one of the earliest applications of opinion sampling in Israel. In addition, the election surveys carried out by the author going back to 1969 were utilized. Until 1981, these surveys were conducted by the Louis Guttman Israel Institute of

Applied Social Research, and since then by the Dahaf Research Institute, with the author writing the questions and analyzing the responses.

For 1987–90, a panel design was used: the same respondents were asked the same questions at different points in time. Data were available for this type of analysis from the answers of 416 respondents from the 1987 and 1988 samples who were interviewed twice. The first wave of interviews was conducted between December 9, 1987 (the day on which the intifada, or Arab uprising, began), and January 4, 1988; the second was held in October 1988. In 1990, 213 of these same respondents were reinterviewed. The original 1987–8 interview was part of the larger survey of 1,116 respondents, and 416 of these respondents were reinterviewed in the weeks before the November 1, 1988 elections. The 213 interviewed again during the October 1989–March 1990 were part of that national survey. The interview period was so long because the reinterviews were also part of a national sample. An unanticipated consequence of this protracted interview period was that 54 percent of the interviews for the 1990 sample were conducted before August 2, the day the Iraqis invaded Kuwait, and 46 percent afterward. Careful analyses indicated that the panel respondents were representative of both the general population and the larger samples in terms of sociodemographic characteristics and policy distribution.

The Dahaf Research Institute, an independent organization, uses a stratified sampling method to represent the major demographic groups of the adult Jewish population of Israel. Three criteria of stratification are employed: (1) four geographical areas, including Haifa and the north, Tel Aviv and the center, Jerusalem, Beer Sheva and the south; (2) size of settlement, including the four major cities, other cities and towns, villages, and rural *moshavim* (cooperative settlements); (3) age of the settlement (established until 1948 and after 1948).

Specific areas of the larger cities and towns are chosen to represent various socioeconomic and ethnic groups, based on the reports of the Central Bureau of Statistics. Sampling in each selected area is based on the size of the population relative to the total adult Jewish population. Goodness-of-fit tests for each sample indicated that the demographic characteristics of the respondents were representative of the total Jewish population of Israel.

Streets are randomly chosen. Interviewers are instructed to choose respondents based on the Kish method (Kish 1965). Sampling is carried out in two stages: (1) apartments are sampled based on specified sampling fractions; (2) a list of adults residing in the sampled apartments is prepared, and from that list respondents are chosen according to the specified sampling fraction.

Appendix II: Policy Scale Questions

1. There are three long-range solutions for the territories held since the 1967 war. With which do you agree most? (Constructed from two questions, the first asking preference with a "leave as is" option, with a follow-up for those respondents, forcing a choice.)

A. In exchange for peace, give up the territories as long as Israel's security interests were provided for
B. Leave the situation as it is, but if Israel had to choose, give up territories if security was provided for
C. Leave the situation as it is, but no choice if Israel had to choose
D. Leave the situation as it is, but if Israel had to choose, annex
E. Annex the territories

Table II.1

Response	1984 %	1985 %	1986 %	1987 %	1988 %	1990 %	1991 %	1992 %	1993 %
A	35	37	30	32	40	44	51	50	54
B	10	8	9	11	10	7	7	7	6
C	2	4	4	3	2	3	2	2	2
D	30	23	34	26	23	17	18	16	15
E	23	27	23	28	26	30	22	25	23
Effective N	1,228	1,103	1,137	1,081	846	1,235	1,098	1,153	1,184

1A. There are three long-range solutions for the territories held since the 1967 war. With which do you agree most? (Constructed from two questions, the first asking preference with an "autonomy" option, with a follow-up for those respondents, forcing a choice.)

A. In exchange for peace, give up the territories as long as Israel's security interests were provided for
B. Autonomy for the Arabs in the territories, but if Israel had to choose, give up territories if security was provided for
C. Autonomy for the Arabs in the territories, even if Israel had to choose between the two other alternatives

D. Autonomy for the Arabs in the territories, but if Israel had to choose, annex
E. Annex the territories

Table II.1A

Response	1994 %
A	28
B	21
C	15
D	14
E	23
Effective N	1,184

2. If the territories are eventually annexed to the State of Israel, are you in favor of granting more civil rights to the Arab inhabitants than they have today, or decreasing them, or leaving them as they are today?

A. Increase including right to vote in Knesset elections
B. Increase without right to vote
C. Leave things as they are now
D. Decrease their civil rights

Table II.2

Response	1984 %	1985 %	1986 %	1987 %	1988 %	1990 %	1991 %	1992 %	1993 %	1994 %
A	6	5	18	20	15	23	23	22	25	27
B	17	15	25	33	31	33	31	31	32	32
C	60	56	46	26	39	32	27	31	28	28
D	11	24	11	21	16	13	18	16	15	13
Effective N	1,237	1,104	1,130	1,098	843	1,215	1,096	1,145	1,157	1,216

3. Do you think that Israel should agree or should not agree to the establishment of a Palestinian state in Judea, Samaria, and the Gaza Strip as part of a peace agreement?

A. Should definitely agree
B. Probably
C. Probably not
D. Should definitely not agree

Table II.3

Response	1987 %	1988 %	1990 %	1991 %	1992 %	1993 %	1994 %
A	7	6	9	10	10	15	13
B	14	20	19	24	19	20	24
C	27	28	27	21	23	23	20
D	52	46	45	46	48	42	42
Effective *N*	1,103	859	1,236	1,116	1,175	1,191	1,220

4. The way things are today, do you think that Israel should or should not be willing to conduct peace negotiations with the PLO?

A. Israel should be willing
B. Israel should not be willing

Table II.4

Response	1987 %	1988 %	1990 %	1991 %	1992 %	1993 %	1994[a] %
A	33	34	40	29	43	52	60
B	66	66	60	71	57	48	40
Effective *N*	1,097	858	1,238	1,124	1,183	1,188	1,189

[a] A four-category answer: certainly agree – 24%; agree – 36%; disagree – 21%; definitely disagree – 19%.

4A. (For those respondents who opposed negotiations in Question 4):

A. Israel should be willing if the PLO undergoes basic changes and announces that it recognizes the state of Israel and will completely give up acts of terror.
B. Israel should not be willing under any conditions

Table II.4A

Response	1986[a] %	1987 %	1988 %	1992 %	1993 %
A	50	49	35	45	51
B	50	51	65	55	49
Effective *N*	1,145	833	873	731	666

[a] Asked of all respondents.

4B. (For those respondents who opposed negotiations in Question 4):
Under what conditions should the state of Israel agree to negotiate with the
PLO?

A. If the PLO unilaterly recognizes the state of Israel
B. If the PLO recognizes the state of Israel and completely gives up acts of terror
C. If the PLO recognizes the state of Israel, completely gives up acts of terror, and
   stops the intifada
D. If the PLO recognizes the state of Israel, completely gives up acts of terror, stops
   the intifada, and rescinds the PLO charter.
E. Israel should not agree under any conditions

Table II.4B

Response	1990 %	1991[a] %
A	4	8
B	8	8
C	18	13
D	29	20
E	42	51
Effective N	834	1,113

[a] Asked of all respondents.

5. Do you agree or disagree that Israel should encourage the Arabs to
leave the country?

A. Definitely agree
B. Agree
C. Do not agree
D. Definitely do not agree

Table II.5

Response	1987 %	1988 %	1990 %	1991 %	1992 %	1993 %	1994 %
A	34	27	26	28	28	27	27
B	35	38	38	35	37	35	32
C	24	27	29	25	25	26	28
D	7	9	6	11	10	12	13
Effective N	1,096	848	1,221	1,094	1,184	1,189	1,224

6. To prevent a war with the Arab countries, Israel should

A. Try to initiate peace negotiations
B. Increase her military power

Table II.6

Response	1986 %	1987 %	1988 %	1990 %	1991 %	1992 %	1993 %	1994 %
A	64	68	64	64	74	72	64	52
B	36	32	36	36	27	28	36	48
Effective *N*	1,127	1,083	839	1,180	1,085	1,097	1,163	1,141

7. There is a suggestion to have an international peace conference with the big powers participating. To what extent do you support this suggestion?

A. Definitely support
B. Support
C. Do not support
D. Definitely do not support

Table II.7

Response	1987 %	1988 %	1990 %	1991[a] %	1992 %	1993[b] %
A	19	17	11	17	49	56
B	46	36	44	51	43	33
C	23	24	28	21	6	6
D	12	24	18	21	2	5
Effective *N*	1,093	848	1,208	1,052	1,164	1,199

[a] To be convened by the superpowers.
[b] Should participation be continued?

8. Recently there has been much talk about situations in which there is a contradiction between the principle of the rule of law and the security interests. On the following scale, "1" represents the opinion which states that when there is a conflict like that, security interests are to be given priority, while "7" represents the opinion that in that case the rule of law is always to be preferred. Where on this scale would you place yourself?

Table II.8

Year	Mean	Security				Rule of law			Effective N
		1	2	3	4	5	6	7	
1987	3.6	14	14	18	27	11	9	7	1,094
1988	3.0	22	24	20	15	9	5	5	854
1990	3.3	18	19	19	23	8	7	7	1,232
1991	3.4	21	13	17	24	10	8	7	1,103
1992	3.4	19	16	21	17	10	9	8	1,161
1993	3.1	26	18	12	24	7	6	7	1,185
1994	3.4	24	13	16	22	8	9	8	1,188

9. In the following scale, rank 1 represents the position that the Israel Defense Force's presence in Judea, Samaria, and the Gaza Strip has a negative effect on the army's fighting ethic and the seventh rank is that the Israel Defense Force's presence in Judea, Samaria, and the Gaza Strip has a positive effect. Where would you rank yourself on the scale?

Table II.9

Year	Mean	Negative					Positive		Effective N
		1	2	3	4	5	6	7	
1986	4.2	4	8	13	44	13	9	9	1,172
1987	4.2	10	9	10	37	12	12	11	1,105
1988	3.8	10	14	14	32	12	11	8	851
1990	3.6	13	15	15	32	9	8	8	1,229
1991	3.9	15	11	12	29	9	10	14	1,109
1992	3.2	17	21	17	29	7	5	5	1,166
1993	3.6	19	17	18	26	8	5	8	1,182
1994	3.4	18	17	15	27	9	6	7	1,186

Notes

2. OVERCOMING THREAT

1. On perceptions of Israeli Arabs see Rouhana 1989; Smooha 1989, 1992; Al-Haj 1993.
2. For the 1967–79 period, see Stone (1982, 36–44).
3. Using oblique factor analysis on the 1986 data set, the coefficient of correlation of the two factors was −.144. The Pearson correlation of the two constructs was .13. See Arian, Talmud, and Hermann (1988, 47).
4. All of these correlations were statistically significant above .001.
5. See Kats 1982; Shmotkin 1990, 1991. There were slight variations in the application of the method over the years. (1) In 1969 and 1988, only the series of questions relating to the personal ladder was asked; national ratings were omitted. (2) Until 1981, the range of the ladder was from rung 0 to rung 10; after 1986, the range was from 1 through 9; rungs 0, 1, 9, and 10 were almost never mentioned and, accordingly, 0 and 1 were collapsed together as were 9 and 10 in these analyses. (3) In the 1981 survey, rung 1 was the top of the ladder, and 10 the base. (4) The 1969 and 1981 surveys used a four- rather than a five-year interval. (5) Since 1986, the wording of the national question specified national security; before that, the inquiry regarded the state of the nation.
6. See Stone (1982, chapter 4) for a measure of mood for this period in Israel.
7. Until 1981, the range of the ladder was from rung 0 to rung 10; after 1986, the range was from 1 through 9. In both cases, rung 5 was the median.
8. The data for the trend lines of Figures 2.3–2.5 are given in Table N2.1.

Table N2.1

	Beta	Adjusted R^2	Significance
Figure 2.3. *Past ladder means*			
National	.83	.66	.000
Personal	.80	.61	.000
Figure 2.4. *Present ladder means*			
National	–	–	not significant
Personal	.80	.61	.000
Figure 2.5. *Future ladder means*			
National	.64	.36	.020
Personal	–	–	not significant

9. In addition to the methodological issues discussed in the previous note, there may also have been an effect due to a slight variation in question wording. The wording was not precisely identical in each application. In the surveys before 1986, respondents were asked about the state of the nation in a general fashion; since 1986, the questions more specifically asked about the security situation of Israel. It could be argued that there was a narrower range of ladder means because people were more consistent regarding the more focused topic of security than about the country in a vaguer sense. But this explanation is unacceptable because the first evidence of narrowing is in 1981, a year in which the broader wording was still used. If the wording explanation is to be accepted, the shift should have occurred when the wording change was introduced.

3. PEACE AND WAR

1. For a comparison with European countries, see Rabier et al. 1986.
2. Israeli public opinion is, of course, not unique in that respect; for a good summary of American data, see Page and Shapiro 1992.
3. For an analysis of American public opinion regarding the Vietnam war, see Verba and Brody 1970; Zaller 1992.
4. For the United States, see Mandelbaum and Schneider 1979; Schneider 1983, 1984, 1985, 1987; Hurwitz and Peffley, 1987, 1991; Shapiro and Page, 1988; Wittkopf 1990; Hinckley 1992. For European countries, see Merritt 1973; Avarbanel and Hughes 1975; Daniel 1978; de Boer 1981, 1985; Capitanchik and Eichenberg 1983; Dalton 1988; Flynn 1985a, 1985b; Eichenberg 1985, 1989; Graham and Kramer 1986; Risse-Kappen 1991; and for Japan, Bobrow 1991.
5. The corresponding figures for 1988 were 37% no change, 27% more moderate, 35% more hardened. The apparent differences between 1988 and 1990 may be the result of a larger movement in the initial period, and more stability later. In any event, for both time periods, hardening was more likely than moderation.
6. In 1988, 6% thought that the intifada improved their own mood, and 5%, the national mood. On the other hand, 41% reported their mood had soured as a result of the intifada, and 59% said the national mood had become worse; 71% said that the intifada had not changed their desire to live in Israel, and 17% reported it had strengthened this desire, while 12% thought it had decreased it; 4% were more positive about both Israeli and territories Arabs, and 45% felt more negative about both groups.
7. The February 20–21, 1991, survey was designed by Mina Zemach, and Carol Gordon was the author of the March 26–27, 1991, survey. Both were conducted by the Dahaf Research Institute.
8. Women, those with children, and Tel Aviv area residents had significantly higher fear. On a 4-point scale (1 = greatest fear), the mean for women was 2.5 and for men 3.4 (t-score of difference of means 9.52, significance $p <$ .001), in agreement with the general tendency of women having significantly higher fear of death than men (Ungar et al., 1990). The difference between those with children (mean = 2.6) and those without (mean = 2.9) was smaller but still significant ($t = 2.6$, $p < .01$). There was also a significant difference between those who lived in Tel Aviv (mean = 2.6) and those who lived elsewhere (mean = 3.0; $t = 3.4$, $p < .001$).

4. CHANGE IN SECURITY ATTITUDES

1. For a different composite measure, see Katz and Al-Haj 1990.
2. Shamir and Shamir (1992) applied the spiral of silence theory proposed by Noelle-Neumann (1984) to Israel and found it wanting. This spiral is the product of social pressures, and it highlights perceptions of opinion and expectations about future trends in producing a "climate of opinion."
3. The use of fathers is a long-standing practice of the government's Central Bureau of Statistics. Apologies to all who have mothers.
4. The data for the trend lines for Figures 4.3, 4.4, and 4.5 are given in Table N4.1. The differences between the means of the groups was not significant, reinforcing the contention of concurrent change.

Table N4.1

	Beta	Adjusted R^2	Significance
Figure 4.3. *Territories by continent of birth*			
Total	−.85	.69	.003
Ashkenazi	−.85	.68	.004
Sephardi	−.93	.84	.000
Israeli	−.63	.31	.069
Figure 4.4. *Territories by age*			
Total	−.85	.69	.003
Under 30	−.91	.81	.000
Over 60	−.81	.60	.008
Figure 4.5. *Policy scale by continent of birth*			
Total	−.86	.67	.029
Ashkenazi	−.87	.70	.024
Sephardi	−.82	.59	.046
Israeli	−.94	.85	.006

5. The total number of respondents switching between Likud and Labor was small. Among them, the number of those who shifted from Labor to Likud was 11, almost twice the number (6) who moved in the opposite direction. Compare Campbell et al. 1960; Butler and Stokes 1969; Jennings and Niemi 1978; Converse and Markus 1979; Markus 1979; Goldberg et al. 1991.
6. The alpha reliability coefficients for the policy scale in the national samples were .72, .80, and .75 in 1987, 1988, and 1990 respectively. In the panel data the corresponding figures were .69, .81, and .77.

5. POLITICS

1. Labor ran alone in 1992, but in previous years the list had other names. In 1965, Mapai and Ahdut Haavoda ran on a joint list called the Alignment. In 1968, Mapai, Ahdut Haavoda, and Rafi merged to form Labor. Between 1969 and 1984, Labor and Mapam put up a joint list called the Alignment. In 1988, Labor and Mapam each offered separate lists. In 1992, Labor ran alone, Mapam joined

with the Civil Rights movement and Shinui to form Meretz. The Likud was formed in 1973 and was a joint list of Herut, the Liberal party, La'am, and others.

2. These are sizable groups, comprising 15% of the 1988 Likud voters in 1992, and 36% of the 1973 Labor voters in 1977. By leaving them out, we implicitly assume that they were similar to those who decided earlier, which we regard as plausible. Although others may not agree with this assumption, in the absence of additional data, this is the only way we can treat these respondents.

3. It is interesting to note that the profile of young first-time voters is broadly the same as the general patterns for 1988 Likud voters. In terms of ethnicity, a third of the Likud and right voters were sephardi, compared to 22% of Labor voters. The major difference among these groups was with regard to their attitude regarding the future of the territories.

4. The application of regression analysis to a dichotomous dependent variable is not straightforward, yet given certain assumptions we were willing to make, it is appropriate. The results of a parallel discriminant analysis are, of course, equivalent. See also note 5(c), which is also relevant to the use of R^2.

5. The relations between the issues and demographic variables were measured with Pearson correlations.

    (a) Since the vote variable is dichotomous (Labor-Likud), there is an upper bound on the size of the correlations, which is lower than 1 (J. Cohen 1983).

    (b) Correlations indicate how far and in what direction two variables covary. In other words, how much of the fact that some voters preferred Likud, and others preferred Labor, "was due" to variations in the explanatory variables (e.g., to age differences among them). Since we do not assume that the "true model" is bivariate, r measures association, not the structural effect of X on Y. For relevant discussions of the meaning and use of standardized measures, see Achen 1982; King 1986; Luskin 1991.

    (c) When comparing correlations (or other standardized measures) across samples, one must check variances of the variables involved, because the correlations are affected by this variance in addition to the relationship in which one is interested. For most sociodemographic variables, the standard deviations across the samples changed very little. The standard deviation of ethnicity has increased slightly since the 1981 survey and has been constant since. This does not interfere with the pattern of correlations obtained. The standard deviation on the religious issue decreased in 1988 and 1992, meaning that the pattern of increasing relations indicated by the correlations could only be more pronounced. The standard deviation of the socialism-capitalism issue changed but in no specific direction, and not in any consistent way with the correlations. The standard deviation of the territories questions is much higher for 1984 and on, compared to the earlier elections, about 1.5 to 1.7 times higher. This means there are two reasons why the correlations have increased: first, there is more polarization and variance on this issue compared to before, and second, the relationship has increased. The standard deviation of the dependent vote variable is quite constant, although it has increased by about 10% since the 1977 election, again, not interfering with our interpretation of the correlation pattern in Table 5.6.

6. One territories question was used through 1981, and another one since 1984. Luckily the 1984 and 1988 questionnaires contained both question formats. The correlations for the early question (not given in Table 5.6) were of a magnitude

similar to those presented in the table: .53 in 1984, and .47 in 1988; this compares to correlations in the .20 range in the earlier elections. There can be no doubt, then, that a real change occurred in 1984, and that the correlation is not simply a methodological artifact.

7. These figures are based on the Central Bureau of Statistics data, pertaining to the Jewish population over the age of 20. See *Israel, Demographic Characteristics 1977, 1978*, 14–15; *Israel, Statistical Abstract – 1992*, 94–95.

8. Since many voters said that everything had an effect on them, the only way to read the results is comparatively: compare the items in terms of relative importance to voters, and compare voters with different voting records as to how different items influenced decisions.

9. In order to minimize the chances for a response set of "spend more" on all items, we asked first whether the respondent supported a tax increase, which would mean paying more taxes. Even though 72% opposed paying more taxes, on six of the nine items, majorities wanted to spend more, and for seven of them the quotient (found by subtracting the percent which wanted less expenditure from the percent wanting more) was positive (see Table 5:9). The results should be compared across issues and across voting groups.

10. We looked at Likud-Labor voters as they are the most interesting and most relevant for our discussion of wedge issues. See note 5 on the use of regression with a dichotomous dependent variable.

11. In both regressions reported here, the two variables had weaker effects on the vote among the 1988 Likud voters than in the total population.

6. A PEOPLE APART

1. On the rhetoric of Menachem Begin, see Gertz 1983.

2. Data used in this chapter are from the 1987 survey, unless otherwise noted.

3. The data in Figure 6.1 are for election years (except for 1962). The corresponding percentages for 1994 were 27% and 39%. These same questions have also been asked by the Louis Guttman Israel Institute of Applied Social Research. For their 1993 findings, see Levy, Levinsohn, and Katz (1993).

4. The 30 attitudinal variables generated three clear factors: the God-and-us construct (5 questions), the go-it-alone construct (6 questions), and authoritarianism (8 questions).

5. On the right-to-the-land response, see Chapter 2 of this volume.

6. This is a revised version of the policy scale presented in Chapter 4 based on the 1987 sample. The standardized alpha reliability coefficient was .681. The hardline pole of the measure includes support for annexing territories, not participating in an international conference for peace chaired by the superpowers, denying civil rights to inhabitants of the territories, not granting autonomy to the territories, opposing the establishment of a Palestinian state, not returning the Golan Heights to Syria for peace, supporting the death penalty for terrorists, justifying the use of nuclear weapons, preferring security interests over the rule of law, and assessing that army activities in the territories have a positive impact on its effectiveness.

7. Operationalized as the sum of the responses to the questions regarding the possibility of peace between Israel and the Arab countries in the near future, Israel's ability to influence the Arabs' willingness for peace, and the assessment

of Arab aspirations. Those in the high category regarded peace as unlikely and the goals of the Arabs far-reaching.

7. THREAT AND POLICY

1. Singer 1958; Pruitt 1965; Tedeschi 1970. Deutsch discussed threat in terms of "ill-intent on the part of the threatener" (1973, 124).
2. Using the autonomy wording in the 1994 sample (see Chapter 4 and Appendix II), 49% agreed to return the territories, 65% reported being threatened if the territories were returned, and 77% thought the chances were high that they would be returned.
3. The corresponding correlations for 1994, all statistically significant, were −.47, −.20, and .22, respectively.
4. This is an abridged form of the threat measure discussed in Chapter 2. The question about Israel's ability to influence the Arabs' willingness for peace was not replicated for the religious domain.
5. The Pearson correlation between level of observance and agreement with the low rate of casualties as a miracle statement was .41 (p = .000, N = 1,092).
6. The respective correlations were .11 and .17, and statistically significant.

8. VALUES

1. In a 1988 survey (Katz 1988), 97% said that it was important or very important that the Jewish character of the state be preserved (that there be a Jewish majority). See also Liebman and Don-Yehiya 1983.
2. In the Katz 1988 survey, 82% said it was important or very important that the democratic character of the state be maintained (i.e., that every resident have equal rights).
3. The value rankings ranged from 1, the value mentioned last, to 4, the most highly ranked value. Although they are clearly ordinal-level measures, we treat these rank orders throughout the analysis as interval-level variables, following common practice; see Alwin and Krosnick 1985; O'Brien 1979. The standard deviation for Jewish majority was the smallest in both general surveys, as well as for the panel. The differences in the standard deviations of the four value rankings in the general surveys ranged between 0.92 and 1.16 in 1988, and between 0.99 and 1.10 in 1990. In the panel data, these figures were 0.87 and 1.14.
4. Even the classic valence dimension of economic stability and development may become a position dimension when juxtaposed with a competing value such as the environment; see Inglehart 1990.
5. Applying a paired t-test to the responses of the panel showed that the difference in the mean scores of the 1988 and 1990 rankings was higher (and statistically significant) for Jewish majority and peace, while it was smaller and not significant for the two lower-ranked and conflictual values, greater Israel and democracy.
6. The right-left self-placement scale ranged from 1 to 7, with 1 being extreme right, and 7 extreme left. As is commonly done, we regarded it as interval level. On the right-left scale, see Inglehart and Klingemann 1976; Arian and Shamir 1983; Huber 1989; Inglehart 1990; Ventura and Shamir 1992.
7. By 1994, the correlations were larger and the patterns altered. The correlations

with right-left were Jewish majority .21; democracy −.33; peace −.42; greater Israel .53. Peace was no longer an abstract value. It had become politicized because it was being negotiated and defined by the Labor-left government.

8. Pearson's r correlations were used to indicate the degree and in what direction the variables covary. One-way causality was not assumed: right-left self-identification and value priorities both measure political and ideological world-view. Since correlations (as other standardized measures) are a function of both the covariance and the variances of the variables, the relative order of the correlations as discussed in the text held also when the differences in the value rankings' variances were taken into account.

9. Right wing settler groups argued about whether or not they should make explicit their preference for greater Israel over peace. Sensing that peace was highly valued, many were not willing to concede in their public relations campaigns that there was a possible trade-off between land and peace (see Harel 1991). Only at the time of the 1991 peace conference did spokesmen of the extreme right begin to speak in terms that might move peace from a being "valence" to a "position" dimension.

10. These value packages are ideologically constrained, notwithstanding their political roots. Land and people are basic notions in all nationalist right-wing ideologies, and in Israel they are also tied to religious tradition. The recognition of the rights of others stems from universalistic standards, and brings together democracy and the willingness to compromise on land. In a study of the meanings attached to left and right in Israel, Ventura and Shamir (1992) showed that the issue of the territories is the major conflict dimension in contemporary Israeli politics, but that right-wingers define it more often with reference to the land, whereas on the left there is more reference to the Palestinians or Arabs, that is, to the people and not to the land.

11. The alpha reliability coefficients for the policy scale in the national samples were .72, .80, and .75 in 1987, 1988, and 1990, respectively. In the panel data the corresponding figures were .69, .81, and .77. We used correction for attenuation formulas to check whether the changes in the reliability of the policy scale over time altered any of our substantive conclusions in this section and the next one. All estimates of R and R^2 increased, of course, but their relative magnitude did not change.

12. Results for the panel respondents are presented in addition to the general samples in order to establish their equivalence, as later analyses depend more heavily on the panel data.

13. The relative order of the correlations as discussed in the text held also when the differences in the value rankings' variances were taken into account.

14. A proper interpretation of the R^2s requires an examination of the variances of the variables, and these variances of the independent variables measured at different time points were all very similar. There was also no difference among the variances of the territories question at the three points in time. On the policy scale, the variance is somewhat higher for 1988 and 1990 than in 1987, peaking in 1988. The effect of these differences runs in the opposite direction of the results, thus presenting no interference with the validity of our interpretation. The regressions used only cases with valid values on all variables.

The other attitudinal factors included constructs which have been shown to have an effect on policy positions in the Israeli context: God-and-us, go-it-alone, threat, and overcome; see Chapter 6.

The last stage in both analyses contained all important socioeconomic variables: education, ethnic background, income, density of living conditions, religiosity, age, and sex. In addition, we included the psychological construct of dogmatism, shown in previous research to have considerable impact on positions toward the territories and related attitudes (Shamir and Sullivan 1983).

The socioeconomic and psychological variables were considered causally prior to the attitudinal predictors of policy position, and were therefore entered in the third and final stage.

15. A problem of interpretation would arise if the importance of values would be low in 1987 and high in 1988, and the opposite pattern were to hold for the God-and-us and go-it-alone constructs. The charge of deficient measurement would be plausible and hard to dismiss. But, as seen in Tables 8.4 and 8.5, this was not the case.

16. While the value rankings account for similar proportions of the variance of the policy scale and of the territories question, the other variables are able to account for more of the policy scale's variation than of the territories question. The R^2s for the policy scale range in the .40s and one even exceeds .60. On the average, our regression equations "explain" almost half of the variance in the policy scale. The R^2s for the territories question vary between .24 and .46, averaging .34.

The figures in Table 8.4 are R^2s. Since we have 15 predictors in the full equations, and the panel samples were quite small, it is wise to check the adjusted R^2s. They are lower by .01–.02 for the estimates of the value rankings' contributions (rows 2 and 3). The two averages, when we take the adjusted R^2s into account, are .22 and .10, instead of .23 and .11. As to the total R^2s, the corresponding adjusted R^2s are .37, .56, and .39 for the policy scale in the three panel samples, and .15, .39, and .30 for the territories question.

17. In the first stage, the lagged dependent variable was regressed on all the variables included in the cross-sectional equations (Table 8.5) at t and t+1. The predicted values from this first stage then served as the instrumental variable, replacing the actual lagged dependent variable in the second stage of the regression analysis. This two-stage least squares procedure produces consistent estimators for the coefficients in the model.

18. The sociodemographic and psychological variables were not included in these equations, as they were assumed to be constant; indirectly they have an effect through the lagged policy position. For the go-it-alone and God-and-us constructs, the 1987 scores were used as indicators for 1988 values.

19. The adjusted R^2s are lower than the raw R^2s by .01–.02 for the value rankings' contributions. The adjusted R^2s for the full equations are .51, .36, .34, and .28 (first row).

Bibliography

Abelson, Robert, and Ariel Levi, "Decision Making and Decision Theory," in Gardner Lindzey and Elliot Aronson (eds.), *The Handbook of Social Psychology*, 3rd edition. Hillsdale, NJ: Lawrence Erlbaum, 1985.

Abramson, Paul, "Demographic Change and Partisan Support," in Asher Arian and Michal Shamir (eds.), *The Elections in Israel – 1988*. Boulder, CO: Westview, 1990.

Achen, Christopher H., *Interpreting and Using Regression*, Sage Series: Quantitative Applications in the Social Sciences. Beverly Hills, CA: Sage, 1982.

Aharoni, Yair, *The Economy of Israel*. New York: Routledge, 1991.

Ajzen, Icek, "Attitude Structure and Behavior," in Anthony R. Praktanis, Steven J. Breckler, and Anthony G. Greenwald (eds.), *Attitude Structure and Function*. Hillsdale, NJ: Lawrence Erlbaum, 1989, pp. 241–74.

Ajzen, Icek, and Martin Fishbein, "Attitude-Behavior Relations: A Theoretical Analysis and Review of Empirical Research," *Psychological Bulletin* 84:1977, 888–918.

Al-Haj, Majid, "The Political Behavior of the Arabs in Israel in the 1992 Elections: Integration vs. Segregation," in Asher Arian and Michal Shamir (eds.), *The Elections in Israel – 1992*. Albany: State University of New York Press, 1995.

Almond, Gabriel, *The American People and Foreign Policy*. New York: Praeger, 1960.

Alwin, Duane F., and Jon A. Krosnick, "The Measurement of Values in Surveys: A Comparison of Ratings and Rankings," *Public Opinion Quarterly* 49:1985, 535–52.

Antonovsky, Aaron, and Alan Arian, *Hopes and Fears of Israelis: Consensus in a New Society*. Jerusalem: Jerusalem Academic Press, 1972.

Arian, Alan, *Ideological Change in Israel*. Cleveland: Case Western Reserve University Press, 1968.

Arian, Asher, *Politics in Israel: The Second Generation*, 2nd edition. Chatham, NJ: Chatham House, 1989a.

Arian, Asher, "A People Apart: Coping with National Security Problems in Israel," *Journal of Conflict Resolution* 33:1989b, 605–31.

Arian, Asher, "Security and Political Attitudes in Israel: 1986–1991," *Public Opinion Quarterly* 56:1, Spring 1992, 116–28.

Arian, Asher, "Democracy and National Security: Public Opinion in Israel," in Avner Yaniv, (ed)., *National Security and Democracy in Israel*. Boulder, CO.: Lynne Reiner, 1993, pp. 129–51.

Arian, Asher, and Carol Gordon, "Political and Psychological Impact of the Gulf War on the Israeli Public," in Stanley Renshon (ed.), *The Gulf War: Leaders, Publics, and the Process of Conflict*. Pittsburgh: University of Pittsburgh Press, 1993.

Arian, Asher, and Michal Shamir, "The Primarily Political Function of the Left-Right Continuum," *Comparative Politics* 15:1983, 139–58.

Arian, Asher, and Michal Shamir, "Two Reversals: Why 1992 Was Not 1977," *Electoral Studies* 12:1993, 315–41.

Arian, Asher, Michal Shamir, and Raphael Ventura, "Public Opinion and Political Change: Israel and the Intifada," *Comparative Politics* 24:1992, 317-35.

Arian, Asher, Ilan Talmud, and Tamar Hermann, *National Security and Public Opinion in Israel*. Boulder, CO: Westview, and *The Jerusalem Post* (JCSS Study #9), 1988.

Aronson, Shlomo, "Nuclearization of the Middle East," *Jerusalem Quarterly* 2:1977, 27–44.

Aronson, Shlomo, "The Nuclear Dimension of the Arab-Israeli Conflict: The Case of the Yom Kippur War," *The Jerusalem Journal of International Relations* 7:1–2, 1984, 107–42.

Avarbanel, M., and B. Hughes, "Public Attitudes and Foreign Policy Behavior in Western Democracies," in W. Chittick (ed.), *The Analysis of Foreign Policy Outputs*. Columbus, OH: Charles Merrill, 1975.

Avgar, Amy, "Lessons From the Gulf War: What Price Did Women Pay?," *Na'amat Woman*, September 1991, 29.

Bar-Tal, Daniel, "The Masada Syndrome: A Case of Central Belief," in Norman A. Milgram (ed.), *Stress and Coping in Time of War*. New York: Brunner/Mazel, 1986, pp. 32–51.

Bar-Tal, Daniel, "Contents and Origins of Israelis' Beliefs About Security," *International Journal of Group Tensions* 21:1991, 237–61.

Bartolini, Stefano, and Peter Mair, *Identity, Competition and Electoral Availability: The Stabilisation of European Electorates 1885–1985*. Cambridge: Cambridge University Press, 1990.

Barzilai, Gad, "National Security Crises and Voting Behavior: The Intifada and the 1988 Elections," in Asher Arian and Michal Shamir (eds.), *The Elections in Israel – 1988*. Boulder, CO: Westview, 1990, pp. 65–76.

Barzilai, Gad, and Efraim Inbar, "Do Wars Have an Impact?: Israeli Public Opinion After the Gulf War," *The Jerusalem Journal of International Relations* 14:1992, 48–64.

Begin, Menachem, *The Revolt* (Hebrew). Tel Aviv: Ahiasaf, 1950.

Ben-Gurion, David, *Things as They Are* (Hebrew). Tel Aviv: Am Hasefer, 1965.

Ben-Meir, Yehuda, "The Effect of the War on the Home Front," in *War in the Gulf: Implications for Israel*, Report of a JCSS Study Group. Tel Aviv: Papyrus, 1991.

Ben-Rafael, Eliezer, and Stephen Sharot, *Ethnicity, Religion and Class in Israeli Society*. Cambridge: Cambridge University Press, 1991.

Benvenisti, Meron, *The Sling and the Club*. Jerusalem: Keter (Hebrew), 1988.

Benvenisti, Meron, with Z. Abu-Zayed and D. Rubinstein, *The West Bank Data Base Project*. Boulder, CO: Westview, 1986.

Berelson, Bernard R., Paul R. Lazarsfeld, and William N. McPhee, *Voting*. Chicago: University of Chicago Press, 1954.

Beres, Louis R. (ed.), *Security or Armageddon: Israel's Nuclear Strategy*. Lexington, MA: Lexington Books, 1986.

Bialer, Uri, "David Ben Gurion and Moshe Sharett – Two Political-Security Orientations in Israeli Society," *State, Government and International Relations* (Hebrew), Fall 1972, 71-84.

Birnbaum, K., "Threat Perceptions and National Security Policies," in S. Lodgaard and K. Birnbaum (eds.), *Overcoming Threats to Europe: A New Deal for Confidence and Security*. Oxford: Oxford University Press, 1987, pp. 39–67.

Blalock, H. M., (ed.), *Causal Models in the Social Sciences*. Chicago: Aldine, 1970.

Bobrow, Davis, "Japan in the World: Opinion from Defeat to Success," in Hans Rattinger and Don Munton (eds.), *Debating National Security: The Public Dimension*. Frankfurt am Main: Peter Lang, 1991, pp. 27–71.

Boulding, Kenneth, "Toward a Theory of Peace," in R. Fischer (ed.), *International Conflict and Behavioral Science*. New York: Basic Books, 1964.

Brecher, Michael, *The Foreign Policy System of Israel: Setting, Images, Process*. London: Oxford University Press, 1972.

Brecher, Michael, *Decisions in Crisis: Israel, 1967 and 1973*. Berkeley: University of California Press, 1980.

Brinkley, Joel, "Majority in Israel Oppose P.L.O. Talks Now, a Poll Shows," *New York Times*, April 2, 1989, 1–2.

Butler, David, and Donald E. Stokes, *Political Change in Britain*. London: Macmillan, 1969.

Campbell, Angus, Philip E. Converse, Warren E. Miller, and Donald E. Stokes, *The American Voter*. New York: Wiley, 1960.

Campbell, Mary, *Harvard Graphics*. Berkeley, CA: Osborne McGraw-Hill, 1990.

Cantril, Hadley, "Trends of Opinion During World War II: Some Guides to Interpretation," in B. Berelson and M. Janowitz (eds.), *Reader in Public Opinion and Communication*. New York: Free Press, 1953, pp. 83–94.

Cantril, Hadley, *The Pattern of Human Concerns*. New Brunswick, NJ: Rutgers University Press, 1965.

Capitanchik, David, and Richard C. Eichenberg, *Defense and Public Opinion*, Chatham House Papers in Foreign Policy 20. London: Royal Institute of International Affairs and Routledge & Kegan Paul, 1983.

Caspari, W., "The 'Mood' Theory," *American Political Science Review* 64:1970, 536–47.

Cattell, Raymond B., "Psychological Measurement: Ipsative, Normative and Interactive," *Psychological Review* 51:1944, 292–303.

Clemans, W. V., "An Analytical and Empirical Examination of Some Properties of Ipsative Measures," *Psychometric Monographs* 14:1966.

Cohen, Avner, "Nuclear Weapons, Opacity and Israeli Democracy," in Avner Yaniv (ed)., *National Security and Democracy in Israel*. Boulder, CO: Lynne Reiner, 1993, pp. 197–225.

Cohen, Erik, "Citizenship, Nationality and Religion in Israel and Thailand," in Baruch Kimmerling (ed.), *The Israeli State and Society: Boundaries and Frontiers*. Albany: State University of New York Press, 1989a, pp. 66–92.

Cohen, Erik, "The Changing Legitimations of the State of Israel, *Studies in Contemporary Jewry* 5:1989b, 148–65.

Cohen, J., "The Cost of Dichotomization," *Applied Psychological Measurement* 7:3, 1983, 249–53.

Cohen, Steven P., and Herbert Kelman, "Evolving Intergroup Techniques for Conflict Resolution: An Israeli-Palestinian Pilot Workshop," *Journal of Social Issues* 33:1977, 165–88.

Conover, J. Pamela, and Stanley Feldman, "The Origin and Meaning of Liberal/ Conservative Self-Identifications," *American Journal of Political Science* 25:1981, 617–45.

Converse, Philip E., "The Nature of Belief Systems in Mass Publics," in David Apter (ed.), *Ideology and Discontent*. New York: Free Press, 1964, pp. 206–61.

Converse, Philip E., "Attitudes and Non-Attitudes: Continuation of a Dialogue," in Edward R. Tufte (ed.), *The Quantitative Analysis of Social Problems*. Reading, MA: Addison-Wesley, 1970, pp. 168–90.

Converse, Philip E., and George B. Markus, " 'Plus ca change . . . ': The New CPS Election Study Panel," *American Political Science Review* 73:1979, 32–49.

Coplin, W., "Domestic Politics and the Making of Foreign Policy," in *Introduction to International Politics*. Chicago: Markham, 1974.

Dahl, Robert A., *Controlling Nuclear Weapons: Democracy Versus Guardianship*. Syracuse: Syracuse University Press, 1985.

Dalton, Russell J., *Citizen Politics: Public Opinion and Political Parties in the United States, United Kingdom and West Germany*. Chatham, NJ: Chatham House, 1988.

Dalton, Russell J., Scott C. Flanagan, and Paul Allen Beck (eds.), *Electoral Change in Advanced Industrial Democracies: Realignment or Dealignment?* Princeton: Princeton University Press, 1984.

Daniel, Donald C. (ed.), *International Perceptions of the Superpower Military Balance*. New York: Praeger, 1978.

Dayan, Moshe, *Breakthrough: A Personal Account of the Egypt-Israel Peace Negotiations*. New York, Knopf, 1981.

De Boer, Connie, "The Polls: Our Commitment to World War III," *Public Opinion Quarterly*, 45:1981, 126–34.

De Boer, Connie, "The Polls: The European Peace Movement and Deployment of Nuclear Missiles," *Public Opinion Quarterly* 49:1985, 119–32.

Deutsch, Morton, *The Resolution of Conflict*. New Haven: Yale University Press, 1973.

Diskin, Abraham, *Elections and Voters in Israel*. New York: Praeger, 1991.

Duncan, O. D., "Path Analysis: Sociological Examples," *American Journal of Sociology* 72:1966, 1–16.

Eban, Abba, *My Country* (Hebrew). Jerusalem: Weidenfeld & Nicolson, 1972.

Eichenberg, Richard C., "Public Opinion and National Security in Europe and the United States," in Linda Brady and Joyce Kaufmann (eds.), *NATO in the 1980s*. New York: Praeger, 1985, pp. 226–48.

Eichenberg, Richard C., *Public Opinion and National Security in Western Europe*. Ithaca: Cornell University Press, 1989.

Encyclopedia Britannica Yearbooks. Chicago: Encyclopedia Britannica.

Feifel, H., *The Meaning of Death*. New York: McGraw-Hill, 1959.

Feldman, Shai, *Israeli Nuclear Deterrence*. New York: Columbia University Press, 1982.

Feldman, Shai, and Heda Rechnitz-Kijner, *Deception, Consensus and War: Israel in Lebanon*, Tel Aviv University, Jaffee Center for Strategic Studies Paper No. 27, October 1984.

Feldman, Stanley, "Structure and Consistency in Public Opinion: The Role of Core Beliefs and Values," *American Journal of Political Science* 32(2):1988, 416–40.

Feldman, Stanley, and John Zaller, "The Political Culture of Ambivalence: Ideological Responses to the Welfare State," *American Journal of Political Science* 36:1992, 268–307.

Festinger, Leon, *A Theory of Cognitive Dissonance*. Stanford, CA: Stanford University Press, 1957.

Fiorina, Morris, *Retrospective Voting in American National Elections*. New Haven: Yale University Press, 1981.

Fishbein, Martin, and Icek Ajzen, *Belief, Attitude, Intention and Behavior*. Reading, MA: Addison-Wesley, 1975.

Flappan, Simha, *The Birth of Israel*. New York: Pantheon, 1987.

Flynn, Gregory (ed.), *NATO's Northern Allies: The National Security Policies of Belgium, Denmark, the Netherlands, and Norway*. Totowa, NJ: Rowman & Allanheld, 1985a.

Flynn, Gregory, and Hans Rattinger (eds.), *The Public and Atlantic Defense*. Totowa, NJ: Rowman & Allanheld, 1985.

Flynn, Gregory, et al., *Public Images of Western Security*. Paris: Atlantic Institute for International Affairs, 1985b.

Foa, E. B., G. Steketee, and B. Olasov-Rothbaum, "Behavioral/Cognitive Conceptualizations of Post-Traumatic Stress Disorder," *Behavior Therapy* 20:1989, 155–76.

Franklin, Mark N., Thomas T. Mackie, and Henry Valen, *Electoral Change: Responses to Evolving Social and Attitudinal Structures in Western Countries*. Cambridge: Cambridge University Press, 1992.

Freedman, Robert O. (ed.), *The Intifada*. Miami: Florida International University Press, 1991.

Friedlander, Dov, and Calvin Goldscheider, *The Population of Israel*. New York: Columbia University Press, 1979.

Gertz, N., "Few Against Many – Rhetoric and Structure in the Election Speeches of Menachem Begin," *Siman Kr'ia – Literary Quarterly* (Hebrew) 16–17:1983, 106–26.

Gildemeister, Joan E., and Hans Furth, "Attitudes Toward Nuclear Issues: Perspective of 'Hard Liner' and 'Soft Liner' College Students," paper presented at the International Society of Political Psychology, Tel Aviv, 1989.

Goldberg, Giora, Gad Barzilai, and Efraim Inbar, *The Impact of Intercommunal Conflict: The Intifada and Israeli Public Opinion.* Jerusalem: The Leonard Davis Institute for International Relations, Policy Studies No. 43, February, 1991.

Goldscheider, Calvin, "Demographic Transformations in Israel: Emerging Themes in Comparative Context," in Calvin Goldscheider (ed.), *Population and Social Change in Israel.* Boulder, CO: Westview, 1992a.

Goldscheider, Calvin. *Israel's Changing Society – Population, Ethnicity, and Development.* Westview, 1992b.

Gordon, Carol, "Mutual Perceptions of Religious and Secular Jews in Israel," *Journal of Conflict Resolution* 33:1989, 632–51.

Gordon, Carol, "Perceived Threat in a Prolonged Social Conflict: The Case of the Conflict Between Religious and Secular Jews in Israel," paper presented at International Society of Political Psychology, San Francisco, 1992.

Gorny, Yosef, *Zionism and the Arabs, 1882–1948.* Oxford: Clarendon Press, 1987.

Graham, Thomas W., and Bernard M. Kramer, "The Polls: ABM and Star Wars: Attitudes Toward Nuclear Defense, 1945–1985," *Public Opinion Quarterly* 50:1986, 125–34.

Guttman, Louis, *The Israel Public, Peace and Territory: The Impact of the Sadat Initiative.* Jerusalem: Jerusalem Institute for Federal Studies, 1978.

Haberman, Clyde,"For Israel's Aged Survivors, A Day of Particular Anguish," *New York Times*, April 19, 1993, A10.

Handel, Michael, *Israel's Political Military Doctrine.* Cambridge, MA: Harvard University Center for International Affairs, 1973.

Harel, Israel, *Ha'aretz* (Hebrew), September 6, 1991.

Harkabi, Yehoshafat, *Arab Attitudes Toward Israel.* New York: Hart, 1986.

Harkabi, Yehoshafat, *Israel's Fateful Decisions.* London: I. B. Tauris, 1988.

Heider, F. *The Psychology of Interpersonal Relations.* New York: Wiley, 1958.

Heller, Rachael F., Herbert D. Saltzstein, and William B. Caspe, "Heuristics in Medical and Non-medical Decision-making," *The Quarterly Journal of Experimental Psychology* 44A(2):1992, 211–35.

Heradstviet, D., *Arab and Israeli Elite Perceptions.* New York: Humanities Press, 1974.

Herman, Simon, *Jewish Identity: A Social Psychological Perspective.* Beverly Hills, CA: Sage, 1977.

Hinckley, Ronald L., *People, Polls, and Policymakers: American Public Opinion and National Security.* New York: Lexington, 1992.

Hofnung, Menachem, *Israel – Security Needs vs. The Rule of Law* (Hebrew). Jerusalem: Nevo, 1991.

Holsti, Ole R., and James N. Rosenau, *American Leadership in World Affairs: Vietnam and the Breakdown of Consensus.* London: Allen & Unwin, 1984.

Holsti, O. R., and James N. Rosenau, "Consensus Lost. Consensus Regained?:

Foreign Policy Beliefs of American Leaders, 1976–1980," *International Studies Quarterly* 30:1986a, 375–409.

Holsti, Ole R., and James N. Rosenau, "The Foreign Policy Beliefs of American Leaders: Some Further Thoughts on Theory and Method," *International Studies Quarterly* 30:1986b, 473–84.

Horowitz, Dan, "Israel Defense Forces: A Civilized Military in a Partially Militarized Society," in R. Kalkowitz and A. Korbuski (eds.), *Soldiers, Peasants and Bureaucracy*. London: G. Allen & Unwin, 1982, pp. 77–106.

Horowitz, Dan, "The Israeli Concept of National Security," in Avner Yaniv (ed)., *National Security and Democracy in Israel*. Boulder, CO.: Lynne Reiner, 1993, pp. 11–53.

Horowitz, Dan, and Baruch Kimmerling, "Some Social Implications of Military Service and the Reserve System in Israel," *European Journal of Sociology* 15:1974, 262–76.

Horowitz, Dan, and Moshe Lissak, *Origins of the Israeli Polity: Palestine Under the Mandate*. Chicago: University of Chicago Press, 1978.

Horowitz, Dan, and Moshe Lissak, *Trouble in Utopia: The Overburdened Polity of Israel*. Albany: State University of New York Press, 1987.

Huber, J., "Values and Partisanship in Left-Right Orientations: Measuring Ideology," in *European Journal of Political Research* 17:1989, 599–631.

Huckfeldt, R. R., "The Social Context of Political Change: Durability, Volatility, and Social Influence," *American Political Science Review* 77:1983, 929–44.

Hurwitz, Jon, and Mark Peffley, "How are Foreign Policy Attitudes Structured? A Hierarchical Model," *American Political Science Review* 81:1987, 1099–1120.

Hurwitz, Jon, and Mark Peffley, "American Images of the Soviet Union and National Security Issues," in Hans Rattinger and Don Munton (eds.), *Debating National Security: The Public Dimension*. Frankfurt am Main: Peter Lang, 1991, pp. 101–38.

Inbar, Efraim, "Israel and Nuclear Weapons since October 1973," in Louis R. Beres, (ed.), *Security or Armageddon: Israel's Nuclear Strategy*. Lexington, MA: Lexington Books, 1986, pp. 61–78.

Inbar, Efraim, "The 'No Choice War'' Debate in Israel," *Journal of Strategic Studies* 12:1989, 22–37.

Inbar, Efraim, *War and Peace in Israeli Politics: Labor Party Positions on National Security*. Boulder, CO: Lynne Rienner, 1991.

Inglehart, Ronald, "Aggregate Stability and Individual-Level Flux in Mass Belief-Systems: The Level of Analysis Paradox," *American Political Science Review* 79:1985, 97–116.

Inglehart, Ronald, *Culture Shift in Advanced Industrial Society*. Princeton: Princeton University Press, 1990.

Inglehart, Ronald, and Hans D. Klingemann, "Party Identification, Ideological Preference and the Left-Right Dimension Among Western Mass Publics," in Ian Budge et al. (eds.), *Party Identification and Beyond*. London: Wiley, 1976, pp. 243–73.

Israel, *Demographic Characteristics of the Israeli Population, 1977, 1978*, Special Report 634. Jerusalem: Central Bureau of Statistics, 1980.

Israel, *Statistical Abstracts of Israel*. Jerusalem: Central Bureau of Statistics.

Janda, Kenneth, Jeffrey M. Berry, and Jerry Goldman, *The Challenge of Democracy*, 3rd edition. Boston: Houghton Mifflin, 1993.

Jennings, M. Kent, and Gregory B. Markus, "The Effect of Military Service on Political Attitudes: A Panel Study," *American Political Science Review* 71:1977, 131–47.

Jennings, M. Kent, and Richard G. Niemi, "The Persistence of Political Orientations: An Over-Time Analysis of Two Generations," *British Journal of Political Science* 8:1978, 333–96.

Jennings, M. Kent, and Richard G. Niemi, *Generations and Politics*. Princeton: Princeton University Press, 1981.

Jervis, Robert, *Perception and Misperception in International Politics*. Princeton: Princeton University Press, 1976.

Juergensmeyer, Mark, *Religious Nationalism Confronts the Secular State*. Berkeley: University of California Press, 1992.

Kahane, Meir, *Uncomfortable Questions for Uncomfortable Jews*. Secaucus, NJ: L. Stuart, 1987.

Kahneman, Daniel, and Amos Tversky, "Prospect Theory: An Analysis of Decision Under Risk," *Econometrica* 47:1979, 263–91.

Kahneman, Daniel, and Amos Tversky, "Choices, Values, and Frames," *American Psychologist* 39:1984, 341–50.

Kastenbaum, R., and R. Aisenberg, *The Psychology of Death*. New York: Springer, 1972.

Kats, Rachel, "Concerns of the Israeli: Change and Stability from 1962 to 1975," *Human Relations* 35:1982, 83–100.

Katz, Elihu, "Forty-nine Percent Lean Towards 'Transfer' of Arabs," *The Jerusalem Post* (International Edition), August 20, 1988.

Katz, Elihu, "Majority Hawkish, But Dovish Trend Seen," *The Jerusalem Post* (International Edition), February 18, 1989, 5.

Katz, Elihu, and Michael Gurevitch, *The Secularization Leisure: Culture and Communication in Israel*. Cambridge, MA: Harvard University Press, 1976.

Katz, Elihu, and Majid Al-Haj, *Research Report 1988 & 1989*. Jerusalem: The Louis Guttman Israel Institute of Applied Social Research, 1990, p. 17.

Katz, Elihu, and Paul F. Lazarsfeld, *Personal Influence*. New York: Free Press, 1955.

Katz, Elihu, Hanna Levinson, and Majid Al-Haj, "Attitudes of Israelis (Jews and Arabs) Towards Current Affairs." Jerusalem: The Louis Guttman Israel Institute of Applied Social Research Press Release, January 10, 1991, pp. 11–15.

Kegley, Charles W., Jr., "Assumptions and Dilemmas in the Study of Americans' Foreign Policy Beliefs: A Caveat," *International Studies Quarterly* 30:1986, 447–72.

Keis, Naomi, "The Influence of Public Policy on Public Opinion – Israel 1967–1974," *State, Government and International Relations* (Hebrew) 8:1975, 36–53.

Kerlinger, Fred N., *Liberalism, Conservatism and the Structure of Social Attitudes*. Hillsdale, NJ: Lawrence Erlbaum, 1984.

Kessler, Ronald C., and David F. Greenberg, *Linear Panel Analysis: Models of Quantitative Change*. New York: Academic Press, 1981.

Key, V. O., Jr., *Public Opinion and American Democracy*. New York: Knopf, 1961.

Key, V. O., Jr., *The Responsible Electorate: Rationality in Presidential Voting, 1936–1960*. Cambridge, MA: Harvard University Press, 1966.

Kimmerling, Baruch, *Zionism and Territory*. Berkeley: University of California Press, 1983.

Kimmerling, Baruch, *The Interrupted System: Israeli Civilians in War and Routinetime*. New Brunswick, NJ: Transaction, 1985a.

Kimmerling, Baruch, "Between the Primordial and the Civil Definitions of the Collective Identity: 'Eretz Israel' or the State of Israel?," in Erik Cohen et al. (eds.), *Comparative Social Dynamics*. Boulder, CO: Westview, 1985b, pp. 262–83.

Kimmerling, Baruch, "Patterns of Militarism in Israel," *Archives of European Sociology* 34:1993, 196–223.

King, Gary, "How Not to Lie with Statistics: Avoiding Common Mistakes in Quantitative Political Science," *American Journal of Political Science* 30:1986, 666–87.

Kirkpatrick, S., and J. Regens, "Military Experience and Foreign Policy Belief Systems," *Journal of Political and Military Sociology* 6:1978, 29–47.

Kish, Leslie, *Survey Sampling*. New York: Wiley, 1965.

Kluckhohn, Clyde, "Values and Value Orientations in the Theory of Action," in Talcott Parsons and Edward A. Shils (eds.), *Toward a General Theory of Action*. Cambridge, MA: Harvard University Press, 1951.

Kremnitzer, Mordechai, "National Security and the Rule of Law: A Critique of the Landau Commission's Report," in Avner Yaniv (ed.), *National Security and Democracy in Israel*. Boulder, CO.: Lynne Reiner, 1993, pp. 153–72.

Krosnick, Jon A., and Duane F. Alwin, "A Test of the Form-Resistant Correlation Hypothesis: Ratings, Rankings and the Measurement of Values," *Public Opinion Quarterly* 52:1988, 526–38.

Lahav, Pnina, "The Press and National Security," in Avner Yaniv (ed.), *National Security and Democracy in Israel*. Boulder, CO.: Lynne Reiner, 1993, pp. 173–95.

Lamare, James W., "Gender and Public Opinion: Defence and Nuclear Issues in New Zealand," paper presented at the American Political Science Association meeting, Atlanta, 1989.

Levite, Ariel, *Offense and Defense in Israeli Military Doctrine*. Boulder, CO: Westview, 1990.

Levy, Gideon, "As If Israel Had Not Been Established," *Ha'aretz*, January 24, 1994, B1.

Levy, Shlomit, Hanna Levinsohn, and Elihu Katz, *Beliefs, Observances and Social Integration Among Israeli Jews*. Jerusalem: The Louis Guttman Israel Institute of Applied Social Research, 1993.

Liebman, Charles, and Eliezer Don-Yehiya, *Civil Religion in Israel: Traditional Judaism and Political Culture in the Jewish State*. Berkeley: University of California Press, 1983.

Lijphart, Arend, *Democracies*. New Haven: Yale University Press, 1984.

Linz, Juan J., and Alfred Stepan (eds.), *The Breakdown of Democratic Regimes*. Baltimore: Johns Hopkins University Press, 1978.

Lukes, Steven, "Some Problems About Rationality," in B. R. Wilson (ed.), *Rationality*. Oxford: Basil Blackwell, 1974, pp. 194–213.

Luskin, Robert C. " 'Abusus Non Tollit Usum': Standardized Coefficients, Correlations and R^2s," *American Journal of Political Science* 35:1991, 1032–46.

MacKuen, Michael, and Courtney Brown, "Political Context and Attitude Change," *American Political Science Review* 81:1987, 471–90.

Madison, James, "Candid States of Parties," in *National Gazette*, March 5, 1792. Reprinted in Marvin Meyers (ed.), *The Mind of the Founder: Sources of the Political Thought of James Madison*. Indianapolis: Bobbs-Merrill, 1973.

Majtabai, A. G., *Blessed Assurance: At Home with the Bomb in Amarillo, Texas*. Boston: Houghton Mifflin, 1986.

Mandel, Robert, "Psychological Approaches to International Relations," in Margaret Hermann (ed.), *Political Psychology*. San Francisco: Jossey-Bass, 1986, pp. 251–78.

Mandelbaum, Michael, and William Schneider, "The New Internationalisms: Public Opinion and American Foreign Policy," in Kenneth A. Oye, Donald Rothchild, and Robert J. Lieber (eds.), *Eagle Entangled: U.S. Foreign Policy in a Complex World*. New York: Longman, 1979, pp. 34–88.

Mannheim, Karl, *Ideology and Utopia*. New York: Harcourt Brace, 1949.

Marcus, G., J. Sullivan, and E. Theiss-Morse, "Political Tolerance and Threat: Affective and Cognitive Influences," paper presented at Midwest Political Science Association meeting, Chicago, 1990.

Margalit, Avishai, "The Honor of Israel," *The New York Review of Books*, June 2, 1988, 17–20.

Markus, Gregory B., *Analyzing Panel Data Sage Series: Quantitative Applications in the Social Sciences*. Beverly Hills, CA: Sage, 1979.

Maslow, A. H., *Motivation and Personality*. New York: Harper, 1954.

Mayer, William G., *The Changing American Mind: How and Why American Public Opinion Changed Between 1960 and 1988*. Ann Arbor: University of Michigan Press, 1992.

McGuire, William J., "Attitudes and Attitude Change," in Gardner Lindzey and Elliot Aronson (eds.), *The Handbook of Social Psychology*, 3rd edition. Hillsdale, NJ: Lawrence Erlbaum, 1985.

Meir, Golda, *My Life* (Hebrew). Tel Aviv: Ma'ariv, 1975.

Merritt, Richard., "Public Opinion and Foreign Policy in West Germany," in P. McGowan (ed.), *Sage International Yearbook of Foreign Policy Studies*. Beverly Hills, CA: Sage, 1973, pp. 255–74.

Mikulincer, Mario, Victor Florian, and Rami Tolmacz, "Attachment Styles and Fear of Personal Death: A Case Study of Affect Regulation," *Journal of Personality and Social Psychology* 58:1990, 273–80.

Miller, Arthur H., and Martin P. Wattenberg, "Throwing the Rascals Out: Policy and Performance Evaluations of Presidential Candidates, 1952–1980," *American Political Science Review* 79:1985, 359–72.

Miller, Warren, and Donald Stokes, "Constituency Influence in Congress," *American Political Science Review* 57:1963, 45–56.

Morris, Benny, *The Birth of a Palestinian Refugee Problem, 1947–1949*. Cambridge: Cambridge University Press, 1988.

Mueller, John E., *War, Presidents, and Public Opinion*. New York: Wiley, 1973.

Negbi, Moshe, *Above the Law* (Hebrew). Tel Aviv: Am Oved, 1987.

Nie, Norman H., Sidney Verba, and John R. Petrocik, *The Changing American Voter*. Cambridge, MA: Harvard University Press, 1979.

Niemi, Richard G., and Herbert F. Weisberg (eds.), *Controversies in Voting Behavior*. Washington: CQ Press, 1993.

Nincic, Miroslav, "New Perspectives on Popular Opinion and Foreign Policy," *Journal of Conflict Resolution* 36:1992, 772–89.

Noelle-Neumann, Elizabeth, *The Spiral of Silence*. Chicago: University of Chicago Press, 1984.

O'Brien, Conor Cruise, *The Siege: The Saga of Israel and Zionism*. New York: Simon & Schuster, 1986.

O'Brien, Robert M., "The Use of Pearson's R with Ordinal Data," *American Sociological Review* 44:1979, 851–7.

Organski, A. F. K., *The $36 Billion Bargain: Strategy and Politics in US Assistance to Israel*. New York: Columbia University Press, 1990.

Page, Benjamin I., and Robert Y. Shapiro, *The Rational Public: Fifty Years of Trends in Americans' Policy Preferences*. Chicago: University of Chicago Press, 1992.

Page, Benjamin I., Robert Y. Shapiro, and Glenn R. Dempsey, "What Moves Public Opinion?," *American Political Science Review* 81:1987, 23–43.

"Palestinian Elections and the Declaration of Principles: Results of a Public Opinion Poll (December 12, 1993)," no author. Nablus: Center for Palestine Research and Studies, mimeo.

Pappe, Ilan, "Moshe Sharett, David Ben Gurion and the 'Palestinian Option,' 1948–1956," *Studies in Zionism* 7/1:1986, 77–96.

Pappe, Ilan, *Britain and the Arab-Israeli Conflict 1948–51*. New York: St. Martin's Press, 1988.

Peri, Yoram, *Between Battles and Ballots*. Cambridge: Cambridge University Press, 1983.

Pruitt, D. G., "Definition of the Situation as a Determinant of International Action," in Herbert C. Kelman (ed.), *International Behavior: A Social Psychological Analysis*. New York: Holt, 1965.

Putnam, Robert D., *Making Democracy Work: Civic Traditions in Modern Italy*. Princeton: Princeton University Press, 1993.

Quandt, William, *Camp David: Peacemaking and Politics*, Washington, DC: Brookings, 1986.

Quattrone, George A., and Amos Tversky, "Contrasting Rational and Psychological Analyses of Political Choice," *American Political Science Review* 82:3,1988, 719–36.

Rabier, Jacques-Rene, Helene Riffault, and Ronald Inglehart, *Euro-Barometer 24*. Ann Arbor: Inter-University Consortium for Political and Social Research, 1986.

Rabin, Yitzhak, "Text of Leaders' Statements at the Signing of the Mideast Pacts," *New York Times*, September 14, 1993, A12.

Rabinovich, Itamar, *The Road Not Taken*. New York: Oxford University Press, 1991.

Rabinowitz, George, and Stuart E. MacDonald, "A Directional Theory of Issue Voting," *American Political Science Review* 83:1989, 93–121.

Rabinowitz, George, Stuart E. MacDonald, and Ola Listhaug, "New Players in an Old Game: Party Strategy in Multiparty Systems," *Comparative Political Studies* 24:1991, 147–86.

Raiffa, Howard, *Decision Analysis: Introductory Lecures on Choices Under Uncertainty*. Reading, MA: Addison-Wesley, 1968.

Rattinger, Hans, "Change Versus Continuity in West German Public Attitudes on National Security and Nuclear Weapons in the Early 1980s," *Public Opinion Quarterly* 51:1987, 495–521.

Richards, David A. J., *A Theory of Reasons for Action*. Oxford: Clarendon Press, 1971.

Risse-Kappen, Thomas, "Public Opinion, Domestic Structure, and Foreign Policy in Liberal Democracies," *World Politics* 43:1991, 479–512.

Rokeach, Milton, *The Open and Closed Mind*. New York: Basic Books, 1960.

Rokeach, Milton, *Beliefs, Attitudes and Values*. San Francisco: Jossey-Bass, 1970.

Rokeach, Milton, *The Nature of Human Values*. New York: Free Press, 1973.

Rokeach, Milton (ed.), *Understanding Human Values*. New York: Free Press, 1979.

Rokeach, Milton, and Sandra J. Ball-Rokeach, "Stability and Change in American Value Priorities: 1968–1991," *American Psychologist* 44:1989, 775–84.

Rose, Richard, and Ian McAllister, *Voters Begin to Choose*. Beverly Hills, CA: Sage, 1986.

Rouhana, Nadim, "The Political Transformation of the Palestinians in Israel: From Acquiescence to Challenge," *Journal of Palestine Studies* 18:3, 1989, 38–59.

Rubinstein, Amnon, *The Constitutional Law of the State of Israel* (Hebrew), 4th edition. Jerusalem: Schocken, 1991.

Russett, Bruce, *Controlling the Sword: The Democratic Governance of National Security*. Cambridge, MA: Harvard University Press, 1990.

Russett, Bruce, and Donald R. DeLuca, " 'Don't Tread On Me': Public Opinion and Foreign Policy in the Eighties," *Political Science Quarterly* 96:1981, 381–99.

Ryan, A., "Maximising, Moralising and Dramatising," in C. Hookway and P. Pettit (eds.), *Action and Interpretation*. Cambridge: Cambridge University Press, 1972, pp. 65–80.

Sartori, Giovanni, *Parties and Party Systems: A Framework for Analysis*. London: Cambridge University Press, 1976.

Schattschneider, E. E., *Party Government*. New York: Rinehart, 1942.

Schattschneider, E. E., *The Semisovereign People: A Realist's View of Democracy in America*. Hinsdale, IL: Dryden Press, 1975.

Schiff, Ze'ev, and Ehud Ya'ari, *Israel's War in Lebanon*. New York: Simon & Schuster, 1984.

Schiff, Ze'ev, and Ehud Ya'ari, *Intifada*. New York: Simon & Schuster, 1989.

Schild, E. O., "On the Meaning of Military Service in Israel," in M. Curtis and M. S. Chertoff (eds.), *Israel: Social Structure and Change*. New Brunswick, NJ: Transaction, 1973, pp. 419–32.

Schneider, William, "Conservatism, Not Interventionism: Trends in Foreign Policy Opinion, 1974–1982," in Kenneth A. Oye, Robert J. Lieber, and Donald Rothchild (eds.), *Eagle Defiant: United States Foreign Policy in the 1980s*. Boston: Little, Brown, 1983, pp. 33–64.

Schneider, William, "Public Opinion," in Joseph S. Nye, Jr. (ed.), *The Making of America's Soviet Policy*. New Haven: Yale University Press, 1984, pp. 11–35.

Schneider, William, "Public Opinion and Foreign Policy: The Beginning of Ideology?," *Foreign Policy* 17:1985, 88–120.

Schneider, William, " 'Rambo' and Reality: Having it Both Ways," in Kenneth A. Oye, Robert J. Lieber, and Donald Rothchild (eds.), *Eagle Resurgent*. Boston: Little, Brown, 1987.

Schuman, Howard, and Stanley Presser, *Questions and Answers in Attitude Surveys*. San Diego: Academic Press, 1981.

Schuman, Howard, and Jacob Ludwig, and Jon Krosnick, "The Perceived Threat of Nuclear War, Salience, and Open Questions," *Public Opinion Quarterly* 50:1986, 519–36.

Shachar, Roni, and Michal Shamir, "Modelling Victory : The 1992 Elections in Israel," in Asher Arian and Michal Shamir (eds.), *The Elections in Israel – 1992*. Albany: State University of New York Press, 1995.

Shafir, Gershon, "Ideological Politics or the Politics of Demography: The Aftermath of the Six-Day-War," in Ian S. Lustick and Barry Rubin (eds.), *Critical Essays on Israeli Society, Politics and Culture*. Albany: State University of New York Press, 1991.

Shalev, Aryeh, *The Intifada: Causes and Effects*. Boulder, CO: Westview, 1991.

Shalev, Michael, *Labour and the Political Economy in Israel*. Oxford: Oxford University Press, 1992.

Shamir, Jacob, and Michal Shamir, "The Dynamics of Public Opinion on Peace and the Territories," report to the Tami Steinmetz Center for Peace Research, Tel Aviv University, 1992.

Shamir, Michal, "Realignment in the Israeli Party System," in Asher Arian and Michal Shamir (eds.), *The Elections in Israel – 1984*, New Brunswick, NJ: Transaction, 1986, pp. 267–96.

Shamir, Michal, "Political Intolerance Among Masses and Elites in Israel," *The Journal of Politics* 53:4, November 1991, 1018–43.

Shamir, Michal, and Asher Arian, "Ethnicity in the 1981 Elections in Israel," *Electoral Studies* 1:1982, 315–32.

Shamir, Michal, and Asher Arian, "The Intifada and Israeli Voters: Policy Preferences and Performance Evaluations," in Asher Arian and Michal Shamir (eds.), *The Elections in Israel – 1988*. Boulder, CO: Westview, 1990, pp. 77–92.

Shamir, Michal, and Asher Arian, "Competing Values and Policy Choices: Israeli Public Opinion on Foreign and Security Affairs," *British Journal of Political Science* 24: 1994, 111–33.

Shamir, Michal, and John L. Sullivan, "The Political Context of Tolerance: The United States and Israel," *American Political Science Review* 77:1983, 911–28.

Shapira, Anita, *Land and Power: The Zionist Resort to Force, 1881–1948*. New York: Oxford University Press, 1992.

Shapiro, Robert Y., and Benjamin I. Page, "Foreign Policy and the Rational Public," *Journal of Conflict Resolution* 32:1988, 211–47.

Sharett, Moshe, *Personal Diary* (Hebrew). Tel Aviv, Ma'ariv, 1978.

Shimshoni, Jonathan, *Israel and Conventional Deterrence*. Ithaca, NY: Cornell University Press, 1988.

Shlaim, Avi, *Collusion Across the Jordan: King Abdallah, the Zionist Movement and the Partition of Palestine*. Oxford: Oxford University Press, 1988.

Shmotkin, Dov, "Subjective Well-Being as a Function of Age and Gender: A Multivariate Look for Differentiated Trends," *Social Indicators Research* 23:1990, 201–30.

Shmotkin, Dov, "The Role of Time Orientation in Life Satisfaction Across the Life Span, *Journal of Gerontology* 46:1991, 243–50.

Simon, Herbert A., "Human Nature in Politics: The Dialogue of Psychology with Political Science," *American Political Science Review* 79:1985, 293–304.

Singer, J. David, "Threat-Perception and the Armament-Tension Dilemma," *Journal of Conflict Resolution* 2:1958, 90–105.

Smith, Eric R. A. N., *The Unchanging American Voter*. Berkeley: University of California Press, 1989.

Smith, Tom W., "Nuclear Anxiety," *Public Opinion Quarterly* 52:1988, 557–75.

Smooha, Sammy, *Israel: Pluralism and Conflict*. Berkeley: University of California Press, 1978.

Smooha, Sammy, *Social Research on Jewish Ethnicity in Israel, 1948–1986*. Haifa: University of Haifa Press, 1987.

Smooha, Sammy, *Arabs and Jews in Israel. Vol. I: Conflicting and Shared Attitudes in a Divided Society*. Boulder, CO: Westview, 1989.

Smooha, Sammy, "Minority Status in an Ethnic Democracy: The Status of the Arab Minority in Israel," *Ethnic and Racial Studies* 13:1990, 389–413.

Smooha, Sammy, *Arabs and Jews in Israel. Vol. 2: Change and Continuity in Mutual Intolerance*. Boulder, CO: Westview, 1992.

Sniderman, Paul M., and Philip E. Tetlock, "Interrelationship of Political Ideology and Public Opinion," in Margaret G. Herman (ed.), *Political Psychology*. San Francisco: Jossey-Bass, 1986, pp. 62–96.

Sniderman, Paul M., Richard A. Brody, and Philip E. Tetlock, *Reasoning and Choice: Explorations in Political Psychology*. Cambridge: Cambridge University Press, 1991.

Sprinzak, Ehud, *The Ascendance of Israel's Radical Right*. New York: Oxford University Press, 1991.

Stimson, James A., *Public Opinion in America: Moods, Cycles, and Swings*. Boulder, CO: Westview, 1991.

Stokes, Donald E., "Spatial Models of Party Competition," *American Political Science Review* 57:1963, 368–77.

Stone, Russell A., *Social Change in Israel: Attitudes and Events, 1967–79*. New York: Praeger, 1982.

Tedeschi, J. T., "Threats and Promises," in P. Swingle (ed.), *The Structure of Conflict*. New York: Academic Press, 1970.

Templer, D., "Death Anxiety: Extroversion, Neuroticism, and Cigarette Smoking," *Omega* 3:1972, 53–56.

Tetlock, Philip E., "Cognitive Style and Political Ideology," *Journal of Personality and Social Psychology* 45:1983, 118–26.

Tetlock, Philip E., "A Value Pluralism Model of Ideological Reasoning," *Journal of Personality and Social Psychology* 50:1986, 819–27.

Tetlock, Philip E., "Structure and Function in Political Belief Systems," in Anthony R. Praktanis, Steven J. Breckler, and Anthony G. Greenwald (eds.), *Attitude Structure and Function*. Hillsdale, NJ: Lawrence Erlbaum, 1989, pp. 129–51.

Touval, Saadia, *The Peace Brokers: Mediators in the Arab-Israel Conflict, 1948–1979*. Princeton: Princeton University Press, 1982.

Truman, David, *The Governmental Process: Political Interests and Public Opinion*. New York: Knopf, 1951.

Ungar, Lea, Victor Florian, and Esther Zernitsky-Shurka, "Aspects of Fear of Personal Death, Levels of Awareness, and Professional Affiliation Among Dialysis Unit Staff Members," *Omega* 21:1990, 51–67.

Ventura, Raphael, and Michal Shamir, "Left and Right in Israeli Politics," *State, Government and International Relations* (Hebrew) 35:1992, 21–50.

Verba, Sidney, and Richard Brody, "Participation, Political Preferences and the War in Vietnam," *Public Opinion Quarterly* 34:1970, 325–32.

Wald, Emanuel, *The Wald Report: The Decline of Israeli National Security Since 1967*. Boulder, CO: Westview, 1992.

Weber, Max, *Economy and Society*. Los Angeles: University of California Press, 1978.

Weimann, Gabriel, "Caveat Populi Quaestor: The 1992 Pre-Elections Polls in the Israeli Press," in Asher Arian and Michal Shamir (eds.), *The Elections in Israel – 1992*. Albany: State University of New York Press, 1995.

Weizman, Ezer, *The Battle for Peace*. New York: Bantam, 1981.

Wittkopf, Eugene R., *Faces of Internationalism: Public Opinion and American Foreign Policy*. Durham, NC: Duke University Press, 1990.

Yaari, M., *Tests of Our Time* (Hebrew). Merchavia: Sifriyat Hapoalim, 1957.

Yaniv, Avner, *Deterrence Without the Bomb: The Politics of Israeli Strategy*. Lexington MA: D. C. Heath, 1987a.

Yaniv, Avner, *Dilemmas of Security: Politics, Strategy and the Israeli Experience in Lebanon*, New York: Oxford University Press, 1987b.

Yaniv, Avner (ed)., *National Security and Democracy in Israel*. Boulder, CO: Lynne Reiner, 1993.

Yaniv, Avner, and F. Pascal, "Doves, Hawks, and Other Birds of the Feather: The Distribution of Parliamentary Opinion on the Future of the Occupied Territories, 1967–77," *British Journal of Political Science*, 1980, 10.

Yankelevich, Daniel, and John Doble, "The Public Mood: Nuclear Weapons and the USSR," *Foreign Affairs* 63:1984, 33–46.

Yariv, Aharon, "Strategic Depth," *Jerusalem Quarterly* 17:Fall 1980, 3–12.

Yishai, Yael, *Land or Peace: Whither Israel?* Stanford, CA: Hoover Institution, 1987.

Zaller, John R., *The Nature and Origins of Mass Opinion.* Cambridge: Cambridge University Press, 1992.

Zaller, John, and Stanley Feldman, "A Simple Theory of the Survey Response: Answering Questions Versus Revealing Preferences," *American Journal of Political Science* 36:1992, 579–616.

Zilboorg, G., "Fear of Death," *Psychoanalytic Quarterly* 12:1943, 465–75.

Zuckerman, Alan, "New Approaches to Political Cleavages," *Comparative Political Studies* 15:1982, 131–44.

Index